*S*THE PIRIT
HELPS US
PRAY

A Biblical Theology of Prayer

Robert L. Brandt

Zenas J. Bicket

Stanley M. Horton, Th.D.
General Editor

LOGION
P R E S S
Springfield, Missouri

02–0678

Unless otherwise indicated, all Scripture quotations are taken from the HOLY BIBLE: NEW INTERNATIONAL VERSION®; NIV®. Copyright ©1973, 1978, 1984 by International Bible Society. Used by permission of Zondervan Publishing House. All rights reserved.

5th Printing 1999

©1993 by Gospel Publishing House, Springfield, Missouri 65802-1894. All rights reserved. No part of this book may be reproduced, stored in a retrieval system, or transmitted in any form or by any means—electronic, mechanical, photocopy, recording, or other-wise—without prior written permission of the copyright owner, except brief quotations used in connection with reviews in magazines or newspapers.

Logion Press books are published by Gospel Publishing House.

Library of Congress Cataloging-in-Publication Data

Brandt, Robert L.
    The spirit helps us pray : a biblical theology of prayer / Robert L. Brandt, Zenas J. Bicket ; Stanley M. Horton, general editor.
        p.   cm.
    Includes bibliographical references and indexes.
    ISBN 0-88243-678-3
    1. Bible—Prayers.   2 Prayer.   I. Bicket, Zenas J.
II. Horton, Stanley M.   III. Title
    BS680.P64B73   1993
    248.3'2—dc20

                                    92-40276

Printed in the United States of America

THE SPIRIT HELPS US PRAY: A BIBLICAL THEOLOGY OF PRAYER

THE SPIRIT HELPS US PRAY: A BIBLICAL THEOLOGY OF PRAYER

Apollos was "a learned man, with a thorough knowledge of the Scriptures" (Acts 18:24). Goodspeed says he was "skillful in the use of the scriptures" (v. 25). The RSV says he "taught accurately." We still have men like this today to help us in understanding the Scriptures, in this particular instance, to understand what God's Word has to say about every aspect of prayer. For Robert L. Brandt and Zenas J. Bicket are gifts to the Church of our time as Apollos and Paul were gifts to the Church of their time.

Having been a colleague of Dr. Bicket in college teaching, administration, and especially in prayer ministries, I can echo Luke's sentiment about Apollos as I consider Dr. Bicket: "He was a great help to those who by grace had believed" (v. 27). Bicket, a man of dedication, discipline, and strength of character, has contributed to a monumental work on prayer.

Robert L. Brandt has been a long-time acquaintance and of one of the families of the Assemblies of God who have stood like giants of character and spiritual leadership. A fearless searcher after truth, dedicated to following it whatever the price, he is, like Paul, a man of vision, and has not been disobedient to that vision.

Spiritual leadership requires a practical, working knowledge of prayer, a knowledge that has given the Word of God precedence and then been integrated into life. For prayer is what we are more than what we say. Thus, in the case of prayer, the medium of the message is man. And in the case of Robert L. Brandt, when he writes about prayer, he is writing about himself. To be with him makes you want to pray. We are fortunate to have leadership like this, that influences us into the presence of God! As a ministerial colleague, as a fellow member of various boards, and as a consultant on matters of the Spirit, Brother Brandt has been a model of spiritual life and leadership.

In the Lord's prayer of John 17, Jesus speaks about "those you have given me to be with me where I am," a phrase that expresses the preciousness of fellowship with men like Bicket and Brandt.

From Genesis to Revelation, from Adam to John the Beloved, these authors cover the trail of revelation meaningfully and efficiently. God's conversations with Adam, Jesus' revelation to John, become patterns for a life and practice of prayer under the influence of the Holy Spirit. Layers of tradition, culture, and self-interests are stripped away and we are introduced to sublime communion with God. A deeper understanding of the work of the Holy Spirit is the result.

Perhaps the optimum contribution of this inclusive volume is in chapters 11 and 12, where the authors spotlight the ministry of the Holy Spirit in praying with and through the Spirit-filled believer. It is here that we leave the company of many traditional writers on this most blessed privilege of communion with God (who is Spirit).

With conviction the authors state, "Pentecostals . . . see room for the gift of tongues to be involved . . ." (p. 271). They talk about praying in the supernatural, that is, with tongues, as well as the need for interpretation of tongues. This special emphasis merits a serious and careful reading of this book by believers who wish to enjoy praying in the Holy Spirit.

What makes this book comprehensive is the practical instruction it offers, detailing the single manifestation in the assembly as well as the offering of public prayer. The passages in Ephesians, which deal with the individual as well as the body of which he is a member, are especially pregnant with guidance. "Do not get drunk; be filled with the Spirit," and (as some writers have concluded that Ephesians 5:19 is indicative of Early Church liturgy) "Speak to one another with psalms, and hymns and spiritual songs. Sing and make music in your heart to the Lord always giving thanks to God." This gives wide dimensions to ways of praying.

Angels and their ministry are included in this book. Though not a common aspect of prayer to many authors, Rev. Brandt and Dr. Bicket are right at home in speaking about the ministry of angels to the saints. Their specific concern is to discover how angelic intervention may occur in response to prayer.

And in support of the reader in quest of how to pray and how God answers prayer today, the authors supply contemporary stories of people who have prayed and how God gave them miraculous answers. This adds immeasurably to the value of this significant book on prayer.

Scores of books have been written on prayer, some on the Holy Spirit, but few like this on the Holy Spirit and prayer. The message of this book is decidedly Pentecostal. It is about the Holy Spirit's relationship to prayer. This Pentecostal view of the topic has been long awaited. At the same time, readers should not think of this as a parochial treatment, but rather as a sound, biblically accurate interpretation.

Further, this book is skillfully written: beautiful sentences, logical structure, colorful diction. Its masterful writing adds great value to the prolific literature on this great subject of prayer. All who minister will be pleased with the indexes and bibliography, helping them make their way around in the book and on to others.

This book should be in every church, college, and home of those who want to enjoy the full blessings of praying in the Holy Spirit. It will be a gold mine for all those who seek to grow in grace and minister to others in the power of the Spirit. I use it next to my Bible.

J. ROBERT ASHCROFT
PRESIDENT EMERITUS
OF BEREAN COLLEGE

THE SPIRIT HELPS US PRAY: A BIBLICAL THEOLOGY OF PRAYER

This study seeks to explore, mainly from a biblical perspective, the entire scope of prayer. The goal is not merely to provide academic understanding, but the higher purpose of developing a corps of people who pray and who therefore make a difference for God in the world. As they are burdened and inspired to pursue diligently an active prayer ministry, they will enrich their own lives, impact their ministry to Christ and His Church, and consequently generate waves of spiritual influence to the ends of the earth.

We want also to encourage a distinctive Pentecostal perspective, having a twofold emphasis: (1) that all Spirit-filled believers take advantage of their access into the very throne room of God through our Savior and Mediator Jesus Christ and (2) that prayer become a power of supernatural dimensions through the help of the indwelling Holy Spirit. In this way prayer moves out of ritual and into reality. "Praying in the Spirit" becomes more than a biblical phrase; It becomes a conduit of divine intervention. Ph is spirit

Communication with God is among the earliest recorded practices of humankind. It seems to have been as natural to Adam as nursing to a newborn. God's evident intent was to be in constant and vital communion with those He created in His own image. He did not intend for people to

15

have to make it on their own. Communion with Him was to be the umbilical cord through which His offspring would be sustained and joined to Deity.

But this communion became an early prey of evil. Though Adam and Eve began their earthly sojourn in holy and harmonious fellowship with their Creator, they do not appear to have lived long before they were endeavoring to hide from God rather than wanting to walk with Him "in the cool of the day" (Gen. 3:8). Such has become the pattern through the passing millenniums of history. Because of neglect or the pernicious influence of evil, people have failed to avail themselves of the divine provision. Consequently, prayer has been commanded, as well as offered as a privilege.

Why are people still so reticent to experience the potential, the adventure, the almost unparalleled challenge, of prayer? Do they not comprehend the divine purpose of prayer? Are they strangely blinded to its value and benefit? Or do they simply not perceive the magnificent potential of prayer, both for the present and the future?

Whatever the case, we will probe deeply the many aspects of prayer in order to uncover a theology of prayer, applying it to the spiritual warfare in which all believers are engaged.

As you begin this book, seek not only to be informed, but also to be motivated. You need not wait until you finish reading the entire text before you put the principles into practice. Day by day submit to the Holy Spirit and depend upon Him. Let the Spirit speak to you along the way about when and how you should pray. Stop at the slightest prompting and pray for that which the Spirit drops into your mind—in the way that the Spirit prompts. Set before you is a most exciting, intriguing, and challenging adventure. Pursue it prayerfully and with an open heart.

In line with the usage of both the KJV and the NIV, "Lord" is used in capitals and small capitals where the Hebrew of the Old Testament has the personal, divine

name of God, Yahweh (which was probably pronounced
'ya-wā).[1]

In quoted Scripture, words the authors wish to emphasize are highlighted with italics.

For easier reading, Hebrew, Aramaic, and Greek words
are all transliterated with English letters.

A few abbreviations have been used:

BAGD: Bauer, Arndt, Gingrich, Danker *(A Greek-English
Lexicon of the New Testament and Other Early Literature)*

Gk.: Greek

Heb.: Hebrew

ISBE: *International Standard Bible Encyclopedia*

KJV: King James Version

LB: *The Living Bible*

NASB: *New American Standard Bible*

NIV: New International Version

NKJV: New King James Version

Phillips: *The New Testament in Modern English,* Translated by J. B. Phillips

RSV: Revised Standard Version

Special thanks to Glen Ellard and his editing staff at Gospel Publishing House and to all who assisted in preparing
this book.

---

[1]The Hebrew wrote only the consonants YHWH. Later traditions followed the New Latin JHVH and added vowels from the Hebrew for
"Lord" to remind them to read *Lord* instead of the divine name. This
was never intended to be read "Jehovah."

THE SPIRIT HELPS US PRAY: A BIBLICAL THEOLOGY OF PRAYER

Prayer is the most intimate expression of the Christian life. Why, then, is it so neglected?

We live in an age that avoids intimacy and close relationships. The disposition to avoid self-exposure and deep friendships affects spiritual as well as interpersonal relationships. Without being fully aware that this spirit of the age has crept into the church, some Christians feel uncomfortable getting too close to God. Prayerlessness is the result.

Then, too, we are busy. We live to perform rather than to be. We admire the active life more than character and relationships. Success is measured by what one accomplishes; so we run, run, run—trying to accomplish all that we can in our waking hours. More concerned about performing than about being, we refuse to accept the biblical reality that human achievement is temporary and fleeting. Only the work of the Spirit is permanent and eternal. Prayerlessness keeps us from achieving the very thing we so desperately need to achieve. Prayerlessness is really godlessness.

Failure to understand the purpose of the Pentecostal experience and the primary role of prayer in maintaining the vitality of that experience also results in prayerlessness.

19

Introduction

The Spirit-filled believer walks and talks with God; he or she may be perceived by other people as a mystic, a prophet, an alien from another world. That is, in fact, the reality: Citizenship in the dominion of the Spirit is just as real as citizenship in the material world.

An understanding of the nature of prayer and its importance in our becoming effective representatives of Christ is essential as we begin this study. This chapter serves, therefore, as a launching pad, not unlike Cape Canaveral, where even the smallest detail of preparation is given close attention.

For the sake of easy reference, terms relating to prayer will be introduced alphabetically, with no intent to indicate sequence or importance by the order.

Adoration

The word "adoration" is not to be found in either Testament of the KJV or NIV. Yet the concept is a vital part of prayer and is actually found in the Bible in such terms as "awe," "fear of the Lord," and "worship." "Adoration" is the demonstration of great love, devotion, and respect; for the Christian, it is worshiping or paying homage to God. Adoration sets the tone for one's prayer life. It reminds the one who prays of the Person he is addressing, of His attributes and personal concern.

How does a believer who desires a richer prayer life begin adoring God? Recounting His attributes is a good start. A new Christian may need to spend a little time studying those attributes, pondering what it really means to be conversing with an all-powerful, all-knowing, always-present God. The Book of Psalms is full of statements about the nature of God. It should be read as a personal affirmation of God's eternal glory and His compassionate, understanding reach toward the person who believes in Him. Adore God by personalizing the words with which the Psalmist adored Him.

Communication

Even though the English words "communicate" and "communication" are not used in Scripture (KJV or NIV) to describe prayer, the idea is inherent. On the one hand, prayer is the transmission of private or public information by human beings to God. Note, for example, Daniel 9:3–6:

I turned to the Lord God and pleaded with him in prayer and petition, in fasting, and in sackcloth and ashes. I prayed to the LORD my God and confessed: "O Lord, the great and awesome God, who keeps his covenant of love with all who love him and obey his commands, we have sinned and done wrong.... We have not listened to your servants the prophets, who spoke in your name to our kings, our princes and our fathers, and to all the people of the land."

On the other hand, prayer is the two-way exchange of information and ideas between God and his people. Note Acts 9:10–16:

In Damascus there was a disciple named Ananias. The Lord called to him in a vision, "Ananias!" "Yes, Lord," he answered. The Lord told him, "Go to the house of Judas on Straight Street and ask for a man from Tarsus named Saul, for he is praying. In a vision he has seen a man named Ananias come and place his hands on him to restore his sight." "Lord," Ananias answered, "I have heard many reports about this man and all the harm he has done to your saints in Jerusalem. And he has come here with authority from the chief priests to arrest all who call on your name." But the Lord said to Ananias, "Go! This man is my chosen instrument to carry my name before the Gentiles and their kings and before the people of Israel. I will show him how much he must suffer for my name."

The earliest recorded two-way communication between the Creator and His highest creation, humanity, is found in Genesis 3, as Adam and Eve sought to avoid the God they had disobeyed.

Then the man and his wife heard the sound of the LORD God as he was walking in the garden in the cool of the day, and they hid from the LORD God among the trees of the garden. But the LORD God called to the man, "Where are you?" He answered, "I heard you in the garden, and I was afraid because I was naked; so I hid" (Gen. 3:8–10).

Therefore, for study, the words "communicate" and "communication" will be used to describe prayer in any one of three senses: ① people speaking to God, ② people and God in dialogue, and ③ God speaking to people in a circumstance in which they are inclined to hear His voice.

Communion

For describing prayer, one dictionary definition of "communion" is especially appropriate: "intimate fellowship or rapport." The idea of people communing with God is very evident in Scripture, the first instance after the Fall being recorded in Exodus 25:22 as God speaks to Moses: " 'There, above the cover between the two cherubim that are over the ark of the Testimony, I will meet with you and give you all my commands for the Israelites.' "

The word "commune," used in the KJV of this passage, is *davar* the ordinary Hebrew word for "speak." Consequently, the Hebrew phrase which literally means "speak with you all my commands" is simplified in the NIV to "give you all my commands." When two beings commune, they meet and speak. The application to prayer is obvious. The Greek word *koinōnia* ("fellowship" or "communion") has a similar application to prayer when there is a close relationship between God and a person. Paul uses the word in 2 Corinthians 13:14: "May the grace of the Lord Jesus Christ, and the love of God, and the fellowship of the Holy Spirit be with you all." The same Greek word is translated "fellowship" in other passages, e.g., Philippians 2:1 and 1 John 1:3.

For the purposes of our study, the word "communion" indicates fellowship and social intercourse at its most intimate. It carries the idea of a close partnership or a merging of spirits into a blessed oneness, like the intertwining of cords into a single rope. As a level of prayer, communion goes beyond ordinary communication. It suggests an uncommon intimacy, for example, as seen in Abraham's involvement with God over Sodom and Gomorrah (see Gen. 18:17,23–33).

Confession

Confession is simply the acknowledgment of a fact about oneself or another. That acknowledgment can be either a disclosure of one's sins as an act of penance or an affirmation of God's greatness and goodness. Both meanings are found in Hebrew and in Greek as well as in English. Thus "to confess . . . 'Jesus is Lord'" (Rom. 10:9) means to affirm that Christ is God's Son sent to the world to become our Savior and Lord.

At least two Hebrew words are translated "confession" in the Old Testament. The first, _todah,_ is derived from the second, _yadah._ Both words carry a suggestion of the two meanings of "confession." The context must determine which is meant. "Ezra the priest stood up and said to them, 'You have been unfaithful, . . . adding to Israel's guilt. Now make _confession_ [todah] to the LORD'" (Ezra 10:10–11). Both _todah_ and _yadah_ are based on the literal meaning of "extending the hand." Hands can be extended in worship to God, or wrung in grief over one's sins. In the 111 occurrences of _yadah_ in the Old Testament, both meanings of "confession" seem to be present. This need not be of concern, however, for praise is appropriate in the midst of confessing sin, just as confessing sin is appropriate when we come to God with our praise. We need ever to acknowledge all the truth God reveals to us—our own sinfulness as well as His holiness and majesty. "I prayed to the LORD my God and confessed: 'O Lord, the great and awesome God, who keeps his covenant of love with all who love him and obey his commands, we have sinned and done wrong'" (Dan. 9:4–5).

The two meanings of "confession" are represented in New Testament usage by the Greek _homologia_ (and its related forms): "that which is acknowledged or confessed." (Rom. 10:9 has already been noted.) The other meaning of "confession" is illustrated in 1 John 1:9: "If we _confess_ our sins, he is faithful and just and will forgive us our sins and purify us from all unrighteousness."

The meaning of "confess" as used in the following chapters is primarily the acknowledgment of sin before both God and people as an essential of effective praying. This meaning was indelibly impressed on the Israelites through the annual ritual of releasing a goat into the wilderness on the Day of Atonement.

> [Aaron] is to lay both hands on the head of the live goat and *confess* over it all the wickedness and rebellion of the Israelites— all their sins—and put them on the goat's head. He shall send the goat away into the desert in the care of a man appointed for the task. The goat will carry on itself all their sins to a solitary place; and the man shall release it in the desert (Lev. 16:21–22).

This symbolized not only God's having covered their sins with the redemption price of shed blood; their sins were gone, never to be remembered by God any more.

An outstanding example of confession in prayer is found in Psalm 51:3–4: "For I know my transgressions, and my sin is always before me. Against you, you only, have I sinned and done what is evil in your sight, so that you are proved right when you speak and justified when you judge."

Contrition

Contrition is the act of grieving and being truly sorry for one's sins or shortcomings. In the Hebrew, *dakka'* means "crushed," "bruised," "contrite." Old Testament examples of the adjectival use include the following:

> The LORD is close to the brokenhearted and saves those who are *crushed* [contrite, KJV] in spirit (Ps. 34:18).

> For this is what the high and lofty One says—he who lives forever, whose name is holy: "I live in a high and holy place, but also with him who is *contrite* and lowly in spirit, to revive the spirit of the lowly and to revive the heart of the *contrite*" (Isa. 57:15).

Contrition is an attitude of the heart involving humility, brokenness of spirit, admission of sin, and grief for short-comings; at the same time it implores God for His mercy.

Entreaty

"Intreat," used in the KJV, is the archaic form of "entreat." The word means "to plead or ask urgently, especially in order to persuade." It is the translation of five different

Hebrew words translated in other passages in the KJV as "to make intercession," "to pray," and "to make supplication." In the NIV they are usually translated "ask," "exhort," "intercede," "pray," "seek," or "urge." An Old Testament passage appropriate to our study is found in Moses' experience with Pharaoh:

Entreat

Introduction

Pharaoh summoned Moses and Aaron and said, "Pray to ["Entreat," KJV] the LORD to take the frogs away from me and my people, and I will let your people go to offer sacrifices to the LORD. Moses said to Pharaoh, "I leave to you the honor of setting the time for me to pray for ["entreat," KJV] you and your officials and your people that you and your houses may be rid of the frogs, except for those that remain in the Nile" (Exod. 8:8–9).

Four Greek words are translated "entreat" in the KJV. In other passages these same words are translated "beseech," "exhort," "ask," and "pray." Note the use of the concept in James 3:17: "The wisdom that comes from heaven is first pure; then peace-loving, considerate, submissive ["easy to be intreated," KJV], full of mercy and good fruit, impartial and sincere." This description of "the wisdom that comes from heaven" characterizes the God who is all-wise.

Intercession

46 Times O.T. KJV James person
4 Times
NIV = 1 Time

The Hebrew word *paga'* occurs forty-six times in the Old Testament. It is translated "intercession" in the NIV one time (four times in the KJV). The verb form means literally "to encounter," "to meet," "to put pressure on"; then "to plead." The causative form with *le,* "for," means "to intercede for." Examples of Old Testament usage include the following:

Therefore I will give him a portion among the great, and he will divide the spoils with the strong, because he poured out his life unto death, and was numbered with the transgressors. For he bore the sin of many, and made *intercession* for the transgressors (Isa. 53:12).

In the New Testament, "intercession" comes from the Greek *entugchanō,* meaning "to appeal to," "to plead for,"

Introduction

"to make intercession," "to pray." Two very familiar and precious passages include the term:

In the same way, the Spirit helps us in our weakness. We do not know what we ought to pray for, but the Spirit himself *intercedes* for us with groans that words cannot express. And he who searches our hearts knows the mind of the Spirit, because the Spirit *intercedes* for the saints in accordance with God's will (Rom. 8:26–27).

I urge, then, first of all, that requests, prayers, *intercession* and thanksgiving be made for everyone (1 Tim. 2:1).

Throughout our study of prayer, we will understand "intercession" to mean "the act of one or more persons, human or divine, making entreaty to God in behalf of another person or persons."

Intercession

Meditation

To meditate is to focus one's thoughts on, reflect on, or ponder over something. Forms of three Hebrew words are translated "meditate" or "meditation" in the Old Testament. These same words are also translated "consider," "muse," "be deep in thought," "ponder," "contemplate," "think," or "mutter [to oneself]." Familiar passages from the Book of Psalms portray meditation as a communication linkage between God and a person:

Blessed is the man who does not walk in the counsel of the wicked or stand in the way of sinners or sit in the seat of mockers. But his delight is in the law of the LORD, and on his law he *meditates* day and night (Ps. 1:1–2).

My soul will be satisfied as with the richest of foods; with singing lips my mouth will praise you. On my bed I remember you; I think of ["meditate on," KJV] you through the watches of the night (Ps. 63:5–6).

Marvin R. Vincent says "meditation is a talking within the mind."[1] Paul advises Timothy, "Be diligent in ["Medi-

---

[1]Marvin R. Vincent, *Word Studies in the New Testament,* vol. 4 (Grand Rapids: Wm. B. Eerdmans Pub. Co., 1946), 253.

tate upon," KJV] these matters; give yourself wholly to them, so that everyone may see your progress" (1 Tim. 4:15). As used in this study, "meditate" means "to rehearse and ponder in the mind for the purpose of a more complete understanding, assimilation, and application of truth."

Petition

A petition is "an earnest request," "something asked for or requested." Four different Hebrew words are translated "petition" in the Old Testament (three in KJV), though two of them share a common root *tehinnah* and *tahnun.* Both are also translated "request," "supplication," and "cry for mercy." Another, *she'elah,* is also translated "request." The verb *baqash,* translated "petition" in Ezra 8:23, is more often translated "seek," or "search for." In speaking to Hannah, Eli said, "Go in peace, and may the God of Israel grant you what you have asked ["thy petition," KJV] of him" (1 Sam. 1:17).

The word "petition" occurs three times in the New Testament, translating three different Greek words, *deēsis* (Phil. 4:6), *emphanizō* (Acts 23:15), and *hikatēria* (Heb. 5:7). The KJV also uses it to translate *aitēma* ("requests," NIV). Two of the usages of *aitēma* relate specifically to prayer: "Do not be anxious about anything, but in everything, by prayer and petition, with thanksgiving, present your *requests* to God" (Phil. 4:6).

The common understanding of the word "petition," in contemporary usage as well as in the biblical Testaments, will be the definition used in this study.

Praying in the Spirit

Although the expression "praying in the Spirit" is more than a single word, a clear understanding of the meaning of the phrase is essential to our study. The expression is derived mainly from Jude 20: "You, dear friends, build yourselves up in your most holy faith and *pray in the Holy Spirit.*" It probably also has its roots, to some extent, in Paul's statement in 1 Corinthians 14:15: "I will *pray with my spirit,* but I will also pray with my mind."

In the first instance (Jude 20), the Holy Spirit seems

Introduction

quite clearly to be the means of the praying; but in Paul's case, the means seems to be his own spirit—*"my* spirit prays" (1 Cor. 14:14). The apparent discrepancy is removed when it is understood that in praying with his spirit, Paul signified he was praying in tongues. "For if I pray in a tongue, my spirit prays" (1 Cor. 14:14). Relate this to Acts 2:4—"All of them were filled with the Holy Spirit and began to speak in other tongues as the Spirit enabled them"—and the sense emerges that praying in tongues is made possible by the enablement of the Holy Spirit.

Therefore, "praying in the Spirit" is defined as that praying which springs from the merging of the human spirit with the Holy Spirit, issuing in a prayerful utterance in an unknown tongue. In addition to the passages already cited, note Ephesians 6:18: *"Pray in the Spirit* on all occasions with all kinds of prayers and requests."

Submission

Submission is not so much a means of prayer as a condition of effective prayer. The submissive person humbly accepts the authority and lordship of the One to whom He prays. Yet a believer in fulfilling this precondition to effective praying needs to submit also to the leaders God has placed over him: "Obey your leaders and submit to their authority. They keep watch over you as men who must give an account. Obey them so that their work will be a joy, not a burden, for that would be of no advantage to you" (Heb. 13:17).

Supplication

Supplication is the act of making humble and earnest entreaty for favor, especially to God. Three Hebrew words from the root *hanan* are translated "supplication" or "supplications." They frequently include the idea of intercession, petition, and strong request. In some passages they are translated "prayer," "beg for mercy," and "beg for favor." Two Old Testament usages are derived from *hanan:*

"When your people Israel have been defeated by an enemy because they have sinned against you, and when they turn back to you and confess your name, praying and *making supplication* to you in this temple, then hear from heaven and forgive the sin of your people Israel and bring them back to the land you gave to their fathers" (1 Kings 8:33–34).

To you, O LORD, I called; to the LORD I cried for mercy [made supplication, KJV] (Ps. 30:8).

The Greek word *deēsis* is translated "supplication" six times in the KJV (which also translates it "prayer," "prayers," or "request," as is the case twelve times in the NIV). In some of the key passages on prayer, *deēsis* indicates a more importunate, passionate pleading with God.

Thanksgiving   *Todah yadah*

O.T.

Thanksgiving is a public acknowledgment or celebration of divine goodness, an expression of gratitude. The Hebrew verb *yadah* and the related noun *todah* are associated with thanks and thanksgiving in the Old Testament. These same words are also translated in other passages "praise" and "confession." The role of thanksgiving in giving honor to God is illustrated in Psalm 69:30: "I will praise God's name in song and glorify him with thanksgiving."

In the New Testament, the word "thanksgiving" is the translation of the Greek *eulogia*, which speaks primarily of praise, and the translation of *eucharistia*, "gratitude," derived from *eu* ("well," "good") and *charis* ("favor," "grace," "graciousness," "goodwill," "thanks"). The association of thanksgiving with prayer is plain in Philippians 4:6: "In everything by prayer and petition, with thanksgiving, present your requests to God."

Thanksgiving as an element of prayer may be greatly undervalued. Still today, devout Jews punctuate the entire day with short sentence prayers. Over a hundred blessings can be recited, usually beginning, "Blessed are you, O Lord, King of the universe." An observant Jew expresses a brief thanks to God upon receiving good (and bad) news, smelling a fragrant flower, eating food, seeing a rainbow, and experiencing a thunderstorm. Throughout the day, the devout Jew praises and thanks God for all things with sentence prayers. Paul's admonition to "pray continually"

(1 Thess. 5:17) makes much more sense when we understand the Jewish background from which Paul was writing. In the following chapters, "thanksgiving" is the acknowledgment of divine goodness, the prayerful expression of gratitude to God, whether spoken or unspoken, in song, music, or an unknown tongue.

Travail

"Travail" is used in the KJV to refer to painful or laborious work, or toil, either physical or mental. In the Old Testament, the idea is frequently associated with childbirth; by extension, travail in prayer is toil that brings forth a response from God. Other translations of the most frequently occurring Hebrew words for "travail" include "labor," "business," "misery," "trouble," and "sorrow."

The words translated "travail" in the New Testament (KJV) also carry meanings associated with childbirth: "deliver," "bring forth," "bear," and "pain." Paul likened his prayerful concern for the spiritual health of the Galatian believers to the pangs of childbirth: "My dear children, for whom I am again in the *pains* of childbirth until Christ is formed in you . . ." (Gal. 4:19). For purposes of our study, "travail" should be understood as that intense application by prayer to the point of inward agony and pain in behalf of spiritual pursuits, including the birthing and development of souls and ministries in the kingdom of God.

Worship

Worship is reverence extended to an esteemed supernatural being; it is also the act of expressing that reverence, admiration, or devotion. Four Old Testament words are translated by some form of the word "worship." These original words are translated by a large number of alternative English words, including "serve," "bow down," "pay homage," "pay honor," "fear," and "revere." Psalm 29:2 is a typical translation of the most common Hebrew word for worship, *chawah* [or shachah], which has the basic meaning "to bow down deeply in homage": "Ascribe to the LORD the glory due his name; *worship* the LORD in the splendor [glorious grandeur] of his holiness."

At least a dozen Greek words are translated as some form of "worship" in the New Testament. Most commonly used is *proskuneō,* "to fall down prostrate in reverence and homage." A related word, *proskunētēs,* means "a worshiper." Speaking to the Samaritan woman, Jesus defined true worship (and prayer) as a spiritual linkage between God and a person: "True worshipers . . . worship the Father in spirit and truth, for they are the kind of worshipers the Father seeks. God is spirit, and his worshipers must worship him in spirit and in truth" (John 4:23–24).

Introduction
N. T.

The preceding fifteen words and phrases are fifteen aspects of prayer. No one of them will provide a comprehensive definition of this great discipline of the Christian life. But as each of them is understood and practiced, a vital prayer life is not only possible but to be expected. Review your mastery of these terms by listing them on a separate sheet of paper and then writing in the definitions. Then check to see if you included all essential parts of each definition.

There are many questions concerning prayer that will go unanswered until we meet face to face the One to whom we pray. Biblical prayer includes travail, intercession, and importunity. But it also includes submission and trust. It is both wrestling with God and resting peacefully in His arms. Prayer may include arguing and complaining to God; He understands that we are human. But if we never learn to submit, our prayers will accomplish nothing. As you study the biblical prayers and teachings on prayer treated in the following chapters, keep the tension of these questions in the back of your mind. Ask the Spirit to use that tension, and any other unanswered questions you may have about prayer, to lead you into a deeper devotional life and a more intimate fellowship with the One who can answer every human question.

Questions for Study

1. What are the causes and results of prayerlessness?
2. What is the difference between communion and communication?
3. What are the key terms that describe the chief aspects of prayer and how are they related to one another?
4. What attitudes should characterize prayer?

PART

1

Prayer In The Old Testament

PRAYERS OF THE PATRIARCHS AND THEIR CONTEMPORARIES

"All religions pray. God and prayer are inseparable. Belief in God and belief in prayer are elemental and intuitive. The ideas may be crude and cruel in primitive and pagan peoples, but they belong to the universal institutions of the human race. The teaching of the Old Testament is full of the subject of prayer."[1]

Prayer, as already noted, stands among the earliest practices of humankind. It makes its debut in the book of beginnings—Genesis—and is strikingly evident all the way from there to Malachi.

Of all God's creatures, only people pray. Prayer is God's gift to us. It is our link with our Creator. Consequently, in studying prayer from an Old Testament perspective, our focus will be upon the people who prayed, the occasions for their praying, how they approached and addressed God, how God's names and attributes may have affected their praying, and the outcome and accomplishments resulting from their praying. We will look in detail at Old Testament accounts in which individuals had personal communication with God.

---

[1]Samuel Chadwick, *The Path of Prayer* (New York: Abingdon Press, 1931), 7.

PART 1

Chapter 1
Prayers
of the
Patriarchs
and Their
Contem-
poraries

Adam

The first record of communication between the Creator and those He created in His image is found in Genesis 1:28: "God blessed them and said to them, 'Be fruitful and increase in number; fill the earth and subdue it. Rule over the fish of the sea and the birds of the air and over every living creature that moves on the ground.' " It was God who took the initiative in addressing humankind, thus establishing a fundamental principle: Hearing God's word, knowing His will, is at least as important as our addressing our concerns to Him—and perhaps of greater consequence.

Although the term "prayer" is not used in the account of Adam and Eve, communication between God and the two people created in His image is clearly evident. It should also be noted that these earliest human beings communicated not only with God, but with the fallen angel, Satan, as well (see Gen. 3:2–5; Rev. 12:9; 20:2). God and Satan both speak, and we must learn to discern between the two. Effective praying is based on what God has said, but it may be hindered if we listen to what Satan says.

The moment people heed Satan's voice, they throw up a communications barrier between themselves and the God who desires to bless them. Though God walked with Adam and Eve "in the garden in the cool of the day" (Gen. 3:8), they could not bear such close communion after the Fall and their consciences caused them to try to hide. The breach between God and sinners finds no remedy until they, by their own confession, make possible the opening of the door of mercy: "[Adam] answered, 'I heard you in the garden, and I was afraid because I was naked; so I hid.' . . . [then] The Lord God made garments of skin for Adam and his wife and clothed them" (Gen. 3:10,21).

Seth

While the Bible is virtually silent about any praying by Adam and Eve, it does hint that for a period of time, following their failure and expulsion from Eden, there was a dearth of calling upon God: "Seth also had a son, and he named him Enosh. At that time men began to call on the name of the LORD" (Gen. 4:26).

There appears some connection between Seth's naming his child Enosh and people beginning to call on the name of the Lord, for "Enosh" means "man," or "people," with an emphasis on the fact they are mortal and finite. By this time it must have become obvious that death was the common lot of mankind. The people of that generation were aware of their weakness and the fragile nature of human life. It may be too that they were aware of hindrances to their relationship with God. Such an awareness is often the forerunner of spiritual pursuit and renewal, as it was in the case of Seth, when people began "to call on the name of the Lord." Here is another basic principle of prayer: Our recognizing our need is prerequisite to our meaningful calling upon God.

The Hebrew also implies calling down a blessing in the name of the Lord and calling themselves by the name of the Lord; that is, they recognized God's good purpose and they took their place as His people.

Of particular significance, too, is the fact that people began to call on "the name of the Lord." "Lord" is "Yahweh," the personal, covenant-keeping name that draws attention to His being with us. The consequences of praying are directly related to the One addressed in prayer. Compare, for example, the praying of Baal's prophets with the praying of Elijah:

They called on the name of Baal from morning till noon. "O Baal, answer us!" they shouted. But there was no response; no one answered. And they danced around the altar they had made (1 Kings 18:26).

At the time of sacrifice, the prophet Elijah stepped forward and prayed: "O LORD, God of Abraham, Isaac and Israel, let it be known today that you are God in Israel and that I am your servant and have done all these things at your command. Answer me, O LORD, answer me, so these people will know that you, O LORD, are God, and that you are turning their hearts back again." Then the fire of the LORD fell (1 Kings 18:36–38).

The prophets of Baal prayed to the lifeless, powerless

PART 1

Chapter 1
Prayers
of the
Patriarchs
and Their
Contem-
poraries

PART 1

Chapter 1
Prayers
of the
Patriarchs
and Their
Contem-
poraries

invention of human hands—Baal. Elijah prayed to the Lord Yahweh, the self-existent, eternal, covenant-keeping God who had made promises to Abraham, Isaac, and Israel—as well as to all the families of the earth (Gen. 12:3). The practice of calling upon the name of the Lord, which began with Seth, was zealously carried forward by his son, Enosh. It was still effective in the days of Elijah.

Enoch

While Scripture does not state specifically that Enoch prayed, it does indicate a superior relationship with God: "Enoch *walked* with God" (Gen. 5:22). The Hebrew word *halak*, here translated "walked," contains the idea of following, adhering to, and so being conversant or communing with God. Enoch's communing was of such proportion that it led to his translation. "Enoch walked with God; then he was no more, because God took him away" (Gen. 5:24).

The writer of Hebrews expands on the Genesis reference:

By faith Enoch was taken from this life, so that he did not experience death; he could not be found, because God had taken him away. For before he was taken, he was commended as one who pleased God. And without faith it is impossible to please God, because anyone who comes to him must believe that he exists and that he rewards those who earnestly seek him (Heb. 11:5–6).

Enoch's testimony that he pleased God is clearly linked to his faith. It is reasonable to conclude that Enoch believed God was real, and believed it to the degree that he diligently sought God by constant prayer and communion. He was rewarded by physical removal from earth, never experiencing death. His praying led him directly into heaven, and also into faith's hall of fame (Heb. 11) for all the world to review.

Noah

As in the case of Enoch, Scripture does not state specifically that Noah "prayed." However, the spiritual pursuits of Noah are identified in the same terms used of Enoch: "He walked with God" (Gen. 6:9).

The account of Noah leaves no doubt that he maintained vital contact and communication with God. Repeatedly, Scripture indicates God spoke to Noah (see Gen. 6:13; 7:1). In turn, Noah responded with implicit obedience: "Noah did all that the LORD commanded him" (Gen. 7:5).

There is a profound lesson in this for every believer who desires prayer communion with God: Hearing from God is directly related to a willingness to obey God; the reason for His silence may be simply that one's heart is uncommitted to Him. In his generation, only Noah had a heart for God. With his contemporaries it was totally different: "The LORD saw how great man's wickedness on the earth had become, and that every inclination of the thoughts of his heart was only evil all the time" (Gen. 6:5). Little wonder then that God could not speak to such people. Prayer was foreign to them. God was not in their thoughts. The idea of walking with God, living for God, and relating to Him was pure folly to them, even as it is to vast multitudes today. We remember the words of Jesus when He said:

"As it was in the days of Noah, so it will be at the coming of the Son of Man. For in the days before the flood, people were eating and drinking, marrying and giving in marriage, up to the day Noah entered the ark; and they knew nothing about what would happen until the flood came and took them all away. That is how it will be at the coming of the Son of Man" (Matt. 24:37–39).

Found in the account of Noah is the first mention of an altar in Scripture: "Noah built an altar to the LORD. . . . He sacrificed burnt offerings on it" (Gen. 8:20). Noah's altar introduced the practice of altar building. The burnt offering signified dedication to God and exaltation of God. The altar denoted relationship and worship; it is vitally linked to prayer. This connection is set forth in Revelation 8:3–4: "Another angel, who had a golden censer, came and stood at the altar. He was given much incense to offer, with the prayers of all the saints, on the golden altar before the throne. The smoke of the incense, together with the prayers of the saints, went up before God from the angel's hand."

Of this altar in Revelation, W. Shaw Caldecott observes:

PART 1

**Chapter 1
Prayers
of the
Patriarchs
and Their
Contem-
poraries**

PART 1

Chapter 1
Prayers
of the
Patriarchs
and Their
Contem-
poraries

It is described as "the golden altar which was before the throne," and, with the smoke of its incense, there went up before God the prayers of the saints. This imagery is in harmony with the statement of [Luke] that as the priests burnt incense, "the whole multitude of people were praying without [outside] at the hour of incense" [Luke 1:10]. In this way both history and prophecy attest the abiding truth that salvation is by sacrificial blood, and is made available through the prayers of saints and sinners offered by a great High Priest.[2]

By divine revelation Noah perceived that his acceptance by God and his effectual prayer to God were dependent upon a blood sacrifice. The same principle applies today, but the blood is that which was shed once and for all at Calvary. That is why Jesus said, "No one comes to the Father except through me" (John 14:6). When prayer is made "in the name of Jesus," we assume not only the power and glory of Jesus Christ but also the access and acceptance provided by the divine sacrifice and the shed blood of the Son of God. By faith Noah understood this principle when he built his altar and made his sacrifice upon it. (See also Heb. 9:21; 10:19.)

Abraham

Though others before him had true faith in God and demonstrated it by their praying and altar building, it is Abraham who can be called the founder of the faith. Never in Scripture are those of "the faith" or "the faithful" identified as children of Adam, or of Seth, or of Enoch, or of Noah. Invariably they are identified (by themselves or others) as "children of Abraham" (e.g., Gal. 3:6–9). Israelites who prayed to God in generations after Abraham commonly addressed the Lord as "the God of Abraham."

Archaeological excavations at Ur of the Chaldees show that Abram (Abraham) lived his earlier years in a very idolatrous, materialistic culture. The name "Ur" may be derived from a root word meaning "light." The city was a center of the worship of the moon god Sin (also called

---

[2]James Orr, ed., *International Standard Bible Encyclopedia,* vol. 1 (Grand Rapids: Wm. B. Eerdmans Publishing Co., 1939), 112.

Nanna by the earlier Sumerians). Since this is the case, it is even more to Abraham's credit that he became so devoted to the true God. Abraham's lineage is traced all the way back to Seth (Gen. 11). It may be that Abraham's faith was the full-bloomed flower of Seth's faith, when people began "to call on the name of the Lord" (Gen. 4:26).

PART 1

Chapter 1
Prayers
of the
Patriarchs
and Their
Contem-
poraries

Why did this single patriarch, with a somewhat dubious heritage, rise to such an esteemed and enormous spiritual stature with continuing influence? For two evident reasons: (1) his obedience to the word of the Lord and (2) his building of altars for public worship and for calling upon the name of the Lord. These two evidences of an unshakable belief in God made Abraham a giant of faith and the father of the faithful.

The Significance of an Altar

Notice the references to Abraham's activity of building altars to the Lord:

The LORD appeared to Abram, and said, "To your offspring I will give this land." So he built an altar there to the LORD, who had appeared to him. From there he went on toward the hills east of Bethel.... There he built an altar to the LORD and called on the name of the LORD (Gen. 12:7–8).

He went from place to place until he came to Bethel ... where he had first built an altar. There Abram called on the name of the LORD (Gen. 13:3–4).

Each instance of building an altar anticipates a meeting between humanity and divinity. In the previous passages notice that Abraham "called on the name of the LORD" at the site of the altar, indicating his awareness that in building an altar he was making preparation for a special relationship with God. Abraham built another altar in Hebron (Gen. 13:18) and another, his most memorable, on Mount Moriah: "When Abraham and his entourage reached the place God had told him about, Abraham built an altar there and arranged the wood on it. He bound his son Isaac and laid him on the altar, on top of the wood" (Gen. 22:9).

Hearing the word of the Lord, worshiping at an altar, and showing faith in Almighty God are inseparable in the

██████████

PART 1

Chapter 1
Prayers
of the
Patriarchs
and Their
Contem-
poraries

Old Testament narratives. There can be physical altars without a corresponding faith in the supernatural, but it is doubtful there can be genuine faith without hearing the Word of the Lord (Rom. 10:17) and setting apart a meeting place with God.

Abraham is identified by God as "my friend" (Isa. 41:8). Friendship indicates close relationship and communion. In studying the life of this remarkable patriarch, one is struck with the evidences of an ongoing intimacy with God. Note the interaction between God and Abraham in this passage:

After this, the word of the LORD came to Abram in a vision: "Do not be afraid, Abram. I am your shield, your very great reward." But Abram said, "O Sovereign LORD, what can you give me since I remain childless and the one who will inherit my estate is Eliezer of Damascus?" And Abram said, "You have given me no children; so a servant in my household will be my heir." Then the word of the LORD came to him: "This man will not be your heir, but a son coming from your own body will be your heir" (Gen. 15:1–4).

When Abram was ninety-nine years old, the Lord appeared to him and said, "I am God Almighty; walk before me and be blameless. I will confirm my covenant between me and you and will greatly increase your numbers." Abram fell face down, and God said to him, "As for me, this is my covenant with you . . ." (Gen. 17:1–3).

Note the signposts of communion between Abraham and God in later verses of Genesis 17:
"God also said to Abraham . . ." (v. 15).
"Abraham said to God . . ." (v. 18).
"Then God said . . ." (v. 19).
"When he had finished speaking with Abraham, God went up from him" (v. 22).
Out of intimacy with God sprang Abraham's impassioned intercession for Sodom and Gomorrah. He maintained such a vital relationship with God that God was able to share with Abraham His very heart regarding those two cities: "The LORD said, "Shall I hide from Abraham what I am about to do?" (Gen. 18:17). And because of this intimacy Abraham became the mighty intercessor (Gen. 18:23–33). And

so was launched the practice of intercession, a ministry reinforced by New Testament instruction that makes such a ministry incumbent on God's servants even today.

Abraham's intercessions, though they did not prevent God's wrath falling upon those extremely wicked cities, did avail to deliver Lot and his family: "When God destroyed the cities of the plain, he remembered Abraham, and he brought Lot out of the catastrophe" (Gen. 19:29). The lesson for us is this: Meaningful intercession comes only from a heart which through intimacy with the divine senses the burden of God's heart.

PART 1

Chapter 1
Prayers
of the
Patriarchs
and Their
Contem-
poraries

When Abraham Did Not Pray

Though Abraham was the epitome of a person of faith, he still bore the burden of his own humanity. While he could and did rise to great heights in his relationship with God, he was nonetheless vulnerable to failure when he did not pray. More than once he failed because he presumed and leaned on his own resources. With Sarah his wife, Abraham tried to fulfill God's promise through human means: "She said to Abram, ... 'Go, sleep with my maidservant [Hagar]; perhaps I can build a family through her.' Abram agreed to what Sarai said" (Gen. 16:2). The results of this episode were not merely the birth of a child, Ishmael, but the launching of a line of descendants who would often be a thorn in the side of Israel (see Gal. 4:22–29).

Again, in his meeting with Abimelech, king of Gerar (Gen. 20), Abraham acted according to his own counsel. He thought, but he did not pray. Fearing for his life, he decided to call Sarah his sister. When his deceit became known, Abraham rationalized his action: " 'I said to myself [I thought," KJV], "There is surely no fear of God in this place and they will kill me because of my wife" ' " (Gen. 20:11).

By his folly and failure, which were so out of character for this stalwart of the faith, Abraham created a dangerous circumstance for Abimelech. "God came to Abimelech in a dream one night and said to him, 'You are as good as dead because of the woman you have taken; she is a married woman' " (Gen. 20:3).

We can neither probe God's mind nor understand why

PART 1

Chapter 1
Prayers
of the
Patriarchs
and Their
Contem-
poraries

He dealt so harshly with the king who unwittingly became a victim of Abraham's deception, but we should at least learn that our prayerlessness can lead to choosing a course of action that will inflict loss and harm, not only to ourselves but to innocent persons around us. While Abraham did fail by his own prayerlessness, he did not allow that failure to discourage further praying. Instead, he seized upon the opportunity to discover a new dimension in prayer—prayer for healing—and found God's ear open to his appeal: "Abraham prayed to God, and God healed Abimelech, his wife, and his slave girls so they could have children again, for the LORD had closed up every womb in Abimelech's household because of Abraham's wife Sarah" (Gen. 20:17–18).

Eliezer _God of help_

The spiritual influence of Abraham was reflected in the life of his trusted servant, Eliezer. Eliezer's parents, probably from Damascus, were evidently servants of Abraham when Eliezer was born: "Abram said, 'O Sovereign Lord, what can you give me since I remain childless and the one who will inherit my estate is Eliezer of Damascus? ... A servant in my household will be my heir' " (Gen. 15:2–3).

From Eliezer's infancy the faith and prayer life of Abraham exerted a strong influence on the child. Whoever chose his name—which means "God of help"—gave evidence of a strong faith and belief in God. Apparently Abraham's praying was not only a private encounter with God, but also a household practice involving his servants. The truth inherent in the relationship between Abraham and Eliezer is self-evident: We "spur one another on toward love and good deeds" (Heb. 10:24) by our example and practice.

Consequently, years later, when Abraham's servant (most probably Eliezer) was commissioned to find a bride for Abraham's son, Isaac, he invoked divine guidance and assistance just as his master had taught him to do: "He prayed, 'O LORD, God of my master Abraham, give me success today, and show kindness to my master Abraham' " (Gen. 24:12). Surely God desires involvement in the affairs of ordinary people and is pleased to participate when they acknowledge their dependence upon Him and pursue His intervention.

Although Western culture does not generally subscribe to the manner of bride selection followed by Abraham for his son Isaac, the principle of inviting divine involvement in the process is not outdated. A return to earnest entreaty and dependence on God in mate selection could well reverse the detestable divorce rate that in many countries threatens to bring about the collapse of the God-ordained home and family.

The means of guidance followed by Eliezer deserves thoughtful attention, for it is used (and sometimes abused) when believers today seek to discover God's will and direction for other decisions:

> "See, I am standing beside this spring, and the daughters of the townspeople are coming out to draw water. May it be that when I say to a girl, 'Please let down your jar that I may have a drink,' and she says, 'Drink, and I'll water your camels too'—let her be the one you have chosen for your servant Isaac. By this I will know that you have shown kindness to my master" (Gen. 24:13–14).

It is certainly possible for God to guide today through circumstances one dictates (as in Eliezer's experience); however, we must be aware of guidelines which seem more appropriate and applicable in the New Testament era. (These will be discussed in later chapters. Note especially chapters 11 and 16.) But despite any questions we may have about the appropriateness of following Eliezer's example in the use of prayer, we must not forget that God honored his faith and his prayer and caused a response from Rebekah in exact harmony with the petition. Eliezer was not left in wonder or doubt. He was also quick to acknowledge God's intervention and divine guidance: "The man bowed down and worshiped the LORD, saying, 'Praise be to the LORD, the God of my master Abraham, who has not abandoned his kindness and faithfulness to my master. As for me, the LORD has led me on the journey to the house of my master's relatives' " (Gen. 24:26–27).

PART 1

**Chapter 1
Prayers
of the
Patriarchs
and Their
Contem-
poraries**

PART 1

Chapter 1
Prayers
of the
Patriarchs
and Their
Contem-
poraries

Isaac

Like Eliezer, Isaac carried the imprint of his father's godly influence. He was also an altar builder and a person of prayer. "The LORD appeared to him and said, . . . 'Do not be afraid, for I am with you; I will bless you and will increase the number of your descendants for the sake of my servant Abraham.' Isaac built an altar there and called on the name of the LORD" (Gen. 26:24–25).

Very little is written of Isaac's praying, although his intimate relationship with God cannot be questioned. He knew God. He heard His voice, he obeyed, and he experienced God's blessings. Indeed, he had personally observed God's intervention at his father's altar, when he himself was the sacrifice, and it no doubt marked him forever. He could have no gnawing question of God's reality. What a foundation for effective praying. "Anyone who comes to him [God] must believe that he exists" (Heb. 11:6).

The biblical record of Isaac's praying is limited to a single request, though that in no way should be construed to mean that he did not have a consistent prayer experience. "Isaac prayed to the LORD on behalf of his wife, because she was barren . . . and his wife Rebekah became pregnant" (Gen. 25:21). The word "prayed" used here suggests more than a casual petition. It derives from the Hebrew 'atar, which in earliest usage was related to a sacrifice. Isaac's prayer was not just a polite request; with intense application he interceded on Rebekah's behalf. The Hebrew also indicates continued or repeated pleading during the twenty years between their marriage and the birth of the twins. He did not give up.

His wife's barrenness was no small concern to both Rebekah and Isaac. For Rebekah, barrenness imposed an especially heavy burden. In those days many felt it indicated divine displeasure; at the least, her barrenness deprived her of every Hebrew woman's highest ambition—giving birth to a son. And for Isaac, it meant being deprived of an heir. His concern no doubt paralleled that of his father, Abraham, when he despaired, "You have given me no children; so a servant in my household will be my heir" (Gen. 15:3). And as we come face to face with Isaac's consuming passion, we learn a very meaningful lesson on how to confront life's major problems: Prayer that receives a divine answer is personal and intense.

PART 1

Chapter 1
Prayers
of the
Patriarchs
and Their
Contem-
poraries

An interesting sidelight is found in the phrase "on behalf of his wife." The literal meaning is "directly in front of his wife." The implication is that Isaac united with Rebekah in supplication over their mutual problem. So here we have an introduction to a prayer principle of major significance: Agreement of as few as two in prayer greatly increases the effectiveness of the praying. For "if two of you on earth agree about anything you ask for, it will be done for you by my Father in heaven" (Matt. 18:19).

Although Scripture only once speaks directly of Isaac's praying, tucked away in the record is a statement that suggests a prayer-related practice worthy of emulation: "[Isaac] went out to the field one evening to meditate" (Gen. 24:63). Here is the earliest mention of the practice of meditation in Scripture. In various Old Testament passages, the word carries the meaning of reflection on God's works and His Word. Meditation can be a substantial support of prayer, for it sharpens one's perception of the problem or need and at the same time focuses on God and His ability to intervene. David engaged in something akin to meditation when in the face of great opposition he "found strength in the Lord his God" (1 Sam. 30:6).

Jacob

Jacob's God was the God of his grandfather Abraham. Godliness has a way of passing from generation to generation, although, as a result of Adam and Eve's sin (Gen. 3), a natural downward declension seems always present, almost like a spiritual law of gravity. Jacob gives proof of this fact, for despite the solid evidence that the faith of his forefather Abraham dwelt in him, there is also evidence of deterioration, or at least an exaggerated conflict between walking after the Spirit (i.e., faith) and walking after the flesh.

Jacob was a curious combination. In him is seen the domination of the Adamic nature, with its bent toward self-seeking, deception, subtlety, and prayerlessness. At the same

PART 1

Chapter 1
Prayers
of the
Patriarchs
and Their
Contem-
poraries

time, as if ever present and ready to burst through the crust of depravity, was that unfeigned faith in the one true God and the belief in His promise. Jacob apparently found it natural and easy to go in his own strength, to rely on his own ingenuity, rather than submit to God. But it is to his credit that when the pressure was on, his faith engaged like an auxiliary generator when the power supply fails. Indeed, Jacob had a heart for God and the tenacity to hold onto God in prayer, when circumstances demanded, until his faith was rewarded. So while there is good reason to believe that Jacob's prayerlessness paved the way for the many subtle and destructive manifestations of sinful flesh in his life, there is also concrete evidence that prayer, when he finally resorted to it, enabled him to escape the snares of the flesh and attain a coveted spiritual stature.

Early evidence of Jacob's communing with God is seen in Genesis 28. By this time, Jacob had already engaged in some devious activity. He had deceived his own father. He had wrenched the birthright from his older brother. Now he was fleeing to Haran to avoid Esau's wrath. The location was Bethel. Despite these fleshly escapades, God saw beyond to Jacob's heart and the fulfillment of a higher divine purpose. God visited Jacob in a dream, telling him that he would be directly involved in the fulfillment of the Abrahamic covenant. As a consequence, Jacob prayed, expressing his gratitude for God's promise in the form of a vow:

Jacob made a vow, saying, "If [or "Since"] God will be with me and will watch over me on this journey I am taking and will give me food to eat and clothes to wear so that I return safely to my father's house, then the LORD will be my God and this stone that I have set up as a pillar will be God's house, and of all that you give me I will give you a tenth" (Gen. 28:20–22).

Making a vow to God is often a part of praying, and it carries with it serious obligations. "You will pray to him, and he will hear you, and you will fulfill your vows" (Job 22:27; see also Num. 30:2 and Eccles. 5:4–5).

Jacob's greatest praying occurred at the time of his greatest stress, when he feared for his life. Even though he had been commanded by God to return to his country and kindred after spending many years away from home, he fell into the vicious grip of fear. Would Esau spare his life? Nearly overcome by fear and distress, Jacob divided his people, flocks, herds, and camels into two groups so that some would escape if Esau should come against him violently:

Jacob prayed, "O God of my father Abraham, God of my father Isaac, O Lord, who said to me, 'Go back to your country and your relatives, and I will make you prosper,' I am unworthy of all the kindness and faithfulness you have shown your servant. I had only my staff when I crossed this Jordan, but now I have become two groups. Save me, I pray, from the hand of my brother Esau, for I am afraid he will come and attack me, and also the mothers with their children" (Gen. 32:9–11).

PART 1

Chapter 1
Prayers
of the
Patriarchs
and Their
Contem-
poraries

His fear was well-founded. His brother was moving in his direction with four hundred armed men. This was the same brother from whom by deception he had stolen both the birthright and the blessing. Fear is terrible. It gnaws at the core of a person. It chases away sleep and inflames the brain. John the Beloved wrote, "Fear has to do with punishment" (1 John 4:18). And we might add, fear always enlarges the problem.

What should we do with our fear? Let Jacob be our mentor: He prayed. And his prayer was most exemplary. First, he identified his God: " 'O God of my father Abraham, God of my father Isaac.' " Then he identified God's promise to him: " 'O Lord, who said to me, "Go back to your country and your relatives, and I will make you prosper." ' " Next, he identified his own unworthiness of God's goodness and blessings: " 'I am unworthy of all the kindness and faithfulness you have shown your servant.' " Finally, he identified his petition and his fear: " 'Save me . . . from the hand of my brother . . . for I am afraid.' "

Jacob was not content just to pray. He did all in his power to heal the breach between himself and his brother. But having done everything he could to make peace with his brother, he still had a deep-seated uncertainty and a growing awareness that his foremost problem was not his brother, but himself. What an agonizing experience it is to have to admit to one's true condition. Such a realization

PART 1

Chapter 1
Prayers
of the
Patriarchs
and Their
Contem-
poraries

and agony can be settled only by God. "Jacob was left alone, and a man wrestled with him till daybreak" (Gen. 32:24).

Who was the man Jacob wrestled? Jacob soon recognized him: "Jacob called the place Peniel, saying, 'It is because I saw God face to face, and yet my life was spared'" (Gen. 32:30). Recalling Jacob's experience years later, Hosea made the same identification: "He struggled with the angel and overcame him; he wept and begged for his favor. He found him at Bethel and talked with him there—the LORD God Almighty, the LORD is his name" (Hos. 12:4–5).

The simple fact is that Jacob struggled with God. It is not difficult to determine the reason. Jacob wanted God's blessing, but at the same time Jacob was the reason God could not honor the desperate pleas. All night the battle raged. All night Jacob cried, "Bless me." All night God responded, "What is your name?" The flesh is weak and strong at the same time. It is weak in that it cannot bow to God and die; it is strong in that it insists on living. Dying is never easy, especially dying to one's sinful, fleshly self.

"What is your name?" Why should God be so insistent? Why should the struggle go on all night? Didn't God know his name? Indeed He did. But to admit the name was to expose the whole problem—Jacob himself, the liar, the supplanter, the deceiver. Jacob could admit unworthiness and need (Gen. 32:10), but how utterly humiliating to appear naked before the Almighty, without any self-fabricated covering.

It was only after God disabled the resisting flesh (Gen. 32:25) that the flesh surrendered and the confession came. Finally, the stubborn wrestler admitted, "I am Jacob." That was all God required; that swung wide the door for God's blessing. Jacob's finally confessing his identity was the key to becoming the person God desired him to be. God said, "Your name will no longer be Jacob, but Israel, because you have struggled with God and with men and have overcome'" (Gen. 32:28).

By his praying and wrestling, Jacob prevailed and became Israel, God's victor and prince. As he came to grips with his own human nature and let God give him a new nature for the old, Jacob's problem with his brother was also resolved. The principle is still vital: The external problems we bring to God in prayer are sometimes answered by a miracle of internal change.

Jacob never forgot his Peniel experience. He was never the same again. Years later he expressed his gratitude for God's faithfulness by returning to the site of another supernatural experience—Bethel—and there building an altar to God (Gen. 35:3).

Although the Book of Job appears much later in the canon, there is great uncertainty about its date and the time Job lived. We include it here simply because it has the setting and sound of the Patriarchal period. For example, like the patriarchs, Job offered his own sacrifices. Job's wealth was measured like Abraham's, in terms of livestock and servants. And his life span was similar to that recorded for the patriarchs.

Prayer takes on a whole new dimension in this most remarkable account of someone tested almost beyond human endurance. From Job we may well learn both how not to pray and how better to pray when confronted with circumstances defying all rational explanation. "'Oh, that I might have my request, that God would grant what I hope for, that God would be willing to crush me, to let loose his hand and cut me off!' " (Job 6:8–9).

Desperate people lose sight of life. Not uncommonly, they pray to die (cf. Num. 11:11–15; 1 Kings 19:4; Jon. 4:3). Yet nowhere in Scripture is there a single instance of God honoring such a request. Job's problem, as with those of all mortals, was his inability to discern the divine purpose and to see beyond the present. At such times, the truth of God can scarcely set foot in the human heart, and one must wrestle with Satan, a master at accentuating darkness. Yet Christians have the blessed Paraclete (Comforter, Helper, Counselor) for help and comfort. "The Spirit helps us in our weakness. We do not know what we ought to pray for, but the Spirit himself intercedes for us with groans that words cannot express" (Rom. 8:26).

How then should we approach life's darkest hours and most severe tests? What should we do when we seem

PART 1

**Chapter 1
Prayers
of the
Patriarchs
and Their
Contem-
poraries**

PART 1

Chapter 1
Prayers
of the
Patriarchs
and Their
Contem-
poraries

utterly unable to find an answer to a prevailing condition, when all hope of recovery has fled, when death seems the only way out? James tells us: "The testing of your faith develops perseverance. Perseverance must finish its work so that you may be mature and complete, not lacking anything. If any of you lacks wisdom, he should ask God, who gives generously to all without finding fault, and it will be given to him" (James 1:3–5).

God's Purposes

Immediate deliverance may not be the will of God; but, if that be the case, God can give us wisdom so that we can grasp His intent and then submit to it. Fierce circumstances drive people to searching inquiry; and it may be concluded, at least in part, that this is one reason for the circumstances. When there is no extreme pressure, no shining diamonds of eternal value emerge.

"What is man that you make so much of him, that you give him so much attention, that you examine him every morning and test him every moment? Will you never look away from me, or let me alone even for an instant? If I have sinned, what have I done to you, O watcher of men? Why have you made me your target? Have I become a burden to you? Why do you not pardon my offenses and forgive my sins? For I will soon lie down in the dust; you will search for me, but I will be no more" (Job 7:17–21).

Job, in this instance, sought to reason with God about His attention to mere human beings. Why, after all, should the eternal God concern himself with such insignificant creatures as we are? The Greek Epicurean philosophers held that God paid no attention whatever to this world, or to what happened in it, but instead dwelt in security and tranquility, with nothing vexing, disturbing, or displeasing Him. Yet Job perceived the opposite to be true and wondered why. "Why, God, are you such a people-watcher? Why do you make so much over an individual like me?" he questioned.

We may find ourselves praying the same prayer in the midst of seemingly unending tests and trials. Yet God does

God is a people watcher

PART 1

**Chapter 1
Prayers
of the
Patriarchs
and Their
Contem-
poraries**

in fact concern himself with the good and evil seemingly so inextricable about us that we can't discern one from the other. The opposite view, that God does not know, or does not care, about human circumstances, actually degrades rather than exalts deity.

Expression in Times of Despair

The person bewildered by circumstances beyond human remedy is tempted to blame God for the suffering. If God can relieve suffering, but does not, the human mind reasons, He must accept responsibility for the unrelieved pain. Inflamed and confused with its own wrestling, the human mind yields to the superior opponents of frustration and despair. So it was with Job, whose extreme sorrow had clouded his vision, distorting his view of God.

"If I say, 'I will forget my complaint, I will change my expression, and smile,' I still dread all my sufferings, for I know you will not hold me innocent. Since I am already found guilty, why should I struggle in vain? Even if I washed myself with soap and my hands with washing soda, you would plunge me into a slime pit so that even my clothes would detest me. He is not a man like me that I might answer him, that we might confront each other in court. If only there were someone to arbitrate between us, to lay his hand upon us both, someone to remove God's rod from me, so that his terror would frighten me no more" (Job 9:27–34).

Suffering can bring a person close to losing mental and emotional equilibrium. We cannot hold Job in derision for the bitterness of soul reflected in his praying.

"I loathe my very life; therefore I will give free rein to my complaint and speak out in the bitterness of my soul. I will say to God: Do not condemn me, but tell me what charges you have against me.... Your hands shaped me and made me. Will you now turn and destroy me? ... If I am guilty—woe to me! Even if I am innocent, I cannot lift my head, for I am full of shame and drowned in my affliction. If I hold my head high, you stalk me like a lion and again display your awesome power against me.... Why then did you bring me out of the womb? I wish I had died before any eye saw me. If only I had never come into

PART 1

Chapter 1
Prayers
of the
Patriarchs
and Their
Contem-
poraries

being, or had been carried straight from the womb to the grave! Are not my few days almost over? Turn away from me so I can have a moment's joy before I go to the place of no return, to the land of gloom and deep shadow" (Job 10:1–2,8,15–16,18–21).

Job readily recognized God's ascendancy over him; nevertheless, he could not resolve the mystery of his own circumstances. People are sometimes so occupied with their circumstances that they cannot see beyond them. Could Job have seen the end of his experience, his attitude would have changed completely. At the same time, God's glorious purpose would have been short-circuited, and Job himself would never have realized God's best. Those who know God also know that the glorious end is in His hands. That confidence breeds trust and peace. When facing a trial like Job's, we must focus not on the present dilemma but on the assurance that the end is designed by a loving God.

Desperate people pray to die or, at the very least, to escape through flight (see Ps. 55:6). But escapism seldom produces a worthy solution. Think of what Job would have lost if this prayer of his had been answered: " 'If only you would hide me in the grave and conceal me till your anger has passed! If only you would set me a time and then remember me! If a man dies, will he live again? All the days of my hard service I will wait for my renewal to come' " (Job 14:13–14).

Although there are confrontational elements in this prayer, when such a prayer grows out of an honest confusion and intensity of suffering God is not offended or angered. It appears that Job was struggling over the full meaning of life and death. He appealed for light about the future: "If a man die, shall he live again?" Deep trials and fierce struggles forces one to face issues squarely. The Christian, however, has a grand advantage, for our Savior Jesus Christ has "destroyed death and has brought life and immortality to light through the gospel" (2 Tim. 1:10).

In such times a person does well to recall Solomon's admonition, "Trust in the LORD with all your heart and lean not on your own understanding" (Prov. 3:5). In due season, the clouds will disappear (as they did for Job) and God

PART 1

**Chapter 1
Prayers
of the
Patriarchs
and Their
Contem-
poraries**

will be seen for who He truly is: the God of great wisdom as well as mercy.

Submission to God's Sovereignty

The morbid and embittered tone of Job's praying eventually changed. Something precipitated a turnabout. Job himself explained the cause: " 'My ears had heard of you but now my eyes have seen you' " (Job 42:5). His perspective on the whole of life, and even death, was vastly altered when he beheld God as He truly is:

"I am unworthy—how can I reply to you? I put my hand over my mouth. I spoke once, but I have no answer—twice, but I will say no more" (Job 40:3–5).

"I know that you can do all things; no plan of yours can be thwarted.... My ears had heard of you but now my eyes have seen you. Therefore I despise myself and repent in dust and ashes" (Job 42:1–2,5–6).

No longer did Job attempt to match wits with God and to resolve rationally his own problem. No longer did he plead his own righteousness. No longer did he wrestle with frustrations over circumstances that seemed to have no end. Instead, he began to see himself in an entirely new light, which is indeed what always happens when people see God (see Isa. 6:1–5). Now he saw himself as "unworthy." His confession was humble and honest: "I have spoken too much. Who was I to argue and debate with God? Surely I sought to deal with matters far beyond my puny ability, matters of which I was plainly ignorant, matters upon which I should have had the good sense to be silent" (paraphrase). Genuine confession leads to, or may indeed be a part of, true repentance. " 'Therefore I ... repent in dust and ashes' " (42:6).

The patriarchs were persons of prayer. Though they preceded the formalized pattern of worship and forgiveness given through Moses, they knew that God demanded sacrifice and obedience. Meeting these requirements, they enjoyed a communion which demonstrates that God speaks to and accepts worship from those who sincerely seek His face.

PART 1

Chapter 1
Prayers
of the
Patriarchs
and Their
Contem-
poraries

Questions for Study

1. What are some examples from the patriarchs that show how prayer and faith are related?

2. What are some examples from the patriarchs that show how prayer and obedience are related?

3. Are there characteristics of the prayers of Abraham that are a good example for us to follow today? Explain.

4. What is the value of meditation, and how can we incorporate it more effectively in our prayer life?

5. Is there a sense in which we, like Jacob, must wrestle in prayer? How can we increase the intensity of our prayers in a more positive manner?

6. What are the chief lessons we can learn from Job's prayers?

THE PRAYERS OF MOSES

Prayer Communion & God

With the founding of Israel as a nation, the Patriarchal Period ended and God began dealing with His people under a national covenant given to Moses at Sinai. Yet access into God's presence was no more difficult than it was before. God is ever seeking to restore fellowship with mankind, even though He may at various times use different means to provide forgiveness for sin and to commune intimately with those who obey His word and desire to know Him.

Of all the personalities of the Old Testament who engaged in prayer to the Lord, it is doubtful that any can compare to Moses, either in results of prayer or in profound impact on the theology of prayer. We might well expect this, for Moses prophesied that another prophet like himself, whom Peter identified as Christ Jesus, would be raised up as God's voice to His people: " 'The Lord your God will raise up for you a prophet like me from among your own people; you must listen to everything he tells you' " (Acts 3:22; cf. Deut. 18:18).

Prayer and communication with God were virtually Moses' sole occupation, especially following his emancipation of Israel from Egyptian bondage. His ear was so tuned to God that Scripture is peppered with the statement, "as the Lord commanded Moses." The expression can be

████████
PART 1
Chapter 2
The
Prayers
of Moses

found eighteen times in Exodus 39 and 40 alone. Moses' entire life as Israel's leader and deliverer was marked by intimate communion with God. (Although the scope of this study will not permit the examination of every instance of dialogue between God and Moses, such a study would be immensely rewarding.)

Although it is not mentioned in Scripture, Moses' praying very likely began at the knee of his godly mother. This habit, along with his early knowledge of the experiences of Abraham, Isaac, and Jacob, provides the clue to understanding his superior godly stature that manifested itself so profoundly in the face of unbelievable pressures and temptations:

By faith Moses, when he had grown up, refused to be known as the son of Pharaoh's daughter. He chose to be mistreated along with the people of God rather than to enjoy the pleasures of sin for a short time. He regarded disgrace for the sake of Christ as of greater value than the treasures of Egypt, because he was looking ahead to his reward (Heb. 11:24–26).

Responding to God's Call

The first record of Moses' praying is found in Exodus 3. God, however, took the initiative here, for it was God who spoke first.

Moses was tending the flock of Jethro his father-in-law, the priest of Midian, and he led the flock to the far side of the desert and came to Horeb, the mountain of God. There the angel of the LORD appeared to him in flames of fire from within a bush. Moses saw that though the bush was on fire it did not burn up. So Moses thought, "I will go over and see this strange sight—why the bush does not burn up." When the LORD saw that he had gone over to look, God called to him from within the bush, "Moses! Moses!" And Moses said, "Here I am" (Exod. 3:1–4).

It should be noted that people never pray so well as when they have first heard from God. This is not to suggest that people should wait for a burning bush before they pray, but rather give attention to the Word of God, which can inspire prayer.

No sooner had Moses responded to God than he was

Responding to God's Call **59**

confronted with a divine command: "Do not come any
closer" (Exod. 3:5). The order may appear strange at first
thought, especially in light of James 4:8: "Come near to
God and he will come near to you." Moses, however, had
to learn early that coming near to the mighty God of the
universe, who includes in His very essence holiness and
justice, requires reckoning with His virtues. In other words,
the stage was now set for Moses's future revelations about
access to God.

Though it is well-established that Moses already had an
implicit faith in God, it is apparent also that he had gaps
in his understanding about God: "Moses said to God, 'Suppose I go to the Israelites and say to them, "The God of
your fathers has sent me to you," and they ask me, "What
is his name?" Then what shall I tell them?' " (Exod. 3:13).
Believers today have the full revelation of both the Old
and New Testaments, but like Moses they have an urgent
need for ever greater experiences of His mighty being.
Effective prayer and spiritual leadership are largely determined by our perception of God. Consequently, God was
pleased to impart to His servant an all-encompassing view
of himself: "God said to Moses, 'I AM WHO I AM. This is what
you are to say to the Israelites: "I AM has sent me to you" ' "
(Exod. 3:14). "I am" is a Hebrew form indicating progres-
sive action. It really means "I will demonstrate who I am
by what I will do." In verse 12 the same Hebrew word is
translated "I will be," and thus the name of God is closely
connected with the promise "I will be with you."

God then went on to reveal what He would do to deliver
Israel. One would think that with such a fresh and awesome
revelation of God, Moses would have been so assured as
to face his new challenge with utter confidence. But it was
not so. Nor do our perceptions of God, be they ever so
lofty, inoculate us from fear of our own inadequacies. Often
the opposite is true: the greater our vision of Him, the great
I AM, the greater our vision of ourselves as I-am-nots.

Moses had two major concerns, both of them springing
from his new assignment. First he confessed, "I am not able
to contend with the unbelief of the people" (see Exod.
4:1). Then he complained, "I am not eloquent" (see Exod.
4:10). But for each of these feelings of inferiority, God had

PART 1
Chapter 2
The
Prayers
of Moses

an answer. For every "I am not," God has an "I am." For Moses there was to be supernatural manifestation and supernatural enablement. Should we expect less today? "The disciples went out and preached everywhere, and the Lord worked with them and confirmed his word by the signs that accompanied it" (Mark 16:20).

Timing of Divine Intervention

Moses set out on his mission. One might expect that with God's clear call and positive assurance of enablement, the promised deliverance of Israel would occur without any faltering. Many today tend to make that wrong assumption, and some, when things do not go as anticipated, despair totally and lose heart. But God views the circumstances differently: "'For my thoughts are not your thoughts, neither are your ways my ways,' declares the LORD. 'As the heavens are higher than the earth, so are my ways higher than your ways and my thoughts than your thoughts' " (Isa. 55:8–9). Instead of an immediate and miraculous deliverance, Moses found the exact opposite. Israel's plight grew worse instead of better, and Moses himself received the complaint and wrath of the people: "When they left Pharaoh, they found Moses and Aaron waiting to meet them, and they said, 'May the LORD look upon you and judge you! You have made us a stench to Pharaoh and his officials and have put a sword in their hand to kill us' " (Exod. 5:20–21).

Those who pray today often confront such delays. Why should that be? We can only say that such a deliberate, divine delay has often proven to be a demonstration of divine wisdom beyond human comprehension.

When Moses could not understand, he prayed. Note the passage closely: "Moses returned to the LORD and said, 'O LORD, why have you brought trouble upon this people? Is this why you sent me? Ever since I went to Pharaoh to speak in your name, he has brought trouble upon this people, and you have not rescued your people at all' " (Exod. 5:22–23).

The providence of God is certain, though His timing may, and often does, generate human perplexity. With our hu-

▬▬▬▬
PART 1
Chapter 2
The
Prayers
of Moses

man limitations we see dimly, and then primarily only the present. But God has the whole scene in clear view: the multiplied complexities, the past and present and future aspects, and the many and complicated actions and reactions of people. We dare not charge God with unreasonableness or injustice. "Will not the Judge of all the earth do right?" (Gen. 18:25).

Do not forget that Egypt had served Israel well. It had provided food during Israel's time of famine. It had honored a Hebrew, Joseph, with the highest office in the land next to the pharaoh. It had made room for Israel and its growth, preserving God's people for four hundred years. True, Egypt had exploited Israel under the new pharaoh, enslaving the people and laying impossible burdens upon them. Nevertheless, God was merciful toward the oppressors of His people; His justice allowed time and space for repentance. Longsuffering and patient, He was and is unwilling that any should perish (see 2 Pet. 3:9).

But judgment will not wait forever. In His time, God does act:

The LORD said to Moses, "Now you will see what I will do to Pharaoh: Because of my mighty hand he will let them go; because of my mighty hand he will drive them out of his country." God also said to Moses, "I am the LORD. . . . I have heard the groaning of the Israelites, whom the Egyptians are enslaving, and I have remembered my covenant. Therefore, say to the Israelites: 'I am the LORD, and I will bring you out from under the yoke of the Egyptians. I will free you from being slaves to them, and I will redeem you with an outstretched arm and with mighty acts of judgment. I will take you as my own people, and I will be your God. Then you will know that I am the LORD your God, who brought you out from under the yoke of the Egyptians' " (Exod. 6:1,2,5–7).

How difficult it is for people to be patient, to allow God time to accomplish His purpose. Hope seems to die so quickly when evil surrounds us. The present darkness seems to shout, "The sun will never rise again!" Moses spoke to the Israelites as God had instructed him, "but they did not listen to him because of their discouragement and cruel bondage" (Exod. 6:9).

In the end, Pharaoh, the self-centered monarch of Egypt, was without excuse. He had been given every conceivable opportunity to acknowledge and submit to the one true God. He had witnessed God's might and miracles. He had seen the prayers of Moses answered again and again:

> After Moses and Aaron left Pharaoh, Moses cried out to the LORD about the frogs he had brought on Pharaoh. And the LORD did what Moses asked. The frogs died in the houses, in the courtyards, and in the fields (Exod. 8:12–13).

> Moses left Pharaoh and prayed to the LORD, and the LORD did what Moses asked: The flies left Pharaoh and his officials and his people; not a fly remained (Exod. 8:30–31; see also 9:27–35; 10:16–20).

Finally Pharaoh reached the point of no repentance. There is a time to pray, and there is a time when further prayer is to no avail. John calls it "a sin that leads to death" (1 John 5:16). Pharaoh and his servants had sinned unto death and had sealed their fates. Entreaty could no longer help. Pharaoh had cut himself off from divine mercy, saying to Moses, " 'Get out of my sight! . . . The day you see my face you will die.' 'Just as you say,' Moses replied, 'I will never appear before you again' " (Exod. 10:28–29).

While there is still the slightest hope, prayer should be made. But when every possibility of an answer has fled, one must commit the circumstance to God.

Prayer—Then Action

Moses knew from repeated experience that when he prayed, God acted. But prayer is not the only thing God expects of a person. Along with believing prayer must come action, a stepping out in faith.

> Moses answered the people, "Do not be afraid. Stand firm and you will see the deliverance the LORD will bring . . . The LORD will fight for you; you need only to be still." Then the LORD said to Moses, "Why are you crying out to me? Tell the Israelites to move on" (Exod. 14:13–15).

Coming against Israel from the rear was the enraged Pharaoh and his well-equipped army; in front of Israel was the formidable Red Sea. On Moses rested the burden of a vast and despairing multitude. As was his custom, Moses cried out to the Lord; and as usual, he got an answer: "Quit crying and act! Tell the children of Israel to go forward."

Moses had ordered, "Stand firm. . . . Be still [remain at rest]." But God gave marching orders, "Move on!" There is a subtle danger in passivity, in a let-God-do-it attitude. Yes, there is a time to stand still, to do nothing but rest; but a command to action must be obeyed.

Although God gave a command contrary to the one Moses gave, we must not overlook the demonstration of faith in Moses' command. Though the Israelites went out of Egypt "armed for battle" (Exod. 13:18), God recognized they were not ready for war (13:17). As slaves in Egypt they had had no training for it. Also, they had women and children with them. A professional army could have made quick work of them. But Moses placed his confidence in God. God would deliver them. Moses believed this, even though God had not yet revealed how deliverance would come.[1]

God generally works through people, not apart from them. Our temptation when we pray, as it was with Moses, is to repudiate responsibility, to hope that in some mysterious way God will do what He has already commissioned us to do. But God will not do what He has asked us to do. At His command, we must move on.

Definite and undeniable answers to prayer generate and stimulate faith both in those who observe and in those who pray. "When the Israelites saw the great power the Lord displayed against the Egyptians, the people feared the Lord and put their trust in him and in Moses his servant" (Exod. 14:31). Moses did more than entreat or intercede. He acknowledged God's intervention and was an example in worship and thanksgiving. His song of praise (Exod. 15:1–19) stirred a worshipful response from Miriam and the women of Israel: "Miriam . . . took a tambourine in her hand, and all the women followed her, with tambourines and

---

[1]Umberto Cassuto, *A Commentary on the Book of Exodus,* trans. Israel Abrahams (Jerusalem: The Magnus Press, The Hebrew University, 1967), 163–164.

■■■■■
PART 1
Chapter 2
The
Prayers
of Moses

dancing. Miriam sang to them: 'Sing to the LORD, for he is highly exalted. The horse and its rider he has hurled into the sea' " (Exod. 15:20–21). The lesson from their response is obvious: Spiritual leaders must set the example if they are to see followers involved in the celebration of praise.

Continued Dependence on God

Instances of divine intervention are often the forerunners of problems and untenable circumstances. Though we may bemoan this fact of life, it is no doubt aimed toward our ultimate good. No sooner had the rejoicing over Pharaoh's defeat ended than Moses had to confront new problems: water shortage, bitter waters, complaining people. A person of lesser spiritual stature, faced with similar difficulties, might have been tempted to blame God foolishly. But not Moses. Prayer was his immediate response and resource. Surely the Lord who had permitted Israel to come into the new crisis would lead them through. So Moses prayed and received an immediate answer: "... the LORD showed him a piece of wood. He threw it into the water, and the water became sweet" (Exod. 15:25). Years later Moses was to remind the Israelites of how God had used one crisis after another to humble and test them:

He led you through the vast and dreadful desert, that thirsty and waterless land, with its venomous snakes and scorpions. He brought you water out of hard rock. He gave you manna to eat in the desert, something your fathers had never known, to humble and to test you so that in the end it might go well with you (Deut. 8:15–16).

Spiritual leadership is costly. It is certainly not for the fainthearted and faithless. When things went well, God received glory; but when things did not go well, the leaders bore the wrath of the people: "There was no water for the people to drink. So they quarreled with Moses and said, 'Give us water to drink' " (Exod. 17:1–2). People tend to see only their circumstances and their leadership—seldom anything beyond. In this crisis they blamed Moses for their plight. From their point of view, Moses (not God) had brought them out of Egypt. They forgot that Moses was only God's servant. So Moses was the object of their wrath: "'Why did you bring us up out of Egypt to make us and our children and livestock die of thirst?'" (Exod. 17:3).

How should spiritual leaders respond when people turn on them? The example of Moses is the one to follow. He might have answered back sharply. He might have argued and explained. He might have succumbed to self-pity and despair. Instead, he did what spiritual leadership must always do: "Moses cried out to the LORD, 'What am I to do with these people? They are almost ready to stone me'" (Exod. 17:4). Prayer was the one thing he could do without fear of doing the wrong thing. To have done any of the things his human nature might have dictated would not have solved the problem. It would only have agitated and inflamed the people more, and Moses might have lost his life. But when he chose to pray, God immediately responded. God knows the right course of action for every situation, and He instructed Moses about what he should do:

"Walk on ahead of the people. Take with you some of the elders of Israel and take in your hand the staff with which you struck the Nile, and go. I will stand there before you by the rock at Horeb. Strike the rock, and water will come out of it for the people to drink." So Moses did this in the sight of the elders of Israel (Exod. 17:5–6).

Human beings are by nature bound largely by the five senses. What people can see and hold they believe. Consequently, many want to worship a god they can see. They have problems with the invisible. Yet until a person can escape the bondage of the material world, he or she will not rightly relate to the God of the supernatural. Paul captured this truth succinctly: "So we fix our eyes not on what is seen, but on what is unseen. For what is seen is temporary, but what is unseen is eternal" (2 Cor. 4:18).

Perhaps one of Moses' greatest strengths was his ability to comprehend the invisible God and then relate to Him: "The people remained at a distance, while Moses approached the thick darkness where God was" (Exod. 20:21). The people drew back, but Moses drew near. Darkness is not always evil; in this instance, God was in it. Yet why would God wrap himself in a mantle of thick darkness? Darkness cannot be in God (John 1:5), but He can be in the darkness. Out of the "thick darkness" God spoke to Moses, giving him commandments for the people, instructions on altar building, and promises of His blessing.

The very angels veil their faces before the Lord of Hosts, and feel themselves unworthy to gaze upon the Divine perfections. But where love increases, fear diminishes. Let love grow, and become strong, and glow within the heart like a flame of fire—by degrees fear changes its character, ceases to be a timorous dread, and becomes awe.... Love draws us towards God more than awe keeps us back. Love ... rejoices that it may "go boldly to the throne of grace.".... "Moses drew near into the thick darkness where God was." The loving soul presses towards God—would "see him face to face"—and "know even as it also is known."[2]

Moses, the Intercessor

The overwhelming tone of Moses' praying was totally unselfish. It was concerned primarily with Israel's relationship with God. This concern for Israel is especially evident in his prayers in Exodus 32.

Interceding for Transgressors

The first of Moses' prayers for Israel occurred while he was still on Sinai, holding in his hands the tables of the Law, newly engraved by God. God had revealed to Moses the gross idolatry of Israel. His request of Moses seems strange, from our point of view: " 'Now leave me alone so that my anger may burn against them and that I may destroy them. Then I will make you into a great nation' " (Exod. 32:10).

At that moment Moses faced a painful dilemma. On the one hand he was the advocate for a people who had flagrantly offended divine justice; on the other hand he was

---

[2]H. D. M. Spence and Joseph S. Exell, eds., *The Pulpit Commentary* (Grand Rapids: Wm. B. Eerdmans Pub. Co., 1950), vol. 1, *Exodus,* by George Rawlinson, 163.

the advocate for divine integrity and justice. We should understand that God was neither commanding nor instructing Moses to allow divine justice to run its course. Rather, God was provoking Moses to that kind of advocacy which would justify His sparing Israel and preserve His integrity in the eyes of the Egyptians. The true advocate and intercessor can be an instrument to influence the final outcome: "The LORD relented and did not bring on his people the disaster he had threatened" (Exod. 32:14).

The second prayer (Exod. 32:30–35) followed Moses' return to the camp of the congregation. God was not going to destroy Israel en masse, as justice seemed to require; but He would sift the congregation and require that individuals publicly declare their allegiance. "He [Moses] stood at the entrance to the camp and said, 'Whoever is for the LORD, come to me' " (Exod. 32:26). The stage seemed set for God's judgment.

Once again Moses was overwhelmed with the obvious plight of his people. He identified so profoundly with them that he was ready to die with them. Nevertheless, he quickly learned that deep concern for the transgressor's fearful lot can go only so far. Though he was willing to die for his sinning followers, in the end each of them would (each of us will) have to give a personal account before the Almighty. "The LORD replied to Moses, 'Whoever has sinned against me I will blot out of my book' " (Exod. 32:33). (The only exception to this divine principle came at Calvary, when God gave His Son to die for the sin of all mankind. But even now, each person is responsible for receiving or rejecting divine grace and mercy.)

Aaron could well be thankful he had a praying brother. While Moses was up on Mount Sinai receiving the Ten Commandments, Aaron succumbed to the carnal desires of the people in molding the golden calf.

The LORD was angry enough with Aaron to destroy him, but at that time I prayed for Aaron too.... I lay prostrate before the LORD those forty days and forty nights because the LORD had said he would destroy you. I prayed to the LORD and said, "O Sovereign LORD do not destroy your people, your own inheritance that you redeemed by your great power and brought out of Egypt *ask God too*

with a mighty hand. . . . Overlook the stubbornness of this people, their wickedness and their sin. Otherwise, the country from which you brought us will say, 'Because the LORD was not able to take them into the land he had promised them, and because he hated them, he brought them out to put them to death in the desert' " (Deut. 9:20,25–28).

If Moses had not been a faithful intercessor, Aaron might have been destroyed as well as the rest of the Israelites. He was fortunate indeed. At the same time, what a sacred responsibility it is for spiritual believers to be intercessors (cf. Gal. 6:1 and James 5:16–20)!

faithful intercessor

Of special significance is the intensity of Moses' intercession for Israel. His was no simple "Lord, spare my people" prayer, followed by a hasty "Amen." Rather it was forty days and nights of awful travail, prompted by the sentence of judgment: "The Lord had said he would destroy you" (Deut. 9:25). Do we comprehend that as we approach the end of the age difficult times are ahead and God's judgments will fall on the world? How grave is the need for intercessors who pray as Moses prayed.

Another intercessory prayer of Moses is recorded in Exodus 33:12–23. It was precipitated by God's declaration to Moses, " 'I will not go with you, because you are a stiffnecked people and I might destroy you on the way' " (Exod. 33:3). Moses was devastated by this frightening revelation. From the day of his call, he had coveted and counted upon the divine Presence. He had heard God say, " 'I will be with you' " (Exod. 3:12). Now he was faced with the prospect of being alone, without God's presence:

Moses said to him, "If your Presence does not go with us, do not send us up from here. How will anyone know that you are pleased with me and with your people unless you go with us? What else will distinguish me and your people from all the other people on the face of the earth?" And the LORD said to Moses, "I will do the very thing you have asked, because I am pleased with you and I know you by name" (Exod. 33:15–17).

The terrible truth is that sinful humanity cannot endure the holy "Presence," for it can well consume them. The Israelites were in such a sinful state that the justice of God could rightly require their destruction. Moses perceived that there was but one ray of hope—God's grace. And that became the ground for his plea. He knew he could not plead for Israel on the basis of law or justice. But in his inmost being he was beginning to catch a glimpse of God's grace and compassion:

The LORD said, "I will cause all my goodness to pass in front of you, and I will proclaim my name, the LORD, in your presence. I will have mercy on whom I will have mercy, and I will have compassion on whom I will have compassion" (Exod. 33:19).

Long before the writer of Hebrews was prompted by the Holy Spirit to pen the truth, Moses had come "with confidence" to the throne of grace, finding mercy and grace to help in the time of need (see Heb. 4:16).

Personal Revelation for the Intercessor

Through God's marvelous grace Moses gained the re-assurance of the Presence (Exod. 33:14); but grace manifested only whets the appetite for more. Thus followed Moses' bold plea, " 'Now show me your glory' " (33:18). We might paraphrase his response, "I have had a glimpse; show me more." What greater prayer could be uttered? Surely this prayer of Moses is a worthy prayer for every child of God, since all believers need an enlarged understanding of the glory and majesty of God.

God was ready to accommodate the prayer (33:19–23). We might paraphrase His response: "Yes, Moses, I will do as you ask, but know that even you cannot bear the full manifestation of My glory. I will permit you enabling glimpses, sufficient for your role as leader of My people. I will enlarge your vision and your faith." There is encouragement for all believers in this answer to Moses' prayer.

The word "glory" is somewhat elusive for finite human beings, probably because it encompasses practically all that God himself is. It is almost synonymous with God. Note verse 22: "When my glory passes by" and "Until I have passed by." God and His glory are inseparable. Where one is, there also is the other. Therefore, Moses saw more than a blinding brilliance. He saw also in the glorious essence

■■■■■■■
PART 1

Chapter 2
The
Prayers
of Moses

of Deity, mercy, truth, holiness, love, patience, and goodness.

[The Lord] passed by in front of Moses, proclaiming, "The LORD, the LORD, the compassionate and gracious God, slow to anger, abounding in love and faithfulness, maintaining love to thousands, and forgiving wickedness, rebellion and sin" (Exod. 34:6–7).

Such a response by God to Moses' anguished plea adequately equipped His servant for the journey ahead. A new revelation of God inspired a new confidence in his intercessory prayer. Moses could never have prayed the words that next came from his lips if he had not experienced his special and personal revelation of God. God's response was far removed from His prior determination to destroy the stubborn Israelites:

"O Lord, if I have found favor in your eyes," he [Moses] said, "then let the Lord go with us. Although this is a stiff-necked people, forgive our wickedness and our sin, and take us as your inheritance." Then the LORD said: "I am making a covenant with you. Before all your people I will do wonders never before done in any nation in all the world. The people you live among will see how awesome is the work that I, the LORD, will do for you" (Exod. 34:9–10).

Dealing with Human Frailties

A mark of good leadership is the ability to handle crises; Moses got plenty of opportunity to demonstrate his good leadership. Having journeyed from Sinai to Kadesh-barnea, Moses again confronted a crisis. "The people complained about their hardships in the hearing of the LORD, and when he heard them his anger was aroused. Then fire from the LORD burned among them" (Num. 11:1).

Sin and God's presence are incompatible; they cannot coexist. Moses had earnestly entreated God for His continued presence with Israel, but now ironically that very Presence, like a mighty inferno, was burning among the people. Sin is always fuel for the "consuming Fire" (Heb. 12:29). Israel was learning by experience that there is no escaping an offended God, and that only one among them had the ear of God: "When the people cried out to Moses, he prayed to the LORD and the fire died down" (Num. 11:2).

Moses might well have said to them, "Enough is enough. You never learn, so bear the consequences." Instead, he must have remembered the revelation of Mount Sinai: God is merciful, gracious, longsuffering. Courage for another prayer of intercession rose in his heart. The fire ceased to burn. We too have an Intercessor like that. Bearing the burden of a vacillating people can so cloud a godly leader's perceptions and so capture his gaze that he begins to express his frustrations instead of trusting God:

> He [Moses] asked the LORD, "Why have you brought this trouble on your servant? What have I done to displease you that you put the burden of all these people on me? . . . I cannot carry all these people by myself; the burden is too heavy for me. If this is how you are going to treat me, put me to death right now . . . and do not let me face my own ruin" (Num. 11:11,14–15).

As mentioned in the previous chapter, others of God's servants have fallen victim to their own frail humanity and have prayed to die: Elijah (1 Kings 19:4), Job (Job 6:8), Jonah (Jon. 4:3). Fortunately, God does not accommodate such expressions, but He does deal with the underlying issues. He knows our frailties. He remembers we are but dust (Ps. 103:14). Though we may have frustrations, He does not condemn. Gently He told Moses He would take of the same Holy Spirit that was on him and put it on seventy elders to share the burden. And there would be no less of the Spirit on Moses. Moses needed to know that the Holy Spirit is powerful enough to take care of any situation. Even in the face of human failure, God's mercy is still faithful.

Only Moses and Jesus are identified in Scripture as being meek or humble (Num. 12:3; Matt. 11:29). And humility shines brightest when the jealous and ambitious attack. The proud and self-possessed fight back; the haughty seek revenge. But the humble pray for their adversaries. Aaron and Miriam had criticized their brother Moses and had sought to usurp his God-appointed position. In so doing, they provoked God. Miriam, who was the chief offender,[3] was punished with dreaded leprosy. A lesser person might have concluded she was receiving her just deserts. But Aaron confessed their sin and pleaded with Moses for Miriam. So "Moses cried out to the LORD, 'O God, please heal her!' " (Num. 12:13).

What an example of praying "for those who persecute you" (Matt. 5:44)! Bishop Hall, the seventeenth-century English cleric, said of Miriam,

> Her foul tongue is justly punished with a foul face, and her folly, in pretending to rival Moses, is manifest to all. Moses interceded for his smitten sister. Affectionately and sincerely he pleaded for her. Moses prayed as one who, from his heart, had fully forgiven the jealousy of Miriam and Aaron.[4]

Note the plea of Moses: *"Please* heal her." Although God honored the plea for healing, He was not pleased to grant it immediately. Those who pray for the sick and afflicted can so desire the healing that the reason for the affliction is overlooked. Miriam's leprosy was the result of a serious offense. Her healing had to be delayed lest a lack of consequence lead to a careless repeat of her sin. She had a lesson to learn.

Israel never seemed to learn from its disobedience and punishment. Yet the compassionate, tenacious Moses never gave up. Despite his almost utter despair earlier, he again became the leader of strength and faith. His concern was no longer with himself, but with God's reputation and God's people. This became very clear when God tested him by suggesting that He would destroy the Israelites and start over by making a new nation from Moses.

> Moses said to the LORD, "Then the Egyptians will hear about it! ... And they will tell the inhabitants of this land about it. They have already heard that you, O LORD, are with these people. ... If you put these people to death all at one time, the nations who

---

[3]The verb "began to talk" is third person feminine singular, showing Miriam was doing the talking, while Aaron stood beside her.

[4]Quoted in Herbert Lockyer, *All the Prayers of the Bible* (Grand Rapids: Zondervan Publishing House, 1959), 42.

have heard this report about you will say, 'The LORD was not able to bring these people into the land he promised them on oath; so he slaughtered them in the desert.' Now may the Lord's strength be displayed, just as you have declared: ... In accordance with your great love, forgive the sin of these people, just as you have pardoned them from the time they left Egypt until now." The LORD replied, "I have forgiven them, as you asked" (Num. 14:13–20).

Like Miriam and Aaron, Korah, Dathan, and Abiram presented a challenge to leadership. They instigated an underhanded mutiny, attempting to establish a priestly order apart from divine authority (Num. 16:1–21). In the face of this challenge, Moses perceived the need for (1) confirmation of God's duly constituted leaders, Moses and Aaron, and (2) judgment upon the usurpers. At the same time, he feared the woeful consequences that were sure to visit the easily swayed congregation. "Moses and Aaron fell facedown and cried out, 'O God, God of the spirits of all mankind, will you be angry with the entire assembly when only one man sins?' " (Num. 16:22). With this prayer, Moses and Aaron agonized in intense intercession. Yet rebellion may become such depravity that no intensity of intercession will deliver from judgment. The earth opened and swallowed the rebels, confirming God's appointment of spiritual leadership and judging the human effort to usurp authority (Num. 16:31–35).

How utterly fickle people can be. Although judgment had literally devoured the rebels, the very next day "the whole Israelite community grumbled against Moses and Aaron. " 'You have killed the LORD's people' " (Num. 16:41). Surely God's wrath burns towards such rashness. Paul describes such vain people in Romans 1:32—"Although they know God's righteous decree that those who do such things deserve death, they not only continue to do these very things but also approve of those who practice them." Witnessing divine judgment upon the rebels was one thing; defending them was quite another. It virtually solicited God to destroy them (Num. 16:45).

But Moses and Aaron were men of unrelenting prayer and intercession; they again "fell facedown" (16:45). The persistence of the two leaders is an example to be emulated by all spiritual leaders. Focused on the need of the people, Moses told Aaron, "Hurry to the assembly to make atonement for them." And Aaron "stood between the living and the dead, and the plague stopped" (16:48).

On another occasion, what were largely a new generation of Israelites were plagued with fiery serpents because of their grumbling: "The people came to Moses and said, 'We sinned when we spoke against the LORD and against you. Pray that the LORD will take the snakes away from us.' So Moses prayed for the people" (Num. 21:7). The anguished plea of the people is noteworthy. This is the single recorded incident in which the people openly begged for Moses' intercession. In their dire emergency they expressed complete confidence in Moses' intercession. Such confidence had been learned by repeated experience.

But Moses' prayer was not answered as the people had supposed it should have been. They wanted the serpents removed. God wanted those bitten by the serpents to participate in obtaining the answer. "The Lord said to Moses, 'Make a snake and put it up on a pole; anyone who is bitten can look at it and live' " (Num. 21:8). Prayer is of little value unless it is mixed with faith, and faith is not present where works are absent (cf. James 2:14–18).

Divine Appointment of Leadership

Although the Book of Numbers records the end of Moses' life and leadership, Deuteronomy provides some further insights related to Moses' prayer ministry. In Deuteronomy 3 Moses pleads with God: " 'O Sovereign LORD, you have begun to show to your servant your greatness and your strong hand. For what god is there in heaven or on earth who can do the deeds and mighty works you do? Let me go over and see the good land beyond the Jordan' " (Deut. 3:24–25). Addressing God as "Sovereign LORD," or "Lord Yahweh (Jehovah)," is significant. "LORD" suggests ownership rights and power. The choice of "Yahweh" (Jehovah), the covenant-keeping name, speaks of the intimate relationship between God and Israel; consequently, there is an atmosphere of grace about it. The impassioned plea is for God to reverse His decision. Moses had flagrantly dishonored and disobeyed God. Having been totally frustrated and provoked by the rebellious Israelites, Moses had failed to declare belief and trust in God and then angrily struck the rock instead of speaking to it (see Num. 20:1–13). As a result, he had evoked God's harsh response: " 'Because you did not trust in me enough to honor me as holy in the sight of the Israelites, you will not bring this community into the land I give them' " (20:12).

God's answer to Moses' request for reconsideration was no. " 'Do not speak to me anymore about this matter' " (Deut. 3:26). We are inclined to say, "God, You are too severe. Why not honor Your servant's request?" We may not fully understand God's refusal, but we must know that the Sovereign does what is best, not only for His servant, but also for His people. Had God accommodated Moses, it might have generated more rebellion in those who had provoked Moses to his angry reaction. Whatever the case, it is better to pray and be denied than not to pray at all.

"Man is destined to die once" (Heb. 9:27). Everyone will die except Christians who are alive at the Rapture (see 1 Thess. 4:17). Few, however, are told by God the place and hour of their decease as Moses was (see Num. 27:12–13). Yet even in the face of his certain death, the greatness and godliness of this devoted servant again shine forth. Though he had longed to enter the Promised Land, that joy was withheld because of his failure. And even though Moses was denied his request for clemency, he abandoned his personal interests and prayed for the people.

Moses said to the LORD, "May the LORD, the God of the spirits of all mankind, appoint a man over this community to go out and come in before them, one who will lead them out and bring them in, so the LORD's people will not be like sheep without a shepherd" (Num. 27:15–17).

The very man who had been set over the congregation by God recognized that only God could provide the necessary leadership. What humility! What total awareness of God's singular ability! Moses might have requested that his successor be a person he had selected, perhaps his own son. But instead his plea was "May the LORD, the God of

■■■■■■

PART 1

**Chapter 2
The
Prayers
of Moses**

the spirits" do the choosing. Only God knows the spirit of a person; thus His choice is always the best.

Here is a valuable lesson in the selection of spiritual leadership. People who look on externals tend to choose on the basis of appearance, education, ability, charisma; God, however, chooses on a totally different basis: He sees the heart. Moses' example of deferring to God is a worthy pattern for selecting a shepherd for a flock of believers.

Moses was indeed a giant in God's Who's Who of Praying People, but he also became God's agent for revealing, in terms mankind can understand, the pathway into God's presence. In its highest manifestation, prayer is finite, sinful people coming into the presence of an infinite, holy God. But the perplexing question arises: How can this paradoxical and apparently impossible connection between the sinful and the holy occur? Even by the most ingenious scheming, no one can placate or escape the judgment of a holy God. None of our "fig leaves" can withstand the "consuming Fire." No one is worthy to approach Him. Then how can we, who are by nature and sinful intent afar off, draw near to a holy God?

Moses was shown the way. Under God's instruction, he was given a road map, a blueprint, a pattern, explaining the way into the Holy Presence. "Moses was warned when he was about to build the tabernacle: 'See to it that you make everything according to the pattern shown you on the mountain' " (Heb. 8:5).

The tabernacle in the wilderness was according to God's design. It charted the way, step by step, into the Holy of Holies, wherein dwelt the glorious Presence. The tabernacle stood in the midst of the encamped congregation of Israel. Each tribe had its assigned location on either the east, south, west, or north side (see Num. 2:1–31)—except the tribe of Levi, the priests, who surrounded the tabernacle, interposed between it and the other tribes. "The Levites, however, are to set up their tents around the tabernacle of the Testimony so that wrath will not fall on the Israelite community. The Levites are to be responsible for the care of the tabernacle of the Testimony" (Num. 1:53). East of the tabernacle, Moses and Aaron and his sons camped, "toward the sunrise, in front of the Tent of Meeting. They were responsible for the care of the sanctuary on behalf of the Israelites" (3:38).

At the heart of the encampment was the tabernacle, and at the heart of the tabernacle was the Holy of Holies, where dwelt the presence of God. But though God's presence was at the center, the ordinary Israelite could not approach Him directly; access was only through a mediatory ministry and a blood sacrifice. Access into God's presence, for each Israelite, involved three human elements: the congregation, the general priesthood, and the high priest. Individual members of the congregation brought animals to the east entrance of the tabernacle, indicating their desire to worship the God who was in their midst as well as acknowledging their own sin-laden conscience and dependence upon blood sacrifice for expiation. The Levitical priests were charged with the actual offering of "gifts and sacrifices" (see Heb. 9:9), including both daily sacrifices and those brought by individuals, and with the service of the tabernacle. But only the high priest could make the ultimate atonement and actually appear in the presence of God and that only once a year. (The diagram provides an elementary understanding of the tabernacle, its setting, and the step-by-step approach to God it symbolized.)

1. The tents of the Israelites surrounded the tabernacle at a distance. "The Israelites are to camp around the Tent of Meeting some distance from it, each man under his standard with the banners of his family" (Num. 2:2). The expression "some distance" at the very least implies separation between the congregation and their God. Because of their sinful state, the people could approach no nearer than the court entrance unless they were bringing a sacrifice. Then both men and women would come to the entrance of the tabernacle itself. To violate the rule was to invite wrath.

2. Entrance to the tabernacle was limited to the Levitical priests, including the high priest. They entered the court and immediately upon doing so, they encountered the bronze altar where, even for them, a blood sacrifice had to be made before they could proceed farther.

3. The bronze altar required payment. The bronze of this altar (an alloy of copper and tin) symbolized judgment (cf.

the bronze serpent in Num. 21:9). Before sinful humanity dared approach the holy God, its sin had to be dealt with properly. The penalty for sin was death—the death either of the transgressor or of an acceptable substitute.

This wholly burnt sacrifice ... serves as a solemn proclamation ... that every man is deeply guilty before God, and never can approach him or secure his favor except by bloody and consuming expiation. Blood—*blood*—BLOOD—is the perpetual and exacting cry of the law against every violator of its precepts; and until that cry is hushed, and that demand satisfied, no one can see the face of God, and live.[5]

4. The laver stipulated cleansing. Beyond the bronze altar, but still outside the holy place, each priest who would enter the holy place encountered the laver, or basin, overlaid with the polished bronze from the mirrors of the women (see Exod. 38:8). Intended to reflect any uncleanness or defilement, the basin was a place of necessary and perpetual cleansing. Every priest had to wash before entry into the place of communion, worship, and prayer.

5. The Holy Place contained three items: (a) the table of showbread (the golden table of the bread of the Presence), foreshadowing Him who is the Bread of Life, (b) the golden lampstand, providing light for activities in the Holy Place, representing the One who lights our pathway toward God, and (c) the golden altar of incense, at the far end of the Holy Place next to the veil, typifying the ascending prayers of God's people and symbolizing the entering into God's presence through prayer and praise.

The Levitical priests, except for the high priest, dared go no further. They could sacrifice, they could wash, they could partake of the bread of the Presence, they could burn incense, but there they had to stop, for before them hung the curtain of separation.

6. The Holy of Holies was the holiest of all places, inhabited by God. It carried for the Israelite the ultimate evidence of God's presence. The descendants of Adam (who,

---

[5]Joseph A. Seiss, *Gospel in Leviticus* (Philadelphia: Lindsay and Blakiston, 1860; reprint, Grand Rapids: Kregel Publications, 1981), 29–30 (page references are to reprint edition).

even after the Fall, bear the image of God [Gen. 9:6] and are thus capable of fellowship with Him) could never be totally fulfilled, or experience fullness of joy, until they could return to that coveted relationship with the manifest presence of God. Yet, for sinners the abode of the "consuming Fire" was a most dreaded place. The role of the earthly tabernacle, pointing ahead to the future access of God's people into the very presence of God, is described in Hebrews:

Only the high priest entered the inner room, and that only once a year, and never without blood, which he offered for himself and for the sins the people had committed in ignorance. The Holy Spirit was showing by this that the way into the Most Holy Place had not yet been disclosed as long as the first tabernacle was still standing (Heb. 9:7–8).

Even though God provided in the pattern of the tabernacle a profound picture of access to himself, His children in the desert never did enjoy the access which is ours today. They had but the shadow; we have the reality. They had the type; we have the fulfillment of that type:

Therefore, brothers, since we have confidence to enter the Most Holy Place by the blood of Jesus, by a new and living way opened for us through the curtain, that is, his body, and since we have a great priest over the house of God, let us draw near to God with a sincere heart in full assurance of faith, having our hearts sprinkled to cleanse us from a guilty conscience and having our bodies washed with pure water (Heb. 10:19–22).

Fortunate are the followers of a praying leader. As the Lord uses you in spiritual leadership, always keep prayer as the highest priority. To conclude your study of this prayer giant of the Old Testament, meditate on his prayer of thanksgiving in Deuteronomy 26 and on his prayer song in Deuteronomy 32 and 33.

Questions for Study

1. Why were some of Moses' prayers not answered immediately?

2. What factors characterized Moses' intercessory prayers?

3. Why were some of Moses' prayers not answered exactly as he asked?

4. What lessons do you learn about prayer and access to God from the study of the tabernacle and its furniture?

5. On what occasions should we not pray?

6. What are some reasons that spiritual leaders must keep prayer as a priority?

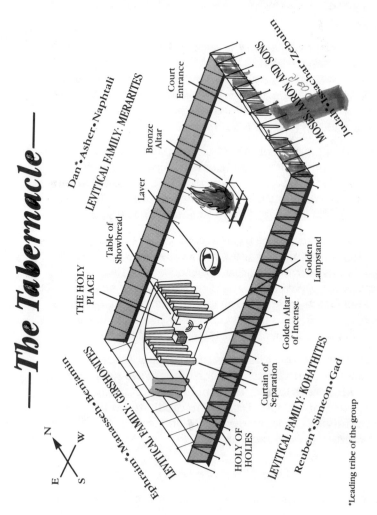

The Tabernacle

Dan*•Asher•Naphtali

LEVITICAL FAMILY: MERARITES

Court Entrance

Bronze Altar

Laver

Table of Showbread

THE HOLY PLACE

MOSES, AARON AND SONS

Judah*•Issachar•Zebulun

Golden Lampstand

Golden Altar of Incense

Curtain of Separation

HOLY OF HOLIES

LEVITICAL FAMILY: KOHATHITES

Reuben*•Simeon•Gad

LEVITICAL FAMILY: GERSHONITES

Ephraim*•Manasseh•Benjamin

N
W — E
S

*Leading tribe of the group

THE PERIOD FROM JOSHUA TO KING SAUL

Under Joshua, Israel entered the Promised Land and subdued it, and the land was divided among the tribes. Each tribe was then to complete the conquest of their assigned territory. However, after the death of Joshua and the rest of his generation, "another generation grew up, who knew neither the LORD nor what he had done for Israel" (Judg. 2:10). That is, they knew about the Lord and the crossing of the Red Sea and the other miracles, but they did not know the Lord or His mighty power in their own experience. This implies a lack of communion with God, a lack of prayer.

As a result, the tribes fell apart, turned to idolatry with its immoral standards, and without godly leadership, "everyone did as he saw fit" (Judg. 17:6; 21:25). This brought God's judgment in the form of defeat and foreign tyranny. When the people finally would repent and cry out to the Lord for help, God would answer their prayers and raise up a judge as deliverer. But when the judge died, the people would fall back into idolatry and the cycle was repeated again and again, until Samuel finally united the tribes. His prayers brought a great time of revival and victory (1 Sam. 7:3,5,12–13). After him King Saul attempted to establish the kingdom but failed. In fact, he lost much of what had

81

PART 1

Chapter 3
The
Period
from
Joshua to
King Saul

been gained under Joshua. The whole period from Joshua to King Saul was full of spiritual ups and downs. But God was always there when the Israelites turned in repentance to seek His help through prayer.

Joshua

Although Joshua was Moses' immediate successor, he does not appear to have been the person of prayer that Moses was. That he did pray cannot be doubted, but he seems to have been more a person of action than a person of prayer. "As the LORD commanded his servant Moses, so Moses commanded Joshua, and Joshua did it; he left nothing undone of all that the LORD commanded Moses" (Josh. 11:15).

On at least one occasion, Joshua's lack of prayer resulted in a problem for Israel with lasting consequences. Unwisely and unadvisedly, Joshua entered into a covenant with men from Gibeon. "The men of Israel sampled their provisions but did not inquire of the LORD" (Josh. 9:14).

Even so, Joshua did pray. His first recorded encounter with Yahweh was at the very outset of his new role as Israel's commander-in-chief. The initiative seems to have been totally of the Lord, for there is no record of Joshua making any petition at the time (see Josh. 1:1–9). Yet hearing is a vital part of praying. He who hears well might very well require less petition.

Joshua's first prayer, a prayer of recognition, is recorded in Joshua 5:13–15:

Now when Joshua was near Jericho, he looked up and saw a man standing in front of him with a drawn sword in his hand. Joshua went up to him and asked, "Are you for us or for our enemies?" "Neither," he replied, "but as commander of the army of the LORD I have now come." Then Joshua fell facedown to the ground in reverence, and asked him, "What message does my Lord have for his servant?" The commander of the LORD's army replied, "Take off your sandals, for the place where you are standing is holy." And Joshua did so.

The whole of Joshua's praying in this instance is recorded in two questions: "Are you for us or for our enemies?" and

"What message does my Lord have for his servant?" The answers received are somewhat of a revelation. The answer to the first question seems, "It is not a question of who I am for or against, but of who is for me." Issues of disagreement among God's children are best resolved not by taking sides against each other but by seeking and choosing the Lord's side.

The second question revealed the heart of Joshua. He was ready to obey—indeed, to be the Lord's servant—and he got his answer (v. 15). In telling Joshua to take off his sandals, the divine visitor was saying, "Give due recognition to Him in whose presence you stand." There is no higher instruction for those who would truly be His servants.

Joshua's next recorded prayer was prompted by Israel's defeat at Ai.

> Joshua tore his clothes and fell facedown to the ground before the ark of the LORD, remaining there till evening.... And Joshua said, "Ah, Sovereign LORD, why did you ever bring this people across the Jordan to deliver us into the hands of the Amorites to destroy us? If only we had been content to stay on the other side of the Jordan! O Lord, what can I say, now that Israel has been routed by its enemies? The Canaanites and the other people of the country will hear about this and they will surround us and wipe out our name from the earth. What then will you do for your own great name?" (Josh. 7:6–9).

Paul's observation about prayer fits Joshua's circumstance perfectly: "We do not know what we ought to pray for" (Rom. 8:26). The utter humility of Joshua and Israel's elders in the face of desperate circumstances is most commendable, but blaming God for their plight was extreme folly. How dimly we human beings see! How poorly we perceive! How unwisely we blame God!

Joshua's appraisal of what Israel's enemies would say about the defeat of God's people was accurate. And his jealousy for the name of the Lord was admirable. However, his judgment of the cause for the disaster was quite inaccurate. Yet the Lord did not reprimand Joshua for his faulty praying. Though we may not always pray with a proper understanding of the facts, God is honored when we pray,

PART 1

Chapter 3
The
Period
from
Joshua to
King Saul

and in turn He honors our praying with an adjustment of our course.

There is a time to pray. But there are times when praying will not, by itself, yield a solution to the problem, even though it may bring to light things that must be changed so the problem can be resolved. "The LORD said to Joshua, " 'Stand up! What are you doing down on your face? Israel has sinned' " (Josh. 7:10–11). Sin had dealt defeat to Israel; victory depended on bringing sin to judgment (see Josh. 7:13 to 8:1; cf. James 5:16).

Another prayer of Joshua's incited the interruption of nature. Few mortals have wrought exploits by prayer as recorded in Joshua 10:12–14:

> Joshua said to the LORD in the presence of Israel: "O sun, stand still over Gibeon, O moon, over the Valley of Aijalon." So the sun stood still, and the moon stopped, till the nation avenged itself on its enemies.... The sun stopped in the middle of the sky and delayed going down about a full day. There has never been a day like it before or since, a day when the LORD listened to a man. Surely the LORD was fighting for Israel!

The answer to Joshua's prayer indicates the degree to which God is willing to be involved in the battle against evil. If need be, He can put the perpetual motion of His universe on hold in order to assure the enemy's defeat. What faith-inspiring encouragement to all who by prayer engage in spiritual warfare!

Deborah

Women played a significant role in Israel's history. And none was more prominent than Deborah, whose name literally translated is "bee," having "a sting for her foes, and honey for her friends."[1]

Prayer can take any of a number of forms, from articulate petition to "groans that words cannot express" (Rom. 8:26). Deborah's recorded prayer might scarcely be judged a prayer at all. It is a song of praise rehearsing God's mighty

---

[1]Herbert Lockyer, *All the Prayers of the Bible* (Grand Rapids: Zondervan Publishing House, 1959), 54.

acts. Yet, considered as a prayer, it offers an inspiring pattern for regenerating faith. Anyone who prays can profit greatly by recounting the many things God has done—for His Kingdom and for His people.

On that day Deborah ... sang this song: "When the princes in Israel take the lead, when the people willingly offer themselves—praise the LORD! ... I will sing to the LORD, I will sing; I will make music to the LORD, the God of Israel" (Judg. 5:1–2).

PART 1

**Chapter 3
The
Period
from
Joshua to
King Saul**

Gideon

During the period of the Judges the Israelites did not serve the Lord in a consistent manner. We can see a cycle repeated where for a time they would serve Him fervently and faithfully. Then came the blessings of the Lord with attendant prosperity and triumph over the enemy. But generally this would not continue long, for soon would come departure from the Lord's commandments, including the practice of idolatry and other evils. As a consequence, chastisement by the Lord followed, including defeat by their enemies (see, for example, Judg. 6:1). Finally the people would repent and beg God for deliverance.

God's dealings with Gideon were in direct response to Israel's cry of desperation during a period of servitude to foreigners. The word of the angel to Gideon—" 'The LORD is with you, mighty warrior' " (Judg. 6:12)—did not make sense to this young farmer timidly beating out wheat in the security of a wine press.

"But sir," Gideon replied, "if the LORD is with us, why has all this happened to us? Where are all his wonders that our fathers told us about when they said, 'Did not the LORD bring us up out of Egypt?' But now the LORD has abandoned us and put us into the hand of Midian." The LORD turned to him and said, "Go in the strength you have and save Israel out of Midian's hand. Am I not sending you?" ... Gideon replied, "If now I have found favor in your eyes, give me a sign that it is really you talking to me." ... When Gideon realized that it was the angel of the LORD, he exclaimed, "Ah, Sovereign LORD! I have seen the angel of the LORD face to face!" (Judg. 6:13–14,17,22).

PART 1

Chapter 3
The
Period
from
Joshua to
King Saul

Gideon's prayer flowed from an awareness of his heritage and a longing for its return, as well as from a sense of inability and unworthiness (6:15). He expressed utter bewilderment to God, but forthrightly and openly. Such honest humility was a shining light in Israel's darkness. Noting his sense of weakness and humility, God selected Gideon for a great mission. Self-confidence can be the greatest enemy to dependence upon God.

Gideon's request, "give me a sign" (6:17), may seem at first to be an unworthy petition. However, Gideon's plea for a sign sprang more from his own self-distrust than from his lack of faith. He had to be certain it was indeed the Lord who was directing him, and that he was not the victim of some illusion or delusion.

Pure terror overtook Gideon as he realized he had truly confronted God (6:22). Yet God will not reveal himself beyond our ability to bear such a revelation. "The LORD said to him, 'Peace! Do not be afraid. You are not going to die' " (6:23). The magnitude of God's revelation was itself a revelation of God's appraisal of Gideon. Immediately Gideon built an altar to the Lord and named it "Yahweh [Jehovah] shalom," "The Lord is Peace," for God was at peace with him. When the Lord said to Gideon, "Peace!" Gideon gained a broadened perception of God. Gone was his feeling that God had abandoned Israel. Then he built an altar as evidence of his new relationship with the Lord.

Gideon's fleece was not a device for finding God's will. He already knew God's will. He simply wanted reassurance. Although Gideon's request was honored by God, the "fleece" has been unwisely applied by well-meaning but misguided Christians who try to use it as a substitute for being guided by God's Word.

"Look, I will place a wool fleece on the threshing floor. If there is dew only on the fleece and all the ground is dry, then I will know that you will save Israel by my hand, as you said." And that is what happened. Gideon rose early the next day; he squeezed the fleece and wrung out the dew—a bowlful of water. Then Gideon said to God, "Do not be angry with me. Let me make just one more request. Allow me one more test with the fleece.

This time make the fleece dry and the ground covered with dew"
(Judg. 6:37–39).

PART 1

Chapter 3
The
Period
from
Joshua to
King Saul

For Gideon, making such a request was acceptable, and
God honored it. For us, a similar request might be dangerous and misleading. Imagine the dilemma Gideon faced.
He was being asked to lead a revolt against the authority
of the ruling Midianites. To readers today, it seems natural
that God would want to deliver His people from foreign
oppression. But Israel had sinned, and invasion by an enemy was the promised penalty. For seven years Israel had
suffered the judgment of God (6:1–6). How could Gideon
be sure that God wanted him to resist authority that God
himself had placed over His disobedient people? In such
an instance, when one feels that God may be leading in an
unusual direction or asking one to do something contrary
to good judgment or usual divine activity, an action like
Gideon's may be in order.

In other words, when Gideon laid out his fleece, he
already knew what God had asked him to do (6:14). But
he had difficulty believing what he had heard. Was it really
God speaking to him? Might he not be imagining what many
Hebrew young men had dreamed of doing—delivering Israel from the Midianites? Was God, who gave authority to
Gentile as well as Hebrew leaders, asking him to resist that
authority? Would God really want to use such a weak and
unimportant person as Gideon? With all these reasons for
not recognizing the validity of the divine instructions he
had earlier received, the use of the fleece may have had a
legitimate purpose. Though there may be instances of similar divine intervention in more recent history, other guidelines for discovering God's will are established by both
example and precept for the New Testament church.

Jabez

Scripture records very little about Jabez. First Chronicles
4:9 calls him "more honorable than his brothers," but to
gain greater insight into him we must rely on his one
recorded prayer.

Jabez cried out to the God of Israel, "Oh, that you would bless

PART 1

Chapter 3
The
Period
from
Joshua to
King Saul

me and enlarge my territory! Let your hand be with me, and keep me from harm so that I will be free from pain." And God granted his request (1 Chron. 4:10).

How people pray, not who they may or may not be, is what gains heaven's attention and response. Jabez's prayer is simple, yet direct in recognizing that God is the source of any blessing or personal success. One is struck with Jabez's godly outlook and spirit, so evident in his four earnest petitions.

1. For God's blessing. We ought to covet the blessing of God, and to treasure it above gold (cf. Gen. 32:26; Prov. 10:22).

2. For enlargement of territory. Everyone ought to desire spiritual posterity, disciples, and influence (cf. 1 Thess. 2:19). Opportunities for greater service should be viewed as possible answers to this prayer.

3. For enablement. We all ought to ask earnestly for God's direction in our affairs, and for the enablement of His hand in our undertaking (cf. Gen. 24:12–14; Acts 4:29–30).

4. For preservation from evil and its hurt. Mankind ought to cry to God for deliverance from evil and its sorry consequences (cf. Matt. 6:13; 1 Thess. 4:3–4).

Jephthah

Jephthah's prayer should sound an alarm for everyone who prays. Making a vow to God is not an uncommon part of praying. In both the Old Testament and the New Testament a vow is a promise, or pledge, made to God, never to a person. It is always a voluntary expression of faith, not a bribe. Jephthah's vow, as he prayed to God, expressed an unusual devotion and commitment.

Jephthah made a vow to the Lord: "If you give the Ammonites into my hands, whatever comes out of the door of my house to meet me when I return in triumph from the Ammonites will be the Lord's, and I will sacrifice it as a burnt offering" (Judg. 11:30–31).

It is of no small consequence to make a promise to God, nor should it be done lightly or without forethought. Jephthah's vow, although made with the best of intentions and with the purpose of giving honor to God, was made without due consideration of possible eventualities. He was shocked when his daughter was the first to come out of his door. There is much debate about how Jephthah carried out his vow. Some believe that in those dark days Jephthah actually sacrificed his daughter. However, Leon Wood gives rather convincing arguments to show that Jephthah "offered her in the sense of devoting her to the Tabernacle for continual service and perpetual celibacy."[2]

PART 1
Chapter 3
The
Period
from
Joshua to
King Saul

Manoah

The natural concern of a Christian parent should be the spiritual nurture and normal development of sons and daughters. The prayer of Manoah is certainly worthy of emulation by every prospective parent.

Manoah prayed to the LORD: "O Lord, I beg you, let the man of God you sent to us come again to teach us how to bring up the boy who is to be born. . . . So Manoah asked him, "When your words are fulfilled, what is to be the rule for the boy's life and work?" (Judg. 13:8,12).

Manoah's prayer was explicitly answered (13:13–14). Parents who sincerely desire to please God and rear their children to honor God are well advised to pray exactly as Manoah did: " 'Teach us how to bring up the boy who is to be born' " (13:8). " 'What is to be the rule for the boy's life and work?' " (13:12).

Samson

Strange as it may seem, there is only one biblical account of Samson's praying prior to his prayer at the time of his death. After killing a thousand Philistines with the jawbone of a donkey, a thirsty and spent Samson called on the Lord: " 'You have given your servant this great victory. Must I now die of thirst and fall into the hands of the uncircumcised?' " (Judg. 15:18).

Here is a person whose record of exploits is such that his name is still synonymous with superhuman strength.

---

[2]Leon Wood, *Distressing Days of the Judges* (Grand Rapids: Zondervan Publishing House, 1975), 287–295.

PART 1

Chapter 3
The
Period
from
Joshua to
King Saul

Here is a person of such remarkable faith that he earned a place in the famous faith chapter of Hebrews (11:32). And yet Samson was also someone whose personal degradation brought him to shame, blindness, and bondage. We wonder why. Could it be that his prayerlessness led to his downfall?

Samson knew how to yield to God's Spirit. He knew how to exercise unusual faith. But he did not know how to subdue his own fleshly passions, and he evidently failed to employ the available resources of prayer, for ultimately "he did not know that the Lord had left him" (Judg. 16:20). Jesus knew the weakness of human nature when He told the disciples, "'Watch and pray so that you will not fall into temptation. The spirit is willing, but the body is weak'" (Matt. 26:41). Let every believer in God take heed!

Samson's final words were addressed to God. He had failed miserably, but he still knew the source of his strength:

"O Sovereign LORD, remember me. O God, please strengthen me just once more, and let me with one blow get revenge on the Philistines for my two eyes. . . . Let me die with the Philistines!" (Judg. 16:28,30).

God's chastening had been bitter, but in the end it yielded the peaceable fruit of righteousness. The awful blindness, bondage, servitude, and humiliation of the Gaza prison had pressed Israel's mighty judge to repentance and to a renewal of relationship with the God unto whom he had been separated from his mother's womb. Once again he was in a position of usefulness. Now he could pray effectively and deliver a defeat to God's enemies beyond anything he had accomplished in his lifetime. Prayer is the key to renewal and restoration.

The Children of Israel

Until now our attention has focused on the praying of individuals. However, some corporate prayers of Israel are recorded and should be noted. The following passage should be read against the backdrop of Judges 19 and 20, as Israel sought God's guidance in moving against the tribal immorality of Benjamin.

PART 1

Chapter 3
The
Period
from
Joshua to
King Saul

The Israelites went up to Bethel and inquired of God. They said, "Who of us shall go first to fight against the Benjamites?" The LORD replied, "Judah shall go first" (20:18). [After being routed by the Benjamites, the Israelites again prayed.] The Israelites went up and wept before the LORD until evening, and they inquired of the LORD. They said, "Shall we go up again to battle against the Benjamites, our brothers?" And the LORD answered, "Go up against them" (20:23). [After another great defeat, the Israelites fasted and inquired of God.] They asked, "Shall we go up again to battle with Benjamin our brother, or not?" The LORD responded, "Go, for tomorrow I will give them into your hands" (20:28).

Failure after apparently receiving a sense of direction from the Lord in response to prayer is not foreign to the experience of God's children, difficult as it may be to understand. In such times God ought not to be rashly blamed, but people ought the more earnestly to inquire. In this way, failure can become the harbinger of a greater success, as happened to Israel (see 20:46).

On the surface, Israel's prayer appears strange indeed. After an initial defeat, "Shall we go up again to battle against . . . our brothers?" and God's answer in the affirmative, leading to the second defeat, appear no less mysterious and out of keeping with God's character. Yet it must be understood that His purposes are not subject to human judgment. In God's economy there may have been a need for learning complete dependence upon God; or God may have seen something in the Israelites (as well as the Benjamites) that needed purging, lest the whole lump be defiled (cf. 1 Cor. 5:5–7). It is only by God's enablement that His highest purpose is accomplished.

The people went to Bethel, where they sat before God until evening, raising their voices and weeping bitterly. "O LORD, the God of Israel," they cried, "why has this happened to Israel? Why should one tribe be missing from Israel today?" (Judg. 21:2–3).

Israel's great sorrow and distress over Benjamin's plight showed their concern over the covenant bond between the tribes. What they did to secure wives for the remaining Benjamites seems cruel, but they felt it was necessary, and

PART 1

Chapter 3

The
Period
from
Joshua to
King Saul

the Bible reminds us that this was not God's direction, for "in those days Israel had no king; everyone did as he saw fit" (Judg. 21:25).

Hannah

Deborah's praying, as we have seen, was in the form of magnification and exaltation of the Lord, a commemorative song, along the lines of Miriam's (see chapter 2, pp. 63–64). By contrast, Hannah's words are more easily recognized as prayer. In fact, one source identifies Hannah's prayer as "the first recorded instance of a woman at prayer."[3] Although many other godly women had surely engaged in prayer from earliest time, it may be that Hannah's is recorded more for its consequences than for any other reason. Her prayer produced one of Israel's most influential prophets, Samuel, who was to become God's agent in the selection and anointing of the incomparable King David.

In bitterness of soul Hannah wept much and prayed to the LORD. And she made a vow, saying, "O LORD Almighty, if you will only look upon your servant's misery and remember me, and not forget your servant but give her a son, then I will give him to the Lord for all the days of his life, and no razor shall ever be used on his head." ... Hannah was praying in her heart, and her lips were moving but her voice was not heard. Eli thought she was drunk (1 Sam. 1:10–11,13).

The heart's deepest desire sometimes becomes the means of affecting the divine purpose. On the one hand was a grieving childless woman, Hannah; on the other was the Lord, about to send to Israel a prophet who would forever alter her history. An unspoken prayer was the link between the two.

Weeping and praying, tears and triumph, often go hand in hand. Of Jesus, the most eminent of praying people, Scripture says, "He offered up prayers and petitions with loud cries and tears to the one who could save him from death, and he was heard because of his reverent submission" (Heb. 5:7). Tears announce the soul's anguish and

---

[3]Lockyer, *All the Prayers,* 60.

its intensity, and the two together elicit response from a compassionate God (cf. 2 Kings 20:5).

PART 1

Chapter 3
The
Period
from
Joshua to
King Saul

In Hannah's prayer we have a mingling of petition and promise, almost a holy bargaining: "If you will ... then I will give." This was not merely cheap bartering. The soul's intensity is measured by the sacrifice it is willing to make to gain its desired goal.

Unique to Hannah's praying was the fact that "her lips were moving but her voice was not heard" (1 Sam. 1:13). Tears came from her eyes, but the prayer came from her heart. This is the first recorded instance of mental, or silent, prayer. And thus we note that the effectiveness of prayer is not dependent upon the petitioner's volume. God, who "sees what is done in secret" (Matt. 6:6), needs no shouting to gain His attention. He needs only the soul's intense desire. (Of course, intense desire may express itself also in loud petition [see Mark 10:46–47].) Although Hannah did not give voice to her prayer, she most certainly did articulate her burden in her mind, for she said to Eli, the high priest, " 'I have been praying here out of my great anguish and grief' " (1 Sam. 1:16).

And Hannah received her answer (1 Sam. 1:17–18). It came first in a divine word from Eli: " 'Go in peace, and may the God of Israel grant you what you have asked of him' " (1 Sam. 1:17). All who pray may learn from Hannah's example. She needed no tangible evidence in order to believe; she needed only a word from the Lord, "and her face was no longer downcast" (1 Sam. 1:18). Hannah's faith rested on that word, and in due season Samuel was born. Even then her faith was evident, for the name she gave her son meant "the Name of God." In this way she honored the name (including the character and nature) of the faithful God who heard and answered her prayer. It also expressed her desire for her son to have a godly name and character.

Prayer need not always be petition. Hannah's second prayer began in highest exaltation of her Lord and ended in inspired prophetic utterance.

"My heart rejoices in the LORD; in the LORD my horn is lifted high. My mouth boasts over my enemies, for I delight in your

PART 1

Chapter 3
The
Period
from
Joshua to
King Saul

deliverance. There is no one holy like the LORD; there is no one besides you; there is no Rock like our God.... The LORD is a God who knows, and by him deeds are weighed.... The LORD brings death and makes alive; he brings down to the grave and raises up. The LORD sends poverty and wealth; he humbles and he exalts. He raises the poor from the dust and lifts the needy from the ash heap; he seats them with princes and has them inherit a throne of honor.... He will guard the feet of his saints, but the wicked will be silenced in darkness. It is not by strength that one prevails; those who oppose the LORD will be shattered. He will thunder against them from heaven; the LORD will judge the ends of the earth. He will give strength to his king and exalt the horn of his anointed" (1 Sam. 2:1–3,6–10).

From silent and unvoiced petition, this godly mother in Israel rose perhaps to loudly articulated praise and prophetic declaration encompassing the coming Messiah. Her praise is reminiscent of Mary's Magnificat (Luke 1:46–55).

Samuel 2 yrs old

Samuel was a mere child when he learned to pray. "The LORD came and stood there, calling as at other times, " 'Samuel! Samuel!' Then Samuel said, 'Speak, for your servant is listening' " (1 Sam. 3:10). But before Samuel entered into this dialogue with God, Eli had taught him to pray: " 'If he calls you, say, "Speak, LORD, for your servant is listening" ' " (3:9).

Eli's instruction was at once profoundly simple and simply profound. It confronted life's central issue—hearing God's voice ("Speak, LORD") and obeying it ("your *servant* is listening"). Here was the launching pad for Samuel's godly and illustrious ministry. Christian parents (as priests over their own homes) might well bless their children, and the world, by imparting to their offspring a simple awareness of God's voice through His Word, and by urging upon them a ready and willing response to the divine call.

But God's message could not be given to the young and tender Samuel until he could recognize its source, and with this he needed help. The Source of the speaking is as important as the message spoken. Both Samuel and Eli needed to know that it was indeed God who had spoken. Eli needed to know that what was reported was not from a childish imagination. Thus the child who was given to the Lord because his mother was "heard of God" was himself readied to respond to God and hear from Him. First, he heard from God; then God heard a response acknowledging Samuel's awareness of the Source of what he had heard. Having learned to recognize the voice of God and to communicate with Him in prayer, Samuel was fit for his task of spiritual leadership.

PART 1

Chapter 3
The
Period
from
Joshua to
King Saul

Later, Samuel was used to bring spiritual revival as well as victory to Israel. Samuel said, "Assemble all Israel at Mizpah and I will intercede with the LORD for you." When they had assembled at Mizpah, . . . they fasted and there they confessed, "We have sinned against the LORD.". . . They said to Samuel, "Do not stop crying out to the LORD our God for us, that he may rescue us from the hand of the Philistines.". . . He [Samuel] cried out to the LORD on Israel's behalf, and the LORD answered him (1 Sam. 7:5–6,8–9).

Israel had departed from the Lord. Their allegiance leaned toward foreign gods. The Philistines were prevailing. There was no way they could obtain God's help until their present course was corrected. Under Samuel's leadership they took three steps. They (1) fasted (7:6), (2) confessed (7:6), and (3) acknowledged their need for divine intervention (7:8). Prayer might yield far greater results if those who pray would first recognize and act upon the already revealed will of God.

The description of Samuel's praying is noteworthy. Samuel "cried out . . . and the LORD answered" (7:9). Prayer to be effective need not be wordy or complicated. It needs only to reflect utter need and total dependence. And when God hears, He acts (see 7:10–14).

Godliness, however, is no guarantee of exemption from disappointment, nor does it always assure complete loyalty of others to the divinely instituted precepts which the godly readily espouse. The fact that Samuel's sons "did not walk in his ways" but "turned aside after dishonest gain and accepted bribes and perverted justice" (1 Sam. 8:3) no doubt was a great personal disappointment to Samuel. But add to that disappointment the request of the elders of Israel for a king to rule over them (8:5), and one begins

PART 1

Chapter 3
The
Period
from
Joshua to
King Saul

to feel the ache that Samuel must have felt. Nevertheless, he continued to conduct the business of the Lord. "When they said, 'Give us a king to lead us,' this displeased Samuel; so he prayed to the LORD" (1 Sam. 8:6). Despite his disappointment and displeasure, Samuel prayed. "It was as prophet that he thus acted as mediator between the people and God; and he gave his services in this his highest capacity as faithfully when the question was one injurious to himself as he had ever done on more pleasing occasions."[4]

The answer Samuel received was both consoling and disconcerting: " 'It is not you they have rejected, but they have rejected me' " (1 Sam. 8:7). They had chosen the dominion of a visible, earthly potentate in place of the invisible, omnipotent Jehovah. Then they greedily pursued monarchy with all of its attendant evils, in place of theocracy with all of its glorious provision and promise. What pitiful deals people make when they follow the counsels of their own desire instead of seeking the counsel of Him who does all things in one's best interest! Israel was to learn by bitter experience of the divine displeasure:

Samuel called upon the LORD, and that same day the LORD sent thunder and rain. So all the people stood in awe of the LORD and of Samuel. The people all said to Samuel, "Pray to the LORD your God for your servants so that we will not die, for we have added to all our other sins the evil of asking for a king" (1 Sam. 12:18–19).

A lesser person than Samuel might have left the Israelites to their own devices, abandoning God's people to suffer the consequences of their decisions. But Samuel sought rather to encourage and comfort his erring people, to aid them despite their folly. To them he also pledged his prayer and continued leadership: " 'Far be it from me that I should sin against the LORD by failing to pray for you. And I will teach you the way that is good and right' " (1 Sam. 12:23). Samuel perceived that it was sin against the Lord to stop praying for his people. Does it matter whether we pray or

---

[4]H. D. M. Spence and Joseph S. Exell, eds., *The Pulpit Commentary* (Grand Rapids: Wm. B. Eerdmans Pub. Co., 1950), vol. 4, *1 Samuel,* by R. Payne Smith, 143.

not? It matters so much that to neglect it is to sin against Almighty God. Samuel's concern for Israel is captured in emotionally charged lines that likely describe at one time or another the feeling of every true spiritual leader who considers the congregation of the Lord through His eyes:

PART 1

Chapter 3
The
Period
from
Joshua to
King Saul

> For her, my tears shall fall;
> For her, my prayers ascend,
> To her, my cares and toils be given,
> Till toils and cares shall end.[5]

Deep and sorrowful disappointment over the failure of God's servants in high places is not an uncommon lot for a godly person. " 'I am grieved that I have made Saul king, because he has turned away from me and has not carried out my instructions.' Samuel was troubled, and he cried out to the Lord all that night" (1 Sam. 15:11).

One expositor says of this passage:

He [Samuel] . . . spent a whole night in interceding for him [Saul], that this decree might not go forth against him. When others were in their beds sleeping, he was upon his knees praying and wrestling with God. He did not . . . deprecate his own exclusion from the government; nor was he secretly pleased, as many a one would have been, that Saul, who succeeded him, was so soon laid aside, but on the contrary prayed earnestly for his establishment, so far was he from desiring that woeful day. The rejection of sinners is the grief of good people; God delights not in their death, nor should we.[6]

Between Samuel and God there was unimpeded communication. Samuel spoke; God responded. God spoke; Samuel responded.

The LORD said to Samuel, "How long will you mourn for Saul, since I have rejected him as king over Israel? Fill your horn with oil and be on your way; I am sending you to Jesse of Bethlehem. I have chosen one of his sons to be king." But Samuel said, "How can I go? Saul will hear about it and kill me." The LORD said,

---

[5]Lockyer, *All the Prayers,* 64.

[6]*Matthew Henry's Commentary on the Whole Bible,* vol. 2 (New York: Fleming H. Revell Co., n.d.), 360.

PART 1

Chapter 3
The
Period
from
Joshua to
King Saul

"Take a heifer with you and say, 'I have come to sacrifice to the LORD' " (1 Sam. 16:1–2).

For those willing to be led, there is ready guidance (cf. John 7:17). The committed heart and the trained ear do not find it difficult to hear the Lord's gentle " 'This is the way; walk in it' " (Isa. 30:21). Fear is the enemy not only of the ungodly, but sometimes of the godly as well. Yet only the godly have a ready panacea. They need but "approach the throne of grace with confidence . . . in . . . time of need" (Heb. 4:16). Samuel did, and he found an immediate solution.

King Saul

Saul is an enigma, a strange combination of God-consciousness, impetuosity, altar-building, and prayer. Though he was God-conscious, he was not godly. Though he did pray at times, he cannot be considered a person of prayer. It is possible that his flagrant acts of disobedience and rashness were but the fruits of his neglect of those means of grace to which his successor, David, would resort.

One instance of his altar building and prayer is noteworthy.

Saul built an altar to the LORD; it was the first time he had done this. . . . Saul asked God, "Shall I go down after the Philistines? Will you give them into Israel's hand?" But God did not answer him that day (1 Sam. 14:35,37).

Because of Saul's disobedience Samuel had said the kingdom would not continue in Saul's line (1 Sam. 13:14). Instead of repenting, Saul tried to act more religious. Without any direction from God, he placed his soldiers under oath not to eat anything until evening (1 Sam. 14:24). Because of Jonathan's daring, a victory was won; but when evening came the soldiers were so famished that they began to kill and eat captured livestock without draining the blood as the Law required. When this was reported to Saul, he had them bring the animals to a large stone, so that the blood could drain out. Then he built his first altar, probably as an attempt to compensate for the breaking of the Law.

But offerings to God do not compensate for an unacceptable life-style and disobedience.

Yet Saul, satisfied with himself, proposed going against the Philistines again. But the priest urged him to seek the Lord first. When God "did not answer him that day," Saul concluded that some sin was creating an obstacle. But he failed to consider that the problem might be within himself rather than his people. So he set out to discover the culprit, whoever he might be (1 Sam. 14:39). Using lots, the lot fell on Jonathan, who, without knowing about his father's oath, had eaten a bit of honey. This was not wrong in itself, nor did the lot mean that Jonathan deserved death. It simply identified him as the one who had eaten something and allowed the rest of the army to go free. Nevertheless, Saul, again without prayer, made another rash oath that Jonathan must die. But the intercession of the people saved him (1 Sam. 14:44–45). How much God is displeased when we rationalize our selfish actions and use outward forms of religion as a substitute for genuine obedience. Had Saul sought and obeyed the will of God, he would not have found God silent. The same lesson must be learned by people today.

Saul was almost a spiritual Jekyll and Hyde. In a single day he could act in deliberate, outright disobedience, and just a short time later plead with Samuel that his worship be accepted. Actually, his real purpose was to try to make a good impression on the people. "Saul replied, 'I have sinned. But please honor me before the elders of my people and before Israel; come back with me, so that I may worship the LORD your God.' So Samuel went back with Saul, and Saul worshiped the LORD" (1 Sam. 15:30–31).

We need not think this too strange or unusual, for even the demon-possessed of Jesus' day worshiped Him (see Mark 5:6). Such worship is unacceptable, nor does it compensate for disobedience.

Saul did pray. But God's response was always the same: "He [Saul] inquired of the LORD, but the LORD did not answer him by dreams or Urim or prophets" (1 Sam. 28:6). We may wonder why there was no response, especially since Scripture indicates that at one point God had "changed Saul's heart" (1 Sam. 10:9). We know that in the natural

PART 1

Chapter 3
The
Period
from
Joshua to
King Saul

PART 1

**Chapter 3
The
Period
from
Joshua to
King Saul**

world of heart transplants it is not uncommon for the human body to reject a new heart. Perhaps in spite of his new heart, Saul retained his power of choice to his own hurt; his own rebellion and disobedience toward God left no place for repentance or recovery. What a fearful prospect!

Consequently, Saul could get no answer. Though he continued as Israel's king for nearly thirty years after his rejection, he was a person cut off from God. No means or device would work, neither dreams, nor Urim, nor prophets. Heaven was silent. As a final resort, he turned to a spiritist medium (1 Sam. 28:7). Although he did on this occasion get an answer of sorts, he got no solution to his problem and died a miserable suicide. He ended as a self-willed king leading a self-willed people to defeat. What a contrast he was to the godly people of prayer who preceded him: Moses, Deborah, Hannah, Samuel!

Questions for Study

1. Under what circumstances would it be appropriate to follow Gideon's example and lay out some sort of fleece?

2. What application of the prayer of Jabez can you make to your own situation?

3. What are some of the ways God dealt with Israel in order to get them to depend on Him?

4. What are some of the ways intense desire may be expressed in prayer?

5. How and why did Samuel show his continuing concern for the people when they asked for a king?

6. What are some of the reasons God will refuse to answer a person's prayers?

THE PRAYERS OF DAVID AND OTHER PSALMISTS

Considering David's devotion after considering that of Saul's is like coming into the daylight from a dark dungeon. David was a man after God's own heart (Acts 13:22); Saul was a man away from God's own heart, rebellious and disobedient. Therein we see an indispensable key to effective praying, for Saul's life seemed void of answers and David's life seemed full of answers.

David apparently realized that prayer is appropriate in all of life's circumstances. Consequently, his prayers—found both in the narrative accounts of his life and in the Psalms—contain petition, confession, praise, and testimony. Whether circumstances were good or bad, whether trouble loomed or the days were filled with blessing, David prayed.

Reliance on the Lord

Warfare became David's lot early in life (beginning with Goliath), and though he had learned war well, he maintained complete reliance on the Lord. He dared not permit success on the field to breed neglect.

David's first recorded prayer, other than those of the Psalms, is a striking contrast to Saul's: "He [David] inquired of the LORD, saying, 'Shall I go and attack these Philistines?' The LORD answered him, 'Go, attack the Philistines' " (1 Sam.

PART 1

Chapter 4
The
Prayers
of David
and Other
Psalmists

23:2). Saul asked the same question of God and got no answer. David prayed and received an immediate answer. Receiving an answer was not as dependent on the content of the request as upon the content of the heart. The Bible draws particular attention to the fact that God recognized David as a true servant of His, a man after His own heart, who would do all His will (see Ps. 89:19–20; 1 Sam. 13:14; Acts 13:22). The desire and intent to do God's will are essential as we approach God in prayer.

David wanted to be sure he had heard from the Lord. "Once again David inquired of the LORD, and the LORD answered him, 'Go down to Keilah, for I am going to give the Philistines into your hand'" (1 Sam. 23:4). David was no self-assured, overly confident man. He was unlike those who today tell us that praying more than once over a matter evidences a lack of faith. The lives of others were in his hands, and it was an act of prudence to check out the certainty of his previous direction.

David said, "O LORD, God of Israel, your servant has heard definitely that Saul plans to come to Keilah and destroy the town on account of me. Will the citizens of Keilah surrender me to him? Will Saul come down, as your servant has heard? O LORD, God of Israel, tell your servant." And the LORD said, "He will." Again David asked, "Will the citizens of Keilah surrender me and my men to Saul?" And the LORD said, "They will" (1 Sam. 23:10–12).

God imparts necessary knowledge to those who seek Him, but He then expects them to act on it. In the light of the information God shared, David determined his own course of action. He did not become fickle in his praying—as people sometimes do—and become unwilling to take the action obviously required by God's revelation.

Another time "David inquired of the LORD, 'Shall I pursue this raiding party? Will I overtake them?' 'Pursue them,' he answered. 'You will certainly overtake them and succeed in the rescue'" (1 Sam. 30:8).

David's approach to God was by way of Abiathar, a priest, who in turn employed the God-ordained Urim and Thummim to determine the will of the Lord. Today we need no intermediary priests, other than Christ, and no mysterious device, for we have the Holy Spirit to relay to our hearts the divine will.

Elevation from soldier to king did not alter David's practice of praying: "In the course of time, David inquired of the LORD. 'Shall I go up to one of the towns of Judah?' he asked. The LORD said, 'Go up.' David asked, 'Where shall I go?' 'To Hebron,' the LORD answered" (2 Sam. 2:1). It is to one's credit that one's prayer life is so ingrained and established that it is not disturbed by life's vicissitudes. When exaltation comes, some people tend to lessen the very practice that takes them there. But not David. His rank had no bearing on his practice of prayer, except perhaps to intensify it.

David's sensitivity to his need for divine direction is most exemplary. He had no doubts about God's having ordained the destruction of the Philistines. Yet the timing of that destruction and the particular means were always left open. Therefore, he regularly asked for—and got—God's faithful and explicit guidance.

David inquired of the LORD, and he answered, "Do not go straight up, but circle around behind them and attack them in front of the balsam trees. As soon as you hear the sound of marching in the tops of the balsam trees, move quickly, because that will mean the LORD has gone out in front of you to strike the Philistine army" (2 Sam. 5:23–24).

Prayer at a Time of Great Blessing

Nathan the prophet conveyed to King David what has been labeled the Davidic Covenant (see 2 Sam. 7), with its abundant promises and assurance. Yet David did not gloat over the overwhelming revelation; instead, he went to prayer:

King David went in and sat before the LORD, and he said: "Who am I, O Sovereign LORD, and what is my family, that you have brought me this far? And as if this were not enough in your sight, O Sovereign LORD, you have also spoken about the future of the house of your servant.... What more can David say to you? For you know your servant, O Sovereign LORD. For the sake of your word and according to your will, you have done this great thing

PART 1

Chapter 4
The
Prayers
of David
and Other
Psalmists

■■■■■■■ ■

PART 1

Chapter 4
The
Prayers
of David
and Other
Psalmists

and made it known to your servant. How great you are, O Sovereign LORD! There is no one like you, and there is no God but you, as we have heard with our own ears. . . .

"Now, LORD God, keep forever the promise you have made concerning your servant and his house. Do as you promised, so that your name will be great forever. Then men will say, 'The LORD Almighty is God over Israel!' And the house of your servant David will be established before you. O LORD Almighty, God of Israel, you have revealed this to your servant, saying, 'I will build a house for you.' So your servant has found courage to offer you this prayer. O Sovereign LORD, you are God! Your words are trustworthy, and you have promised these good things to your servant. Now be pleased to bless the house of your servant, that it may continue forever in your sight; for you, O Sovereign LORD, have spoken, and with your blessing the house of your servant will be blessed forever" (2 Sam. 7:18–22,25–29; cf. 1 Chron. 17:16–27).

Although the physical posture in prayer may at times have some significance, the spiritual, or heart, posture is of primary concern to the Lord. In this case, David went in and "sat before the LORD" (7:18). (Sitting before the Lord in those days was the privilege of the king; ordinary persons would stand or kneel.)

> 'Tis not to those who stand erect,
> Or those who bend the knee,
> It is to those who bow the heart
> The Lord will gracious be;
> It is the posture of the soul
> That pleases or offends;
> If it be not in God's sight right
> Naught else can make amends.[1]

Among the many lessons to be derived from this prayer of David, these should be noted:

1. The heart attitude of the person praying should be one of deep humility (vv. 18–19).

2. The praying person should recognize that God has

---

[1]Herbert Lockyer, *All the Prayers of the Bible* (Grand Rapids: Zondervan Publishing House, 1959), 82.

total knowledge of His servants and should approach God accordingly (v. 20).

PART 1

Chapter 4
The
Prayers
of David
and Other
Psalmists

3. God makes His plans and intentions known to His servants according to His own heart. In other words, the degree and extent of His revelation is His own province (v. 21).

4. It is to the praying person's advantage, being among other things a most meaningful stimulus to faith, to contemplate and declare the greatness of God (v. 22).

5. Recognition of and appreciation for the redeemed people of God (the family of God), who are forever His, is of paramount importance (vv. 23–24).

6. Our prayers should encompass both the household of God and the household of God's servants (vv. 25–29).

Prayer at Times of Failure

Foolishness and foolhardiness are the common lot of humans. Few, if any, are exempt, not even the devout and mighty King David. David's heart being after "[God's] own heart" (Acts 13:22) was his greatest spiritual asset. Let come anything into his life—failure, faulty judgment, sin, foolishness—his heart, like a compass, always pointed the way out, because deep in his heart he really wanted to do God's will. This always led him to make confession, demonstrate repentance, and receive forgiveness. Yet it should not be thought that his heart was simply an escape mechanism by which he could avoid the consequences of his folly. The account of the aftermath of David's illicit relationship with Bathsheba bears this out. The baby born of their adultery was very sick, sending David to prayer: He "pleaded with God for the child. He fasted and went into his house and spent the night lying on the ground" (2 Sam. 12:16).

Even in the face of utter and devastating failure, the godly pray. David had been literally "at ease in Zion" (cf. 2 Sam. 11:1) while his armies were at war, and it may well be that his vast conquests had for a season caused neglect of his otherwise vital relationship with God. Or if that was not the case, the lesson is that though people do pray, they

PART 1

Chapter 4
The
Prayers
of David
and Other
Psalmists

remain susceptible to their passions and must always be on guard against the unexpected moment of temptation.

Before David prayed, he had mended his spiritual fences. He had confessed his terrible deeds (12:13) and been assured of God's mercy and grace. Without that contrition, his prayer would itself have been presumptuous sin. But even with David's confession, and despite days of fasting and intercession, God refused the request. His will was that the child should die (12:14). Prayer could not blot out the damage done; certain consequences had to follow, complete forgiveness notwithstanding.

Another time, after David foolishly (perhaps proudly) numbered the people of Israel and Judah (see 2 Sam. 24:1–15), bringing God's wrath upon himself, he quickly confessed his sin: "When David saw the angel who was striking down the people, he said to the LORD, 'I am the one who has sinned and done wrong. These are but sheep. What have they done? Let your hand fall upon me and my family'" (2 Sam. 24:17).

A person rarely sins and affects himself alone. The higher the visibility and the greater the responsibility of the person, the greater, the more far-reaching, the impact of the sin. There is anguish over recognizing one's own sin, but that hardly compares with the anguish after realizing its effect upon others. It was that kind of anguish which caused David to pray as he did, and then led him to a measure of relief. The chronicler (probably Ezra) records the restored communion:

David built an altar to the LORD there and sacrificed burnt offerings and fellowship offerings. He called on the LORD, and the LORD answered him with fire from heaven on the altar of burnt offering (1 Chron. 21:26).

God's fire consuming the offerings became David's assurance and evidence of divine approval and acceptance.[2] Although literal fire is no longer God's means of showing

---

[2]This being an Old Testament means of showing divine approval (cf. Lev. 9:24; 2 Chron. 7:1), it was very likely the way God demonstrated His acceptance of Abel's offering while Cain's offering remained rejected and unburned (see Gen. 4:4–5).

His acceptance and imparting assurance to the one b
ing the offering, He yet has a holy fire of confirmatior
assurance for those who offer themselves upon His altar
(Acts 2:1–4).

Prayer in the Midst of Adversity

"During the reign of David, there was a famine for three
successive years; so David sought the face of the LORD. The
LORD said, 'It is on account of Saul and his blood-stained
house; it is because he put the Gibeonites to death' " (2 Sam.
21:1). Adverse conditions—whether they be physical and
earthly (drought, famine, suffering, sickness) or spiritual
(the backsliding of God's people) or the absence of a keen
sense of God's presence—ought to lead to an earnest in-
quiring of the Lord, a sincere seeking of His face. Such
seeking may well uncover the cause of the existing and
persistent condition. David learned that Israel's present
problem had its roots in the previous administration, and
that the present reaping was the fruit of past sowing. Saul,
in his rashness and recklessness, had directed an attack on
the Gibeonites with whom Israel had a covenant (see Josh.
9:15–27); divine justice would not rest the case, though
the perpetrator was dead. Armed with God's view of the
problem, David set out to effect a remedy (2 Sam. 21:3–
6). "After that, God answered prayer in behalf of the land"
(21:14).

Prayer as Expression of Praise

Praise is an essential part of praying, in fact, the highest
form of praying, and in this David was expert. "David sang
to the LORD the words of this song when the LORD delivered
him from the hand of all his enemies and from the hand
of Saul" (2 Sam. 22:1). All of 2 Samuel 22 is a psalm of
praise, David was giving recognition and highest praise to
God for His well-perceived role in David's daily walk. David
recognized the power of God and praised Him for deliverance, especially deliverance from the most life-
threatening circumstances. He honored God for the guidance, the empowering, and the victories He gives. Truly
He is a faithful God who is worthy of all praise! (This aspect

**Chapter ᴛ
The
Prayers
of David
and Other
Psalmists**

PART 1

**Chapter 4
The
Prayers
of David
and Other
Psalmists**

of David's prayer life will be amplified in the treatment of individual psalms.)

The Public Prayer of a Godly Leader

First Chronicles 29 records a magnificent prayer of David as he stood before the congregation of Israel:

David praised the LORD in the presence of the whole assembly, saying, "Praise be to you, O LORD, God of our father Israel, from everlasting to everlasting. Yours, O LORD, is the greatness and the power and the glory and the majesty and the splendor, for everything in heaven and earth is yours. Yours, O LORD, is the kingdom; you are exalted as head over all. Wealth and honor come from you; you are the ruler of all things. In your hands are strength and power to exalt and give strength to all. Now, our God, we give you thanks, and praise your glorious name. . . .

"We are aliens and strangers in your sight, as were all our fore-fathers. Our days on earth are like a shadow, without hope. O LORD our God, as for all this abundance that we have provided for building you a temple for your Holy Name, it comes from your hand, and all of it belongs to you. I know, my God, that you test the heart and are pleased with integrity. All these things have I given willingly and with honest intent. And now I have seen with joy how willingly your people who are here have given to you. O LORD, . . . keep this desire in the hearts of your people forever, and keep their hearts loyal to you. And give my son Solomon the wholehearted devotion to keep your com-mands, requirements and decrees and to do everything to build the palatial structure for which I have provided" (1 Chron. 29:10–13,15–19).

This great prayer, a model for any servant who prays in public, divides readily into five earnest expressions of the heart of a burdened leader:

(1) David models confident entry into God's presence (vv. 10–13). What a delightful and inspiring example for the leaders of congregations! Acknowledging God's greatness and power, hallowing His heavenly majesty, and giving praise to His glorious name are always appropriate ways to begin public prayer.

(2) David recognizes divine enablement (vv. 14–16). Apart

PART 1

Chapter 4
The
Prayers
of David
and Other
Psalmists

from God's supply, none would have anything to give: "It comes from your hand, and all of it belongs to you." There is no room for any of us to glory in our own giving; like David, we can glory only in God's enablement (2 Cor. 9:8). To recognize this truth before God is to court ever larger enablement to share what God has given.

3. David confesses that God takes pleasure in the righteous heart (1 Chron. 29:17). Any leader of people might well linger long over David's understanding that God sees the thoughts and intents of every heart. God draws special pleasure from hearts that willingly offer themselves, their abilities, and their possessions for His service.

4. David petitions for a continuing spirit of liberality among God's people (v. 18). Liberality is Godlike. Little wonder that it should generate such joy—in God and in the giver. David's plea and ours might well be: May this quality prevail perpetually.

5. David prays for other leadership (v. 19). He prayed that his son might be, like himself, a man after God's own heart and carry out the vision of the father. Let every parent kneel beside this godly giant and offer a similar petition.

To give full attention to each of the prayers of David and others in the Book of Psalms would require, by itself, a sizable volume. Therefore, we will look at only selected prayers for the drawing out of major lessons from David's practice. However, this should not be a theoretical study. "Poetry, like music, may be analyzed and dissected, yet ultimately it must be appreciated and experienced, and to divorce the element of subjectivity from the understanding of poetry is to divest it of its power."[3]

Sincere prayer is an accurate measurement of one's true self, a revelation of the heart. Consequently, the Psalms provide an accurate picture of David (2 Sam. 23:2), the

---

[3]Peter C. Craigie, *Psalms 1–50,* vol. 19, Word Biblical Commentary Series (Waco, Tex.: Word Books, 1983), 36. Even though this study will not examine all the psalms, the reader is urged to do so, personally praying their words whenever they are appropriate. The discipline of reading the Book of Psalms for spiritual encouragement and profit is strongly recommended. Three psalms each day, in addition to other Bible study, will strengthen your prayer life.

PART 1

Chapter 4
The
Prayers
of David
and Other
Psalmists

prince of praying people, and other psalmists, as the Spirit spoke through them (1 Chron. 25:1). For all were used by the same Holy Spirit to bless us.

Recognizing God

Prayer is hardly prayer at all apart from an appropriate recognition of the God to whom it is addressed. Prayer in the Psalms is most exemplary in this regard.

For command of appropriate language, the standard of excellence of the prayer expression of the Psalms cannot be superceded. Within them we have "the very thesaurus of devotional terms." Their grace and elegance of expression provide us with a rich vocabulary for use as we draw nigh to God.[4]

Notice how David and the other psalmists repeatedly honor God for His majestic power and glory, for His faithfulness, justice, and unfailing love. He is the Creator and Sustainer of all things. He is a good God, full of mercy and ready to forgive. Because He is eternal, He is always present, always available. We can always approach Him with confidence, for He cares for us (see Nah. 1:7; Eph. 5:29; Heb. 4:16; 1 Pet. 5:7). Praise brings us into His presence as we recognize who He is and what He has done and can do.

O LORD, our Lord, how majestic is your name in all the earth! You have set your glory above the heavens (8:1).

Your love, O LORD, reaches to the heavens, your faithfulness to the skies. Your righteousness is like the mighty mountains, your justice like the great deep.... How priceless is your unfailing love! (36:5–7).

Great is the LORD, and most worthy of praise, in the city of our God, his holy mountain (48:1).

[God is] the hope of all the ends of the earth, ... who formed the mountains by your power, having armed yourself with strength, who stilled the roaring of the seas, the roaring of their waves, and the turmoil of the nations (65:5–7).

---

[4]Lockyer, *All the Prayers,* 103.

Proclaim the power of God, whose majesty is over Israel, whose power is in the skies. You are awesome, O God, in your sanctuary; the God of Israel gives power and strength to his people. Praise be to God! (68:34–35).

You are forgiving and good, O Lord, abounding in love to all who call to you.... You, O Lord, are a compassionate and gracious God, slow to anger, abounding in love and faithfulness (86:5,15).

The LORD reigns, he is robed in majesty; the LORD is robed in majesty and is armed with strength. The world is firmly established; it cannot be moved. Your throne was established long ago; you are from all eternity (93:1–2).

The LORD is the great God, the great King above all gods. In his hand are the depths of the earth, and the mountain peaks belong to him. The sea is his, for he made it, and his hands formed the dry land (95:3–5).

Praise the LORD, O my soul. O LORD my God, you are very great; you are clothed with splendor and majesty. He wraps himself in light as with a garment; he stretches out the heavens like a tent and lays the beams of his upper chambers on their waters. He makes the clouds his chariot and rides on the wings of the wind. He makes winds his messengers, flames of fire his servants. He set the earth on its foundations; it can never be moved (104:1–5).

Our perceptions of God bear heavily upon our praying. And even though David seemed to recognize God for the exhalted One He truly is; at the same time, he had a gift for making God relevant to the circumstances of life. The wealth of descriptive terms used for God is impressive:

A shield, bestower of glory, the lifter of my head [that is, in victory over enemies] (3:3)

My strength, my rock, my fortress, my deliverer, my shield, my stronghold (18:1–2)

My shepherd (23:1)

My help (54:4)

My hope (71:5)

PART 1

Chapter 4
The
Prayers
of David
and Other
Psalmists

PART 1

Chapter 4
The
Prayers
of David
and Other
Psalmists

My portion[5] (73:26)
My King from of old (74:12)
My God, a sun and shield (84:11)
My father (89:26)
Our dwelling place (90:1)
My song (118:14)
Your shade at your right hand [that is, right there to
    protect you], your keeper (121:5,7)
My loving God (144:2)

Praise and Worship

Praise and worship are essential ingredients in prayer.
David was the pacesetter of all time for this high and holy
exercise; other psalmists followed his example.

I will praise you, O LORD, with all my heart; I will tell of all your
wonders. I will be glad and rejoice in you; I will sing praise to
your name, O Most High (9:1–2).

I love thee, O LORD, my strength. The LORD is my rock, my fortress
and my deliverer; my God is my rock, in whom I take refuge.
He is my shield and the horn of my salvation, my stronghold. I
call to the LORD, who is worthy of praise, and I am saved from
my enemies (18:1–3).

It is good to praise the LORD and make music to your name, O
Most High, to proclaim your love in the morning and your faithfulness at night, to the music of the ten-stringed lyre and the
melody of the harp. For you make me glad by your deeds, O
LORD; I sing for joy at the works of your hands. How great are
your works, O LORD, how profound your thoughts! (92:1–5).

Praise the LORD, O my soul; all my inmost being, praise his holy
name. Praise the LORD, O my soul, and forget not all his benefits—
who forgives all your sins and heals all your diseases, who re-
deems your life from the pit and crowns you with love and
compassion, who satisfies your desires with good things so that
your youth is renewed like the eagle's (103:1–5).

I will exalt you, my God the King; I will praise your name for

---

[5]Asaph as a Levite had no inherited portion in the Land (see Num.
18:20–21). The Lord provided for them however.

ever and ever. Every day I will praise you and extol your name for ever and ever. Great is the LORD and most worthy of praise; his greatness no one can fathom (145:1–3).

PART 1

Chapter 4
The
Prayers
of David
and Other
Psalmists

Again we see how David and the other psalmists praised the Lord in all things and with all means, especially including instrumental music and song. Their praise was no formal repetition of a few set phrases. Though the psalms were often composed for congregational worship, or to celebrate specific occasions, the psalms came from hearts moved and inspired by the Holy Spirit. They encouraged the worshipers to put the whole heart and soul into their worship and to honor God for His provision for every aspect of life.

Petition

Besides practicing praise and worship, David and the other psalmists made supplication. Even though their praying is marked by balance (unlike that of many people), the psalms are loaded with petition. And characteristically they encompass a great variety of situations and circumstances. They practiced the admonition of Jesus long before the words of our Savior were recorded: "Disciples ... should always pray" (Luke 18:1). At all times and in all circumstances, prayer is the divine instruction for God's children.

For Guidance: Lead me, O LORD, in your righteousness because of my enemies—make straight your way before me (5:8).

For Mercy: Be merciful to me, LORD, for I am faint; O LORD, heal me, for my bones are in agony. My soul is in anguish. How long, O LORD, how long? (6:2–3).

For Understanding: Why, O LORD, do you stand far off? Why do you hide yourself in times of trouble? (10:1).

For Consolation: How long, O LORD? Will you forget me forever? How long will you hide your face from me? How long must I wrestle with my thoughts and every day have sorrow in my heart? How long will my enemy triumph over me? (13:1–2).

For Deliverance from Evil Men: Rise up, O LORD, ... rescue me from the wicked by your sword. O LORD, by our hand save me from such men, from men of this world whose reward is in this life (17:13–14).

Chap.

The
Prayers
of David
and Other
Psalmists

For God's Help in Time of Distress: In my distress I called to the LORD; I cried to my God for help. From his temple he heard my voice; my cry came before him, into his ears (18:6).

For Cleansing from Hidden and Willful Sin: Who can discern his errors? Forgive my hidden faults. Keep your servant also from willful sins; may they not rule over me. Then will I be blameless, innocent of great transgression (19:12–13).

For Right Words and Thoughts: May the words of my mouth and the meditation of my heart be pleasing in your sight, O LORD, my Rock and my Redeemer (19:14).

For Forgiveness: Look upon my affliction and my distress and take away all my sins (25:18).

For Help from the Lord: Hear, O LORD, and be merciful to me; O LORD, be my help (30:10).

For God's Blessing: Let your face shine on your servant; save me in your unfailing love (31:16).

For God's Perpetual Presence: O LORD, do not forsake me; be not far from me, O my God. Come quickly to help me, O Lord my Savior (38:21–22).

For Deliverance from God's Judgment: Save me from all my transgressions; do not make me the scorn of fools. . . . Remove your scourge from me; I am overcome by the blow of your hand. You rebuke and discipline men for their sin; you consume their wealth like a moth. . . . Hear my prayer, O LORD, listen to my cry for help; be not deaf to my weeping. . . . Look away from me, that I may rejoice again before I depart and am no more (39:8,10–13).

For Light and Truth: Send forth your light and your truth, let them guide me; let them bring me to your holy mountain, to the place where you dwell (43:3).

For a Pure Heart and a Steadfast Spirit: Create in me a pure heart, O God, and renew a steadfast spirit within me (51:10).

To Retain God's Presence and the Holy Spirit: Do not cast me from your presence or take your Holy Spirit from me (51:11).

For Restoration of the Joy of Salvation: Restore to me

the joy of your salvation and grant me a willing spirit, to sustain me (51:12).

For God's Favor to Return Toward His People: You have rejected us, O God, and burst forth upon us; you have been angry—now restore us! (60:1).

To See God's Power and Glory: O God, you are my God, earnestly I seek you; my soul thirsts for you, my body longs for you, in a dry and weary land where there is no water. I have seen you in the sanctuary and beheld your power and your glory (63:1–2).

For God's Help When Overwhelmed: Save me, O God, for the waters have come up to my neck. I sink in the miry depths, where there is no foothold. I have come into the deep waters; the floods engulf me. I am worn out calling for help; my throat is parched. My eyes fail, looking for my God (69:1–3).

For Help in Old Age: Even when I am old and gray, do not forsake me, O God, till I declare your power to the next generation, your might to all who are to come (71:18).

For God's Attentive Response When One Is in Trouble: Hear my prayer, O LORD; let my cry for help come to you. Do not hide your face from me when I am in distress. Turn your ear to me; when I call, answer me quickly (102:1–2).

For God's Examination and Correction: Search me, O God, and know my heart; test me and know my anxious thoughts. See if there is any offensive way in me, and lead me in the way everlasting (139:23–24).

Confession

Confession is an essential ingredient in prayer, for it unlocks mercy's door and unleashes God's forgiveness (see 2 Sam. 12:13). The prayers in the Psalms incorporate significant occurrences of confession.

I acknowledged my sin to you and did not cover up my iniquity. I said, "I will confess my transgressions to the LORD"—and you forgave the guilt of my sin (32:5).

Have mercy on me, O God, according to your unfailing love; according to your great compassion blot out my transgressions.

PART 1

Chapter 4
The
Prayers
of David
and Other
Psalmists

PART 1

Chapter 4
The
Prayers
of David
and Other
Psalmists

Wash away all my iniquity and cleanse me from my sin. For I know my transgressions, and my sin is always before me. Against you, you only, have I sinned and done what is evil in your sight, so that you are proved right when you speak and justified when you judge. Surely I was sinful at birth, sinful from the time my mother conceived me (51:1–5).

Thanksgiving

Thanksgiving played a major role in the prayers of the Psalms, just as it should in ours. Thanklessness is a subtle enemy of the soul, ever leading deeper into darkness (Rom. 1:21).

You . . . clothed me with joy, that my heart may sing to you and not be silent. O LORD my God, I will give you thanks forever (30:12).

I will praise God's name in song and glorify him with thanksgiving (69:30).

I will sacrifice a thank offering to you and call on the name of the LORD (116:17).

A final note before ending our overview of the prayers recorded in the Psalms: David had learned the demanding discipline of habitual prayer, recording his practice on at least two occasions.

In the morning, O LORD, you hear my voice; in the morning I lay my requests before you and wait in expectation (5:3).

Evening, morning and noon I cry out in distress, and he hears my voice (55:17).

Doubtless such practice began during his youthful years. It is reasonable to believe that before David ever ended his shepherding days he had already become a person of prayer. For surely there is no substitute for solitude when learning and practicing the holy art of prayer.

Questions for Study

1. Why was David called a man after God's own heart?
2. When is it a lack of faith to repeat a prayer and when is it an expression of faith?

3. What do David's prayers show about the importance of the attitude of the heart?

4. Can you summarize what you have learned about public prayer from David's example?

5. What does David's example show us about how we should approach God in prayer?

6. What are some of the other lessons that can be learned from the prayers in the Book of Psalms?

PART 1

Chapter 4
The
Prayers
of David
and Other
Psalmists

THE PRAYERS OF SOLOMON AND LATER LEADERS OF ISRAEL

Solomon

Some of the most exemplary praying in all the Bible is that of King Solomon, David's son and successor to the throne. Unlike David's prayers, very few of Solomon's prayers are recorded, but for each recorded prayer, there is also a recorded answer. The earliest account of his praying is found in 1 Kings (see also 2 Chron. 1:7–13).

A Humble Prayer for Wisdom

At Gibeon the LORD appeared to Solomon during the night in a dream, and God said, "Ask for whatever you want me to give you." Solomon answered, "You have shown great kindness to your servant, my father David, because he was faithful to you and righteous and upright in heart. You have continued this great kindness to him and have given him a son to sit on his throne this very day. Now, O LORD, my God, you have made your servant king in place of my father David. But I am only a little child and do not know how to carry out my duties. Your servant is here among the people you have chosen, a great people too numerous to count or number. So give your servant a discerning heart to govern your people and to distinguish between right and wrong.

PART 1

Chapter 5
The
Prayers
of
Solomon
and Later
Leaders
of Israel

For who is able to govern this great people of yours?" (1 Kings 3:5–9).

Of particular interest is God's word to the young king: " 'Ask for whatever you want me to give you.' " Asking is important both to us and to God, to us because it acknowledges dependence upon God and to God for in some way He has made His working contingent on our exercise of faith. Jesus instructed, " 'Ask and it will be given to you' " (Matt. 7:7). But the receiving is dependent upon the kind of asking. "This is the confidence we have in approaching God: that if we ask anything according to his will, he hears us" (1 John 5:14). "When you ask, you do not receive, because you ask with wrong motives [badly]" (James 4:3).

Before Solomon ever launched his petition, he made several notable acknowledgments:

1. God had shown great mercy and kindness to his father, David (1 Kings 3:6).

2. It was God who had made him king in his father's place (v. 7).

3. He was utterly unable to lead God's chosen people, "too numerous to count" (vv. 7–8).

It is quite understandable that Solomon should feel overwhelmed by his responsibility. To his credit, however, he did not reckon his heritage (son of the mighty King David) as ample enablement for the task. What a lesson to be learned by the sons and daughters of prominent and able parents when in one way or another the children become heirs to their parent's roles of leadership!

Note Solomon's petition (v. 9). God's attention is gained not only by a humble attitude but also by unselfish petition. A lesser individual might have asked for that which would bring personal benefit: riches, power, honor. But not Solomon. His prayer was concerned solely with the welfare of his people. He did not consider the people his, but God's. He took the place of an undershepherd, willing to carry out God's will and work in behalf of God's people. He desired wisdom so he could judge with discrimination and administrate with fairness the affairs of the kingdom. And "the Lord was pleased that Solomon had asked for this" (v. 10). To an affirmative answer to Solomon's request,

God also added what Solomon had not asked for: "riches and honor" and "a long life" (vv. 11–14).

PART 1

**Chapter 5
The
Prayers
of
Solomon
and Later
Leaders
of Israel**

A Renewal of the Covenant

After the completion of the temple of the Lord, which took seven years, Solomon had the priests place the ark of the Lord in the inner sanctuary, the Most Holy Place (1 Kings 8:6). When the priests left the sanctuary, a cloud filled the temple so that the priests couldn't perform their service. Then Solomon offered a prayer of dedication (1 Kings 8:22–53), which is one of the longest recorded prayers in Scripture. It should be read in its entirety, but for this discussion, selected portions provide its tone and content:

Solomon stood before the altar of the LORD in front of the whole assembly of Israel, spread out his hands toward heaven and said:

"O LORD, God of Israel, there is no God like you in heaven above or on earth below—you who keep your covenant of love with your servants who continue wholeheartedly in your way.
. . .

"But will God really dwell on earth? The heavens, even the highest heaven, cannot contain you. How much less this temple I have built! Yet give attention to your servant's prayer and his plea for mercy, O LORD my God. Hear the cry and the prayer that your servant is praying in your presence this day. May your eyes be open toward this temple night and day, this place of which you said, 'My Name shall be there,' so that you will hear the prayer your servant prays toward this place. Hear the supplication of your servant and of your people Israel when they pray toward this place. Hear from heaven, your dwelling place, and when you hear, forgive.

"When a man wrongs his neighbor . . . then hear from heaven and act. Judge between your servants, condemning the guilty. . . . Declare the innocent not guilty, and so establish his innocence.

"When your people Israel have been defeated by an enemy because they have sinned against you, and when they turn back to you and confess your name, praying and making supplication to you in this temple, then hear from heaven and forgive the sin of your people Israel and bring them back to the land you gave to their fathers.

PART 1

Chapter 5
The
Prayers
of
Solomon
and Later
Leaders
of Israel

"When the heavens are shut up and there is no rain because your people have sinned against you, and when they pray toward this place and confess your name and turn from their sin because you have afflicted them, then hear from heaven and forgive the sin of your servants, your people Israel. Teach them the right way to live ...

"When a prayer or plea is made by any of your people ... spreading out his hands toward this temple—then hear from heaven, your dwelling place. Forgive and act; deal with each man according to all he does, since you know his heart ...

"As for the foreigner ... when he comes and prays toward this temple, then hear from heaven, your dwelling place, and do whatever the foreigner asks of you, so that all the peoples of the earth may know your name and fear you, as do your own people Israel, and may know that this house I have built bears your Name. ...

"When they sin against you—for there is no one who does not sin—and you become angry with them and give them over to the enemy, who takes them captive to his own land, far away or near; and if they have a change of heart in the land where they are held captive, and repent and plead with you in the land of their conquerors and say, 'We have sinned, we have done wrong, we have acted wickedly;' and if they turn back to you with all their heart and soul ... then from heaven your dwelling place, hear their prayer and their plea, and uphold their cause. And forgive your people, who have sinned against you ... and cause their conquerors to show them mercy. ... (1 Kings 8:22–23,27–36,38–39,41–43,46–50).

Solomon's prayer has three readily identifiable divisions:
1. A general appeal that God would honor His word to David and heed the prayer of His servant Solomon (vv. 22–30).
2. Seven special petitions (vv. 31–50). These were expressed in poetic parallelism. His "ifs" are balanced by "thens," his "whens" by "thens." (Each paired statement reveals a profound theology of prayer; any student of prayer would profit by thoughtful attention to each petition.)
   a. When a man is required to take an oath, then hear from heaven and act (vv. 31–32).

P. 36

b. When the people confess their sin, then hear from heaven and forgive the sin (vv. 33–34).

c. When the people turn from their sin because you have afflicted them, then hear from heaven and forgive the sin (vv. 35–36).

d. When the people examine themselves in times of famine or plague and pray, then deal with each person according to what action or forgiveness he needs (vv. 37–40).

e. When a foreigner comes and prays toward the temple because of your great name, then do whatever the foreigner asks (vv. 41–43).

f. When you send your people to war and they pray, then hear from heaven and uphold their cause (vv. 44–45).

g. When the people sin and you send them to be held captive and they turn from their sin and pray, then hear them and forgive them (vv. 46–51).

3. A concluding appeal for God's careful attention to His separated (chosen) people (vv. 51–53).

PART 1

Chapter 5
The
Prayers
of
Solomon
and Later
Leaders
of Israel

Paramount in Solomon's praying was his awareness that God's blessings and provisions are related to actions and to meeting divine requirements and conditions. To forget this is to pray in vain.

Solomon's prayer posture and physical actions are not without significance. He "spread out his hands toward heaven" (v. 22) and "rose from before the altar of the Lord, where he had been kneeling" (v. 54). The hands stretched out toward heaven show he was open to receiving God's blessing and help. By humbly kneeling (though he was king and could sit before the Lord, cf. 2 Sam. 7:18), he acknowledged God's sovereignty as the divine King and his own unworthiness and total dependence on God.

Verse 27, acknowledging God's omnipresence as it does, reveals Solomon's perception of God's greatness and infinitude, certainly a vital ingredient in effective praying. How completely gratifying to turn from our human limitations to the mighty God who has no equal, who is at once infinite and eternal, who cannot be contained in a mere earthly house, nor even in the highest heaven, who knows no

■■■■■
PART 1

Chapter 5
The
Prayers
of
Solomon
and Later
Leaders
of Israel

constraint of time. He inhabits limitless time and endless years. What a great God is our God!

Elijah

Few people have gained such recognition for their praying as did the prophet Elijah. For when he prayed to his God (the name "Elijah" signifies "My God is Yahweh [Jehovah]"), the results were remarkable.

One of the reasons for this kind of results must have been a relationship of regular communication between him and God, a relationship implied in 1 Kings 17:1: "Elijah the Tishbite ... said to Ahab, 'As the LORD, the God of Israel, lives, whom I serve, there will be neither dew nor rain in the next few years except at my word.' " The phrase "whom I serve" indicates at the very least Elijah's personal relationship to, and his standing as a representative of, God. It suggests also Elijah's communion with Him, as well as his habit of receiving direction from Him.

A Powerful, Effective Prayer

God's hand or His purposes in life's vicissitudes are not always accurately assessed—as in the story of the widow's son who died only to be raised again to life (read 1 Kings 17:8–24)—for we see only "a poor reflection as in a mirror" (1 Cor. 13:12).

He [Elijah] cried out to the LORD, "O LORD my God, have you brought tragedy also upon this widow I am staying with, by causing her son to die?" Then he stretched himself out on the boy three times and cried to the LORD, "O LORD my God, let this boy's life return to him!" The Lord heard Elijah's cry, and the boy's life returned to him, and he lived (1 Kings 17:20–22).

From the widow's viewpoint, her only son's sudden death was punishment for some sin of her youth, long buried in memory's secret chamber; and who is to say that God does not in some cases employ such means for obtaining necessary repentance, thereby freeing the soul for loftier heights? Yet it should be remembered that Satan is a master strategist who delights in taking advantage of life's untoward circumstances by using them to induce condemnation for sins long since forgiven and cleansed (cf. Rom. 8:1,33–34).

As Elijah prayed, he may have also wrongfully charged God with slaying the widow's son. Both mother and prophet were subject to human feelings and limitations. It is quite possible that neither assumed cause of death was totally accurate, that in this instance God's sole purpose was to demonstrate His miraculous power to bring glory to himself (cf. John 9:3; 11:4). But regardless of our assessment of God's reasons for causing or allowing a tragedy to happen, it is certainly within proper bounds to implore God for a solution to the problem. Our error may easily be that we draw our own conclusions, and then pray. Yet the reverse order might spare us from unnecessary anguish and deter us from wrongly accusing God.

Some speculate on Elijah's reason for stretching himself upon the child; it is sufficient to understand that in this act the prophet revealed his intensity and total involvement in gaining the necessary divine intervention. Certainly here is faith in action; the humanly impossible becomes reality as the God of the impossible freely demonstrates His unlimited power. Elijah's unusual behavior was not the cause, but the medium through which the prayer was answered.

"The prayer of a righteous man is powerful and effective" (James 5:16). Elijah was an excellent example of the validity of that inspired statement. He had a single passion as he pled with God for the dead child; he was consumed by his desperate petition. His cry left no doubt about the end he pursued: " 'O LORD my God, let this boy's life return to him!' " (1 Kings 17:21). Elijah's prayer may not conform to our concepts of acceptable prayer; it was a prayer for a temporal miracle, without conditions or alternatives. Yet the Lord heard and answered it.

Reminders of Who God Is

Elijah and 450 prophets of Baal stood before the people to prove who was God, the Lord or Baal. The people decided this would be a good test and made the preparations. Although the prophets called on Baal from morning until

PART 1

Chapter 5
The
Prayers
of
Solomon
and Later
Leaders
of Israel

PART 1

Chapter 5
The
Prayers
of
Solomon
and Later
Leaders
of Israel

evening, they received no answer. Then Elijah stepped forward and began to pray:

O LORD, God of Abraham, Isaac and Israel, let it be known today that you are God in Israel and that I am your servant and have done all these things at your command. Answer me, O LORD, answer me, so these people will know that you, O LORD, are God, and that you are turning their hearts back again" (1 Kings 18:36–37).

How God is addressed is of no little consequence. It can arouse faith in those praying and awaken the hearts of those hearing. Recognizing who God is builds faith in what He can do. He is not a god like Baal, who could give no answer even though his prophets sought his response with utmost earnestness and importunity. In contrast, Elijah's God is the God of Abraham, Isaac, and Israel; each of these patriarchs had received supernatural answers to prayers. Only once before in Scripture is this identification of God as the God of Abraham, Isaac, and Jacob used; and in that instance it was God himself who used it at the burning bush (Exod. 3:6). Our prayers can be enriched by addressing God for who He is. (Note Paul's prayer in Ephesians 1:17: "the God of our Lord Jesus Christ, the glorious Father.")

The content of Elijah's simple prayer, which obtained heaven's immediate and undeniable response (vv. 38–39), reveals the chief passion of the great prophet. Prayer, for us as well as for Elijah, mirrors the heart. From Elijah's perspective, Israel had to know two things: (1) the identity of God and (2) the source of Elijah's authority. They had to know the God of Israel, for the folly of their king had brought utter confusion to the people: " 'Let it be known today that you [the God of Abraham, Isaac, and Israel] are God in Israel.' " It had to be understood, too, that Elijah was not on some self-appointed mission, but that he was merely the servant of God, doing as he had been commanded: " '[Let it be known] . . . that I am your servant and have done all these things at your command.' "

Elijah's sole purpose was to turn the heart of this people back to the true God (18:37). What will it take today for a similar turnaround in the hearts of people the world over? It may require supernatural manifestations, as in Elijah's day. What followed did turn the heart of the people back to the true God. The fire fell and consumed the offering, the wood, the stones, the dust, even the water. "When all the people saw this, they fell prostrate and cried, 'The LORD—he is God! The LORD—he is God!' " (18:39). Literally, they said, "The LORD—He is *the God*" (the one true God). Conversely, they recognized that Baal was no god at all.

PART 1
Chapter 5
The
Prayers
of
Solomon
and Later
Leaders
of Israel

Delays and Persistence

After God's sovereignty over Israel was demonstrated and established, Elijah could announce with confidence that rain to break the drought was on the way. Though the words of his prayer are not recorded, he must have prayed with fervor for God to send the rain:

Elijah climbed to the top of Carmel, bent down to the ground and put his face between his knees. "Go and look toward the sea," he told his servant. And he went up and looked. "There is nothing there," he said. Seven times Elijah said, "Go back." The seventh time the servant reported, "A cloud as small as a man's hand is rising from the sea." So Elijah said, "Go and tell Ahab, 'Hitch up your chariot and go down before the rain stops you.' " (1 Kings 18:42–44).

The posture of the praying prophet denotes the intensity of his prayer. James describes this intensity by using the Greek word *energeó* (from which we get the word "energy"), translated by the KJV as "effectual" and "fervent" and by the NIV as "effective" and "powerful." It has been suggested that Elijah's posture was like that of an Israelite woman in the travail of birth; such a view is not inappropriate, for surely he did travail for the spiritual rebirth of his people.

But the question can be raised: Since God had told Elijah, " 'Go and present yourself to Ahab, and I will send rain on the land' " (1 Kings 18:1), why did he have to pray at all? Had not Elijah obeyed? Indeed he had. Yet there was a time lapse between the promise and the fulfillment. We may well ponder the reason for the delay. God must somehow limit His intervention in human affairs to the active

PART 1

Chapter 5
The
Prayers
of
Solomon
and Later
Leaders
of Israel

involvement of His servants. He looks for their faith and prayers and then releases His benefits. We must conclude that He desires, if not needs, our prayers. How much more glory might come to Him, and how many more might turn to God, if we rightly and consistently prayed!

Here also is a lesson on persistence and perseverance, as well as a gentle rebuke of those who insist that praying for a thing more than a single time indicates lack of faith. Elijah's unrelenting travail and his repeated command, directing his servant to look for the first hint of an answer, were the exact opposite of unbelief. He knew it would rain, but he also perceived that there was an essential role he must play in making it possible. Would that everyone today might pray with the same awareness.

A Time Not to Pray

Here again is illustration of James' assertion that Elijah was human just like us. Here again is our opportunity to identify with him as a person of prayer. One day he can pray down fire and rain, and the next, he can pray to die. (Read 1 Kings 19:1–7.)

He . . . went a day's journey into the desert. He came to a broom tree, sat down under it and prayed that he might die. "I have had enough, LORD," he said. "Take my life; I am no better than my ancestors" (1 Kings 19:4).

There is a time to pray, and (as we noted with Moses before the Red Sea) there is a time not to pray. Prayer when exhaustion and depression have invaded our earthly frame may easily become prayer that is contrary to the Creator's gracious will. It is our good fortune that God knows our humanity, remembering how he formed us (Ps. 103:14). He does not condemn us for our misguided prayers when life has overwhelmed us, nor, thankfully, does he answer them. Had He answered the distraught prophet's plea, think of the loss. God had planned for Elijah to escape earth without dying (2 Kings 2:1); but at this point, Elijah sought to escape earth by dying.

It is for our edification that the Bible tells the whole story, speaking not only of someone's mighty exploits, but also of his frustrations, failures, and defeats. Unlike God, who changes not, people on successive days can be "the glory" and "the scandal" of the universe. The Bible does not whitewash its heroes. It lets us see them as they were, so we can learn from their times of weakness as well as from their success.

PART 1
Chapter 5
The
Prayers
of
Solomon
and Later
Leaders
of Israel

As we have observed, the results of Elijah's prayers were remarkable—so remarkable, perhaps, that they intimidate, instead of inspire, us. Therefore, in addition to studying the recorded prayers of Elijah, we have considered other pertinent biblical comments about him: for example, that of James, the Lord's brother, illustrating effective praying by referring to Elijah (James 5:16–20). The Holy Spirit— as if bent on getting rid of any misconceptions about him— inspired James to encourage us by noting, "Elijah was as completely human as we are" (James 5:17, LB). And so we have seen that he too had to contend with his own humanity and with the lingering passions of the fallen nature that war against the soul.

Elisha

Restoring Life to the Dead

Elisha was a remarkable man of prayer, like Elijah, his predecessor. He received a "double portion" of the spirit of Elijah, that is, the portion of the heir. Consequently, he was recognized as taking Elijah's place as leader among the prophets (2 Kings 2:9,15). Also like Elijah, Elisha experienced an answer to prayer that seldom comes to mortals:

When Elisha reached the house, there was the boy lying dead on his couch. He went in, shut the door on the two of them and prayed to the LORD. Then he got on the bed and lay upon the boy, mouth to mouth, eyes to eyes, hands to hands. As he stretched himself out upon him, the boy's body grew warm. Elisha turned away and walked back and forth in the room and then got on the bed and stretched out upon him once more. The boy sneezed seven times and opened his eyes (2 Kings 4:32–35).

Raising the dead is certainly not the order of the day. Never has it been, nor ever will it be. But this is not to say

PART 1

Chapter 5
The
Prayers
of
Solomon
and Later
Leaders
of Israel

that it cannot happen. God has not changed, nor has His power diminished. Through His might, people have been raised from the dead and will yet be raised from the dead. " 'Why should any of you consider it incredible that God raises the dead?' " (Acts 26:8). Elijah had been used in such a miracle. And certainly Elisha had heard the account from his mentor; consequently his faith rose as the opportunity for a miracle presented itself. His ministry followed the pattern of his predecessor. One can scarcely pray effectively without provoking friends to emulate the practice.

"He ... lay upon the boy" (2 Kings 4:34) as if to communicate some of his vital heat or spirit to him. In this way Elisha, like Elijah (1 Kings 17:21), after asking God for a miracle, expressed the earnestness of his desire and of his trust in that divine power on which he depended for the accomplishment of this great work.

He then turned away from the boy (the Hebrew may indicate he went down into the Shunammite's house), pacing back and forth as one full of concern, wholly intent upon the miracle he was seeking. A second time he stretched himself upon the child (2 Kings 4:35). Those who earnestly desire to impart spiritual life to dead souls must likewise labor fervently in prayer and direct encounter. "Natural means are in our power; those that are supernatural belong to God. We should always do our own work, and beg of God to do his."[1]

A Request for Spiritual Understanding

The king of Aram wanted to capture Elisha because his every secret plan against Israel had been thwarted by God's telling Elisha and Elisha's telling the king of Israel. So one night Aram's men surrounded the city, intent on taking Elisha. Elisha's servant was fearful, but Elisha told him not to be afraid. Then he prayed for the man:

"O Lord, open his eyes so he may see." Then the Lord opened the servant's eyes, and he looked and saw the hills full of horses

---

[1]Adam Clarke, *The Holy Bible Containing the Old and New Testament with a Commentary and Critical Notes,* vol. 2 (London: Ward, Lock & Co., n.d.), 388.

PART 1

Chapter 5
The
Prayers
of
Solomon
and Later
Leaders
of Israel

and chariots of fire all around Elisha. As the enemy came down toward him, Elisha prayed to the LORD, "Strike these people with blindness." So he struck them with blindness, as Elisha had asked (2 Kings 6:17–18).

For the seasoned servant of God to see is one thing; for the beginner to see is another. Therefore, the elder must bear the burden of the younger. Elisha felt none of the hopelessness and despair his servant experienced; his spiritual senses discerned the presence of the hosts of heaven. His servant needed the same vision, and for that Elijah prayed with remarkable results.

But in the next breath Elisha prayed, "Strike these people with blindness." What an irony! For his servant he requests sight; for the enemy he requests blindness. God answered both prayers of His faithful prophet.

On the surface, these answers to prayer may seem to have been capricious. But when viewed against the background of the national political situation they were acts of mighty deliverance. Elisha did not lead the Syrians to Samaria for them to be murdered. . . . Elisha advised the king of Israel to free them and to treat them well. This in turn brought national deliverance because "the bands from Aram stopped raiding Israel's territory" (2 Kings 6:23).[2]

David also prayed that he might understand the deep things of God: "Open my eyes that I may see wonderful things in your law" (Ps. 119:18). Satan is a master at blinding human eyes to reality (cf. 2 Cor. 4:4 and Eph. 4:18). It is of utmost importance that God's servants see clearly and truly. The God-ordained means to this end is prayer.

Asa

Asa called to the LORD his God and said, "LORD, there is no one like you to help the powerless against the mighty. Help us, O LORD our God, for we rely on you, and in your name we have come against this vast army. O LORD, you are our God; do not let man prevail against you" (2 Chron. 14:11; see also 14:9–15).

---

[2]Harold Lindsell, *When You Pray* (Wheaton, Ill.: Tyndale House Publishers, 1969), 141.

PART 1

Chapter 5
The
Prayers
of
Solomon
and Later
Leaders
of Israel

Human comparison is often the parent of fear, and exaggeration is the enemy of faith. When Israel's 12 spies compared themselves with Canaan's giants, 10 of them saw themselves as mere grasshoppers and became victims of their own exaggeration. Asa could have failed in similar fashion, for his army was scarcely half the size of the enemy army. He had 580,000 compared with 1,000,000 Ethiopians. But to Asa, numbers were not significant, because God's people had a supernatural resource. "There is no one like you to help the powerless against the mighty." Faith alters our perspective and brings into play, by the process of prayer, the power of the One against whom the multiplied powers of humanity are no match.

As Asa prayed, he confessed his faith: "We rely on you." Resting, leaning, or relying is a demonstration of active faith. And Asa's declaration, "In your name we have come against this vast army," was the hallmark of confident reliance (cf. 1 Sam. 17:45 and Acts 3:6).

Jehoshaphat

Only fools are fearless. And although fear can paralyze us, it can also be our friend, especially when, as with Jehoshaphat, it drives us to God. Some men had come to Jehoshaphat to inform him that a vast army was approaching.

Alarmed, Jehoshaphat resolved to inquire of the LORD, and he proclaimed a fast for all Judah. The people of Judah came together to seek help from the LORD; indeed, they came from every town in Judah to seek him. Then Jehoshaphat stood up in the assembly of Judah and Jerusalem at the temple of the LORD in the front of the new courtyard and said:

"O LORD, God of our fathers, are you not the God who is in heaven? You rule over all the kingdoms of the nations. Power and might are in your hand, and no one can withstand you. O our God, did you not drive out the inhabitants of this land before your people Israel and give it forever to the descendants of Abraham your friend? They have lived in it and have built in it a sanctuary for your Name, saying, 'If calamity comes upon us, whether the sword of judgment, or plague or famine, we will stand in your presence before this temple that bears your Name and will cry out to you in our distress, and you will save us.'

"But now here are men from Ammon, Moab and M whose territory you would not allow Israel to invade wh came from Egypt; so they turned away from them and destroy them. See how they are repaying us by coming to us out of the possession you gave us as an inheritance. C __r God, will you not judge them? For we have no power to face this vast army that is attacking us. We do not know what to do, but our eyes are upon you."

All the men of Judah, with their wives and children and little ones, stood there before the LORD (2 Chron. 20:3–13).

Here we have the earliest record of a general fast proclaimed by royalty, and evidently kept by all of Judah. The entire nation was aware of the desperate plight that had befallen them, and for no apparent reason. But such is life, whether of a nation, a church, a family, or an individual.

In some wholly unexpected quarter a grave difficulty arises. That power which should have been an ally suddenly becomes an enemy; that very institution which had been the source of sustenance threatens to drag us down with itself into financial ruin; the very men who promised to be, and who were, our best friends on whom we could rely, turn into our opponents and thwart our purposes; the bright, the brilliant morning has become a clouded noon, and a severe storm impends.[3]

Jehoshaphat's prayer (2 Chron. 20:6–12), though unpremeditated, is one of the most elegant prayers of the Old Testament, truly an exemplary model. Addressed to Jehovah, the Self-Existent, the Eternal, the Covenant-Keeper, the ever-present God, this prayer extols God in five ways:

1. He is the [faithful] God of our ancestors (20:6).
2. He is in heaven but rules over all the earth (20:6).
3. He is omnipotent (20:6).
4. He gave the land to His people Israel (20:7).
5. He is their only hope (20:12).

---

[3]H. D. M. Spence and Joseph S. Exell, eds., *The Pulpit Commentary* (Grand Rapids: Wm. B. Eerdmans Pub. Co., 1950), vol. 6, *2 Chronicles,* by P. C. Barker, 242.

PART 1

Chapter 5
The
Prayers
of
Solomon
and Later
Leaders
of Israel

Solomon's dedicatory prayer (1 Kings 8:33–45) is the reference point for Jehoshaphat's impassioned plea (2 Chron. 20:8–9). Note the three divisions of Jehoshaphat's prayer: (1) a reminder of Israel's past mercy toward Ammon, Moab, and Mount Seir according to God's instruction, (2) a cry for God to consider how the Ammonites, Moabites, and Edomites are now returning evil for good, and (3) a petition for God's help and intervention in the light of Judah's present dilemma and her admitted helplessness.

Noteworthy also is Jehoshaphat's confession and affirmation of trust and dependence: " 'Our eyes are upon you' " (20:12). When one prays for divine intervention, eyes fixed on God rather than on the threatening circumstance, God is certain to answer. Then God's Spirit came upon Jahaziel who gave God's directions to Jehoshaphat that brought victory and rejoicing (20:14–28).

Hezekiah

Much is to be learned from Hezekiah's praying (see 2 Kings 18 through 20:11; 2 Chron. 29 through 32; Isaiah 36 through 39). Here is a man who once yielded to the enemy instead of praying to God. "Hezekiah king of Judah sent this message to the king of Assyria at Lachish: 'I have done wrong. Withdraw from me, and I will pay whatever you demand of me' " (2 Kings 18:14). But the enemy is never satisfied with a little yielding; he always demands more.

A Plea for God's Attention

Hezekiah had learned his lesson: to surrender to difficulties is folly. All must learn this lesson. If we yield to our difficulties, they will return, and with renewed force. Surrendering to one difficulty makes the next one harder to resist. Resisting one difficulty makes the next one easier to overcome. And prayer is the indispensable key to overcoming.

Hezekiah's approach to God is a model for all who would secure an answer from the Lord. Faith rises as one recognizes and proclaims the God to whom prayer is directed.

Hezekiah prayed to the LORD: "O LORD, God of Israel, enthroned between the cherubim, you alone are God over all the kingdoms of the earth. You have made heaven and earth. Give ear, O LORD, and hear, open your eyes, O LORD, and see; listen to the words Sennacherib has sent to insult the living God.

"It is true, O LORD, that the Assyrian kings have laid waste these nations and their lands. They have thrown their gods into the fire and destroyed them, for they were not gods but only wood and stone, fashioned by men's hands. Now, O LORD our God, deliver us from his hand, so that all kingdoms on earth may know that you alone, O LORD, are God" (2 Kings 19:15–19; see also the rest of chapter 19; cf. Isa. 37:14–20).

PART 1

Chapter 5
The
Prayers
of
Solomon
and Later
Leaders
of Israel

Note how Hezekiah identifies and proclaims his God:

1. Hezekiah addresses the "LORD God of Israel"—the very God ridiculed by the enemy (cf. 2 Kings 19:10–12).

2. Hezekiah prayed in the house of the Lord, where God was "enthroned between the cherubim" (2 Kings 19:15). How blessed is the person who is aware of the presence of the divine.

3. Hezekiah recognized God as the supreme potentate: "You alone are God over all the kingdoms of the earth." For Hezekiah, this comprehensive view of God included his present enemy, Assyria, and encouraged his faith greatly.

4. Hezekiah identified God as the Creator: "You have made heaven and earth." At least ten times in Bible prayers (mainly in the Old Testament) God is identified as the "Maker of heaven and earth"; but this faith-building confession seems also to have been common in the Early Church (cf. Acts 4:24), and has inspired contemporary songwriters as well (e.g., "How Great Thou Art!").

Hezekiah's plea for God's attention was a mark of His trust in God. He had received a boastful letter from Sennacherib, king of Assyria, casting aspersions upon God and in effect saying that Sennacherib was greater than any god. Hezekiah had seen revival early in his reign; he knew the majesty of the Lord. He also knew that his army could not withstand the Assyrian forces. In faith he immediately took the letter into the temple and spread it out before the Lord (2 Kings 19:14; Isa. 37:14). The handling of threatening letters demands sensitivity to God's leading.

PART 1

Chapter 5
The
Prayers
of
Solomon
and Later
Leaders
of Israel

Hezekiah was not inclined to deny facts. " 'It is true, O LORD, that the Assyrian kings have laid waste these nations and their lands' " (2 Kings 19:17). Some today would label Hezekiah's words a negative confession and an enemy of faith. Yet little is to be gained by a head-in-the-sand attitude. That will not solve the problem. Only God can perform the miracle, and the sooner that reality is acknowledged, the sooner His help will be forthcoming. In the face of the facts (the superiority of Assyria over the gods of the nations), Hezekiah voices his worthy and jealous concern that " 'all kingdoms on earth may know that you alone, O LORD, are God' " (19:19).

Difficult Times amidst Victory

Possibly the most memorable of Hezekiah's prayers is recorded in 2 Kings 20. (See also 2 Chron. 32:24–26 and Isa. 38:1–22.) Isaiah had just told Hezekiah, who was very ill, to put his house in order because he would not recover.

Hezekiah turned his face to the wall and prayed to the Lord, "Remember, O LORD, how I have walked before you faithfully and with wholehearted devotion and have done what is good in your eyes." And Hezekiah wept bitterly (vv. 2–3).

Great victories for God's servants and great defeats for their enemies often include difficult times for God's servants. When Hezekiah took gold from the temple to give Sennacherib as tribute, Hezekiah became "ill and was at the point of death." But his prayer brought assurance that God would deliver Jerusalem from the Assyrians. We may wonder why God allows difficult times; perhaps it is the divine wisdom guarding us lest we become boastful and take to ourselves undue glory (cf. 2 Cor. 12:1–10). (It should be noted here that the Bible finishes up the story of Sennacherib's invasions, then goes back to tell of Hezekiah's sickness, which occurred early in 701 B.C.[4] It is obvious

---

[4]J. Ridderbos, *Isaiah,* trans. John Vriend (Grand Rapids: Zondervan Publishing House, 1985), 315. See also Stanley M. Horton, "A Defense on Historical Grounds of the Isaian Authorship of the Passages in Isaiah Referring to Babylon" (Th.D. diss., Central Baptist Seminary, Kansas City, Kans., 1959), 131.

from the Assyrian field commander's comments in 2 Kings 18:29–31,33, that God had already given Hezekiah the promise of 2 Kings 20:6.)

Note two things about Hezekiah's praying: (1) he turned his face to the wall and (2) he wept bitterly. The turning of his face to the wall no doubt reflected his awareness of a need for privacy and for intense personal communion with God. It is easier to find God in solitude than in company with the multitude. Jesus himself often sought solitude in the mountains or deserted places (e.g. Matt. 14:23; Mark 1:35). Weeping and praying mingle well. It need not be considered unseemly to express our deepest emotions with tears, especially at the altar. Of our Lord it is written that he too "offered up prayers and petitions with loud cries and tears" (Heb. 5:7).

Hezekiah's earnest prayer brought him a fifteen-year extension of life. They were years of great blessed revival. The war party had been discredited by the miraculous defeat of Sennacherib. The people had taken a stand of faith and obedience (2 Kings 18:36). God gave them comfort (Isa. 40:1). Then Isaiah was able to give the wonderful prophecies of Isaiah 40 through 66.

Ezra

Ezra was a spiritual adviser to the Jewish exiles who returned from Babylon to Jerusalem in 457 B.C. As such, he voiced an amazing prayer of confession on behalf of the people.

One commentator has labeled Ezra's prayer in Ezra 9 "a most pathetic address," springing out of Israel's utter failure and unbearable burden. In it is to be found no petition whatever, but a vicarious confession, one of the most profound ever recorded. The prayer voices an intense travail:

Then, at the evening sacrifice, I rose from my self-abasement, with my tunic and cloak torn, and fell on my knees with my hands spread out to the LORD my God and prayed:

"O my God, I am too ashamed and disgraced to lift up my face to you, my God, because our sins are higher than our heads and our guilt has reached to the heavens. From the days of our forefathers until now, our guilt has been great. Because of our

PART 1

Chapter 5
The
Prayers
of
Solomon
and Later
Leaders
of Israel

PART 1

**Chapter 5
The
Prayers
of
Solomon
and Later
Leaders
of Israel**

sins, we ... have been subjected to the sword and captivity, to pillage and humiliation at the hand of foreign kings, as it is today.

"Though we are slaves, our God has not deserted us in our bondage. He has shown us kindness in the sight of the kings of Persia: He has granted us new life. ...

"But now, O our God, what can we say after this? For we have disregarded the commands you gave through your servants the prophets. ... *disobedience*

"What has happened to us is a result of our evil deeds and our great guilt, and yet, our God, you have punished us less than our sins have deserved. ... Shall we again break your commands? ... Would you not be angry enough with us to destroy us, leaving us no remnant or survivor? O LORD, God of Israel, you are righteous! We are left this day as a remnant. Here we are before you in our guilt, though because of it not one of us can stand in your presence" (Ezra 9:5–7,9–11,13–15).

Such a confession, when disobedience has brought the judgment of God, is the divinely appointed remedy for what may seem a hopeless situation. Genuine confession cracks the door of mercy.

From Ezra's example in prayer, we can learn some important lessons on approaching God in repentance:

1. He approached God not with haughtiness but with utmost humility and sorrow, which he expressed by tearing his tunic and cloak (9:3).

2. He displayed total subservience and submission by falling on his knees (v. 5).

3. He understood that no human means was adequate for the enormity of the situation at hand. His only hope for his people, who had invited the rightful wrath of the just God, was the undeserved mercy of that same God. So, like earnest men before him (see Exod. 9:29; 1 Kings 8:22), he spread his empty hands out to the generous Lord God of heaven (v. 5).

The attitude of the person is of more consequence than is the prayer itself, though the prayer reflects the inward condition of the person. Ezra's consummate shame is obvious: "I am too ashamed and disgraced" (9:6). What an indictment upon a generation such as ours, where many seem to know no shame, having a conscience so seared that the ability to blush is completely dead! (Cf. 8:12.)

Ezra's prayer might well be called a prayer of r[ ] as well as of confession. In it he recognizes five

1. The continuing transgression of Israel "from the days of our forefathers" had led to "the sword and captivity, to pillage and humiliation at the hand of foreign kings" (v. 7).

2. God, in His divine grace, had left a remnant of Israel, manifesting his kindness in their bondage and giving them "new life to rebuild the house" of God in Jerusalem (vv. 8–9).

3. God's patience had been shown by punishing the flagrantly disobedient less than they deserved, and His kindness had been shown by sending unearned deliverance (vv. 10–13).

4. If Israel were to again break the commands of God, God's justice rightfully required that the disobedient be destroyed (v. 14).

5. Israel, because of their guilt, had no defense and no claim to make. They were not worthy to stand in God's presence (v. 15).

Ezra's prayer, then, is a pattern for the truly penitent, whether the disobedient individual engaged in deplorable behavior or the selfless intercessor who, like Ezra, approaches God on behalf of his own nation or people.

Nehemiah

God does His greatest works through people with burdened hearts. Nehemiah, like his predecessor Ezra, was such a person. He grieved deeply for his fellow Jews. Public leaders who truly have their people at heart experience sorrows that others escape. God grant us more leaders who experience such sorrows.

Nehemiah was a man given to prayer. His intimacy with God is evidenced by his repeated personal reference to "my God." Effective prayer avoids starchy formality in favor of warm and loving familiarity. That familiarity, however, must never be allowed to become irreverence. Our Maker is our Friend, but our Friend is never anything less than our Maker.

PART 1

Chapter 5
The
Prayers
of
Solomon
and Later
Leaders
of Israel

Intercession for a Nation

While in captivity, Nehemiah discovered that the Jewish remnant had returned to Jerusalem, but its gates had been burned and its walls broken down (Neh. 1:1–3). He became burdened with the plight, the lack of security, of his city and its people. His praying was no lighthearted, soon forgotten activity. Rather, it was a most demanding and serious occupation, involving weeping, mourning, fasting, and praying.

When I heard these things, I sat down and wept. For some days I mourned and fasted and prayed before the God of heaven. Then I said:

"O Lord, God of heaven, the great and awesome God, who keeps his covenant of love with those who love him and obey his commands, let your ear be attentive and your eyes open to hear the prayer your servant is praying before you day and night for your servants, the people of Israel. I confess the sins we Israelites, including myself and my father's house, have committed against you. We have acted very wickedly toward you. We have not obeyed the commands, decrees and laws you gave your servant Moses.

"Remember the instruction you gave your servant Moses, saying, 'If you are unfaithful, I will scatter you among the nations, but if you return to me and obey my commands, then even if your exiled people are at the farthest horizon, I will gather them from there and bring them to the place I have chosen as a dwelling for my Name.

"They are your servants and your people, whom you redeemed by your great strength and your mighty hand. O Lord, let your ear be attentive to the prayer of this your servant and to the prayer of your servants who delight in revering your name. Give your servant success today by granting him favor in the presence of this man" (Neh. 1:4–11).

All true prayer, like Nehemiah's prayer, proceeds from a right perception of God (see v. 5). God is divine, exalted, faithful, and powerful. The more we know of God, the more effective and acceptable our worship and prayer will become. Nehemiah not only knew his God intimately but also how to approach Him:

PART 1

Chapter 5
The
Prayers
of
Solomon
and Later
Leaders
of Israel

1. With sorrow (v. 4). Prayer was intended to be glad communion with God, but sin brought to it a mournful sound. Now it is often bathed with tears; yet the day is coming when without tears (Rev. 7:17; 21:4) we will rejoice in God. Even today, however, the sorrows of prayer are more victorious than the rejoicing of sin.

2. With importunity (vv. 5–6). Nehemiah implored God to hear his prayer. His entire being voiced his devotion. Spiritual realities must be earnestly sought.

3. With persistence (v. 6). Nehemiah prayed day and night. His persistence mirrored that of Jacob: "I will not let you go unless you bless me" (Gen. 32:26).

4. With confession (vv. 6–7). Nehemiah's confession was individual, corporate, and open.

5. With supplication (vv. 8–11). Prayer usually voices some specific petition. It may relate to divine promise or divine mercy.

A Prayer for Judgment against Evil

Nehemiah had received permission from the king, Artaxerxes, to go and rebuild Jerusalem. When Nehemiah and the Jews began to be opposed and ridiculed for their work by the "neighboring peoples" (cf. Ezra 9:1), he went to God: " 'Hear us, O our God, for we are despised. Turn their insults back on their own heads. Give them over as plunder in a land of captivity. Do not cover up their guilt or blot out their sins from your sight, for they have thrown insults in the face of the builders' " (Neh. 4:4–5).

From a New Testament perspective, praying for judgment to fall on evil persons seems inappropriate. Did not our Lord instruct, " 'Love your enemies and pray for those who persecute you' " (Matt. 5:44)? And did not the apostle Paul echo the same sentiment when he taught, "Bless those who persecute you; bless and do not curse. . . . Do not repay anyone evil for evil. . . . Do not take revenge, my friends" (Rom. 12:14,17,19)? How then do we account for such unmerciful imprecations from the lips of this God-fearing man of the Old Testament?

We need to remember that the guidelines from both Jesus and Paul are, and must always be, the general rule;

PART 1

Chapter 5
The
Prayers
of
Solomon
and Later
Leaders
of Israel

but at the same time there is allowance for the exception. We do have the revelation that "there is a sin that leads to death. I am not saying . . . pray about that" (1 John 5:16). And we have an insight regarding a depravity so severe that "God gave them over in the sinful desires of their hearts to sexual impurity" (Rom. 1:24) and "a depraved mind" (Rom. 1:28). Further, there is the Pauline instruction to "hand this man over to Satan, so that the sinful nature may be destroyed and his spirit saved on the day of the Lord" (1 Cor. 5:5).

Nehemiah's prayer for judgment on Israel's enemies was not necessarily the fruit of an overheated spirit; it seems rather to have been provoked by a holy jealousy for God and His cause. David prayed similarly (see Ps. 109:7,14–15). A believer should never, of his own volition, exclude any sinner from his prayer; but on a rare occasion the Holy Spirit might restrain a believer from praying for a sinner's salvation—if the sin that leads to death has been committed. Nehemiah may well have prayed in harmony with God's will, for only God knows when evil people have crossed the line to eternal hopelessness.

Having endured opposition of hostile neighbors, the Jews then experienced a famine and economic hard times. It was brought to Nehemiah's attention that the people were also being taken advantage of by their own officials who were lending money at an exhorbitant rate and accepting various family members as slaves. When confronted, the nobles and officials took an oath to give back what they had taken and to not practice usury any longer. Nehemiah explained what took place next:

I also shook out the folds of my robe and said, "In this way may God shake out of his house and possessions every man who does not keep this promise. So may such a man be shaken out and emptied!" At this the whole assembly said, "Amen," and praised the LORD. And the people did as they had promised (Nehemiah 5:13).

At first glance, this verse seems more a solemn pronouncement of a curse than a prayer. But a closer look reveals Nehemiah's expectation of God to execute judgment on any who might fail to fulfill their promise to the

Lord. Nehemiah was keenly aware of his own inability to enforce the people's promises; but he knew God was abundantly able to, and for this he prayed.

PART 1

Chapter 5
The
Prayers
of
Solomon
and Later
Leaders
of Israel

Asking God to Take Note

At times it may seem that faithful service as well as outright defiance go unnoticed by God. Nehemiah felt that God might not have taken proper note of his faithfulness as well as of the evil deeds of his enemies. Two verses capture his complaint:

Remember me with favor, O my God, for all I have done for these people (Neh. 5:19).

This first petition seems to reflect Nehemiah's feeling that the people for whom he had worked so diligently were ungrateful for his labor. (Such a feeling is not uncommon even in our day.) Even so, Nehemiah relieved his pain by a simple prayer that God, who is not like unappreciative people, would in due time reward him.

The second prayer is the very opposite; it asks that God duly reward the evildoers with whom Nehemiah had to contend.

Remember Tobiah and Sanballat, O my God, because of what they have done; remember also the prophetess Noadiah and the rest of the prophets who have been trying to intimidate me (Neh. 6:14).

Both political leaders and errant prophets were hindering the work of God. What a valuable lesson for us. God should be implored to "remember" and do something about those who try to intimidate us, be they human or devil. It is not for us to avenge ourselves, though that may be our natural bent (see Rom. 12:19). God has reserved the right to execute vengeance, and when He does it, it is done justly (see Lev. 19:18; Deut. 32:35; Ps. 94:1).

A Way Back to God

The Book of Nehemiah records an unusual prayer. It is unusual for two reasons: (1) It is the longest recorded prayer in the Bible and (2) it is voiced by eight people,

PART 1

Chapter 5
The
Prayers
of
Solomon
and Later
Leaders
of Israel

Levites: Jeshua, Kadmiel, Bani, Hashabneiah, Sherebiah, Hodiah, Shebaniah, and Pethahiah.

It is unlikely that these Levites prayed in unison. Although it is not so stated, it is more likely that they each prayed a portion of the entire prayer. What an inspiration it must have been to the people to hear eight spiritual leaders voice expressions that merged into a single cry to God! Only selected portions of the corporate prayer can be included here; however, a full reading of Nehemiah 9:5–38, with an awareness of the distinctiveness of the prayer, can provide new insights into the possibilities of public prayer.

"Stand up and praise the LORD your God, who is from everlasting to everlasting."

"Blessed be your glorious name, and may it be exalted above all blessing and praise. You alone are the LORD. You made the heavens, even the highest heavens, and all their starry host, the earth and all that is on it, the seas and all that is in them. You give life to everything, and the multitudes of heaven worship you.

"You are the LORD God, who chose Abram. . . . You found his heart faithful to you, and you made a covenant with him. . . . You have kept your promise because you are righteous.

"You saw the suffering of our forefathers in Egypt. . . . You sent miraculous signs and wonders against Pharaoh. . . . You divided the sea before them. . . . By day you led them with a pillar of cloud, and by night with a pillar of fire to give them light on the way they were to take.

"You came down on Mount Sinai; you spoke to them from heaven. You gave them regulations and laws that are just and right, and decrees and commands that are good. . . . In their hunger you gave them bread from heaven and in their thirst you brought them water from the rock; you told them to go in and take possession of the land you had sworn with uplifted hand to give them.

"But they, our forefathers, became arrogant and stiff-necked, and did not obey your commands. . . . But you are a forgiving God, gracious and compassionate, slow to anger and abounding in love. Therefore you did not desert them. . . .

"You gave your good Spirit to instruct them. You did not

withhold your manna from their mouths, and you gave them water for their thirst. For forty years you sustained them in the desert; they lacked nothing, their clothes did not wear out nor did their feet become swollen. . . .

"But they were disobedient and rebelled against you; they put your law behind their backs. They killed your prophets, who had admonished them in order to turn them back to you; they committed awful blasphemies. So you handed them over to their enemies, who oppressed them. But when they were oppressed they cried out to you. From heaven you heard them, and in your great compassion you gave them deliverers, who rescued them from the hand of their enemies.

"But as soon as they were at rest, they again did what was evil in your sight. . . . And when they cried out to you again, you heard from heaven, and in your compassion you delivered them time after time.

"You warned them to return to your law, but they became arrogant and disobeyed your commands. They sinned against your ordinances, by which a man will live if he obeys them . . . and refused to listen. . . . But in your great mercy you did not put an end to them or abandon them, for you are a gracious and merciful God.

"Now therefore, O our God, the great, mighty and awesome God, who keeps his covenant of love, do not let all the hardship seem trifling in your eyes—the hardship that has come upon us, upon our kings and leaders, upon our priests and prophets, upon our fathers and all your people, from the days of the kings of Assyria until today. In all that has happened to us, you have been just; you have acted faithfully, while we did wrong. . . .

"But see, we are slaves today, slaves in the land you gave our forefathers so they could eat its fruit and the other good things it produces. . . . We are in great distress.

"In view of all this, we are making a binding agreement, putting it in writing, and our leaders, our Levites and our priests are affixing their seals to it" (Neh. 9:5–13,15–17,20–21,26–29,31–33,36–38).

A great portion of this lengthy prayer is a recital of Israel's early history and a recognition of God and His dealings with His people. Prayer takes on a whole new dimension when God is properly acknowledged—when His mercies,

PART 1

Chapter 5
The
Prayers
of
Solomon
and Later
Leaders
of Israel

PART 1

Chapter 5
The
Prayers
of
Solomon
and Later
Leaders
of Israel

provisions, chastening, and blessings are recounted. In the prayer, God is acknowledged as the only Lord (v. 6); Creator and Maker of all things (v. 6); Preserver of all (v. 6); the One worshipped by heaven's hosts (v. 6); the One who chose Abram (v. 7); the Name Changer (v. 7); the great, mighty, and awesome God (v. 32); the Covenant Keeper (v. 32); and the God of mercy (v. 32).

After an extended rehearsal of Israel's disobedience and rebellion, and of God's patience, mercy, and chastisement, the prayer concludes with a petition ("do not let all this hardship seem trifling in your eyes"), a confession ("you have been just, . . . while we did wrong"), and a covenant ("In view of all this, we are making a binding agreement"). What a pattern for God's people at any time! There is a proper course of action even amid sin and failure; there is a way back to God.

Nehemiah was indeed a man of prayer; his example was reflected even in the duly constituted spiritual leadership of the Levites. Godly leadership is a profound blessing in any nation or government.

"Remember Me"

Nehemiah returned at some point to King Artaxerxes. But while he was serving in the king's court, God's people in Jerusalem once again became complacent in their worship. When Nehemiah returned to Jerusalem (Neh. 13:6–7) he "learned about the evil thing Eliashib [the priest] had done," defiling the temple by allowing Tobiah to store his household goods in the room which was supposed to be used to store the temple articles. (Tobiah had been one who had opposed the Jews at the rebuilding of the city [see Neh. 4:3; 6:19] and was also an Ammonite [see 13:1–2].) Nehemiah also discovered that the house of God had been neglected (Neh. 13:10–11). He put things back in order and then prayed for God to remember his faithfulness:

Remember me for this, O my God, and do not blot out what I have so faithfully done for the house of my God and its services (Neh. 13:14).

■■■■■■
PART 1
Chapter 5
The
Prayers
of
Solomon
and Later
Leaders
of Israel

Then Nehemiah saw the people working and selling on the Sabbath. He rebuked them and warned them of the calamity they were bringing on themselves. He reminded them of when their forefathers had done the same thing. So he commanded them to "keep the Sabbath day holy" (Neh. 13:15–22). Then he prayed from a heart that loved God and desired to keep His Word:

Remember me for this also, O my God, and show mercy to me according to your great love (Neh. 13:22).

Finally, Nehemiah saw some of the men of Judah who married pagan women. The influence of these mothers was so great that the children could not even speak the language of Judah. Because he recalled how Solomon's wives had led him astray, Nehemiah rebuked the men and called down curses upon them. To emphasize the seriousness of what they were doing, he even beat some of them and pulled out their hair. Then he made them take an oath not to let their children marry outside the faith (Neh. 13:23–28). Then, for the third time Nehemiah prays, "Remember me" (13:14,22,31).

Remember me with favor, O my God (13:31).

Nehemiah's task had been to restore not only the city of Jerusalem but the relationship of its people to God. Under his spiritual leadership, we see one of the greatest spiritual renewals in the history of Israel. Nehemiah's requests for God's attention were not prompted by pride or boasting, but were humble appeals for God's faithfulness in noting his obedience and diligent labor.

That is, when Nehemiah asked God to remember him, he was not merely asking God to keep him in mind. God never forgets. But when the Bible speaks of God remembering it always means that God steps into the situation and does something about it that is in line with His promises. Nehemiah was expressing his faith that God would continue to show favor to him in an active way. He was also expressing his personal relation with the Lord when he ends by calling God, "My God." We recall Peter's admonition that believers cast all their anxious worry and care upon God, "because he cares for you" (1 Pet. 5:7).

■■■■■
PART 1

**Chapter 5
The
Prayers
of
Solomon
and Later
Leaders
of Israel**

What great consolation is derived from the knowledge that God is a personal God and does indeed care about us!

Questions for Study

1. What do Solomon's prayers show us about the kind of God we serve?

2. What were the chief characteristics of most of Elijah's prayers?

3. When are we most likely to pray prayers contrary to God's will?

4. What was unusual about Jehoshaphat's prayer?

5. Why would some label Hezekiah's prayer in 2 Kings 19:17 a "negative confession"? Why was Hezekiah right in praying this way?

6. When would a prayer like Ezra's (9:6ff.) be appropriate today?

7. How did the prayer of the eight Levites show they were concerned about finding a way back to God?

8. What prompted Nehemiah's "remember me" prayers?

PRAYER IN THE PROPHETIC BOOKS

God's chosen prophets spoke the very words God gave them to deliver. So they of necessity were individuals of prayer. Although direct mention of prayer is missing from some of the Minor Prophets, it is plain that they had audience with God and heard from Him directly. We look in this chapter at the significant instances of prayer in the lives of these special messengers of God.

Isaiah

Although Isaiah, this prince of prophets, had much to say about prayer (see Isa. 1:15; 12; 55:6–7; 62:6–7), only a few of his prayers are recorded. Immediately after Isaiah's unusual revelation of the holiness of God (Isa. 6:1–4), this exchange between Isaiah and the Lord took place:

"Woe to me!" I cried. "I am ruined! For I am a man of unclean lips, and I live among a people of unclean lips, and my eyes have seen the King, the LORD Almighty."

Then one of the seraphs flew to me with a live coal in his hand, which he had taken with tongs from the altar. With it he touched my mouth and said, "See, this has touched your lips; your guilt is taken away and your sin atoned for."

149

■■■■■■
PART 1

Chapter 6
Prayer in
the
Prophetic
Books

Then I heard the voice of the Lord saying, "Whom shall I send? And who will go for us?"

And I said, "Here am I. Send me!" He said, "Go and tell this people: 'Be ever hearing, but never understanding; be ever seeing, but never perceiving.' Make the heart of this people calloused; make their ears dull and close their eyes. Otherwise they might see with their eyes, hear with their ears, understand with their hearts, and turn and be healed."

Then I said, "For how long, O Lord?" And he answered: "Until the cities lie ruined. . . . As the terebinth and oak leave stumps when they are cut down, so the holy seed will be the stump in the land" (Isa. 6:5–11,13).

This passage consists of prayer mingled with narrative. It records what should be expected whenever human beings receive a revelation of God. Prayer may bring one to an awesome awareness of God, and when it does, one's reaction may well parallel that of the prophet. There is certainly no room for frivolity or irreverence in the presence of Him in whom there is no darkness at all. That awesome light of deity exposes any vestige of darkness and causes the soul to cry out, "Woe to me!"

It is in God's presence that finite humans are (1) convicted of sin (v. 5), (2) purged of sin (vv. 6–7), and (3) called to minister (vv. 8–9). Isaiah's prayer of commitment, following the purifying of his own soul, laid the groundwork for the divine call. A yielded will and purified heart will clear the way for the heavenly commission: "Go and tell this people." It was a difficult message, but there was hope. God would have a remnant—a "holy seed."

Isaiah also gives us examples of prayers of praise, even when the promise has not yet been fulfilled, even while adversity is being endured. Prayers of praise give proper honor to God while at the same time they stimulate the supplicant's faith. One measure of our prayer life is the extent to which it includes the kind of thanksgiving and praise voiced by Isaiah.

O LORD, you are my God; I will exalt you and praise your name, for in perfect faithfulness you have done marvelous things, things planned long ago. . . . Therefore strong peoples will honor you; cities of ruthless nations will revere you. You have been a refuge for the poor, a refuge for the needy in his distress, a shelter from the storm and a shade from the heat. . . . On this mountain the LORD Almighty will prepare a feast of rich food for all peoples. . . . The Sovereign LORD will wipe away the tears from all faces. . . . In that day they will say, "Surely this is our God; we trusted in him, and he saved us. . . . Let us rejoice and be glad in his salvation" (Isa. 25:1,3–4,6,8–9).

PART 1

**Chapter 6
Prayer in
the
Prophetic
Books**

By his prayer of praise, Isaiah left us a glorious example of adoration in prayer. "Since adoration brings man into immediate and direct contact with God, in the role of servant to master, of the created to the Creator, it is foundational to all other kinds of prayer."[1] The prophet becomes a choral leader extolling God's deeds in the past and His victories in the future. What this covenant-keeping God has been in the past is a guarantee of what He will be in the future.

Isaiah included in one of his songs of praise the words of encouragement for the believer in times of stress and adversity. In these times the believer must affirm that God provides perfect peace.

You will keep in perfect peace him whose mind is steadfast, because he trusts in you. . . . The path of the righteous is level; O upright One, you make the way of the righteous smooth. Yes, LORD, walking in the way of your laws, we wait for you; your name and renown are the desire of our hearts. My soul yearns for you in the night; in the morning my spirit longs for you. When your judgments come upon the earth, the people of the world learn righteousness. . . . LORD, you establish peace for us; all that we have accomplished you have done for us (Isa. 26:3,7–9,12).

The Evangelical Prophet, as Isaiah has been called, was praying out of personal experience and desire, out of a mind set upon God, and out of a profound desire that all people may learn righteousness. He understood well that "the fruit of righteousness will be peace; the effect of righ-

---

[1]Harold Lindsell, *When You Pray* (Wheaton. Ill.: Tyndale House Publishers, 1969), 33.

PART 1

Chapter 6
Prayer in
the
Prophetic
Books

teousness will be quietness and confidence forever" (Isa. 32:17).

But few people, no matter how sincerely they may seek the face of the Lord, escape those periods of God's silence, when the heavens are like brass and God seems not to hear a desperate cry for help. Job experienced such times: "If I go to the east, he is not there; if I go to the west, I do not find him. When he is at work in the north, I do not see him; when he turns to the south, I catch no glimpse of him" (Job 23:8–9). It may seem that God has forsaken us; it seemed so to His own Son (Matt. 27:46). Yet we can be confident that everything He is doing is consistent with His unchanging love. He is only pruning and purifying us. God's discipline does not nullify His desire or determination to bless His people. Israel, as a nation, also experienced the silence of God. It was in such a circumstance that Isaiah prayed his last recorded prayer.

Look down from heaven and see from your lofty throne, holy and glorious. Where are your zeal and your might? Your tenderness and compassion are withheld from us. But you are our Father, though Abraham does not know us or Israel acknowledge us; you, O LORD, are our Father, our Redeemer from of old is your name....

Oh, that you would rend the heavens and come down, that the mountains would tremble before you! As when fire sets twigs ablaze and causes water to boil, come down to make your name known to your enemies and cause the nations to quake before you! ...

All of us have become like one who is unclean, and all our righteous acts are like filthy rags; we all shrivel up like a leaf, and like the wind our sins sweep us away. No one calls on your name or strives to lay hold of you; for you have hidden your face from us and made us waste away because of our sins.

Yet, O LORD, you are our Father. We are the clay, you are the potter; we are all the work of your hand. Do not be angry beyond measure, O LORD; do not remember our sins forever. Oh, look upon us, we pray, for we are all your people....

After all this, O LORD, will you hold yourself back? Will you keep silent and punish us beyond measure? (Isa. 63:15–16; 64:1–2,6–9,12).

These petitions seem more like the prayer of a nation than of a lone prophet, for the prophet is giving voice to the heart-cry of his people. One senses a passion in the latter part of Isaiah's prayer: "Oh, that you would rend the heavens and come down" (64:1). The petition was that God, who dwells in heaven, would break the barrier and show himself mighty on earth (64:1–3). Such intensity is always in order for God's children.

Such impassioned praying seems to spring open the door of spiritual insight and revelation and to suggest causes for the prevailing conditions (see 64:5–7). It would certainly be fitting for the Church around the world to pray as Isaiah did, for the need for revival today is just as great as it was in the seventh and eighth centuries B.C.

Once hearts have been searched out and enlightened by the Holy Spirit, then the time is at hand for pursuit of a remedy. Conviction of sin is never intended to impose an unbearable burden from which there is no relief; rather, it is intended to lead to repentance and renewal. Isaiah's prayer concludes with due recognition of the proper relationship between God and His people; we should be clay in the hands of the master Potter (64:8).

Jeremiah

Jeremiah "the weeping prophet" was also a praying prophet. As has been observed, tears and prayer join together very appropriately, if the former occur as indicators of humility. "A broken and contrite heart, O God, you will not despise" (Ps. 51:17). Receiving an answer from God is much more certain when the petition is made with humility and brokenness.

The first recorded prayer of Jeremiah was his response to the divine call (Jer. 1:1–8). "Ah, Sovereign LORD," I said, "I do not know how to speak; I am only a child" (Jer. 1:6). At first, the response may seem to be an excuse; on second thought, it holds a humility that becomes the young prophet's highest recommendation. For as Adam Clarke observes:

Those who are really *called of God* to the sacred ministry are such as have been brought to a deep acquaintance with themselves, feel their own ignorance, and know their own weakness.

PART 1

Chapter 6
Prayer in
the
Prophetic
Books

They know also the awful responsibility that attaches to the work; and nothing but the authority of God can induce such to undertake it.[2]

God's plan in calling Jeremiah, whom he knew, set apart, and appointed before he was born (1:5), was clear: " 'You must go to everyone I send you to and say whatever I command you' " (1:7). So Jeremiah delivered God's message to a backslidden people: "Return, faithless people; I will cure you of backsliding" (3:22). The reply God wanted to hear was: " 'Yes, we will come to you, for you are the LORD our God. Surely the idolatrous commotion on the hills and the mountains is a deception; surely in the LORD our God is the salvation of Israel' " (Jer. 3:22–23).

The folly of the people and the root of their backsliding were one: They had placed their trust in false gods. Jeremiah's message was that they could not pick and choose the gods they wanted to serve. The worship of idols is implied in verse 23 (hence NIV, "Surely the idolatrous commotion on the hills and the mountains is a deception"). Only the one true God, the Lord, could save the people from their sins and their difficult circumstances.

Although there is no indication that Jeremiah's life was in opposition to God, he had received a message to deliver to Israel that the enemy was coming to destroy them (Jer. 4:5–9) and his response to God was accusatory: " 'Ah, Sovereign LORD, how completely you have deceived this people and Jerusalem by saying, "You will have peace," when the sword is at our throats' " (Jer. 4:10).

Not every kind of prayer and worship honors God, nor does all praying and worship gain the requested end. Without a sincere and God-honoring life, prayer is a mockery (see Ps. 66:18 and Isa. 1:11–16). Some able commentators and scholars have sought to exonerate Jeremiah by adjusting the language of his strange prayer; we most likely get nearest to the truth about it when we take it at face value, recognizing that even the most godly may, in mo-

---

[2]Adam Clarke, *The Holy Bible Containing the Old and New Testament with a Commentary and Critical Notes* (London: Ward, Lock & Co., n.d.), 388.

ments of extreme pressure and impatience with God's calculated actions, overreact (cf. Josh. 7:7). From Jeremiah's example we can learn a lesson for our own flawed humanity. We are never justified in tirades against the Almighty. The Lord himself said, " 'My thoughts are not your thoughts, neither are your ways my ways' " (Isa. 55:8). Prayer from an impure heart that presumes to know better than God is sin and must be repented of.

PART 1

Chapter 6
Prayer in
the
Prophetic
Books

At the same time, we do well not to point a judgmental finger at the tender-hearted, disappointed prophet, so deeply desiring fulfillment of a prophecy on behalf of his people that the evident delay provokes a bitter outcry.

In some instances, Jeremiah's weeping over the predicament of God's people is described; on other occasions, his prayer's tone carries the pain and agony.

O LORD, do not your eyes look for truth? You struck them, but they felt no pain; you crushed them, but they refused correction. They made their faces harder than stone and refused to repent (Jer. 5:3).

The prophet here gives voice to his reasons for weeping. His heart was crushed by Israel's unresponsiveness and failure to submit to divine, redemptive discipline. Jeremiah knew that though God was full of tender mercy and great patience there was a point at which judgment could no longer linger, for God was also a God whose eyes were looking "for truth" (cf. Gen. 6:5–7; 18:20–33; 1 Pet. 4:17).

Surely God seeks for likeminded intercessors today, those for whom the depravity in both the church and the nation is a grievous concern. Without such similarly burdened people, the clouds of iniquity and the powers of evil will not be dispelled.

The time may come, however, when people finally refuse to respond to the love God extends. Then intercession must cease and judgment begin. Consequently, God advised Jeremiah, " 'Do not pray for this people nor offer any plea or petition for them; do not plead with me, for I will not listen to you' " (Jer. 7:16).

In addition to pain and agony for the people, Jeremiah experienced the overpowering emotion of grief, knowing

━━━━━━━
PART 1

Chapter 6
Prayer in
the
Prophetic
Books

that the punishment God's people had received was well-deserved. *Jeremiah*

I know, O LORD, that a man's life is not his own; it is not for man to direct his steps. Correct me, LORD, but only with justice—not in your anger, lest you reduce me to nothing (Jer. 10:23–24).

What beauty and perfume come out of the dirt of the earth. The color and smells of woodlands, flowers, and windblown seeds would not be known were it not for the cold earth from which vegetation grows. So it is with the odious experiences of life. A chastened spirit, uttering words of confession and submission, can bring beauty and perfume out of the worst circumstance.

This prayer teaches several relevant concepts: (1) It is good to approach God recognizing our dependence on Him and our need for His guidance. (2) Sin deserves God's anger, but if we come willing to submit to His correction (teaching, training, instruction), we can expect justice, which implies gentleness, fairness, and moderation. As Abraham said, "Will not the Judge of all the earth do right?" (Gen. 18:25). (3) Those who do come under God's anger (because of rebellion and lack of repentance) will be reduced "to nothing," that is, to insignificance. (Jeremiah is identifying himself with the people here, as the prophets often did. The Greek Septuagint translation made before the time of Christ has "us" for "me" in verse 24.)

Even though Jeremiah had a good understanding of God and His character, he, like other great persons of prayer, was at times greatly perplexed. While he glimpsed eternal precepts and reality with a God-given discernment (cf. 1 Cor. 2:13–14), he was still robed in human flesh, which is forever at war with the Spirit (Gal. 5:17). So it was with Jeremiah.

You are always righteous, O LORD, when I bring a case before you. Yet I would speak with you about your justice: Why does the way of the wicked prosper? Why do all the faithless live at ease? You have planted them, and they have taken root; they grow and bear fruit. You are always on their lips but far from their hearts. Yet you know me, O LORD; you see me and test my thoughts about you. . . . How long will the land lie parched and

PART 1

Chapter 6
Prayer in
the
Prophetic
Books

the grass in every field be withered? Because those who live in it are wicked, the animals and birds have perished. Moreover, the people are saying, "He will not see what happens to us" (Jer. 12:1–4).

Jeremiah did not doubt that the Lord would be righteous in judgment, yet his natural view provoked him to debate with God over certain issues. God's treatment of the wicked seemed far more gracious and benevolent than His treatment of Jeremiah. And struggle as he might, there appeared to be no justification for this and no possibility of reconciling God's actions with His character. The writer of Psalm 73 made similar observations (vv. 3–17).

How does one handle such troublesome thoughts? Jeremiah prayed. The Psalmist went into God's sanctuary (73:17). Both faced the issue squarely. Unfortunately, many hush their doubts and thus fall victim to influences that subtly destroy a once-solid faith. To suppress doubt is to strangle openness and sincerity and generate indifference to truth. Doubt is conquered only as it is boldly confronted.

Every believer must early learn that the answer to troublesome doubts may well be far beyond the brightest human intellect; God's ways and wisdom are far superior to the best of mortal understanding (cf. 1 Cor. 1:21). Such doubts, rather than driving us from God, must press us toward Him. Prayer is the key to the infinite wisdom. By this means alone can those multiplying doubts that crowd our minds be reduced to zero, allowing the "Spirit of wisdom and revelation" (Eph. 1:17) to open the eyes of our understanding.

God's prophets, preaching a true but unpopular message, may suffer as they see deceived people running after false prophets. From ancient times there have been false prophets that God's prophets and God's people have had to deal with (cf. Matt. 7:15; Mark 13:22; Rev. 20:10). Jeremiah had to deal with prophets who were saying there would be no suffering but only peace at a time when God's message to him was the opposite.

Although our sins testify against us, O Lord, do something for the sake of your name. For our backsliding is great; we have sinned against you. O Hope of Israel, its Savior in times of distress,

■■■■■■■
PART 1

**Chapter 6
Prayer in
the
Prophetic
Books**

why are you like a stranger in the land, like a traveler who stays only a night? ... You are among us, O LORD, and we bear your name; do not forsake us! ...

The LORD said to me, "Do not pray for the well-being of this people. Although they fast, I will not listen to their cry; though they offer burnt offerings and grain offerings, I will not accept them. Instead, I will destroy them with the sword, famine and plague."

I said, "Ah, Sovereign LORD, the prophets keep telling them, 'You will not see the sword or suffer famine. Indeed, I will give you lasting peace in this place.' "

The LORD said to me, "The prophets are prophesying lies in my name. I have not sent them or appointed them or spoken to them. They are prophesying to you false visions, divinations, idolatries and the delusions of their own minds" (Jer. 14:7–9,11–14).

The blame for this sad state is not totally that of the false prophets. People with an appetite for falsehood, in religion or anything else, will find prophets who will accommodate them. Jeremiah's prayer holds a twofold challenge for us: (1) Those who claim to speak for God must be true prophets, not influenced by those who speak out of their own hearts. (2) God himself will take note of and deal with those who for personal advantage cater to the whims of an errant people.

In addition to listening to false prophets, the people sometimes sought help from false gods in seeking answers or confirmations of things they wanted to hear. Throughout history, the human race has prayed to many different gods. Sometimes even God's people turn to them when they do not seem to hear from the one true God. But Jeremiah labels these false gods accurately—"worthless idols."

Why have you afflicted us so that we cannot be healed? We hoped for peace but no good has come, for a time of healing but there is only terror. O LORD, we acknowledge our wickedness and the guilt of our fathers; we have indeed sinned against you. For the sake of your name do not despise us; do not dishonor your glorious throne. Remember your covenant with us and do not break it. Do any of the worthless idols of the nations bring rain? Do the skies themselves send down showers? No, it is you, O

LORD our God. Therefore our hope is in you, for you are the one who does all this (Jer. 14:19–22).

PART 1

Chapter 6
Prayer in
the
Prophetic
Books

The chief end of prayer is not the getting of desired objects, but the gradual development of a relationship with God, a relationship compatible with His character and authority. Consequently, some prayers ring with despair, while others echo obedience, submission, surrender, to the divine will. Prayer reaches its acme when it speaks forth the sincere heart-cry: "Your will be done!" God's honor, "for the sake of your name" (14:21), must be prayer's ultimate intent. "For Jesus' sake," when it comes from the heart, expresses that goal supremely well.

Jeremiah revealed his character, his faithfulness to his calling, and his struggle as he prayed concerning his persecution, his searching in God's Word for an answer, and his unremoved pain. Scarcely can the one praying be separated from his prayer. They are parts of each other.

You understand, O LORD; remember me and care for me. Avenge me on my persecutors. You are long-suffering—do not take me away; think of how I suffer reproach for your sake. When your words came, I ate them; they were my joy and my heart's delight, for I bear your name, O LORD God Almighty. I never sat in the company of revelers, never made merry with them; I sat alone because your hand was on me and you had filled me with indignation. Why is my pain unending and my wound grievous and incurable? Will you be to me like a deceptive brook, like a spring that fails? (Jer. 15:15–18).

Jeremiah was God's prophet for that time, warning people to turn from their wicked ways and inviting them to receive forgiveness and restoration. The people, however, weren't responding. In fact, the Scripture indicates that Jeremiah suffered reproach from the people (see v. 15).

For the earnest person, there is only one solid fuel for the launching of his communion and petition—the Word of God, the truth—which Jeremiah realized. Until people learn to mingle their prayers with the Holy Word, they have missed a great opportunity: The best prayer is the one prayed from the Word itself. That word Jeremiah ate

PART 1

Chapter 6
Prayer in
the
Prophetic
Books

was his spiritual manna. It was his joy and his "heart's delight." No wonder the Psalmist declared, "The unfolding of your words gives light" (Ps. 119:130).

The one on whom the hand of the Lord rests (15:17), however, may find himself a separated person. "Revelers" may be also translated "laughers" or "jokers," indicating that the youthful prophet was not disposed to run with the flamboyant and sportive set of his generation. Because of God's burden resting upon him, Jeremiah's life took on aspects of solitude, separation, and holy concern, making him incompatible with his fellows in their unconcerned indulgence. Throughout church history, a somewhat similar experience has come to others who by the intensity of their praying entered into the very heart of God and, at times, suffered reproach or misunderstanding because of it. They found themselves so shut in with God as to render them a breed apart. John Knox, David Brainerd, and Watchman Nee are just a few examples. There is yet room and need for more such prayer warriors.

God promised Jeremiah that He would strengthen him in such a way that although the people would fight against him, they would not overcome him (v. 20). Jeremiah depended on God's healing and salvation for himself as well as for the nation of Israel. He demonstrated a conviction that springs from a knowledge that God is alive and answers prayer. Note Jeremiah's simple and firm persuasion: "Heal me, O Lord, and I will be healed; save me and I will be saved" (17:14).

O LORD, the hope of Israel, all who forsake you will be put to shame. Those who turn away from you will be written in the dust because they have forsaken the LORD, the spring of living water. Heal me, O LORD, and I will be healed; save me and I will be saved, for you are the one I praise. They keep saying to me, "Where is the word of the LORD? Let it now be fulfilled!" I have not run away from being your shepherd; you know I have not desired the day of despair. What passes my lips is open before you. Do not be a terror to me; you are my refuge in the day of disaster. Let my persecutors be put to shame, but keep me from shame; let them be terrified, but keep me from terror. Bring on them the day of disaster; destroy them with double destruction (Jer. 17:13–18).

PART 1

**Chapter 6
Prayer in
the
Prophetic
Books**

Those who pray ought always to remind themselves of the greatness of the One to whom they pray; to Jeremiah He was "the hope of Israel." To be reminded is to find faith stimulated. In addition to helping their own faith by renewing an awareness of who God is, those who pray may also help themselves by pondering the outcome of forsaking or not forsaking God. To Jeremiah the difference was between having one's name written in the dust (17:13) and engraved in eternal rock.

To the casual observer, the Book of Jeremiah may show Jeremiah to have a persecution complex and a readiness to call down fire from heaven (cf. Luke 9:54). The prophet, however, was praying very much in harmony with the heart of God.

Listen to me, O LORD; hear what my accusers are saying! Should good be repaid with evil? Yet they have dug a pit for me. Remember that I stood before you and spoke in their behalf to turn your wrath away from them. So give their children over to famine; hand them over to the power of the sword. . . . Let a cry be heard from their houses when you suddenly bring invaders against them, for they have dug a pit to capture me and have hidden snares for my feet. But you know, O LORD, all their plots to kill me. Do not forgive their crimes or blot out their sins from your sight. Let them be overthrown before you; deal with them in the time of your anger (Jer. 18:19–23).

We must remember that what is heaped upon the prophet delivering God's message is actually heaped upon God. The sufferings of this prophet were the sufferings of his Master. Israel's reactions to the prophet's compassion, concern, pleading, and unflinching fidelity to God's message were a virtual invitation to God's fierce wrath. In essence, Jeremiah's prayer represents an amen to God's response and intentions.

However, Jeremiah again, like many who seek an answer from God but do not receive it immediately, had questions about God's faithfulness in keeping His promises to His

PART 1

Chapter 6
Prayer in
the
Prophetic
Books

messenger. He even went so far as to express his discouraged feeling that God had deceived him:

> O LORD, you deceived me, and I was deceived; you overpowered me and prevailed. I am ridiculed all day long; everyone mocks me. . . . If I say, "I will not mention him or speak any more in his name," his word is in my heart like a fire, a fire shut up in my bones. I am weary of holding it in; indeed I cannot. . . . O LORD Almighty, you who examine the righteous and probe the heart and mind, let me see your vengeance upon them, for to you I have committed my cause (Jer. 20:7,9,12).

What a rash prayer! Or was it? "Deceived" may be too strong a word here, for God is in no sense a deceiver. "Enticed" is another way of translating the Hebrew; nevertheless, in times of deep discouragement, one may feel deceived. But God is faithful to teach us in spite of our illusions and false persuasions. It may be that Jeremiah was alluding to his initial hesitation about accepting the prophetic office when he was first called. This is not to say that he had weakened when the pressure and consternation seemed unbearable, though he may have been tempted almost to that point (20:8–9).

When divinely called leaders become disillusioned by difficult circumstances and bend as a tree in a gale, they must lift their eyes to the One who gave the call. Courage will be renewed, as it was in Jeremiah: "The LORD is with me like a mighty warrior" (20:11). That the "mighty warrior" is with us is the sure knowledge that His enemies will be subdued, if not vanquished. The "mighty warrior" (the Hebrew indicates He is master, in control) will make known His power to defend His own.

One does not need to study many Old Testament prayers, either public or private, to observe that most of them, even those filled with intense and desperate requests, begin with a recounting of God's majesty, His mercy, and His great deeds. After Jeremiah followed divine instructions to purchase a field, sign and seal the deed, and deliver it to Baruch as a sign that God would one day restore the land (and property would be bought and sold), Jeremiah prayed this prayer:

PART 1

**Chapter 6
Prayer in
the
Prophetic
Books**

"Ah, Sovereign LORD, you have made the heavens and the earth by your great power and outstretched arm. Nothing is too hard for you. You show love to thousands.... O great and powerful God, whose name is the LORD Almighty, great are your purposes and mighty are your deeds. Your eyes are open to all the ways of men; you reward everyone according to his conduct and as his deeds deserve. You performed miraculous signs and wonders in Egypt and have continued them to this day, both in Israel and among all mankind, and have gained the renown that is still yours. You brought your people Israel out of Egypt with signs and wonders, by a mighty hand and an outstretched arm and with great terror. You gave them this land you had sworn to give their forefathers, a land flowing with milk and honey. They came in and took possession of it, but they did not obey you or follow your law.... See ... the city will be handed over to the Babylonians.... What you said has happened, as you now see. And though the city will be handed over to the Babylonians, you, O Sovereign LORD, say to me, 'Buy the field with silver and have the transaction witnessed' " (Jer. 32:17–25).

For the earnest person there is no greater encouragement or impetus than the review of God's mighty acts. (See 1 Sam. 7:12 and Ps. 78.) Such a practice generously reinforces the conviction that there is nothing too hard for God. It is not a mere whistling in the dark or a clever psychological maneuver for developing assurance or self-confidence, but a spiritual exercise of significant meaning for every child of God. Note God's response to such a recounting of His wonderful deeds: " 'I am the LORD, the God of all mankind. Is anything too hard for me?' " (Jer. 32:27).

The circumstance of Jeremiah's lamentations is the fall of Jerusalem, as he foretold. The enemy from the north (see Jer. 6:22) had been God's agent for punishing a rebellious, unrepentant people. The Book of Lamentations is filled with tears and prayers. Every age has had its share of sorrow and pain, but no age has produced such a heart of sorrow as is reflected in this book.

"See, O LORD, how distressed I am! I am in torment within, and in my heart I am disturbed, for I have been most rebellious. Outside, the sword bereaves; inside, there is only death. People

PART 1

Chapter 6
Prayer in
the
Prophetic
Books

have heard my groaning, but there is no one to comfort me. All my enemies have heard of my distress; they rejoice at what you have done. May you bring the day you have announced so they may become like me. Let all their wickedness come before you; deal with them as you have dealt with me because of all my sins. My groans are many and my heart is faint" (Lam. 1:20–22).

Here is an account of true contrition. Lamentation is the manifestation of this attitude. It is the mourning Jesus referred to in Matthew 5:4—"Blessed are those who mourn, for they will be comforted."

Prayers in the night take on the hue of the darkness around them. Yet God understands, and hears, even when the supplicant accuses Him of causing the terror and destruction; only He knows the heart as well as the words that issue from the mouth.

"Look, O LORD, and consider: Whom have you ever treated like this? Should women eat their offspring, the children they have cared for? Should priest and prophet be killed in the sanctuary of the Lord? Young and old lie together in the dust of the streets; my young men and maidens have fallen by the sword. You have slain them in the day of your anger; you have slaughtered them without pity. As you summon to a feast day, so you summoned against me terrors on every side. In the day of the LORD's anger no one escaped or survived; those I cared for and reared, my enemy has destroyed" (Lam. 2:20–22).

Jeremiah's prayer reflects a double darkness: (1) the burden of a depressing destruction in the land and (2) the spell of a spiritual darkness over the people. For people today who experience such darkness, there is the blessed assurance: "The light shines in the darkness, but the darkness has not understood it [laid not hold of it]" (John 1:5).

Jeremiah continued to lament about the situation of God's people, calling out to God for answers and relief:

You have covered yourself with a cloud so that no prayer can get through. . . .
Streams of tears flow from my eyes because my people are destroyed. My eyes will flow unceasingly, without relief, until the LORD looks down from heaven and sees. . . .
I called on your name, O LORD, from the depths of the pit.

You heard my plea: "Do not close your ears to my cry for relief."
You came near when I called you, and you said, "Do not fear."
O LORD, you took up my case; you redeemed my life. You have
seen, O LORD, the wrong done to me. Uphold my cause! (Lam.
3:44,48–50,55–59).

Along with elements of sincere sorrow, this prayer of
Jeremiah (Lam. 3:41–66) contains a confident note of trust.
Buried in the usual requests that God would judge those
who were afflicting His people so mercilessly is the testimony, "You redeemed my life." What descriptive language
Jeremiah uses to express the fount of tears deep within!
God seemed surrounded by an impenetrable cloud so that
no prayer could pass through to Him; the prophet's eyes
wept rivers, his tears flowed continuously. But Jeremiah
believes that because God heard and answered in the past,
ultimately there will be penetration of the clouds and a
divine response: God will hear; He comes near and speaks
comfort to the burdened prophet, "Do not fear."

The Israelites had experienced the horrors of war: servitude, abuse, famine, humiliation. Jeremiah faced the reality of their situation, and because of it, prayed most effectively. People who ignore or deny their situations become
victims of self-deception, practicing a false religion, which
can never turn the tide and resolve the difficulty.

PART 1

**Chapter 6
Prayer in
the
Prophetic
Books**

Remember, O LORD, what has happened to us; look, and see our
disgrace. Our inheritance has been turned over to aliens, our
homes to foreigners. We have become orphans and fatherless,
our mothers like widows.... Those who pursue us are at our
heels; we are weary and find no rest. We submitted to Egypt and
Assyria to get enough bread. Our fathers sinned and are no more,
and we bear their punishment. Slaves rule over us, and there is
none to free us from their hands. We get our bread at the risk
of our lives because of the sword in the desert.... The crown
has fallen from our head. Woe to us, for we have sinned! Because
of this our hearts are faint, because of these things our eyes grow
dim.... You, O LORD, reign forever; your throne endures from
generation to generation. Why do you always forget us? Why do
you forsake us so long? Restore us to yourself, O LORD, that we
may return; renew our days as of old unless you have utterly

PART 1

Chapter 6
Prayer in
the
Prophetic
Books

rejected us and are angry with us beyond measure (Lam. 5:1–3, 5–9, 16–17, 19–22).

Jeremiah recounted their troubles with a starkness too plain for sacred Scripture, some might think. Yet God does not want our prayer to sugarcoat reality. There is at least one time when we must express ourselves candidly: when we come to God asking for His help and deliverance.

Through it all, Jeremiah was gripped by a passion for the revival of his people. The world today needs the same openness in bringing before the Lord the devastation of our families and our society.

Ezekiel

The prophet Ezekiel lived in complete fellowship with God. Yet the prayer and dialogue between him and God are found less frequently in his book than the prayer and dialogue of the other Major Prophets in their books. Ezekiel received his call to the prophetic ministry in the midst of a vision anticipating the approach of divine judgment: "He said to me, 'Son of man, stand on up your feet and I will speak to you.' . . . He said: 'Son of man, I am sending you to the Israelites, to a rebellious nation that has rebelled against me' " (Ezek. 2:1,3).

Every person of prayer develops unique prayer habits, usually inspired by other godly people who have set an example. Ezekiel's address to God as "sovereign Lord" was probably inspired by the example of Abraham (Gen. 15:2), Moses (Deut. 3:24), Joshua (Josh. 7:7), Gideon (Judg. 6:22), David (2 Sam. 7:18–20, 28–29), Solomon (1 Kings 8:53), and Jeremiah (Jer. 32:17). Undoubtedly that expression (also translated in some versions, "The Lord Jehovah") ignited the fires of faith and enabled Ezekiel to perceive the mighty deity whom he was approaching and beseeching.

Then I said, "Not so, Sovereign Lord! I have never defiled myself. From my youth until now I have never eaten anything found dead or torn by wild animals. No unclean meat has ever entered my mouth" (Ezek. 4:14).

The Lord had described to Ezekiel what he was to do

PART 1

Chapter 6
Prayer in
the
Prophetic
Books

to symbolize the coming destruction of Jerusalem and subjection of Israel. He was to cook his bread over human
dung, for the Jewish people would be defiled in the land
of the Gentiles. Ezekiel's response to God at this is similar
to Peter's (see Acts 10:10–14). Peter, too, was concerned
that he not defile himself with what God had formerly
forbidden. What great souls are those who by every means
seek to avoid defilement and pollution! Pollution of the
soul by sin is the greatest dread of good people. Yet there
can be times when an overly tender conscience fears without cause. Ezekiel had not yet learned that it is not what
goes into the mouth that defiles a person, but what comes
out (see Matt. 15:11). The world today, however, falls far
short of that pure conscience that sincerely seeks to avoid
any suggestion of defilement or pollution.

The Book of Ezekiel later recorded how Ezekiel prayed
for his people with intensity. One who experiences a burden for others may sometimes feel as though God cares
less for the needy than the one praying does. Yet our compassion can never exceed God's, for it is God who gives
the burden to pray for others.

While they [guardian angels] were killing [those who had committed abominations] and I was left alone, I fell facedown, crying
out, "Ah, Sovereign LORD! Are you going to destroy the entire
remnant of Israel in this outpouring of your wrath on Jerusalem?"
(Ezek. 9:8).

Throughout Scripture, falling facedown described the
urgency of desperate intercession. Yet no matter how intense a need the person may feel, God's compassion is
greater still (see Ezek. 18:23,32). The prospect of judgment
on Jerusalem made Ezekiel feel it would be a total disaster.
"God places people in situations of trial where they may
fall, situations which may be disastrous: but the purpose
is not disaster but triumph."[3] God would indeed preserve
a godly remnant of the nation of Israel. The destruction of
Jerusalem and the Babylonian exile were necessary in order to get rid of Israel's idolatry and prepare the way for

[3]Kenneth Leech, *True Prayer: An Invitation to Christian Spirituality*
(San Francisco: Harper & Row, Publishers, 1980), 146.

PART 1

Chapter 6

Prayer in
the
Prophetic
Books

the eventual ministry on earth of Jesus Christ. He could hardly have taught the Sermon on the Mount if the Israelites were still worshiping idols everywhere (as in Jer. 3:13; Ezek. 6:13).

Carrying God's message to His people is not all glamour. God sometimes gives His messengers the burdensome task of pronouncing judgment. Such an assignment is a heavy weight on the prophet. Even as the voice of judgment thunders, the heart of compassion must be breaking.

> As I was prophesying, Pelatiah son of Benaiah died. Then I fell facedown and cried out in a loud voice, "Ah, Sovereign LORD! Will you completely destroy the remnant of Israel?" (Ezek. 11:13).

God had commanded Ezekiel to prophesy against Jaazaniah and Pelatiah (Ezek. 11:2–4). Some commentators suggest that Ezekiel, like Peter in the case of Ananias and Sapphira, pronounced judgment on Pelatiah, who then suddenly died.[4] If that is true, we have here a profound lesson for any who by the exercise of a God-given authority are used by the Almighty to bring His severe judgment. There is no place for gloating; there can only be sadness, and the prayer that the same judgment not come to others.

Another burden carried by God's messengers is that the hearers don't always take the message seriously. Surely when God's servant speaks the very message the Almighty has asked him to deliver, the hearers should repent and receive the instruction. But all too often the opposite happens: The messenger is ridiculed, persecuted, and rejected. At such a time it is easy to question whether one has correctly heard and announced the word of the Lord: "I said, 'Ah, Sovereign LORD! They are saying of me, "Isn't he just telling parables?" ' " (Ezek. 20:49).

Here is a lesson for all of God's servants who are the victims of "they say" and hearsay. Surely the suggestion that Ezekiel spoke fiction rather than truth was simply a self-serving excuse for rejecting his strong and unmistak-

---

[4]See W. Carley, *The Book of the Prophet Ezekiel* (Cambridge, Mass: Cambridge University Press, 1974), 68; and Charles L. Feinberg, *The Prophecy of Ezekiel* (Chicago: Moody Press, 1969), 65; and Douglas Stuart, *Ezekiel* (Dallas: Word Books, 1989), 102.

able condemnation. If people reject God himself, it is little wonder that His anointed messengers sometimes receive the same treatment.

PART 1
Chapter 6
Prayer in
the
Prophetic
Books

Daniel

Daniel was a person of prayer. He stood resolute in his determination to pray, even when to do so meant being thrown into a den of lions. He also relied on God for wisdom and the interpretation of the dreams of Nebuchadnezzar and Belshazzar. To speak before heads of state with such authority and assurance comes only from extended times in the place of prayer.

In the first instance of dream interpretation, Daniel was required not only to tell the interpretation but the dream as well. The four Hebrew wise men of the king's court in Babylon were driven to prayer. Faced with the awful prospect of having their houses destroyed and then being torn limb from limb if they could not interpret Nebuchadnezzar's dreams (Dan. 2:5,12–13), Daniel, Shadrach, Meshach, and Abednego prayed earnestly (2:18; see also 1:7). While the actual words of their prayer are not recorded, the content of the petition is clear.

Daniel returned to his house and explained the matter to his friends Hananiah, Mishael, and Azariah. He urged them to plead for mercy from the God of heaven concerning this mystery, so that he and his friends might not be executed with the rest of the wise men of Babylon (Dan. 2:17–18).

Extreme circumstances have a way of refining prayer to its essence, eliminating excess verbiage directed more to human ears than to God's ears. Furthermore, shared burdens become lighter. The union of forces produces a greater force. The dynamics of united prayer are awesome. Agreeing together in prayer for a particular need produces results. When the Early Church prayed together in unity, the place of prayer was shaken (see Acts 4:31).

As Daniel and his companions prayed, in the distress of the moment it's unlikely that they imagined the answer would dramatically reveal the true God to the fierce king of Babylon. However, Daniel knew that God had given

■■■■■■
PART 1

Chapter 6
Prayer in
the
Prophetic
Books

Nebuchadnezzar the dream in the first place. Therefore, he could confidently declare to the king, " 'There is a God in heaven who reveals mysteries' " (Dan. 2:28). When we pray, though it be in the face of extreme circumstances, we do well to remember that we may be fulfilling a divine role reaching far beyond our limited vision of the moment.

Daniel so proved himself a man of God, interpreting another dream for Nebuchadnezzar, explaining the writing on the wall, distinguishing himself above the other administrators, that "the king planned to set him over the whole kingdom" (6:3). The jealous administrators had to devise a trap to get rid of him, since "he was trustworthy and neither corrupt nor negligent" (v. 4) and they were unable to find gounds for charges against him in governmental affairs. Knowing Daniel was a person of prayer, they had the king sign a decree that for thirty days no one could pray to anyone but the king.

"When Daniel learned that the decree had been published, he went home to his upstairs room where the windows opened toward Jerusalem. Three times a day he got down on his knees and prayed, giving thanks to his God, just as he had done before" (Dan. 6:10). No greater line has been written about Daniel than the one that concludes this verse: ". . . as he had done before." Great individuals have great habits; great habits make great individuals. Communion with God should be the foremost habit of every child of God. Daniel's unswerving devotion in the face of vicious and bloodthirsty persecutors sprang from his long-practiced prayer habit. His habit had put steel in his soul, so that when his life was threatened for practice of the habit, he simply kept up his practice without apology. The strength of the praying person is most evident when he is under siege.

In Daniel 9, Daniel intercedes for captive Israel after meditating on the prophecies of Jeremiah, which said that after seventy years as slaves they would be restored. Daniel "turned to the LORD God and pleaded with him in prayer and petition, in fasting, and in sackcloth and ashes" (v. 3). As Daniel introduced his prayer of confession, he "turned to the Lord God." He made a total commitment to making things right with God, and he had absolute faith in the One to whom the prayer was directed. This was not a formal prayer. It was marked by supplication, intense entreaty. The sackcloth and ashes were marks of complete self-effacement.

"O Lord, the great and awesome God, who keeps his covenant of love with all who love him and obey his commands, we have sinned and done wrong. We have been wicked and have rebelled; we have turned away from your commands and laws. We have not listened to your servants the prophets, who spoke in your name to our kings, our princes and our fathers, and to all the people of the land.

"Lord, you are righteous, but . . . we and our kings, our princes and our fathers are covered with shame because we have sinned against you. The Lord our God is merciful and forgiving, even though we have rebelled against him; we have not obeyed the LORD our God or kept the laws he gave us through his servants the prophets. . . .

"All this disaster has come upon us, yet we have not sought the favor of the LORD our God by turning from our sins and giving attention to your truth. . . .

"O Lord, in keeping with all your righteous acts, turn away your anger and your wrath. . . .

"Give ear, O God, and hear; open your eyes and see the desolation of the city that bears your Name. We do not make requests of you because we are righteous, but because of your great mercy. O Lord, listen! O Lord, forgive! O Lord, hear and act! For your sake, O my God, do not delay, because your city and your people bear your Name" (Dan. 9:4–10,13,16,18–19).

Daniel was the nation's advocate at God's bar of justice. He pleaded for revival and restoration, and the basis for the plea was genuine repentance. He considered as his own sins the sins of rulers, kings, priests, and judges. His prayer could well be a pattern for all who perceive the sorry state of many nations, including ours, in this day. Prayer warriors can have greater influence over national affairs than titular heads of state. A person on knees of prayer is mightier than a king upon his throne. Those who pray as Daniel prayed have access to the audience-chamber of the Most High; like Daniel they hear the pronouncement of the divine will.

Daniel voiced his prayer so earnestly because he knew

PART 1

Chapter 6
Prayer in
the
Prophetic
Books

God's purpose concerning Israel. Knowing God's will does not render prayer unnecessary; it makes it all the more important and effective, since praying in faith always brings a response. As Daniel prayed, he fastened his eyes on God, recalling His character and attributes; as he so prayed, even greater faith arose in his heart.

The Book of Daniel closes with Daniel's vision of end-time events. The world turns to horoscopes, fortune tellers, divination, and various types of occultic practices when seeking glimpses into the future. But that which God wants us to know about the future is contained in His Word, and we must turn to no other source to inquire about that which is to happen. "I heard, but I did not understand. So I asked, 'My lord, what will the outcome of all this be?'" (Dan. 12:8).

Daniel's prayer is a guideline for those who may ponder the meaning of prophecy or may be totally perplexed when seeking to determine the prophetic timetable. Daniel's perception that he "did not understand" led him to the One who knows the end from the beginning. How much better it is to pray to the One who knows the future than to speculate about the end and arrive at wrong conclusions.

Daniel's prayer for understanding was answered. Even though he was not given all the information he might have desired, he got an answer which put his spirit to rest. "'Go your way, Daniel, because the words are closed up and sealed until the time of the end'" (Dan. 12:9). We too can expect peace concerning the future as we inquire of God alone.

Joel

Joel, the prophet through whom God gave a most memorable prophecy about a future outpouring of the Holy Spirit (Joel 2:28–29), was a person who knew how to pray. Though he prophesied of a future time of blessing, he lived in a time of drought and difficulty. He has left for us examples of how to pray.

To you, O LORD, I call, for fire has devoured the open pastures and flames have burned up all the trees of the field. Even the

wild animals pant for you; the streams of water have dr
and fire has devoured the open pastures (Joel 1:19–20).

How does one pray when nature seems to with
essential rain, or sends too much moisture, or shakes
earth with devastating quakes, or destroys and kills through
tornadoes or hurricanes? Some would suggest that it is an
impertinence to interfere with natural laws and events by
our prayers. But Joel's example gives sound instruction.
Whatever the catastrophe or the cause thereof, we may
follow the impulse of our heart, crying out to Almighty
God. The One who guides the affairs of mankind can also
restrain the destruction caused by a fallen creation. He
may turn devastation away and leave a blessing behind. If
not, His comfort and help will come in response to the
prayer for deliverance.

Joel also instructed the priests of Israel where and how
they should pray, just as Jesus taught His disciples how
they should approach God in prayer (see Matt. 6:9–13):
"Let the priests, who minister before the LORD, weep between the temple porch and the altar. Let them say, 'Spare
your people, O LORD. Do not make your inheritance an
object of scorn, a byword among the nations. Why should
they say among the peoples, "Where is their God?" ' " (Joel
2:17).

Dean Stanley's vivid description of this remarkable prayer
scene gives substance to this national cry for deliverance:

The harsh blast of the consecrated ram's horn called an assembly
to an extraordinary fast. Not a soul was to be absent.... It con-
vened old and young, men and women, mothers with infants at
their breasts, the bridegroom and the bride on their bridal day.
All were there stretched in front of the altar.... The priestly
caste, instead of gathering as usual upon its steps and its plat-
form,... lay prostrate, gazing towards the Invisible Presence
within the sanctuary. Instead of the hymns and music which,
since the time of David, had entered into their prayers, there
was nothing heard but the passionate sobs and the loud dissonant
howls of such as only an Eastern hierarchy could utter. ... They

PART 1

Chapter 6
Prayer in
the
Prophetic
Books

waved their black drapery towards the temple, and shrieked aloud, "Spare thy people, O Lord!"[5]

The burden of this prayer, as might well be the burden of all prayer, is God's honor. The pagan cried out in derision, "Where is your God?" Today a similar cry rises from the ungodly. It is time for the Church to pray as Israel prayed, with intensity and earnestness.

Amos

Even in Old Testament times, a person did not need to be a prophet or a son of a prophet to hear from and speak for God. A simple shepherd-farmer, Amos was commissioned to bring a divine message to Israel (see Amos 7:14–15).

On only one occasion was a prayer directed by Amos to God recorded: "I cried out, 'Sovereign LORD, I beg you, stop! How can Jacob survive? He is so small!' " (Amos 7:5). This prayer contains a line of great consequence for all who pray: "He is so small." (See also Amos 7:2.) Israel was in great need of God's help. In their own strength, the people were small. But their admission of utter poverty was the gateway to divine intervention. Jesus said, " 'Blessed are the poor in spirit [those who recognize their own destitution or poverty]: for theirs is the kingdom of heaven' " (Matt. 5:3).

Because of sin, Israel had been demoralized and defeated; God had brought judgment on them. The prayer of Amos shows his spirit. He had to preach judgment, but he preached it out of a broken heart.

Jonah

Jonah was used of God to accomplish something he had not prayed for. In fact, Jonah did not want the Ninevites to repent and be spared. But when God asks His servant to do something he would normally not pray for, the issue

---

[5]H. D. M. Spence and Joseph S. Exell, eds., *The Pulpit Commentary* (Grand Rapids: Wm. B. Eerdmans Pub. Co., 1950), vol. 13, *Joel,* by J. J. Given, 23.

becomes obedience. There are times when God's plan calls for ministry that no one feels a burden for. So Jonah and his shipboard companions were given concerns that compelled them to seek God. Caught in a violent storm at sea, and hearing from Jonah that his presence was somehow the cause of it all, the pagan sailors voiced to God a desperate prayer for personal safety: "They cried to the LORD, 'O LORD, please do not let us die for taking this man's life. Do not hold us accountable for killing an innocent man, for you, O LORD, have done as you pleased' " (Jon. 1:14).

These pagans were imploring the Lord, the one true God, in such a manner as to indicate at least some knowledge of Old Testament Law, which held a murderer responsible for taking the life of an innocent person. With their meager knowledge they were hardly equipped to pray with much understanding; yet, to their credit, they did pray. And, unlike Jonah, they prayed with genuine concern for a fellowman and with submission to God. God is merciful to everyone, especially to those who call upon Him, whether they be benighted pagans or enlightened saints, for they are all His offspring (see Acts 17:29).

Thrown overboard by the sailors, Jonah was swallowed by the great fish prepared by God. We can understand Jonah's feeling that he was in "the depths of the grave [Heb. *Sheol*]," with no prospect of deliverance apart from the supernatural intervention of the God from whom he was running.

"In my distress I called to the LORD, and he answered me. From the depths of the grave I called for help, and you listened to my cry. You hurled me into the deep, into the very heart of the seas, and the currents swirled about me; all your waves and breakers swept over me. I said, 'I have been banished from your sight; yet I will look again toward your holy temple.' The engulfing waters threatened me, the deep surrounded me; seaweed was wrapped around my head.... When my life was ebbing away, I remembered you, LORD, and my prayer rose to you, to your holy temple. Those who cling to worthless idols forfeit the grace that could be theirs. But I, with a song of thanksgiving, will sacrifice to you. What I have vowed I will make good. Salvation comes from the LORD" (Jon. 2:2–5,7–9).

PART 1

**Chapter 6
Prayer in
the
Prophetic
Books**

No more unusual prayer has ever been offered throughout the millennia of history; surely there is no record of prayer being offered in as strange a place as this. The lessons from this memorable prayer are many. First, prayer is appropriate at any time and in any place. One does not need a cloistered chapel or a lofty cathedral to have audience with the Almighty. As a believer practices the constant presence of God, prayer can be made at the kitchen sink or on a busy street, aboard an airplane or at the wheel of an automobile, in a field or in the city, in a place of solitude or amid the surging throng, in foxholes or in prayer closets, in a sanctuary or in a fish's belly. The place where prayer is voiced has little bearing upon God's hearing. Second, one's greatest need often becomes the inspiration for one's greatest praying. Could it be that God in His wise providence permits distress and untoward circumstances to provoke us to prayer and dependence? Third, that prayer, to be effective, must be coupled with submission. A rebellious spirit may bring the sea billows over our souls, but submission will bring deliverance. Fourth, prayer is an exercise of faith. It was for Jonah. He remembered the Lord and promised to look again toward His holy temple (2:4,7). Where there is no genuine faith in God, there will be little praying to God. Often it takes the storm to stir faith into action. Fifth, prayer can bring assurance. Jonah "prayed through" so that even though he was still in the fish's belly he could speak as though he were already delivered. Finally, prayer from the depths is heard in the heights. " 'My prayer rose to you, to your holy temple' " (2:7). Depths are not uncommon to human experience. For some people it is the depth of sorrow; for some the depth of suffering; for some the depth of sin, for others the depth of mental anguish. But there is no depth from which the human cry cannot be heard on high (see Pss. 107:23–28; 139:8–10).

On the other hand, great discouragement can come when God does not act the way a person feels He should. Jonah experienced such a despair, even contemplating suicide.

"O LORD, is this not what I said when I was still at home? That is why I was so quick to flee to Tarshish. I knew that you are a gracious and compassionate God, slow to anger and abounding in love, a God who relents from sending calamity. Now, O LORD, take away my life, for it is better for me to die than to live" (Jon. 4:2–3).

Jonah was a prophet with a good reputation for fulfilled prophecies (2 Kings 14:25). He knew what people would say if he returned and nothing happened to Nineveh. He knew what kind of God he served, but he was more concerned over his own reputation than God's. He could not face what he thought was a personal disgrace. God had spared Nineveh, just as Jonah knew all along that He would. Jonah was disappointed, and he was wrong to pray to die. But he was right to bring his feelings to God. How gently God dealt with him, giving him an insight that has inspired the work of missions even today.

Habakkuk

The questions that trouble a servant of God are sometimes as big as those that trouble others. Habakkuk asked God, "Why are not the prayers of good men immediately answered?" and "Why do the wicked prosper?" Some count only two recorded prayers of Habakkuk; others count three. What may be considered two prayers (Hab. 1:1–11 and 1:12 to 2:20) may actually be the expressing of two problems in one prayer.

How long, O LORD, must I call for help, but you do not listen? Or cry out to you, "Violence!" but you do not save? Why do you make me look at injustice? Why do you tolerate wrong? Destruction and violence are before me; there is strife, and conflict abounds. Therefore the law is paralyzed, and justice never prevails. The wicked hem in the righteous, so that justice is perverted (Hab. 1:2–4).

Though God does not respond directly to Habakkuk's first question, "Why are not the prayers of good men immediately answered?" there are principles which provide a partial answer. Importunity is sometimes necessary before one will value the answer should it come. In other words, if we received an answer at the first petition, the blessing may not be fully appreciated. The gift means much

PART 1

Chapter 6
Prayer in
the
Prophetic
Books

more when the mind is receptive to it. Delay sometimes
adjusts the mind so that true gratitude and praise result
when the answer is received. Prayer itself is the best means
of spiritual growth. Conscious interaction with God is essential to moral and spiritual excellence. True prayer is
the means of becoming more and more like Christ. Ac-
quiescence to the divine will must often come before a
request is granted. At times, we do not understand completely what we should pray for; we may be fortunate that
our prayers are not answered. On occasion, our selfish wills
must yield to the divine will. Jesus prayed that the cup
might pass from him, but it did not. Instead, He yielded to
a higher divine will: "Yet not my will, but yours be done"
(Luke 22:42). We need not be anxious about the absence
of immediate answers to prayer. God will faithfully witness
to our spirits that He is accomplishing a work even in the
delay.

The second question, "Why do the wicked prosper?" has
been asked by many of the Old Testament prophets, including Habakkuk:

O LORD, you have appointed them to execute judgment; O Rock,
you have ordained them to punish. Your eyes are too pure to
look on evil; you cannot tolerate wrong. Why then do you tolerate the treacherous? Why are you silent while the wicked
swallow up those more righteous than themselves? (Hab. 1:12–
13).

God knows what He is doing. When Habakkuk could not
understand why God would use the Babylonians to punish
Israel when they were more wicked than the Israelites,
God made it clear that He knew how bad the Babylonians
were. He would use them and then take care of their punishment in due time. (Cf. Isa. 10:3–12.) We must let God
answer our prayers in His way, recognizing He knows best.

It seems most fitting that the final prayer of the Old
Testament should be eloquent Hebrew poetry extolling
the glories of the Holy One and pleading earnestly for His
mercies. Habakkuk's prayer psalm had two purposes: It was
personal and it was intended for musical praise in the liturgy. (Note the musical instructions.)

Lord, I have heard of your fame; I stand in awe of your deeds, O Lord. Renew them in our day, in our time make them known; in wrath remember mercy. . . . [God's] glory covered the heavens and his praise filled the earth. His splendor was like the sunrise; rays flashed from his hand, where his power was hidden. Plague went before him; pestilence followed his steps. He stood, and shook the earth; he looked, and made the nations tremble. The ancient mountains crumbled and the age-old hills collapsed. His ways are eternal. . . . The mountains saw you and writhed. Torrents of water swept by; the deep roared and lifted its waves on high. Sun and moon stood still in the heavens at the glint of your flying arrows, at the lightning of your flashing spear. . . . You came out to deliver your people, to save your anointed one. . . . You trampled the sea with your horses, churning the great waters. I heard and my heart pounded, my lips quivered at the sound; decay crept into my bones, and my legs trembled. Yet I will wait patiently for the day of calamity to come on the nation invading us. Though the fig tree does not bud and there are no grapes on the vines, though the olive crop fails and the fields produce no food. . . . yet I will rejoice in the Lord, I will be joyful in God my Savior. The Sovereign Lord is my strength; he makes my feet like the feet of a deer, he enables me to go on the heights (Hab. 3:2–6,10–11,13,15–19).

PART 1

Chapter 6
Prayer in
the
Prophetic
Books

Of necessity, prophets prayed; sometimes they prayed for even those against whom they prophesied. Intimately acquainted with the divine intent for the future, they knew better than others what to pray for. Because Habakkuk had found God ready to answer prayer before, he could pray with assurance that God's ear was inclined toward him and toward Judah. The well-known declaration of Habakkuk 2:4 ("the righteous shall live by . . . faith") is quoted three times in the New Testament (see Rom. 1:17; Gal. 3:11; Heb. 10:38) and was rediscovered by Martin Luther in the Protestant Reformation. Faith that included faithfulness was the foundation for Habakkuk's entire life; the righteous do live by faith and by prayer born of that faith, a faith that includes faithfulness.

Although there are no commands about prayer in the Old Testament, as there are in the New Testament, the thread of prayer is prominently interwoven in the super-

PART 1

Chapter 6
Prayer in
the
Prophetic
Books

natural dealings of God with His people. The examples of the patriarchs, prophets, and leaders are sufficient evidence that prayer is not a later invention of imaginative individuals, but a basic means of a person's establishing a relationship with God.

Questions for Study

1. What do you suppose Isaiah would say to people who pray light and frivolous prayers, or to those who address the Lord as "Daddy God"?

2. How should we pray when we feel that somehow God has forsaken us?

3. How did Jeremiah overcome doubt and troublesome thoughts?

4. Why did God tell Jeremiah to stop interceding for his people?

5. Why is it important to mingle the Word of God with our prayers?

6. What is the importance of a pure conscience when we pray?

7. Why did Daniel ask his companions to pray with him?

8. How does knowing God's will help us in our prayers?

9. How should our prayers show our concern for God's honor?

10. How do we know that God will hear the prayers of the unsaved if they pray to Him in sincerity?

11. How did God deal with Habakkuk's questions? Will He condemn us if we have doubts and questions?

PART
2

—The Spirit Helps Us Pray—

Prayer In The New Testament

— *Chapter Seven* —

PRAYER IN THE LIFE AND MINISTRY OF CHRIST

In studying the prayer practice of Christ, we must first contemplate His unique nature. The Lord Jesus Christ was Deity as well as human. He was both the Son of God and the Son of Man, which immediately brings up four questions: To whom did Christ pray? Since Christ is God, was it God praying to God? Since Christ is God, was He praying to himself? Since Christ is God, why did He need to pray at all?

1. To whom did Christ pray? The record is very clear. Eighteen times the Gospels record that Christ directed His prayer to the Heavenly Father. In five of those instances He included a descriptive phrase or term, but there is no hint of any other object to whom His prayer was addressed: "Father, Lord of heaven and earth" (Matt. 11:25; Luke 10:21); "my Father" (Matt. 26:39,42); "Abba, Father" (Mark 14:36); "Holy Father" (John 17:11); "righteous Father" (John 17:25); and "Father" (Matt. 11:26; Luke 10:21; 22:42; 23:34,46; John 12:27–28; 17:1,5,21,24). In responding to the disciples' request that He teach them to pray, Jesus told them to pray, "Our Father" (Matt. 6:9; Luke 11:2). Jesus, however, did not include himself in that prayer, nor did He ever include anyone else when He said, "My Father." On a single occasion, Jesus addressed His prayer to God:

PART 2

Chapter 7
Prayer in
the Life
and
Ministry
of Christ

" 'My God, my God, why have you forsaken me?' " (Matt. 27:46). This, however, was His way of claiming Psalm 22 as an expression of His feelings on the cross (see Ps. 22:7–8,14–17).

2. Since Christ is God, was it God praying to God? The answer to this question is not as simple as the preceding one, because it enters the realm of a rather profound theology. That Jesus was indeed God is soundly established in Scripture (see Matt. 1:23; John 20:28; Heb. 1:8). Nevertheless, He laid aside His glory (but not His Godhood) when He clothed himself with the mantle of humanity (Phil. 2:5–7). In His identification with us He was still fully God as well as fully human. But He accepted the limits of being in a physical body. Consequently, He used His voice to commune with His Father. It should not be overlooked that there is an evident communion within the Godhead (see Gen. 1:26). The nature of this communion is surely beyond human comprehension, but it would seem in content to be something other than the recorded prayers of Jesus to the Father.

3. Since Christ is God, was He indeed praying to himself? Though we do talk to ourselves (e.g., Ps. 42:11), from our vantage point to pray to oneself would be an absurdity. As the Son of God, Christ is indeed God, but He is also the Second Person in the triune Godhead. No, Christ was not praying to himself, since each Person in the Godhead is a distinct Person; therefore, God the Son prayed to God the Father.

4. Since Christ is God, why did He need to pray at all? Although Jesus Christ is God, He was not God only while on earth. He was the God-Man. As God He did not need to pray (except for that communion and fellowship within the Godhead already mentioned), but as man, clothed with a body as a descendant of Abraham (Phil. 2:7; Matt. 1:1), prayer was as essential to Him as it was to Abraham and to all of his offspring.

Nearly fifteen centuries before the beginning of Christ's ministry on earth, Moses announced, "The LORD your God will raise up for you a prophet like me from among your own brothers" (Deut. 18:15). The likenesses of Christ and Moses are numerous and striking. For example, both were miraculously spared in infancy from the wrath of a king, both became savior of their people, and both were described as humble (cf. Num. 12:3; Matt. 11:29). Although we cannot pursue all the similarities between them, we do want to note the clear similarity in their prayer lives. As has been noted in chapter 2, Moses' whole life was governed by and based on prayer. So it was with Christ. Prayer was prominent in every facet and phase of His life and ministry. Scripture cites numerous instances of specific prayer during the short three and one-half years of Christ's ministry, but there is evidence that prayer was the very life-breath of Jesus, just as it was of Moses. Jesus lived a disciplined life. The Gospels note certain habits; one was regular synagogue attendance on the Sabbath Day, which, of course, included prayer time (cf. Matt. 21:13; Luke 4:16). It is not unreasonable to think that Jesus went daily to the synagogue or temple, depending on where He was, for a time of prayer.

Also supporting the idea of Jesus' constancy in prayer is His forthright declaration to His disciples "that they should always pray and not give up" (Luke 18:1). Furthermore, at the very outset of Jesus' ministry, Scripture indicates His commitment to and dependency upon prayer. "Very early in the morning, while it was still dark, Jesus got up, left the house and went off to a solitary place, where he prayed" (Mark 1:35). Other references show that this was a continuing discipline (Matt. 14:23; Mark 6:46; Luke 5:16; 9:18,28). Furthermore, at significant junctures prayer played a particularly important part in His ministry.

Prayer at His Baptism

Although there is no recorded prayer of Jesus before his water baptism at the Jordan, we can be sure that He prayed regularly. But it is appropriate that the first mention of His praying occurred at His baptism, at which time the Holy Spirit descended upon Him. Though every child of God should know how to address the Father, there should be something special about the prayer of the Spirit-filled Christian. Jesus' praying at His water baptism also indicates that baptism should be more than mere ritual, ceremony, or

PART 2

Chapter 7
Prayer in
the Life
and
Ministry
of Christ

formality. It ought rather to be an occasion for high and holy communion with the Father, as it was in this instance. What Jesus prayed is not recorded, but it is of no small consequence that heaven was opened as He prayed and that there was a striking manifestation of the other members of the Trinity.

When all the people were being baptized, Jesus was baptized too. And as he was praying, heaven was opened and the Holy Spirit descended on him in bodily form like a dove. And a voice came from heaven: "You are my Son, whom I love, with you I am well pleased" (Luke 3:21–22).

It should be noted that in numerous instances during the last century, scores of believers have been filled with the Spirit at the time of their water baptism. Although there is no other biblical example of this, there is no scriptural prohibition to disallow its happening.

Prayer in the Wilderness

After He was specially endued by the Holy Spirit, Jesus was driven by that Spirit into the wilderness (Mark 1:12), where he was tempted. There is no record of His praying on that occasion, but there can be no doubt that it was a time of much prayer. Scripture records that after the wilderness experience, "Jesus returned to Galilee in the power of the Spirit" (Luke 4:14). Prayer alone provides power over temptation as well as power for ministry.

The writer of the Book of Hebrews records that Jesus "offered up prayers and petitions with loud cries and tears to the one who could save him from death, and he was heard because of his reverent submission" (Heb. 5:7). Although the obvious reference is to His Gethsemane experience, it is not inappropriate to associate intense prayer with Jesus' temptation experience as well.

Prayer Before Choosing His Apostles

Before Jesus selected His apostles, He prayed. The importance of the occasion is underscored by the extended period of Christ's praying—all night. He was about to select twelve men who would become some of the most significant in history.

PART 2

Chapter 7
Prayer in
the Life
and
Ministry
of Christ

One of those days Jesus went out to a mountainside to pray, and spent the night praying to God. When morning came, he called his disciples to him and chose twelve of them, whom he also designated apostles (Luke 6:12–13).

These men were to be foundation stones in the building of God (Eph. 2:20). They were to have their names inscribed in the foundation of the heavenly city (Rev. 21:14). Upon their shoulders would rest the formation and the future of His Church. They would not only share in His earthly ministry and be taught by Him personally but they would also be eyewitnesses of His death, burial, and resurrection. Beyond that, they would, almost to the last man, be called upon to forfeit their lives for the sake of their witness. The choices Jesus made would have eternal consequences. They had to be made with the counsel of heaven, not the counsel of earth (which too often uses the basis of outward appearance).

Although the content of Jesus' prayer is not recorded, we wonder if the gist of it might have been much like the prayer of the apostles after Judas' tragic failure: " 'Lord, you know everyone's heart. Show us which of these two you have chosen' " (Acts 1:24). The outcome was clear; the twelve were selected on the advice of heaven: "Simon [whom he named Peter], his brother Andrew, James, John, Philip, Bartholomew, Matthew, Thomas, James the son of Alphaeus, Simon who was called the Zealot, Judas son of James, and Judas Iscariot, who became a traitor" (Luke 6:14–16). It is doubtful, when scanning the pedigree of those chosen, that the same choices would have been made by one who had only an earthly viewpoint. Jesus' long and serious praying gave Him the divine perspective that enabled Him to make His appointments unaffected by worldly considerations.

Some may wonder how, after all night in prayer, Jesus could have chosen one who would so utterly fail as did Judas. Did not omniscient God know that Judas would fail? And since He knew he would fail, why did He permit him to be chosen? Assuredly God in His unfathomable wisdom

PART 2

Chapter 7
Prayer in
the Life
and
Ministry
of Christ

does not think and act as we humans might. He has said as much: " 'My thoughts are not your thoughts, neither are your ways my ways,' declares the LORD. 'As the heavens are higher than the earth, so are my ways higher than your ways and my thoughts than your thoughts' " (Isa. 55:8–9). Moreover, we need to remember that His choice does not do away with the exercise of human will, nor does His call guarantee against future rebellion and failure. That He foreknew Judas' fall is certain (Acts 1:20). That He calls people despite His foreknowledge of their rebellion and failure is clear. There can be no question that on another occasion He chose Saul, the son of Kish, to be Israel's king (1 Sam. 10:1); yet Saul rebelled, failed, and was rejected (1 Sam. 15:23).

Prayer for Little Children

The disciples felt that they knew how Jesus should spend His time, and to whom He should minister. Certainly, they reasoned, children should be far down on the agenda. So they rebuked the parents and the little ones for getting in the way. What emotional scars those children might have carried away if Jesus had not intervened on their behalf, touching them in a way they would remember as long as they lived.

Little children were brought to Jesus for him to place his hands on them and pray for them. But the disciples rebuked those who brought them. Jesus said, "Let the little children come to me, and do not hinder them, for the kingdom of heaven belongs to such as these." When he had placed his hands on them, he went on from there (Matt. 19:13–15).

Here we have not only a heartwarming scene of Jesus praying for little children who were brought to Him, but a beautiful precedent for all parents. As ambassadors of Jesus himself, parents and all who minister to children can love and bless these who are held in special care by God (cf. Matt. 18:5–6; Mark 9:42).

What kind of prayer did Jesus pray over the children? We are not told. We read only that "he placed his hands on them." And since the children were brought to Him "to place his hands on them and pray for them," it seems obvious that He did indeed pray. The custom of the time would indicate that the prayer was some form of blessing. It may well have been spontaneous, or it could have been the very benediction that Moses instructed Aaron and his sons to pronounce upon the children of Israel: " 'The LORD bless you and keep you; the LORD make his face shine upon you and be gracious to you; the LORD turn his face toward you and give you peace' " (Num. 6:24–26). How the lives of the children touched by Jesus on this occasion must have been affected! Is it too much to think that some of them may have become stalwarts in the Early Church?

PART 2

Chapter 7
**Prayer in
the Life
and
Ministry
of Christ**

Prayer on the Mount of Transfiguration

The praying of Jesus on the occasion of His transfiguration is of particular interest. By this time, the cross loomed large in the panorama of His earthly mission. His popularity with the crowd was waning, and He had already foretold His frightful prospect (cf. Luke 9:22). Shadows of a nighttime experience were beginning to deepen about Him.

Perhaps His climb up the mountain with the three disciples was not unlike that of Abraham's climb up Moriah, when he was divinely directed to offer his one and only son. Surely there was an uncommon and awesome atmosphere, with perhaps little conversation and none of the excitement that comes from ministering to multitudes. Yet they were on the threshold of experiencing the most unusual and remarkable prayer session they had ever attended. Never before nor since has there been such a prayer meeting on this earth.

As with several other singular occasions in the life of Jesus, no written record reveals the content of the prayer. Gibson speculates:

[M]ay we not with reverence suppose that on that lonely hilltop, as later in the Garden, there might be in His heart the cry, 'Father, if it be possible'? If only the way upward were open now! Has not the kingdom of God been preached in Judaea, in Samaria, in Galilee, away to the very borderlands? and has not the Church been founded? and has not authority been given to the apostles? Is it, then, absolutely necessary to go back, back to Jerusalem,

PART 2

**Chapter 7
Prayer in
the Life
and
Ministry
of Christ**

not to gain a triumph, but to accept the last humiliation and defeat?[1]

Transfiguration

Jesus went up the mountain not to commune with Moses and Elijah, though He did talk with them about his departure (literally His "exodus," His death, resurrection, and ascension). His real purpose was to speak with His Father that He might draw divine strength into His own spirit. The transfiguration prayer of Jesus had a lasting impact on His three disciples. Never again would they be the same. When John the Beloved declared, "We have seen his glory, the glory of the One and Only, who came from the Father, full of grace and truth" (John 1:14), he was, at least in a measure, making reference to that unforgettable hour on the mount. Peter likewise declared the profound effect of the experience on him when he wrote: "He received honor and glory from God the Father when the voice came to him from the Majestic Glory, saying, 'This is my Son, whom I love; with him I am well pleased.' We ourselves heard this voice that came from heaven when we were with him on the sacred mountain" (2 Pet. 1:17–18). Even beyond its deep influence on the three disciples, that prayer experience has cast its awe-inspiring rays upon Christian pilgrims from that day until this.

Prayer for Peter

The prayer Jesus prayed for Peter (Luke 22:32) should encourage every believer, no matter how weak or flawed one may feel. As we wrestle against evil and spiritual wickedness, often in our own desires and lusts, the possibility of spiritual victory seems remote and unlikely. But Jesus knows the strength of the test and will not permit it to overwhelm us (1 Cor. 10:13). He told Peter of His faithful support (calling him Simon rather than Peter, for he was hardly a rock when in his own strength he tried to stand against Satan): " 'Simon, Simon, Satan has asked to sift you as wheat. But I have prayed for you, Simon, that

*spiritual
war*

---

[1]John Monro Gibson, *The Gospel of St. Matthew* (London: Hodder and Stoughton, 1900), 236.

your faith may not fail. And when you have turned back, strengthen your brothers' " (Luke 22:31–32).

The occasion of the Master's praying was the impending failure, so frightening and tragic, of one of the three in His inner circle. Jesus knew exactly what lay ahead, though Peter himself could not even fathom the possibility. He replied, 'Lord, I am ready to go with you to prison and to death' " (Luke 22:33). Not only was he naive, oblivious to his weakness, he was also unaware that there was one seeking to devour him. Nor did he have the faintest notion of how God, in His pure wisdom, allows Satan to place His servants in the sieve of testing, for their own ultimate good. Satan had, no doubt, obtained permission to do this very thing, hoping to bring about the downfall of one of Christ's chosen (Luke 22:31; see also Job 1:6–12; 2:3–7). But though Peter was about to fail miserably, Christ would not forsake him. Though His words to Peter were a blunt prediction of failure, they were spoken from a compassionate heart that was determined to bring Peter through to victory.

There is in Peter's experience a sobering lesson for every believer. All are in some way vulnerable to enemy ambush. None dare think for a moment of being above failure. The possibilities for and propensities to evil are enormous—error, unbelief, pride, vanity, selfishness, self-centeredness, worldliness, intemperance, impurity, and all the sins of the spirit. Regeneration is not a guarantee against Satan's attack and devices. Yet what encouragement, comfort, and consolation spring from Jesus' word to Peter: "I have prayed for you." If Jesus would pray for Peter, is there any reason to believe He will not do the same for all who follow Him? "He always lives to intercede for them" (Heb. 7:25).

Jesus' prayer for Peter deserves careful study. It is significant that He did not ask the Father to let Peter escape Satan's sifting, or that he would never fail. If the Great Intercessor relieved us of all moral responsibility, guaranteeing that we would never fall, we would be mere puppets, bringing no pleasure to our Creator. Though we are utterly weak in the flesh, we must learn, even though it be through our failure, that there are resources available to us. What we must do for ourselves, God will not do for us. The Scriptures show the way. " 'Watch and pray so that

PART 2

Chapter 7
Prayer in
the Life
and
Ministry
of Christ

PART 2

Chapter 7
Prayer in
the Life
and
Ministry
of Christ

you will not fall into temptation. The spirit is willing, but the body is weak' " (Matt. 26:41). "If by the Spirit you put to death the misdeeds of the body, you will live" (Rom. 8:13). "Live by the Spirit, and you will not gratify the desires of the sinful nature" (Gal. 5:16). Jesus' prayer for Peter was brief and simple, yet heartening: "that your faith may not fail."

What a person does immediately after failure bears heavily on his ultimate direction. Then it is that the mettle of a person is tested to the limit and the true condition of the heart is revealed. When we see ourselves for what we are, we are tempted to lose faith in ourselves as well as God. Consequently, the all-compelling concern of Jesus was not Peter's immediate failure, but its possible fruit. Failure in testing can lead to failure of faith, which in turn can lead to the ultimate disaster, as was the case with Judas (Matt. 27:3–5). One might question why Jesus did not pray for Judas as He did for Peter. Could it be that God, whose view penetrates the depths of the human heart, saw in Judas a heart sold-out to the Satanic purpose, while in Peter, though he too failed, He saw a heart desiring to fulfill the divine will? Whether we can fully comprehend Jesus' reason, we can rest assured that He prayed according to what He knew was His Father's will.

There can be little doubt that Peter's faith was tested to the limit. Had he not boldly denied his Lord? Had he not been the ultimate traitor? Had he not done with vengeance what he had so brashly announced he would never do? Indeed he had, and without doubt Satan sought to capitalize on it. Yet Jesus had said, "I have prayed for you, that your faith may not fail." Possibly that prayer became its own answer, for it is not difficult to imagine Peter, adrift in despair, suddenly remembering the very words of His Lord, whom he had disgraced. They must have rung in his heart. They were words of faith to him, turning on again the light of hope in his soul.

The outcome of this prayer of Jesus cannot be measured. Peter's restoration was complete. His faith did not fail. He was not destroyed; instead, he went on to fill his high apostolic office with distinction and to strengthen his brothers, as his Master had directed.

Prayer at Lazarus' Tomb

PART 2

**Chapter 7
Prayer in
the Life
and
Ministry
of Christ**

In the raising of Lazarus from the dead, one of Christ's greatest miracles, we find a manner of prayer different from that accompanying any other of His miracles. The Jews were unable to deny the reality of His miracles, so they ascribed them to the power of the devil. But by praying to the God of heaven, addressing Him as Father, Jesus boldly proclaimed that His miracles were performed by power from above. "Jesus lifted up His eyes and said, 'Father, I thank You that You have heard Me. And I know that You always hear Me, but because of the people who are standing by I said this, that they may believe that You sent Me'" (John 11:41–42, NKJV). Public prayer need not be profound and lengthy if private prayer has been made in advance. Jesus had known for possibly four days (John 11:39) that Lazarus was dead. Much of the intervening time was no doubt occupied with prayer, especially the night hours. Jesus' use of the past tense ("I thank you that you *have heard* me") indicates that before the public prayer was ever uttered, private prayer had been made—and answered. There was no shade of doubt in Jesus' mind.

Martha felt certain that the normal process of decay was already far advanced in the body of her brother. But there is no confirmation that such a stench had permeated the sepulchre. Is it possible that the process of putrefaction had been halted through the earlier private prayer and that the body was awaiting the moment of the public miracle?

The confident testimony of Jesus, "I know that you always hear me," affirms that the prayers He prayed were submissive to the divine eternal will. So He could say later, "'If you remain in me and my words remain in you, ask whatever you wish, and it will be given you'" (John 15:7). In other words, if your desires are submissive to the divine purpose, there is nothing, either material or spiritual, that God is not prepared to give. This is the key to receiving answers to our prayers. We must pray in private until we know that our requests are in harmony with the divine will. This truth sheds meaningful light on the questions of prayer and the human nature of Christ. When we understand the principle of harmony between our requests and

PART 2

Chapter 7
Prayer in
the Life
and
Ministry
of Christ

submission to the eternal will and purpose of God (as Jesus most perfectly demonstrated), the place of prayer in the life of Christ and in our own spiritual life is clearly seen.

"I know that you always hear me" beautifully portrays the divine communion between the Father and the Son. Indeed there is never an impediment to the perfect alignment of their will and purpose. Even His cry on the cross, "Why have you forsaken me?" was an expression to fulfill the entire Psalm 22. No satanic effort can ever short-circuit that eternal relationship of "God the One and Only, who is at the Father's side" (John 1:18). As the Father heard the Son always, even during His earthly mission, so we can be certain He hears Him now, as He is seated at the Father's own right hand in heaven. What confidence then is ours that His intercessions avail for the petitions we place in His hand, for Him the Father hears always.

Jesus looked up to heaven, invoking the supreme God before the disbelieving Jews, so that they might know it was divine power, not satanic counterfeit, that was working a miracle. In addressing the Father, Jesus sought to increase the faith of the multitude in the power of the Most High God. The result of Jesus' prayer was immediate and, no doubt, utterly shocking to all present, for before their incredulous eyes stood a man who had been dead and in the grave four days. Especially noteworthy is the fact that at the tomb Jesus did not pray for Lazarus to be raised to life. He had done that earlier, and when He arrived at the grave site, there was not even a vestige of doubt in His heart. His prayer was only thanksgiving. How glorious for the child of God is that experience of absolute assurance born in prayer, nurtured in thanksgiving, and brought to fulfillment at the strategic moment.

Not only was Lazarus raised, but a greater concern of Jesus was fulfilled: " 'That they may believe that you sent me' " (John 11:42). Just a few verses later, John records, "Therefore many of the Jews who had come to visit Mary, and had seen what Jesus did, put their faith in him" (John 11:45). Nevertheless, the outcome of answered prayer sometimes has negative aspects since not everyone has faith; such people often view the outcome through a different set of eyes:

Some of them went to the Pharisees and told them what Jesus had done. Then the chief priests and the Pharisees called a meeting of the Sanhedrin. "What are we accomplishing?" they asked. "Here is this man performing many miraculous signs. If we let him go on like this, everyone will believe in him, and then the Romans will come and take away both our place and our nation" (John 11:46–48).

Those who pray are well advised to keep in mind this frequent response of skeptics and workers of evil.

PART 2

Chapter 7
Prayer in
the Life
and
Ministry
of Christ

Prayer for Himself and All Believers

An aspiring pianist once desired to take lessons from the great master, Paderewski. Although he was enrolled as a pupil, the chief lesson he received was the privilege of watching and listening to the great pianist practice. This inspired him to practice. In John 17, we are privileged to listen in on "the true Lord's prayer." In what more meaningful way could we gain some of the most profitable lessons in the art of prayer, lessons that can inspire us to pray?

The occasion of Christ's high priestly prayer (John 17) is not recorded. However, some possibilities have been suggested by various expositors. Some feel that Christ concluded the solemn time of the Last Supper (at the Passover meal) with the prayer. Others speculate that the prayer was voiced in some area of the temple as Jesus and His disciples stopped there. No matter what the occasion may have been, the prayer is one of the most significant of Holy Scripture. It was only a matter of hours until Jesus would give His life as a ransom for many.

"Father, the time has come. Glorify your Son, that your Son may glorify you. . . . I have brought you glory on earth by completing the work you gave me to do. And now, Father, glorify me in your presence with the glory I had with you before the world began. . . .

"I have revealed you to those whom you gave me out of the world. They were yours; you gave them to me and they have obeyed your word. . . . I pray for them. I am not praying for the world, but for those you have given me, for they are yours. All I have is yours, and all you have is mine. And glory has come to

PART 2

Chapter 7
Prayer in
the Life
and
Ministry
of Christ

me through them. I will remain in the world no longer, but they are still in the world, and I am coming to you. Holy Father, protect them by the power of your name—the name you gave me—so that they may be one as we are one. While I was with them, I protected them and kept them safe by that name you gave me....

"I am coming to you now, but I say these things while I am still in the world, so that they may have the full measure of my joy within them. I have given them your word and the world has hated them, for they are not of the world any more than I am of the world. My prayer is not that you take them out of the world but that you protect them from the evil one. They are not of the world, even as I am not of it. Sanctify them by the truth; your word is truth. As you sent me into the world, I have sent them into the world. For them I sanctify myself, that they too may be truly sanctified....

"My prayer is not for them alone. I pray also for those who will believe in me through their message, that all of them may be one, Father, just as you are in me and I am in you. May they also be in us so that the world may believe that you have sent me. I have given them the glory that you gave me, that they may be one as we are one: I in them and you in me. May they be brought to complete unity to let the world know that you sent me and have loved them even as you have loved me.

"Father, I want those you have given me to be with me where I am, and to see my glory, the glory you have given me because you loved me before the creation of the world.

"Righteous Father, though the world does not know you, I know you, and they know that you have sent me. I have made you known to them, and will continue to make you known in order that the love you have for me may be in them and that I myself may be in them" (John 17:1,4–6,9–26).

J. C. Macaulay calls this prayer "the *sanctum sanctorum* of Holy Scripture."[2] We, like the disciples, listen in on intimate communion between the Father and the Son just before the offering of the divine sacrifice for our salvation. It almost seems irreverent to analyze such a prayer, but it

---

[2]J. C. Macaulay, *Devotional Studies in St. John's Gospel* (Grand Rapids: Wm. B. Eerdmans Pub. Co., 1945), 209.

is only as we dwell on the content of the prayer that we appreciate its full meaning. We come to it as worshipers, not as grammarians or lexicographers dissecting each inflection.

As the Master prays, three primary concerns occupy His mind: (1) His own glorification (vv. 1–5), (2) His immediate apostolic group (vv. 6–19), and (3) the many believers yet to come (vv. 20–26).

Jesus' central concern and all-encompassing plea in the first section of the prayer (vv. 1–5) is His own glorification. He anticipates the restoration of a condition known to Him "before the world began" (v. 5) but laid aside during His pilgrimage on this earth.

"Glorify" comes from the Greek *doxazō*, which means "to praise," "honor," "magnify," or "clothe in splendor." Our Lord himself provided an insight into the profound depths of His plea for glorification when He prayed, "Glorify me in your presence with the glory I had with you" (17:5). Although the word "glory" has numerous facets, or shades of meaning, and various applications, depending on its setting, Jesus applied it here to the glory He shared with – *one* the Father. Consider also Paul's vivid portrayal of Jesus' condescension (Phil. 2:5–8) or deglorification, whereby, in some incomprehensible way, Jesus laid aside His glory in behalf of His mission of redemption. By the time of this prayer, even though His passion was yet ahead, Christ considered His mission already accomplished. He was anticipating that highest of expectations—His reglorification and return to the Father's throne, where He remains as the God-Man in heaven.

Not to be overlooked is the necessity of His glorification. His longing for His original state was not mere selfish desire. Just as His deglorification was essential for the salvation of the world, so His reglorification was essential to the welfare of His body, the Church. According to John, the glorification of Jesus had to precede the sending of the Holy Spirit as Comforter, or Helper. "Up to that time the Spirit had not been given, since Jesus had not yet been glorified" (John 7:39).

Should we, like Jesus, pray for glorification? J. C. Macaulay observed, "Such a request would be altogether inap-

PART 2

**Chapter 7
Prayer in
the Life
and
Ministry
of Christ**

PART 2

Chapter 7
Prayer in
the Life
and
Ministry
of Christ

propriate and irrelevant on our lips, in any circumstances."[3]
Yet we wonder if in some sense such a prayer might be
acceptable, for it seems that Paul had the glorification of
human creatures in focus when he wrote:

> The creation itself will be liberated from its bondage to decay
> and brought into the glorious freedom of the children of God.
> We know that the whole creation has been groaning as in the
> pains of childbirth right up to the present time. Not only so, but
> we ourselves, who have the firstfruits of the Spirit, groan inwardly
> as we wait eagerly for our adoption as sons, the redemption of
> our bodies (Rom. 8:21–23).

Paul also says, "Just as we have borne the likeness of the
earthly man, so shall we bear the likeness of the man from
heaven" (1 Cor. 15:49). This does not suggest, even re-
motely, that believers will be glorified as Jesus was when
He returned to His exalted position as very God in heaven.
Nor should we pray for such glorification; yet it suggests
that we might well pray to bear His likeness now and that
we will experience an ongoing glorification throughout
eternity (cf. Phil. 3:21).

The second section of the prayer (vv. 6–19) may be
described as a prayer for preservation. First, Jesus recounts
the process by which His closest followers were brought
into an intimate holy relationship. " 'They have obeyed
your word' " (v. 6); " 'I gave them the words you gave me
and they accepted them' " (v. 8); and " 'they believed that
you sent me' " (v. 8). The lesson is obvious. Those who
desire the highest revelation and insight into the divine
realm have a role to play themselves. They must accept
and obey His Word, and they must believe in the One who
has given the Word.

The focus of this prayer was not the world, but the
disciples: " 'I am not praying for the world, but for those
you have given me' " (v. 9). We could clarify the meaning
by simply inserting "now" into the text: "I am not praying
[now] for the world." His intercession at this time was
pinpointing those who were already given to Him and had

---

[3]Ibid., 210.

chosen to believe on Him. What a great consolation for every true believer.

A famous race horse of years ago was considered the most valuable horse in the country. His keeper loudly proclaimed his virtues, letting it be known that not even for a minute, day or night, was the horse without a human eye watching him. To the Lord we are far more valuable, for we have eternal value. His eye is always on His children. Christ's central concern was the keeping of His own after His departure. The work He had begun in and through them had to continue. Paul also reflected similar concern for his immediate followers (see Acts 20:25–32). Spiritual leaders must always show a concern for those they have touched for Christ, though they may be separated by great distances. The means of the keeping is shown in the petition, "Protect them by the power of your name" (17:11). Jesus had been protecting them—even when they thought they were protecting Him.

Now, when that fortress was removed, they would feel the ringing blows of their real adversary. And yet the words of life were alive in them. And these precious powerful words and the transferred guardianship back to the Father would deliver Jesus' ragged and frightened little expeditionary force through the D-day of spiritual warfare and muster them into a vast and willing army of powerful spiritual warriors that would rock the world![4]

Verses 12–15 are a plea that the Father would continue what the Son had begun: I have kept them; now You keep them. " 'While I was with them, I protected them and kept them safe by that name you gave me.... My prayer is not that you take them out of the world but that you protect them from the evil one' " (vv. 12,15). Here is great encouragement for every believer. All who desire to be kept will be kept. So also those who deliberately choose not to be kept will not be kept. The "one doomed to destruction" (v. 12), Judas, was not so by divine determination, but by the direction of his own will. "God, we infer, could have brought about God's purposes without the sacrifice of

PART 2

**Chapter 7
Prayer in
the Life
and
Ministry
of Christ**

---

[4]William David Spencer and Aida Besançon Spencer, *The Prayer Life of Jesus* (Lanham, Md.: University Press of America, Inc., 1990), 188.

PART 2

Chapter 7
Prayer in
the Life
and
Ministry
of Christ

Judas. Judas, Caiaphas, Pilate, the crowds—and we, no doubt, if we had been there—however, lent willing hands."[5]

Escaping from the problems of life was not in Jesus' mind, though it does at times plague the minds of His followers. How much better we think it would be to flee than to fight. How much better the glorious new world than this troublesome old world. Paul described the dilemma well: "I am torn between the two: I desire to depart and be with Christ, which is better by far; but it is more necessary for you that I remain in the body" (Phil. 1:23–24). Likewise, while the world with its animosity and evil is a dark threat, the believer is the means necessary for dispelling that darkness. For this reason, Jesus' prayer is a pattern for our daily prayer.

The third concern of Jesus included us (vv. 20–26). He was interested in those far beyond His immediate circumstance, in fact, to the very end of the Church Age: " 'for those who will believe in me through their [the disciples'] message' " (v. 20). Whether we are aware of it, that prayer reaches all the way to each of us present-day believers. Our prayers are usually confined to the present, or at best, to our lifetime. The lesson here is that we might enlarge the vision of our praying, reaching beyond our generation and encompassing all believers, to the end of the age. Ray C. Stedman expresses his concern "how to convey something of the gripping reality of the requests of Jesus—something of the intense practicality of what Jesus is saying. I am so afraid that we will listen to these words as we would to beautiful poetry or a moving drama, and entranced by their familiarity and beauty, fail to realize that Jesus is actually praying for us here—for what he prays for his disciples he prays for us."[6]

The scope of the intercession now enlarges. Although earlier in His prayer Jesus declared he was not praying for the world (v. 9), He here definitely concerns himself with the world: " 'that the world may believe that you have sent me' " (v. 21). Although Christ's intercession is primarily

---

[5]Ibid., 192.

[6]Ray C. Stedman, *Jesus Teaches on Prayer* (Waco, Tex.: Word Books, 1975), 159.

for believers, it recognizes that sinners become believers through faith in the divine Son of God and His redemptive work.

PART 2

**Chapter 7
Prayer in
the Life
and
Ministry
of Christ**

To comprehend the glory of the Son is to understand the very essence of the unity of Father and Son: " 'the glory that you gave me' " (v. 22). Glory may be defined as the manifestation of the nature, character, and being of God. It is reflected in God's image. Jesus understood that the glory which made Him and the Father one would also make His followers one in fellowship with the triune God and with each other. "[We all] are being transformed into his likeness with ever-increasing glory" (2 Cor. 3:18). Can the believer pray any greater prayer than to ask that the image and glory of God be formed in himself and in all members of Christ's body? Surely there is no more powerful means for gaining the eye and ear of an unbelieving world than for God's image to be fully reflected in His children.

Inherent in God's nature is His supreme love. When demonstrated in believers, that love, Jesus realized, would convince the world that God had indeed sent His Son as an expression of His love. Here is the unparalleled means to world evangelism—the love of God manifested in believers, between believers, and through believers. Carrying God's love to the sinner should be the prayer concern of every believer, even as it was of Jesus.

Prayer in Gethsemane

Preceding His arrest, Jesus went with His disciples to Gethsemane. On this occasion of the overwhelming agony of our Lord, the inner circle of disciples—Peter, James, and John—failed the Master miserably. Not only did they miss the significance of the hour and the great test Jesus was facing, but they also failed to prepare themselves for the testing that was yet ahead for them.

Going a little farther, he fell with his face to the ground and prayed, "My Father, if it is possible, may this cup be taken from me. Yet not as I will, but as you will." Then he returned to his disciples and found them sleeping. "Could you men not keep watch with me for one hour?" he asked Peter. "Watch and pray so that you will not fall into temptation. The spirit is willing, but the body is weak." He went away a second time and prayed, "My Father, if it is not possible for this cup to be taken away unless I drink it, may your will be done." When he came back, he again found them sleeping, because their eyes were heavy. So he left them and went away once more and prayed the third time, saying the same thing (Matt. 26:39–44).

Never has there been a prayer time to match this one. Though the most committed of His disciples were nearby, Jesus had to carry His burden alone to the Father. It was night. The very atmosphere was heavy with foreboding. Mark records that He "began to be deeply distressed and troubled. 'My soul is overwhelmed with sorrow to the point of death'" (Mark 14:34). "Deeply distressed," "troubled," "overwhelmed with sorrow"—what an awful hour for Jesus! What could have reduced the One who had "authority to lay [His life] down, and . . . take it up again" (John 10:18) to such an unfathomable distress? What could cause Him to pray as He did that dreadful night? In Jesus' own words, it was "this cup" (Matt. 26:39,42; Mark 14:36; Luke 22:20,42). We can only surmise what made that cup so frightful. Surely it was not simply the prospect of His physical death; if that were so, many of His followers faced death with greater courage. Furthermore, He had come into the world to die.

The strong implication is that the cup was full of iniquity: the sins and guilt of the world. All the horrible sins of humanity were in that cup. What was happening there was likely foreshadowed in Leviticus:

[Aaron] is to lay both hands on the head of the live goat and confess over it all the wickedness and rebellion of the Israelites—all their sins—and put them on the goat's head. He shall send the goat away into the desert in the care of a man appointed for the task. The goat will carry on itself all their sins to a solitary place; and the man shall release it in the desert (Lev. 16:21–22).

As He faced Calvary, the Son of God was confronted with the indescribable prospect of becoming the Scapegoat for all sinners, past, present, and future. There, too, Isaiah's prophetic insight found its fulfillment: "The LORD has laid on him the iniquity of us all" (Isa. 53:6). Little wonder, then, that the horror-filled prospect and the tortured praying caused blood to spring from the Savior's pores (Luke 22:44).

The contents of Jesus' three successive prayers on this historic occasion are almost identical. Note the similarity by Matthew, Mark, and Luke:

First Prayer: " 'My Father, if it is possible, may this cup be taken from me. Yet not as I will, but as you will' " (Matt. 26:39). " 'Abba, Father,' he said, 'everything is possible for you. Take this cup from me. Yet not what I will, but what you will' " (Mark 14:36). " 'Father, if you are willing, take this cup from me; yet not my will, but yours be done' " (Luke 22:42).

Second Prayer: "He went away a second time and prayed, 'My Father, if it is not possible for this cup to be taken away unless I drink it, may your will be done' " (Matt. 26:42). "Once more he went away and prayed the same thing" (Mark 14:39).

Third Prayer: "So he left them and went away once more and prayed the third time, saying the same thing" (Matt. 26:44).

It is noteworthy that only on this occasion did Jesus address God as He did here: "My Father" (in Matt.) or "Abba Father" (in Mark). One cannot help but feel the anguished appeal of Jesus' soul as He calls upon the only Source of help for Him. But Jesus qualified his request with, " 'If it is possible. . . .' " (Matt. 26:39).

With God all things are possible. But it was not possible to take away that cup of woe if men were to be saved. . . . God will not always take the cup of suffering from us. It may be necessary that we should suffer, for our own good or for the good of others; our sufferings may be contained in God's eternal purpose. Yet we pray for their removal. . . . Only we must pray all the Lord's prayer, not part only. . . . "Not as I will, but as thou wilt."[7]

What was the outcome of Jesus' unprecedented prayer? The author of Hebrews tells us: "He was heard because of

---

[7]H. D. M. Spence and Joseph S. Exell, eds., *The Pulpit Commentary* (Grand Rapids: Wm. B. Eerdmans Pub. Co., 1950), vol. 15, *Matthew,* by A. Lukyn and B. C. Caffin, 543.

PART 2

Chapter 7
Prayer in
the Life
and
Ministry
of Christ

his reverent submission. Although he was a son, he learned obedience from what he suffered and, once made perfect, he became the source of eternal salvation for all who obey him" (Heb. 5:7–9).

Luke provides a further aspect of the event: "An angel from heaven appeared to him and strengthened him" (Luke 22:43). Although there was no way for both the cup to be taken away and the will of God to be accomplished, there was a way for the cup to be borne so the will of God could be done. It is still the same for us today.

Prayer on the Cross

Only two brief prayers issued from Jesus during the horrible ordeal on the cross. In the first we see utter distress over what appeared to the *man* Christ Jesus to be total abandonment by God; in the second we see His declaration of total abandonment to God.

The first prayer on the cross came near the end of the crucifixion: "'*Ēlōi, Ēlōi, lama sabachthani?*'—which means, 'My God, my God, why have you forsaken me?'" (Mark 15:34; see also Matt. 27:46). Experiencing an awful darkness, an almost unbearable physical agony, and a sense of total aloneness, Jesus cried out; in all likelihood, everyone at the scene heard Him. We wonder if those who heard Him ever forgot that anguished cry. For certain, the heart of God must have been torn at that pleading utterance. Yet, to complete redemption's plan the Father had to allow His Son to pass through those dreadful moments. There may still be times when God's servants sense a similar loneliness, if Paul's experience is any indication (see Phil. 3:10).

The prayer, though only a short sentence, provokes the most sober thinking. Had God really forsaken Him? Does God ever forsake His own? Though the Father could not embrace the sin and iniquity His Son bore in our behalf, He still loved His Son. The one who can so call upon God has God with him even when he feels abandoned. The Father responds to the faintest cry or to the most desperate plea. Only the one who cares not that he may be abandoned is truly alone.

PART 2

Chapter 7
Prayer in
the Life
and
Ministry
of Christ

His cry, which quotes Psalm 22:1 in the Aramaic, was also a way of His claiming Psalm 22 as an expression of his suffering on the cross. The psalm should be read with this in mind.

His prayer of desperation was heard (see Heb. 5:7). The awful agony of feeling abandoned was short-lived. It lasted only as long as the purpose of God required. When moments of deep distress visit us, we must remember: God does hear.

The second prayer on the cross was also very brief: " 'Father, into your hands I commit my spirit' " (Luke 23:46). Having prayed those words, Jesus breathed His last. Here is a prayer that few will ever pray, although some have. John Huss, taunted by his enemies as he made his way to be burned at the stake, spoke out with sure faith and theological accuracy: "I commit my spirit into thy hand, O Lord Jesus Christ, who has redeemed me." Although we may never at the point of death find occasion to pray these same words, we may make the commitment of our lives every day that we serve Him.

Questions for Study

1. What reasons did Jesus have for praying regularly?

2. What does Jesus' prayer for Peter teach us about His intercession for us?

3. What does Jesus' prayer at Lazarus' tomb teach us about the relation between public and private prayer?

4. What aspects of Jesus' prayer in John 17 can we apply in our own praying?

5. What was in the cup that Jesus spoke about in His prayer in Gethsemane?

6. Does God ever really abandon or forsake His own?

— *Chapter Eight* —

CHRIST'S TEACHING ON PRAYER

No more meaningful and insightful instructions on prayer can be discovered than those set forth by that One who prayed so effectively, and with such assurance, that He could say, " 'Father, . . . I know that You always hear Me' " (John 11:41–42, NKJV). It is far more important to learn to pray, however, than to learn about prayer. Learning about prayer will be of consequence only if that learning equips us to pray better.

In His teaching on heaven, Jesus told His disciples that they knew how to get to where He was going. Thomas, however, said he didn't even know where Jesus was going, much less the way to get there. Jesus answered him, " 'I am the way. . . . No one comes to the Father except through me' " (John 14:6). No more direct statement about access to God can be found in the teaching of Jesus. This applies not only to salvation but also to prayer, for Jesus alone is "the new and living way" by whom we enter the Most Holy Place (Heb. 10:19–20). This truth is absolute. No one can approach God through any other name, or by any other means. "There is one God and one mediator between God and men, the man Christ Jesus" (1 Tim. 2:5). The liberal (antisupernatural) theologians and philosophers of our world would have us believe that such a view is too narrow

PART 2

**Chapter 8
Christ's
Teaching
on Prayer**

and bigoted. But we must bow to a final court of appeals, the Holy Scriptures.

When we offer prayer in Jesus' name, we must do more than simply attach, especially in a formal or rote manner, the phrase "in Jesus' name." When Jesus talked about asking in His name (John 14:13), He meant more than saying the right words. Since in the Bible the name represents the person and the person's character and nature, when we pray in Jesus' name we must pray in conformity with His person, nature, and will. We must also recognize who He is, submit to His authority, and put complete faith in him. Our desire as we pray, then, will always be to bring glory to both Jesus and the Father (cf. Acts 3:16; 4:30; Rom. 15:6). Further, by praying in Jesus' name we acknowledge that Jesus is our only hope for access to God. Sinful people cannot have access on their own to a holy God. If they were to approach God directly, they would be consumed, for " 'God is a consuming Fire' " (Heb. 12:29). For this reason, Old Testament people never entered the Most Holy Place (see chapter 2). Their only access was by way of the high priest, who was permitted entrance only once each year, and that not without blood (cf. Heb. 9:7–8). Under the new covenant, Jesus is the eternal High Priest with constant and permanent access accomplished by the offering of His own blood (Heb. 9:11–12). We have access to God only because of Christ; in Christ our sin has been removed, and through Him—and through Him alone—we approach God.

BELIEVERS

| *By* the Spirit's Enablement (Rom. 8:26–27) | COME | *Through* Jesus the Only Mediator (1 Tim. 2:5) (John 14:6) | TO | The Father |

Consider now the protocol of prayer. Though the Father, the Son, and the Holy Spirit are One, prayer, according to Scripture, should be addressed to the Father. At the same time, the Father, who considers the condition of the heart more than the correctness of the words, surely does not reject prayer for lack of exact protocol. It is not uncommon for believers to address Jesus or the Holy Spirit in their prayers. Even so, the pattern of prayer should be understood as set forth in Scripture (see diagram on p. 208).

Receiving What We Ask For

Jesus gave instructions on how we can receive what we ask for in prayer: " 'If you remain in me and my words remain in you, ask whatever you wish, and it will be given you' " (John 15:7). What does it mean to "remain ["abide," KJV] in" Christ? In what way can the words of Christ remain, or dwell, in us? We must know the answer to these questions if we are to see the fulfillment of Christ's promise of having what we ask for. John 15:1–11 is perhaps the most comprehensive promise of receiving answers to prayer: "Ask whatever you wish, and it will be given you." But there are conditions. There is a key that must be used to achieve such certainty in answered prayer: "If you remain in me and my words remain in you."

"Remain" is the word of greatest consequence in John 15:7. It is derived from the Greek *menō* and means "to stay" (in a given place, state, or relationship). As used here, it speaks of a relationship between the believer and Christ himself—a union, a oneness, a *koinōnia* (fellowship, sharing, partnership) or being entwined together—in a mystical yet very real fellowship or partnership. That is the condition necessary for a believer to experience this unlimited asking and receiving. Yet the remaining must be more than "staying in Christ." The qualifications are twofold: "If you remain in me *and* my words remain in you." It must also include allowing His words to remain in us. The two are a balanced pair. This should be the Christian norm—the believer remaining in Christ and Christ's Word remaining in the believer. Each complements and enables the other. The "words" mentioned here include more than the words spoken by Jesus, heard by those who followed Him, and recorded almost exclusively in the Gospels. They include the entire Word of God, all of Holy Scripture, given to us by divine inspiration (2 Tim. 3:16). Believers who desire to measure up to the divine intention for their lives must be so saturated by the Word of God that it becomes a veritable part of them, and remains in them. This is possible only through the rigid discipline of living in the Word. Such a discipline does not just happen; it comes from a fixed decision to make it happen.

The prospect of receiving anything we ask for is most appealing, but the temptation is to divorce the promise from the conditions. Human nature likes the ring of the promise: "Ask whatever you wish and it will be given you"; yet it is wishful thinking to suppose that the promise is valid apart from the stated requirements.

The believer in Christ, full of His words, evermore consciously realizing union with Christ, charged with the thoughts, burning with the purposes, filled with words of Jesus, will have no will that is not in harmony with the Divine will. Then faith is possible in the fulfilment of his own desire, and prayer becomes a prophecy and pledge of the answer.... This is the true philosophy of prayer."[1]

Jesus explained that one prayer that would always be answered is the sincere request for the gift of the Holy Spirit. The Holy Spirit is present in the world to convict and convince the sinner and to bring the new birth when a person believes. He then is resident in the believer as "Counselor" (Comforter, Paraclete, Helper; John 14:16), and as witness to the believer's salvation (Rom. 8:16). Then it is important for the believer to ask for the promise of the Father, the gift of the Spirit to provide power for effective witnessing (Acts 1:4,8; 2:4).[2]

But Satan is a master deceiver. He does all within his power to prevent people from partaking of God's blessings and provisions. So it is that he seeks to keep believers from our chief Helper, the Holy Spirit. Using his effective tool of fear, Satan suggests to the earnest seeker of the Holy Spirit, *You may receive a demon, or you may receive a counterfeit, or you may be victim of an inflamed imag-*

[1]H. D. M. Spence and Joseph S. Exell, eds., *The Pulpit Commentary* (Grand Rapids: Wm. B. Eerdmans Pub. Co., 1950), vol. 2, *John,* by H. R. Reynolds, 243.

[2]Stanley M. Horton, *What the Bible Says About the Holy Spirit* (Springfield, Mo.: Gospel Publishing House, 1976), 137–139, 258–259.

ination. For all who are plagued in this way, Jesus has an answer:

*Father
Child
relationship.*

"Which of you fathers, if your son asks for a fish, will give him a snake instead? Or if he asks for an egg, will give him a scorpion? If you then, though you are evil, know how to give good gifts to your children, how much more will your Father in heaven give the Holy Spirit to them who ask him!" (Luke 11:11-13; cf. Matt. 7:11).

Jesus underscores the integrity of God the Father by a simple comparison with the way an earthly parent treats his child. The son, making request of his father, does not receive instead some wholly unacceptable substitute, some fearsome counterfeit, like a snake instead of a requested fish or a scorpion instead of the requested egg. If earthly fathers—who are evil in comparison with God's holiness and goodness—know how to give good gifts, how much greater is our confidence that God will grant our childlike petition for the fullness of the Holy Spirit! We can rest assured that He who is the epitome of good, especially when measured against His fallen creatures, will " 'much more . . . give the Holy Spirit to those who ask him' " (11:13).

Therefore, it is both the privilege and duty of all believers to petition the Father to give them the Holy Spirit, and then to rest in the assurance that when they so pray out of sincere hearts, there will be no deception on God's part. They will receive what they desire and request.

Another promise of Jesus concerning answered prayer seems at first glance to assure our receiving anything we ask for. " 'Again, I tell you that if two of you on earth agree about anything you ask for, it will be done for you by my Father in heaven' " (Matt. 18:19).

The spiritual force of symphonizing, or harmonizing, human spirits is incomprehensible. "Agree," as our Lord employed it here, is from the Greek *sumphōneō,* "to fit with," "match with," "be in harmony," "be of one mind," which in turn comes from *sumphōnos,* "harmonious," "sounding together in harmony," "agreeing." In the divine economy there is a release of power from agreement between as few as two, the lowest possible number needed for agreement. In the natural world we calculate that two of similar strength can exert twice the force of one: Two horses can pull twice the load of one, two tons of dynamite can exert twice the explosive force of a single ton. Yet even in the physical world there are evidences of a disproportionate increase in accomplishment through a special kind of agreement. For example, a study of group dynamics shows that ten minds working in agreement on a given project produce far more results than the same ten minds working separately on the same project. Scripture recognizes the same principle when it observes how one can "chase a thousand," but two can "put ten thousand to flight" (Deut. 32:30). Even though one believer with the Lord's help can chase a thousand, two believers with the same help can put ten times that number to flight.

Agreement, unity, harmony, or being in one accord—all have a profound dynamic in the body of Christ. To underscore that truth, God holds out a promise for even the least possible movement in that direction: "If [only] two of you on earth agree." How greatly heaven must have rejoiced on the Day of Pentecost when 120 were found in perfect harmony and accord.[3] Little wonder then that God, by His Spirit, was able to infuse that group of believers with a manifestation that still impacts the world.

Each believer is a part, a member, of Christ's body (see 1 Cor. 12:27). As such, each of us has the right and the privilege of claiming God's provisions and promises, and indeed ought to do so. Nevertheless, independence and autonomy are not God's intention for His children, for we are "all members of one body" (Eph. 4:25). God is highly pleased with any genuine movement toward oneness of believers, and consequently offers us keys to heaven's treasury if as few as two believers agree.

The agreement, or unity, however, is qualified: "about anything you ask for." The agreement and the asking mesh; the thing asked for becomes the basis for the musical harmony, that holy symphony which touches the heart of God. The condition is more than simple agreement to ask God

---

[3]Some ancient manuscripts read in Acts 2:1 the Gk. *homou*, "together," instead of *homothumadon*, "in one accord." The meaning is not essentially changed in this context.

for something; it is an agreement deeply worked into spirits of people whose spirits have been so fine-tuned each other in a common desire that they are in heaven harmony over that desire.[4] On the surface the phrase "abou anything you ask" appears to be a promise without any restriction or limit. Yet no single verse of Scripture is to be isolated from other clear teachings of Scripture on a subject. Therefore, "anything you ask" must be further qualified by such biblical statements as, "If we ask anything according to his will, he hears us" (1 John 5:14); and "When you ask, you do not receive, because you ask with wrong motives" (James 4:3). It is quite likely that when two believers are brought into such agreement and harmony, as is indicated in the text, their asking will be according to the Master's will, not the brainchild of some illicit or purely human ambition or desire.

Increasing Faith for Answers

When Jesus talked about prayer, he often made reference to faith. Faith is at the heart of all effective praying. It is the prerequisite to answered prayer, since prayer is the language of faith. "Anyone who comes to [God] must believe that he exists and that he rewards those who earnestly seek him" (Heb. 11:6). Nothing is more futile than prayer without faith. On the other hand, nothing a believer does is more productive and meaningful than praying in faith.

2 Cor 7:14

Heb 11:6

"Have faith in God," Jesus answered. "I tell you the truth, if anyone says to this mountain, 'Go, throw yourself into the sea,' and does not doubt in his heart but believes that what he says will happen, it will be done for him. Therefore I tell you, whatever you ask for in prayer, believe that you have received it, and it will be yours" (Mark 11:22–24).

Faith is the prime mover of God's hand. Yet it is altogether too easy to misunderstand how mountain-moving faith is exercised. Some teach that it is automatic when one speaks; in other words, faith rises when one confesses the thing prayed for: "what he says will happen" (11:23).

---

[4]See Appendix 1, "Contemporary Application of Agreeing in Prayer."

Yet much more is involved in the possession and exercise of faith than mere vocalizing. "Saying" is not necessarily believing at all, for it can spring out of the human spirit as the expression of a purely human desire. The "saying" must always be the byproduct of praying. Divorcing "saying" from praying is like trying to make an automobile run without an engine. Furthermore, the "saying" must be compatible with God's revealed will.

This is the confidence we have in approaching God: that if we ask anything according to his will, he hears us. And if we know that he hears us—whatever we ask—we know that we have what we asked of him (1 John 5:14–15).

Mark 11:22–24 contains three lessons on faith. First is Jesus' exhortation, "Have faith in God." It almost sounds like a command; however, "have" is a simple present tense, not an imperative. Some ancient manuscripts read, "If you have faith in God." Certainly Christians often find themselves struggling fiercely to fulfill it. They testify to faith, they announce their faith, they employ a variety of human formulas for faith; yet all the while they tend to overlook the simple biblical means to faith: the Word of God itself. "Consequently, faith comes from hearing the message, and the message is heard through the word of Christ" (Rom. 10:17). Faith's greatest stimulant is the Word of God made alive by the Holy Spirit.

It is not without significance that Jesus did not simply say, "Have faith." He did not intend to say, "Have faith in faith." Such a practice is full of folly. But He clearly said, "Have faith *in God.*" Faith cannot stand alone. It needs something on which or in which it is placed. According to Jesus' instruction, the mighty God of the universe is to be the object of our faith. What greater object could faith desire? The God in whom faith is placed, and upon whom it makes its claims, is the God who, according to Paul, "is able to do immeasurably more than all we ask or imagine" (Eph. 3:20). Yes, He is the same God whose mighty power was "exerted in Christ when he raised him from the dead and seated him at his right hand in the heavenly realms" (Eph. 1:20).

[H]ow vain is the effort to have faith by straining to believe the promises in the Holy Scriptures. A promise is only as good as the one who made it—but it is as good, and from this knowledge springs our assurance. By cultivating the knowledge of God we at the same time cultivate our faith. Yet while so doing we look not at our faith but at Christ, its author and finisher. Thus the gaze of the soul is not in, but out and up to God. So the health of the soul is secured.[5]

2. The second lesson to be learned from Mark 11:22–24 is Jesus' explanation of the awesome power of faith in God and how it operates. "Faith" (Gk. *pistis*) could be translated "faith-obedience." There is no faith in God without obedience to His will and trust in Him. Unfeigned, undiluted faith meets no obstacle too great, since it brings against that obstacle the unlimited, matchless power of our God, with whom nothing is impossible (see Gen. 18:11–14; Jer. 32:17; Luke 1:37; 18:27). The believer who has obedient, trusting faith in that kind of God is able to speak and then see the words fulfilled before his very eyes. It was with this disposition that Jesus spoke to the fig tree (Matt. 21:19); it was with this disposition that Peter spoke to the lame man at the temple gate (Acts 3:6). But before speaking in such a fashion, believers must make certain they have the kind of faith Jesus and Peter had, and that their words are not mere human presumption or wishful thinking.

3. The third lesson comes in Jesus' instruction on the means of having mountain-moving faith. Verse 24 begins with a significant "therefore," connecting it to the thought of the previous verses and identifying the only way such faith can be found: "when you pray." In other words, before we speak to mountains with divine authority, we must speak to God. And before we speak to God of our desires, we must determine by the Word that those desires harmonize with His revealed will. Once the conviction has reached the heart that the request is according to the divine will, the petitioners have but to believe that they will receive

---

[5]A. W. Tozer, *That Incredible Christian* (Calcutta: Evangelical Literature Depot, 1964), 28.

what is desired of the Lord. And Jesus promised, " 'It will be yours.' "

Faith need not be subject to time restraints. Once faith has risen in the heart, delay of the actual answer should be no problem. Faith does not dictate the terms of the answer. It merely assures the answer within the framework of God's will and purpose.

Clearing the Pathway for Prayer

Jesus' instruction on forgiveness is closely tied to His instruction on mountain-moving faith, indicating that such faith is possible only when the petitioner is freed from every impediment. Effective praying and divinely inspired confidence are predicated upon right relationships with other people. Jesus taught that those who desire answers to prayer must carefully evaluate their attitudes toward any who may have wronged them. The slightest holding of any grudge against another can block God's forgiveness and so become an impediment to answered prayer: " 'When you stand praying, if you hold anything against anyone, forgive him, so that your Father in heaven may forgive you your sins' " (Mark 11:25). " 'If you do not forgive men their sins, your Father will not forgive your sins' " (Matt. 6:15). Forgiveness is to be a part of praying: "And when you stand praying, ... forgive." Answered prayer is dependent upon our status as God's forgiven children, but receiving His forgiveness hinges upon our willing forgiveness of others. What a sobering thought in a day when human relations are so often shattered by the prevailing self-centered spirit of the world!

Every prayer rests upon our faith in God's pardoning grace. If God dealt with us after our sins, not one prayer could be heard. . . . God's forgiving disposition, revealed in His love to us, becomes a disposition in us; as the power of His forgiving love [is] shed abroad and dwelling within us, we forgive even as He forgives. If there be great and grievous injury or injustice done us, we seek first of all to possess a Godlike disposition; to be kept from a sense of wounded honor, from a desire to maintain our rights, or from rewarding the offender as he has deserved. In the little annoyances of daily life, we are watchful not to excuse the hasty temper, the sharp word, the quick judgment, with the thought that we mean no harm, that we do not keep the anger long, or that it would be too much to expect from feeble human nature, that we should really forgive the way God and Christ do. No, we take the command literally, *"Even as* Christ forgave, *so also* do ye."[6]

Jesus goes even one step further in instructing us about people who have wronged us. Not only are we to forgive them, we are also to pray for them: " 'Pray for those who mistreat you' " (Luke 6:28). Matthew gives a reason: " 'Pray for those who persecute you, that you may be sons of your Father in heaven' " (Matt. 5:44–45). To forgive and pray for those who wrong us is to follow the example of Jesus (see Luke 23:34), to become true children of God.

Following the Model Prayer

Jesus also dealt with the issue of forgiving others in His instruction to the disciples in response to their request: " 'Lord, teach us to pray, just as John taught his disciples'." (Luke 11:1). Many ask for the same thing today, hoping to find some formula for receiving quick and predictable answers to prayer. But is our request really sincere if we do not take the time to find out what His Word says about prayer, or take the time to put those instructions into practice? So we must give heed to every detail of the model prayer, which Jesus prefaced with the words " 'This, then, is how you should pray' " (Matt. 6:9). While it is commendable to pray what some have labeled the Lord's Prayer, it is of much greater importance to be guided in praying by principles of prayer provided by our Lord. "This" is a translation of the Greek *houtos* and should be understood to mean "in this way or fashion." Jesus was saying, "Be guided by these general concerns when you pray."

"Our Father in heaven, hallowed be your name, your kingdom come, your will be done on earth as it is in heaven. Give us today our daily bread. Forgive us our debts, as we also have

---

[6]Andrew Murray, *With Christ in the School of Prayer* (New York: Fleming H. Revell Co., 1885), 105–106.

■■■■■■
PART 2

Chapter 8
Christ's
Teaching
on Prayer

forgiven our debtors. And lead us not into temptation, but deliver us from the evil one.[7] For if you forgive men when they sin against you, your heavenly Father will also forgive you. But if you do not forgive men their sins, your Father will not forgive your sins" (Matt. 6:9–15).

Addressing God as "Our Father" (v. 9) should remind us of the benevolence of the One we approach. What blessing accrues when, as we pray, our hearts are aware that a loving Heavenly Father is directing His attention toward us, even as we are directing our attention toward Him. He is our Father, "the Father of compassion" (2 Cor. 1:3), and we are His children. "As a father has compassion on his children, so the LORD has compassion on those who fear him" (Ps. 103:13). Identifying God as our Father "in heaven" (v. 9) acknowledges His superiority to the best of earthly fathers. Prayer, practiced by earthly beings, must be directed to a higher being in a higher world.

"Hallowed be your name" (v. 9) is not a statement or a mere prayer wish. It is a genuine request, the first of a list of petitions: "Let Your Name [or Your Person] be treated as holy [or with reverence] among all mankind." This petition will be finally answered when God himself sanctifies His name among all people in the coming Kingdom. (See Ezek. 36:22–23.) Now our part is to balance our personal familiarity with a compassionate Heavenly Father by showing complete reverence and respect. The Greek *hagiazō* means "to make holy," "to treat as holy," "to hold in reverence," "to highly honor." A person's name is more than a mere word; it stands for the person. God's name represents and signifies God himself, including His character, nature, works, and words. For example, Mary, Jesus' mother, associated God's name with holiness and great works: "The Mighty One has done great things for me—holy is his name" (Luke 1:49).

Unfortunately, this hallowing of God's name receives less attention than some of the other petitions of this prayer. Many a person has cried earnestly, "Give me today my

---

[7]A few late manuscripts add 6:13b: "For yours is the kingdom and the power and the glory forever. Amen."

daily bread" or "Deliver me from the evil one." But concern that God's name might be reverenced and honored lags behind our concern about our own welfare. How can we make His name hallowed? Certainly the third commandment must be obeyed: " 'You shall not misuse the name of the LORD your God' " (Exod. 20:7). But we also respect Him by daily life and conduct. Obedience to God and a consistent testimony bring honor to that name: "As obedient children, do not conform to . . . evil desires. . . . But just as he who called you is holy, so be holy in all you do" (1 Pet. 1:14–15; see also Heb. 12:14). We also hold Him in high honor as we join our brothers and sisters in public worship. "You have come to . . . the city of the living God. You have come to thousands upon thousands of angels in joyful assembly, to the church of the firstborn. . . . You have come to God, . . . to Jesus. . . . Therefore . . . let us . . . worship God acceptably with reverence and awe" (Heb. 12:22–24,28). Hymns and songs of praise and testimony bring glory and honor to God's name.

"Kingdom of God" refers to the sphere of God's authority and reign. At present, God's kingdom works through the Church (i.e., believers) in a world that is in rebellion against God. Yet the Church is not the Kingdom. So when we pray, "Your kingdom come" (v. 10), we are praying for that ultimate consummation of the events of time when " 'the kingdom of the world has become the kingdom of our Lord and of his Christ, and he will reign for ever and ever' " (Rev. 11:15).

There should be nothing a believer desires more than the coming of God's kingdom. One Jewish tradition says, "He prays not at all, in whose prayers there is no mention of the Kingdom of God."[8] Yet the Jews who quoted the saying likely thought of the Kingdom only as being similar to those that surrounded them. Even the apostles did not comprehend the true nature of God's kingdom until after they had been baptized in the Holy Spirit (cf. Acts 1:6).

Although we may not say the words "Your kingdom come" in every prayer we voice, the cry for the completed

---

[8]William H. Erb, *The Lord's Prayer* (Reading, Penn.: I. M. Beaver, Publisher, 1908), 87.

Kingdom must always be the foundation on which every petition is lifted; even though God has already defeated Satan, there are remnants of the evil rebellion. Our most earnest desire must be that the enemy of our soul may no more have dominion over us, but that the Holy Spirit may take full possession of our hearts, bringing every thought, word, and deed into subjection to Jesus. "Your kingdom come, O Lord, in the world and in my heart." God's ultimate intention will be attained only as each believer individually, and the Church corporately, invites and permits the kingdom to come according to God's good pleasure. The correlation between the coming of Christ's kingdom and the performance of His will is obvious, since wherever and whenever His will is performed, there also His kingdom is being manifested.

God's kingdom, that is, God's rule, or reign, is also heaven's rule, because it has its source with God in heaven. The desire for God's kingdom, or rule, is not limited to the future millennial reign when Jesus will reign in victory over everything contrary to the will of God. It also expresses a desire for God to rule now in every heart that will subject itself to His will so His will may be done on earth just as it is always done in heaven. This is the secret of having righteousness, peace, and joy in the Holy Spirit (Rom. 14:17).[9]

To say "Your will be done" (v. 10) requires complete submission. As mentioned earlier, in order for Jesus to fulfill His mission, He became submissive to the will of the Father (see Heb. 5:7–9). Submission is perhaps the most basic ingredient in prayer, for where there is unreserved submission, there is no impediment to God's response. It therefore becomes imperative that we pray "Your will be done on earth as it is in heaven" as an expression also of our trust and confidence in a faithful God who knows what He is doing and who will fulfill His promises.

Towering high above our earthly and temporal needs are the heavenly petitions already noted. Nevertheless, we

---

[9]Stanley M. Horton, *The New Testament Study Bible: Matthew*, vol. 2, The Complete Biblical Library (Springfield, Mo.: The Complete Biblical Library, 1989), 109.

are yet in our earthly state; we are beset with earthly needs and concerns, and our Lord has instructed us to petition the Heavenly Father for them:

"Give us today our daily bread" (v. 11) means "supply our basic earthly needs." The petition is itself a recognition of our dependency on God. However, to pray in this way does not lessen the need for human effort (cf. Gen. 3:19 and 1 Tim. 5:8); but it does recognize that God is the source of our temporal supply, no matter how hard we may have worked to supply those needs. The temporal things for which we pray are not to be ends in themselves. They are means by which we can fulfill the purpose for which God has placed us on earth. Without bodily nourishment and basic provisions of physical life we cannot do God's will on earth. The necessities of life are only a means of giving us strength to labor more earnestly in fulfilling all the petitions of this model prayer.

" 'Man does not live on bread alone, but on every word that comes from the mouth of God' " (Matt. 4:4). To live only by natural bread makes life hardly worth living. When we pray, "Give us today our daily bread," we should also mean the Bread of Life. The Israelites ate manna in the desert, but nevertheless died; God in His mercy has provided Bread which gives life, although the natural body may die. God has made us with a physical and spiritual nature and has provided bread for both natures. Christ is the Bread for the spiritual nature. He said, " 'I am the bread of life. He who comes to me will never go hungry' " (John 6:35). Give us today our needed daily spiritual bread.

"Forgive us our debts, as we also have forgiven our debtors" (6:12). Luke uses "sins" (11:4) instead of "debts"; our sins are debts. Therefore, as we pray, we must always be aware of our need for mercy and forgiveness, and must employ the God-provided means to that end: confession (1 John 1:9). A penitent confession humbles the proud and leads to repentance. As we repent, as we pray for the canceling of our debts, we request that they be blotted out of the divine record.

Forgiveness, so essential to an overcoming life, is our first and greatest need. No matter how diligently we may resist temptation and fulfill all our religious obligations, we still come short of God's righteousness. Every child of God must regularly ask for forgiveness. The self-righteous person feels no need to ask God's forgiveness, but as we draw nearer to our Savior and Lord, we feel a great sense of sin and unworthiness. Like Isaiah we cry, " 'Woe to me! ... I am ruined! For I am a man of unclean lips, and I live among a people of unclean lips, and my eyes have seen the King, the LORD Almighty' " (Isa. 6:5).

We ask for forgiveness from God, "as we also have forgiven our debtors" (v. 12). The conjunction "as" does not indicate degree, since we can never forgive perfectly—only God can forgive sin—but we can and must forgive real and imagined wrongs against us. Yet there is a comparison in the conjunction. As we are ready to forgive out of our weakness and sinfulness, God is ready in His perfect holiness to forgive us. Asking God for His forgiveness goes hand in hand with forgiving others. At the moment we ask, we are forgiven—if we have demonstrated our understanding of forgiveness by forgiving the thoughtlessness of others toward our insignificant self. (See Matt. 18:21–35.)

"Forgive us our debts" is a prayer concerning past sins. "Lead us not into temptation, but deliver us from the evil one" (v. 13) is a prayer for protection in the immediate future. A truly repentant person is concerned not only about making the past right, but about remaining righteous after the forgiveness and cleansing. One needs to be set free from not only the penalty of sin, but also the power of sin. The usual definition of "temptation" is "enticement to do wrong." Yet we know full well that God does not influence His children to do evil (James 1:13). The difficulty must lie in a proper understanding of the words "lead" and "temptation." "Lead" (Gk. *eisphero*) is used in the sense of allowing us to be brought into certain circumstances. Benjamin Wilson's version of this phrase reads, "Abandon us not to trial."[10] But the Greek word has no thought of abandoning us. God is faithful; He would never abandon us to Satan's deceit. The key word in this petition is "temptation" (Gk. *peirasmos*). As used in Scripture, it

---

[10]Benjamin Wilson, *The Emphatic Diaglott* (Brooklyn: International Bible Students Association, 1942), 27.

can mean "trial," "test," or "enticement to do wrong." If the next phrase, "Deliver us from the evil one," is a separate petition, the meaning could be either of the two. If, as is more likely, "Deliver us from the evil one" and "Lead us not into temptation" are a single petition, the meaning of enticement is appropriate. Implied in the word "temptation" are not only those violent Satanic assaults, but also those severe afflictions we find ourselves inadequate to bear. In the present evil day, this is a prayer for all to pray; the great beguiler is intensely active. He plants evil thoughts; he generates evil imaginations; he encourages delight in viewing evil; he pressures the will to perform; he incites to lust; he provokes to sin; he lures to death. Our prayer should issue from a true sense of our inherent weakness before the powers of darkness, bent on our destruction. There is certainly a need for defensive praying.

Not only did our Lord instruct us on how prayer ought to begin, but He also taught us how to end it. This expression of praise to God is a brief doxology. It is homage to, and recognition of, Him to whom the prayer has been directed. In this outburst of praise, the soul is assured that God will grant the petitions. In corporate prayer, the doxology would form a fitting conclusion voiced by the entire congregation. "The kingdom, and the power, and the glory" (Matt. 6:13, KJV) all belong to God. The preceding petitions must be voiced in that consciousness if answers are to be received. Each request should be made in the confidence that the answer will bring glory to God and to Him alone.

Having Right Motives

Jesus gave a number of other guidelines for prayer. That He began with a negative word in these instructions must not be taken lightly. The issue He addresses here is motivation.

"And when you pray, do not be like the hypocrites, for they love to pray standing in the synagogues and on the street corners to be seen by men. I tell you the truth, they have received their reward in full. But when you pray, go into your room, close the door and pray to your Father, who is unseen. Then your Father, who sees what is done in secret, will reward you. And when you pray, do not keep on babbling like pagans, for they think they will be heard because of their many words. Do not be like them, for your Father knows what you need before you ask him" (Matt. 6:5–8).

To be effective, prayer must spring from proper motivation. That is the first rule. Prayer voiced only to attract the attention and admiration of people is not prayer at all, but merely exaltation of self. The hypocritical Pharisees wanted their piety to be seen and applauded. Consequently, they, along with the scribes, were denounced for their long public prayers, which they used to cover their mistreatment of widows (see Mark 12:40).

To be accepted by the Father, prayer must be directed toward the ear of the Almighty. Jesus gave three admonitions to help us pray with a proper motivation: (1) Pray without seeking attention (v. 5). (2) Pray in secret (v. 6). (3) Pray without vain repetition (vv. 7–8).

Christ's instruction that His followers should enter their room and shut the door when they pray does not suggest that public prayer is improper. But it does underscore the believer's need for avoiding any thought of using prayer as a means of gaining the admiration of people. The word "room" ("closet," KJV) is a translation of the Greek *tameion* and means literally "innermost room," or "hidden, secret room." It simply means a place of privacy. Even in a busy schedule, with pressing demands coming from many sources, privacy for communion with God must be found. Samuel Chadwick summarized it well:

Some place must be found that shall be a trysting place with God. A hungry heart will find a way. In the open air or in some secluded corner, some inner sanctuary will be found. If this advantage is impossible, the soul must make an open space into which it can withdraw, even in the presence of others, and be alone with God; but the "inner chamber" is an unspeakable boon. ... God wills that men should pray everywhere, but the place of His glory is in solitudes, where he hides us in the cleft of the rock, and talks with man face to face as a man talketh with his friend."[11]

Prayer, like almsgiving and fasting, should be done in secret so that the Heavenly Father, who sees in secret, may reward the act of devotion openly (see Matt. 6:3–4,18). Those like the Pharisees who wanted to be seen while praying on the streets at the scheduled times for prayer have their reward. That is, they got the attention they really wanted and cannot expect anything from God.

Jesus' second admonition is to secret yourself. Then pray to Him who is in secret. "Secret" is from the Greek *kruptō*, "to conceal." As it relates to God "who sees what is done in secret" (v. 6), it calls attention to His omnipresence. Though He is concealed from the human eye, yet He is indeed present in the secret place. Awareness of this reality on the part of the praying person is a great stimulant to faith. God sees the prayer that is so secret, even if it is but a thought. Although the open reward for secret prayer is the divine answer, it is enough that God meets us in our secret room, transforming us into His temple.

> Prayer is the soul's sincere desire,
> Uttered or unexpressed;
> The motion of a hidden fire
> That trembles in the breast.
>
> Prayer is the burden of a sigh,
> The falling of a tear;
> The upward glancing of an eye,
> When none but God is near.[12]

The third admonition is to not "babble" ("vain repetition," KJV), a word which comes from the Gk. *battologeō*, "to speak without thinking." Meaningless and mechanically repeated phrases carry no weight with God; the cry of the heart, rather than the noise from the lips, is what is heard.

---

[11]Samuel Chadwick, *The Path of Prayer* (New York: Abingdon Press, 1931), 30.

[12]W. F. Adeney, in H. D. M. Spence and Joseph S. Exell, eds., *The Pulpit Commentary* (Grand Rapids: Wm. B. Eerdmans Pub. Co., 1950), vol. 15, *Matthew,* by A. Lukyn and B. C. Caffin, 248.

It is not the repeating of prayer that is condemned, but the empty, mindless repetition. Repetition can indicate urgency, but again, it is the cry of the heart that counts. Christ himself prayed, repeating the same words (Matt. 26:44). So did Daniel (9:18–19). Repetition can express our deepest emotions. But the superstitious rehearsing of words, without regard to their sense, displeases God and brings no response. One might well ask, If we are to avoid "many words" and if our Heavenly Father knows our need before we ask, why pray at all? The answer is that prayer is more than an appeal to God. It expresses our submission of the will to God, and is a means of exercising faith toward God, both of which, in a sense, loose the hand of God to act according to our need. Prayerlessness blocks God from providing for us what He knows we need.

Some today reject praying in tongues by saying it is another type of babbling. But prayer in the Spirit is never mere babbling, even though the person exercising the gift may not know the full import of the sounds of the tongue. Spirit-given words are never empty or meaningless repetition. But if one seeks to replicate previous verbal expressions without the prompting of the Holy Spirit, the caution of Jesus about "babbling" certainly applies.

Praying for Workers

Someone has stated that Jesus left only one prayer request for His Church: "When he saw the crowds he had compassion on them, because they were harassed and helpless, like sheep without a shepherd. Then he said to his disciples, 'The harvest is plentiful but the workers are few. Ask the Lord of the harvest, therefore, to send out workers into his harvest field' " (Matt. 9:36–38; cf. Luke 10:2). On another occasion He admonished, " 'Open your eyes and look at the fields! They are ripe for harvest' " (John 4:35).

People without a vision and without compassion do not pray as they ought; but give them a vision, coupled with compassion, and they become like John Knox when he prayed, "Give me Scotland or I die!"

More than a century ago Professor W. F. Adeney wrote: "Never was so large a harvest-field open for the sickle as in our own day; never were so many laborers needed. The great want of the world is apostolic missionaries, men and women with the spirit of Christ in them."[13] Today the vastness of the harvest field defies the imagination. Over five billion people now inhabit the earth. The world's population doubles every thirty years. If this growth rate continues, by the year 2020 there will be over ten billion people on this Earth—each of these is a person for whom Christ died. When the multitude of the Pacific Rim, Eurasia, Africa, North and South America are gathered in, only then will Christ see the result of "the suffering of his soul, and ... be satisfied" (Isa. 53:11).

The question is: How can it be done? How can this incomprehensible harvest be gathered?

"Ask the Lord of the harvest, therefore, that he will send out workers into his harvest field." Workers are the fruit of prayer. How imperative that the church pray in a fashion unparalleled in all of history, and that it pray specifically for the Lord to send out an army of harvesters! Praying for workers to be sent out into the harvest is a magnificent way to multiply the impact of one's prayer. A major task of every worker is prayer. So each added worker is another praying person. The primary qualification for every soul winner is to be a prayer warrior. Prayer is the spiritual force that will bring Christ into full possession of His kingdom, securing for Him the nations as His inheritance and the ends of the earth for His possession (cf. Ps. 2:8). The harvest is the Lord's. He sends out the workers, calling and equipping them by the Holy Spirit. Only He can instill that zealous love for souls needed to reach a world of lost souls.

Praying with Persistence

Jesus taught an important lesson about prayer through the parables of the importunate friend and the unjust judge. Both illustrate the often-quoted promise of Jesus: " 'Ask and it will be given to you; seek and you will find; knock and the door will be opened to you. For everyone who asks receives; he who seeks finds; and to him who knocks,

---

[13]Ibid., 382.

the door will be opened' " (Matt. 7:7–8; cf. Luke 11:9–10). The three key words in Matthew 7:7—"ask," "seek," "knock"—are present active verbs. The sense of the passage therefore is, "Keep on asking until you receive; keep on seeking until you find; keep on knocking until the door is opened." Rather than indicating unbelief, importunity and persistence do just the opposite. They suggest a determination to obtain a desired end and faith that prevails against all obstacles.

Though there seems evidently a climax here, expressive of more and more importunity, each of these terms presents what we desire of God in a different light. We ask for what we wish; we seek for what we miss; we knock for that from which we feel ourselves shut out. Answering to this threefold representation is the triple assurance of success to our believing efforts.[14]

Scripture is replete with examples of persistence in prayer. Elijah prayed seven times on Carmel (1 Kings 18:42–44). Daniel prayed twenty-one days about a single matter (Dan. 10). Jesus prayed three times in Gethsemane concerning the ordeal He was about to face (Matt. 26:36–44). The Early Church kept "earnestly praying" for Peter, chained in prison (Acts 12:5). Paul very likely prayed fourteen days in a storm-tossed ship (Acts 27:21–25). So the teaching of Jesus is readily confirmed. We "should always pray and not give up" (Luke 18:1).

We begin to give up when faith falters before the victory is won. We should not give up and cease praying before we have conquered or received assurance of an answer. Jesus illustrated His teaching that we should persist and not give up by two parables: the friend at midnight and the unjust judge.

Then he said to them, "Suppose one of you has a friend, and he goes to him at midnight and says, 'Friend, lend me three loaves of bread, because a friend of mine on a journey has come to me, and I have nothing to set before him.' Then the one inside an-

---

[14]Robert Jamieson, A. R. Fausset, and David Brown, *A Commentary Critical and Explanatory on the Old and New Testaments,* vol. 5 (New York: George H. Doran Company, 1921), 30.

swers, 'Don't bother me. The door is already locked, and my children are with me in bed. I can't get up and give you anything.' I tell you, though he will not get up and give him the bread because he is his friend, yet because of the man's boldness he will get up and give him as much as he needs" (Luke 11:5–8).

Then Jesus told his disciples a parable to show them that they should always pray and not give up. He said: "In a certain town there was a judge who neither feared God nor cared about men. And there was a widow in that town who kept coming to him with the plea, 'Grant me justice against my adversary.' For some time he refused. But finally he said to himself, 'Even though I don't fear God or care about men, yet because this widow keeps bothering me, I will see that she gets justice, so that she won't eventually wear me out with her coming!' " And the Lord said, "Listen to what the unjust judge says. And will not God bring about justice for his chosen ones, who cry out to him day and night? Will he keep putting them off? I tell you, he will see that they get justice, and quickly. However, when the Son of Man comes, will he find faith on the earth?" (Luke 18:1–8).

These parables are not like Jesus' "other parables, for they teach by contrast, and not by comparison.... The point in common between them is that importunity prevails. If the suppliants were not heard for their much speaking, their persistence had much to do with their prevailing."[15] Jesus did not merely teach importunity or bold urgency in prayer; He also taught that God responds to persistent prayer. R. A. Torrey said, "We should be careful about what we ask from God, but when we do begin to pray for a thing we should never give up praying for it until we get it, or until God makes it very clear and very definite to us that it is not His will to give it."[16]

Combining Prayer with Fasting

Christ's teaching on fasting and prayer is minimal, providing only limited guidance. While He did underscore its

---

[15]Chadwick, *Path of Prayer,* 70.

[16]Reuben A. Torrey, *How to Pray* (New York: Fleming H. Revell Company, n.d.), 66.

importance when preparing to deal with difficult cases, His only direct instruction dealt more with motivation for fasting than with procedures and guidelines. Yet there is no doubt that He recognized the virtues of the practice.

"When you fast, do not look somber as the hypocrites do, for they disfigure their faces to show men they are fasting. I tell you the truth, they have received their reward in full. But when you fast, put oil on your head and wash your face, so that it will not be obvious to men that you are fasting, but only to your Father, who is unseen; and your Father, who sees what is done in secret, will reward you" (Matt. 6:16–18).

The major concern of this teaching about fasting is that believers guard against making it an act of hypocrisy or giving in to the temptation of self-aggrandizement.[17] All who advocate fasting should heed Christ's concerns. Yet, we should not permit the potential pitfalls to become excuses for neglecting this valid spiritual exercise.

The spiritual exercise of fasting and praying at length for an urgent need should not be viewed as a device for obtaining God's approval or attention. While fasting has its reward, that reward relates more to the one who fasts than to the ultimate object of the prayer. There should come a finely tuned spiritual perception and an enlarged faith as a result of prayer and fasting. Prayer and fasting can make valuable contributions to the life of an individual or congregation, though the practice of fasting should never be allowed to degenerate into an empty formality or an attempt to manipulate God.

The poignant and agonizing problem that elicited Jesus' comment " 'This kind can come out only by prayer' "[18]

---

[17]Edgar R. Anderson, "The Holy Spirit's Role in Prayer and Fasting," in *Conference on the Holy Spirit Digest,* vol. 2, ed. Gwen Jones (Springfield, Mo.: Gospel Publishing House, 1983), 225–229.

[18]The words "and fasting" are found in some ancient Gk. mss., but not in others. Textual evidence seems to point to insertion rather than deletion of the words. They are therefore omitted from many contemporary translations. We do know that Jesus said it would be appropriate for His followers to fast after He left them (Matt. 9:15; Mark 2:20; Luke 5:35). Prayer coupled with fasting would indicate an intensity or urgency in the prayer.

(Mark 9:29) can be understood only in light of the context (read Mark 9:14–28). It was in response to the disciples' utter inability to exercise the faith required for accomplishing deliverance from demon possession. In response to the father's plaintive point that he had brought his son to the disciples and they could not cure him, Jesus chided the disciples, " 'O unbelieving and perverse generation, . . . how long shall I stay with you? How long shall I put up with you? Bring the boy here to me' " (Matt. 17:17). Intense, urgent prayer, even to the point of fasting, was the means for achieving the desired deliverance.

Prayer invokes the aid of God, and puts one's self unreservedly in his hands; fasting subdues the flesh, arouses the soul's energies, brings into exercise the higher parts of man's nature. Thus equipped, a man is open to receive power from on high, and can quell the assaults of the evil one.[19]

It is clear from the teaching of Jesus that He considered prayer a primary key to accomplishing God's work on earth. It is essential for warding off temptation and discouragement. It helps the believer reach proper decisions. It provides strength when pressures become so intense that we are inclined to give up. The true center of prayer, according to the teaching of Jesus, is neither our needs nor our wills. It is God and His will. And we pray in the name of the One who taught the importance of prayer—the name of Jesus.

Questions for Study

1. What does it mean to pray in Jesus' Name?
2. How do we maintain a relationship where we are "in Christ"?
3. What are some improper motivations for prayer?
4. What does it mean to pray in faith?
5. What are some of the things (in addition to an unwillingness to forgive) that can hinder our prayers?
6. Should the principles expressed in the model prayer Jesus gave His disciples be expressed in every one of our prayers? Why or why not?

---

[19]Lukyn, *Matthew,* 178.

7. Since Jesus said to pray "Our Father," are there any biblical grounds for praying to Jesus or to the Holy Spirit?

8. When we hallow God's name, what are some of the names of God that we should treat as holy, and what do they show about the nature and character of the one true God?

9. What is the correlation between seeking God's kingdom and doing His will?

10. What needs should have the most prominent place in our prayers?

11. What are some proper motivations for prayer?

12. What is the difference between repeated prayers that are mere babbling and repeated prayers that are "importunate"?

13. Why is it so important that we pray for the Lord to send out an army of harvesters?

14. What is the value of fasting in relation to prayer?

— *Chapter Nine* —

PRAYER IN THE JERUSALEM CHURCH

The Book of the Acts of the Apostles is more than the inspired record of the ministry of a special company of believers. It is the inspired record of the acts of a fledgling Church, of the acts of the Holy Spirit in and through that Church, and of the acts of those evil forces, both human and demonic, that sought to hinder and destroy the Church. The prayers of the Early Church were crucial to the supernatural events marking the early days of this new move of the Spirit.

If there is a primary lesson in this fascinating and intriguing history, it is that prayer was indispensable: Without it there would not have been this awe-inspiring account. The Early Church was launched with a seven- to ten-day prayer meeting (Acts 1:13–14); it continued in prayer (2:42); and prayer was ever its sustaining force.

The Book of Acts sets forth no direct doctrine or theology of prayer; nevertheless, by an unceasing flow of examples it does teach about the subject. Generations have received inspiration and encouragement from the example of these praying apostles who planted the seed and watered it with the tears of prayer. We too can see our labor for the Kingdom increase as we undergird our efforts with

233

■■■■■■■
PART 2

Chapter 9
Prayer in
the
Jerusalem
Church

intercessory prayer. The practical lessons from these prayers and their results are many.

The First Prayer Meeting of the Early Church

The occasion of the first prayer meeting after the ascension of Christ is unmistakably clear (see Acts 1:13–14). The motivation for it came directly from Jesus, the Head of the Church. Although He does not specifically tell them to pray, the disciples knew full well that the time of staying (Luke 24:49) and waiting (Acts 1:4) was to be filled with prayer. "Stay" is a translation of the Greek *kathizō*, meaning "to sit down," "settle down," "stay."

When they arrived, they went upstairs to the room where they were staying. Those present were Peter, John, James and Andrew; Philip and Thomas, Bartholomew and Matthew; James son of Alphaeus and Simon the Zealot, and Judas son of James. They all joined together constantly in prayer, along with the women and Mary the mother of Jesus, and with his brothers (Acts 1:13–14).

The promised gift (see Luke 24:49; Acts 1:5) was well worth waiting for. The intensity of their desire for the promised power of the Holy Spirit is demonstrated by their obedient prayer: "They all joined together constantly in prayer." The actual burden of their prayer is not recorded, except the later request for guidance in choosing Judas' successor. However, their prayer as they waited must have related to the purpose for their waiting—the coming of the Holy Spirit upon them. Praise was also an important part of their worship. Jesus during His appearances after His resurrection had opened their minds so they could understand the Scriptures (Luke 24:45). The meaning of the cross and the resurrection in God's plan of redemption was now wonderfully clear to them. Thus, their hearts were full of praise to God, praise they expressed continually in the Temple, probably at the morning and evening hours of prayer (Luke 24:53; Acts 3:1). Thus, with open hearts and minds they remained in a state of readiness and spiritual harmony and expectation, waiting for God's calendar to be fulfilled. The waiting was important, for God's purpose in baptizing them in the Spirit was to make them

PART 2

**Chapter 9
Prayer in
the
Jerusalem
Church**

powerful witnesses. On the Day of Pentecost the crowds were again gathered in Jerusalem, and with the 120 together in one place, they did indeed present a powerful impact when they were all filled with the Holy Spirit. Then the days of waiting were over. Never again do we read of believers being asked to wait for any period of time before they could be filled with the Spirit.[1]

The Book of Acts portrays the community attitude of the Early Church with the descriptive [Gk.] word *homothumadon*—"with one mind or purpose or impulse" (GELNT[2], p. 566). The KJV often translates it, "with one accord." It is interesting that 11 of its 12 New Testament occurrences are in the Book of Acts. . . . When people were in one accord, it often resulted in a demonstration of God's power.[3]

Of special interest is the constituency of the prayer meeting. There is no hint of any kind of segregation. Apostles and disciples, men and women, they were all there as one body. "All of you who were baptized into Christ have clothed yourselves with Christ. There is neither Jew nor Greek, slave nor free, male nor female, for you are all one in Christ Jesus" (Gal. 3:27–28). There was no suggestion of clamor or quarrel. It was almost a family affair. All who desired to be there were there. None was excluded. So it is in the household of faith.

And when the Holy Spirit was poured out upon them, the same nonexclusiveness prevailed. All were filled. "All of them were filled with the Holy Spirit and began to speak in other tongues as the Spirit enabled them" (Acts 2:4).

---

[1]"Tarrying meetings" in the early part of the twentieth-century Pentecostal revival brought great blessing and helped many who had been taught against a personal baptism in the Spirit. They needed the opportunity to open their hearts and minds to the truth. But many at the Azusa Street mission in 1906 were baptized in the Holy Spirit after only a few minutes of prayer and praise. Myrle (Fisher) Horton, the mother of Stanley M. Horton, received in about ten minutes.

[2]Walter Bauer, *A Greek-English Lexicon of the New Testament and Other Early Christian Literature,* 2d ed. trans. by F. Wilbur Gingrich and Frederick W. Danker (Chicago: University of Chicago Press, 1979).

[3]Tim Munyon, "The Scourge of Individualism," *Advance,* 1 January 1990, 9.

Prayer, too, is for all people. No one need ever feel left out of this glorious privilege and high responsibility. Prayer is the great leveler. Male or female, high or low, rich or poor—all believers meet on common ground before God's throne.

The outcome of this first prayer meeting of the Early Church would forever affect the world. The Holy Spirit was now available to the Church in a way He had never been available before. That He was present in the world before this day cannot be denied. But for Him to come upon so many believers, clothing them with power to be His witnesses, had until then been unknown.

The events of the Day of Pentecost, prepared for by the praying which preceded it, were of tremendous consequence. "Suddenly a sound like the blowing of a violent wind came from heaven and filled the whole house where they were sitting" (Acts 2:2). Wind, a common symbol of the Holy Spirit for any knowledgeable Jew, stirred great excitement among those in prayer.

And quick on the heels of the wind came fire. "They saw what seemed to be tongues of fire that separated and came to rest on each of them" (Acts 2:3). Another readily recognized symbol of divine presence in the Jewish community (see Exod. 3:1–6; 1 Kings 18:38–39), the fire must have reminded them of the words of John the Baptist, " 'He shall baptize you with the Holy Spirit and with fire' " (Luke 3:16).[4] All this remarkable manifestation must have spoken loudly to the 120 that the Holy Spirit was now given, whereupon "all of them were filled with the Holy Spirit and began to speak in other tongues as the Spirit enabled them" (Acts 2:4). All this, and much more that was to follow, is traceable to the promise of God that the extended prayer meeting had been focusing on right up to the Day of Pentecost.

The lessons we learn are important: (1) Prayer is the

---

[4]But John probably used "fire" as a symbol of judgment, while the "tongues of fire" here seems to be a symbol of God's acceptance. See the discussion by Stanley M. Horton in *What the Bible Says About the Holy Spirit* (Springfield, Mo.: Gospel Publishing House, 1976), 140–142.

major key to the outpouring of the Holy Spirit. (2) Extended prayer may be necessary to produce a Body in one accord. (3) Prayer is the prelude to mighty manifestations of God's power.

In the midst of the Church's first extended prayer meeting, the replacement of Judas, a grave matter of its leadership, arose (see Acts 1:15–26). It appears that the apostles were following the desire of Jesus himself when they concluded that their number should be twelve. Judas, one of the original twelve, had ended his life and his apostleship by suicide. So it was now appropriate to replace him. Two men, from among the many present, were chosen. Why or how, we are not told. Both of them must have been qualified according to the conditions that were applied. To fill the high office, one must have been part of Jesus' company from the beginning of His ministry, and have continued until His ascension. He must also have been a witness to His resurrection (see Acts 1:21–22). Very likely, several of the original seventy (see Luke 10:1) met the requirements. Yet only two, Joseph, called Barsabas, and Justus, also known as Matthias, were selected as candidates. "Then they prayed, 'Lord, you know everyone's heart. Show us which of these two you have chosen to take over this apostolic ministry, which Judas left to go where he belongs.' Then they cast lots, and the lot fell to Matthias; so he was added to the eleven apostles" (Acts 1:24–26).

We wonder what may have preceded this prayer and casting of lots. Was an actual vote taken, with each candidate receiving an equal number of votes? or had some other mutually acceptable process been followed? In any case, two men had equal qualifications as far as the one hundred twenty could tell. How should the choice between them be made? Recognizing that only God knew their hearts, and that in the final analysis it is the heart of a person that qualifies for service to God, these pioneers of the Christian faith resorted to prayer. And after prayer "they cast lots, and the lot fell to Matthias" (Acts 1:26). The casting of lots, the placing of fleeces, and the use of any other such device are not God's chosen means of guidance today, however, since we have the Holy Spirit and

PART 2
Chapter 9
Prayer in
the
Jerusalem
Church

the Scriptures to direct us.[5] Yet we can believe that God honored the simple faith of people who turned to those processes for God's direction and for confirmation of His will. They recognized that "the lot is cast into the lap, but its every decision is from the LORD" (Prov. 16:33).

The Regular Discipline of Prayer

The importance of prayer is seldom disputed by believers. But the lack of a regular discipline of praying often contradicts the verbal assent. The disciples in the Early Church practiced a consistent commitment to prayer, and from that discipline came signs and wonders, the miraculous intervention of God, and a mighty growth in the Church (see Acts 2:43). Luke cites an occasion when the apostles were involved in a miracle (see Acts 3:1–8) on their way to the temple for prayer. "One day Peter and John were going up to the temple at the time of prayer—at three in the afternoon" (Acts 3:1). In this brief reference to prayer, we find no mention of a particular burden that may have been compelling them to attend temple prayers; we note only that they were regular in their habit of praying. They had a particular place, the temple, and a particular time, three o'clock in the afternoon, for prayer.

Every believer does well to have a specific time and place for praying. But even more important are the sincerity and conscious communion with God that must infuse the praying. An overly regimented discipline can engender bondage, as it had for the Jewish community with its three established times for daily prayer: nine in the morning, three in the afternoon (the ninth hour of the day), and nightfall (1 Chron. 23:30 speaks only of two times daily; but cf. Ps. 55:17; Dan. 6:10). While such regular practice is commendable, one must always be on guard lest the set times deteriorate into mere form or into an outward show

---

[5]For example, the people chose the seven in Acts 6:5, and the "appointing" of the elders in Acts 14:23 was done by means of an election. The Gk. word used actually means Paul and Barnabas "conducted an election by the show of hands." The context also speaks of prayer and fasting.

of piety. For there is no substitute for sincere and meaningful communion with God at regular times of prayer.

Of special note is the fact that Peter and John went to the place of prayer together; consequently they were together for the remarkable miracle that occurred. Once again we are reminded of Jesus' teaching, " 'If two of you on earth agree about anything you ask for, it will be done for you by my Father in heaven' " (Matt. 18:19; see pp. 211–213). Evidently there was an affinity of spirit between these two men that resulted in the blessed and holy kind of agreement that attracted the eye of the Almighty.

The lessons to be learned from this brief reference to prayer are important: (1) The discipline of prayer is vital for all believers. (2) A specific time and place for prayer are part of that discipline. (3) The door of possibility is opened by joining another in prayer.

PART 2

Chapter 9
Prayer in
the
Jerusalem
Church

Prayer in the Face of Persecution

Peter and John had been God's special instruments for bringing a most remarkable healing to a man who had from birth been crippled and unable to walk (Acts 3). Incensed at what the two were teaching and doing, the priests and the captain of the temple guard and the Sadducees had cast them into prison (Acts 4:1–3). The next day Peter, filled anew with the Holy Spirit (v. 8), preached fearlessly to all of them. Finally, after being threatened by the authorities, Peter and John were let go. They returned to their fellow believers, to whom they reported the prohibition of the chief priests and elders: that they neither speak nor teach any more in the name of Jesus. That edict sent the Early Church to its knees in prayer.

When they heard this, they raised their voices together in prayer to God. "Sovereign Lord," they said, "you made the heaven and the earth and the sea, and everything in them. You spoke by the Holy Spirit through the mouth of your servant, our father David: 'Why do the nations rage and the peoples plot in vain? The kings of the earth take their stand and the rulers gather together against the Lord and against his Anointed One.' Indeed Herod and Pontius Pilate met together with the Gentiles and the people of Israel in this city to conspire against your holy servant Jesus, whom

PART 2

Chapter 9
Prayer in
the
Jerusalem
Church

you anointed. They did what your power and will had decided beforehand should happen. Now, Lord, consider their threats and enable your servants to speak your word with great boldness. Stretch out your hand to heal and perform miraculous signs and wonders through the name of your holy servant Jesus." After they prayed, the place where they were meeting was shaken. And they were all filled with the Holy Spirit and spoke the word of God boldly (Acts 4:24–31).

How the company of believers prayed is not described. One may have led while the others gave affirmation with their amens. Or several may have led in turn. There is also the possibility that all quoted Psalm 2 in unison (see Acts 4:25–26). But whatever the procedure, the unity of their prayer was the key: "They raised their voices together in prayer to God" (v. 24). Their prayer is introduced with due recognition of the God they were addressing: " 'Lord, you made the heaven and the earth and the sea, and everything in them' " (v. 24). The word here for "Lord" is different from the one used in other passages. This one means "master," "sovereign," or "supreme authority." Such acknowledgment honors God as Creator of the universe, and at the same time it generates faith in the hearts of those who pray to so great a God.

In this prayer of the Church undergoing persecution, the believers further recognize God's omniscience and His predetermination of all that had happened to their Master (4:25–28). The suffering and death of Jesus were still at the forefront of their minds. The knowledge of God's omniscience and complete control of all that happens is just as vital for believers today. We are assured that God is fully aware of all of life's vicissitudes and is never taken by surprise. He is still the Majesty on high, the foreseeing, predetermining Sovereign of the universe, who also gives us free choice and lets us know we can fully entrust ourselves to Him. In verse 29 the prayer departs from recognizing God as God of the past, and describes Him as God of the present also. *"Now,* Lord, consider their threats." This small group of persecuted believers knew that the God who demonstrated His control in the past was able also to control the present, the crisis they faced notwithstanding.

PART 2

**Chapter 9
Prayer in
the
Jerusalem
Church**

...ng times when troubles seem ...cern and prayer at such times ...ng or preventing trouble and ... and resolution to meet the ...ss and confidence. To that early ...s the answer to the threat was not ...even a plea that God would stop ...g judgment on those making them. ...for boldness and power to declare ...ving that God was aware of their situ... ...face the opposition with courage and confide... ...od who had commissioned them to declare His message could be asked to authenticate their ministry with signs and wonders: " 'Enable your servants to speak your word with great boldness. Stretch out your hand to heal and perform miraculous signs and wonders through the name of your holy servant Jesus' " (Acts 4:29–30). Miraculous manifestations, they knew, would be a divine amen to their devoted efforts, testifying that God was indeed working with and through them. The answer even today to an insipid, powerless, apologetic witness is still the power of God manifested in demonstrations of Holy Spirit power and God-given healings, signs, and wonders. We must take courage and implore God for such effective witness, never allowing Pentecostal evidences to be relegated to the past.

We are not left to wonder if the prayer of this early group of Christians was heard. The answer was dynamic: (1) The place was shaken where they were assembled together. (2) They were all filled with the Holy Spirit. (3) They spoke the word of God boldly (Acts 4:31). God's answer came by way of the Holy Spirit, even as Jesus had indicated earlier, " 'You will receive power when the Holy Spirit comes on you' " (Acts 1:8). These disciples had received the Holy Spirit on the Day of Pentecost. Yet that special enduement of power did not preclude the need for "fresh fillings, fresh anointings, fresh moves of the Spirit, new manifestations" of the Spirit's power and gifts, and perpetual dependence on the help of the Spirit.[6] The first-century

---

[6]Horton, *What the Bible Says,* 151.

PART 2

Chapter 9
Prayer in
the
Jerusalem
Church

apostles could not subsist in their Christian walk without frequent communion with Deity; neither can twentieth-century believers. God gives grace for the moment, but no reservoir for the future. His followers must practice a constant communion. A consistent and overflowing prayer life is the means to that end.

The ordinary reaction when the Holy Spirit comes upon people is that they speak out (Cf. Luke 1:42 and Acts 2:4; 4:32; 10:46; 19:6). Acts 4:31 declares that after these believers were filled with the Spirit, "they spoke the word of God boldly," exactly what they had prayed for (v. 29). It should be noted that their boldness to speak sprang from their being filled with the Spirit, not from their request for signs and wonders. Signs and wonders, however, did come in answer to their request, confirming the Word which was preached boldly, plainly, and openly; but boldness in witness is a work of the Holy Spirit as well.

The lessons to be learned from this notable passage on prayer and its consequence are many: (1) When persecutions and threats come, get with the people of God and pray. (2) As you pray, strengthen your faith by confessing the greatness of the God to whom you pray. (3) Pray on the basis of God's Word as it applies to your situation. (4) Don't pray merely for self-preservation and escape when persecutions and threats come, but pray that you will have effective ministry in spite of those persecutions and threats. (5) Pray that God will enlarge your capacity to be filled full with the Holy Spirit and that God will confirm His Word with miraculous signs.

A Priority of Prayer

Unless those called to spiritual leadership and ministry exercise great care, they find themselves so quickly entangled in the affairs of people that prayerful waiting on the Lord goes begging. This same problem faced the fledgling Church. In the midst of all the excitement of a rapidly growing church, a problem surfaced: One group of new converts complained to the leadership that their widows were being overlooked in the administration of necessities.

Complained
Widows Being neglected
serious discord

A move of the Spirit that began in unprecedented unity was suddenly confronted with serious discord.

PART 2

Chapter 9
Prayer in
the
Jerusalem
Church

The apostles were concerned about providing support for destitute widows. But they had a higher mission, which they could not set aside. Consequently, they grappled with a question that comes to all spiritual leaders: Shall we allow ministry to temporal needs to supplant ministry to spiritual needs? Their decision was a good one for that day as well as this: " 'It would not be right for us to neglect the ministry of the word of God in order to wait on [money] tables' " (Acts 6:2).[7] This conclusion in no way suggests that the church is not obligated to care for its own; but it does teach that others, besides those engaged in the preaching ministry, must be charged with the benevolence functions of the church (v. 3). Otherwise, the most important function of the ministry, that which deals with the eternal, is exchanged for a less important concern, the temporal.

Acts 6:2/3

We are not told the specific petitions voiced by the apostles, but it seems evident there was a balance between their praying and their preaching: " 'We will turn this responsibility over to them and will give our attention to prayer and the ministry of the word' " (6:4). Each complemented the other. Without prayer, preaching is an exercise in futility; without proclamation, prayer is deprived of a major opportunity for fulfillment, especially in the life of a minister:

A school to teach preachers how to pray, as God counts praying, would be more beneficial to true piety, true worship, and true preaching than all theological schools.... Preachers who are great thinkers, great students, must be the greatest of prayers, or else they will be the greatest of backsliders, heartless professionals, rationalistic, less than the least of preachers in God's estimate.[8]

---

[7]The Gk. word is used of money tables in Matt. 21:12, Mark 11:15, John 2:15, and of a bank in Luke 19:23. In view of Acts 4:35, where money, not food, was distributed, "money tables" are probably referred to here.

[8]E. M. Bounds, *Preacher and Prayer* (Chicago: The Christian Witness, n.d.), 25, 27.

■■■■■■■■
PART 2

Chapter 9
Prayer in
the
Jerusalem
Church

Every form of prayer should be familiar to the preacher. The preacher must learn to plead with God before standing to plead with others. The preacher must delight in communion with God before seeking to communicate the glories of God and the gospel. The preacher must learn to make earnest intercession and supplications before inviting others to come and know the Savior. Speaking of David Brainerd's praying, Jonathan Edwards observed:

> His [life] history shews us the right way to *success* in the work of the ministry.... Animated with love to Christ and the souls of men, how did he "labour always fervently," not only in word and doctrine, in public and private, but in *prayers* day and night, "wrestling with God" in secret, and "travailing in birth," with unutterable groans and agonies, "until Christ were formed" in the hearts of the people to whom he was sent! ... Like a true son of Jacob, he persevered in wrestling, through all the darkness of the night, until the breaking of the day.[9]

How do we resolve the conflict that continues to rage in the present-day church about how much effort should be spent in meeting physical needs and how much in preaching the gospel to lost souls? Those in the preaching ministry must not permit themselves to be sidetracked into becoming caretakers of material needs at the expense of their God-given ministry. Top priority for those called to preach must ever be praying and ministering the Word.

Prayer at the Point of Death

Stephen had just delivered a searching, scorching message to his Christ-rejecting fellow Jews (Acts 7:2–53). He had denounced them boldly, declaring, " 'You stiff-necked people, with uncircumcised hearts and ears! You are just like your fathers: You always resist the Holy Spirit!' " (Acts 7:51). In response, they "gnashed their teeth at him ... covered their ears and, yelling at the top of their voices, ... dragged him out of the city and began to stone him. ... While they were stoning him, Stephen prayed, 'Lord

---

[9]*Memoirs of the Rev. David Brainerd* (New Haven: S. Converse, 1822), 458–459.

PART 2

**Chapter 9
Prayer in
the
Jerusalem
Church**

Jesus, receive my spirit.' Then he fell on his knees and cried out, 'Lord, do not hold this sin against them.' When he had said this, he fell asleep" (Acts 7:54,57–60).

How should we react to persecution and abuse? Should we curse the opposition and call down heaven's wrath on them? A lesser person than Stephen might have responded in that fashion, but not this Spirit-led lay preacher. He was no ordinary worldling, for in him dwelt not "the spirit of the world but the Spirit who is from God" (1 Cor. 2:12). In humble response to the horrible violence of which he was now the victim, he displayed no hint of retaliation in his redeemed spirit. There was only compassion and tender concern for those who in the next instant would snuff out his life.

Stephen's prayer expressed two concerns: (1) the destination of his spirit and (2) the welfare of his enemies. He could hardly have followed his Lord's example more closely. Only a few months earlier, as Jesus was dying at the hands of evil men, His words had echoed from the cross, " 'Father, into your hands I commit my spirit' " (Luke 23:46). Now Stephen cries, "Lord Jesus, receive my spirit." He had already glimpsed the other world (see Acts 7:55–56), and its glory seemed to alleviate the pain of the moment. He also knew that "to be away from the body" was to be "at home with the Lord" (2 Cor. 5:8).

It is of note that Stephen asked for no physical deliverance, no miracle to effect his release. Just as Jesus died according to the will of God, at the hands of wicked men, so might also His servants die. The will of God may be accomplished in dying just as much as in living. His servants, like Stephen, are to be wholly submissive to that will, whatever the outcome may be. Though Stephen did not verbalize the words, he was indeed praying, *Your will be done!*

Having tended to his own spirit, Stephen then directed his sincere concern toward his violently sinning countrymen. He kneeled down, no doubt with his face heavenward, signifying both his great humility and his prayerful approach to the God of heaven. Stephen's prayer, " 'Lord, do not hold this sin against them,' " echos the Lord's prayer on the cross: " 'Father, forgive them, for they do not know

PART 2

Chapter 9
Prayer in
the
Jerusalem
Church

what they are doing' " (Luke 23:34). It must have been an exceedingly sharp sword piercing the hearts of the observers. While they were killing him, he was pleading for them. Unbelievable! Unthinkable! Yet there it was loud and clear. Surely he was fulfilling his Lord's command, " 'Love your enemies and pray for those who persecute you, that you may be sons of your Father in heaven' " (Matt. 5:44–45).

What was the outcome of this unusual praying and this exemplary kind of dying? In that vicious and blood-thirsty crowd was at least one man who was, body and soul, bent on destroying not only fearless Stephen, but also the whole Church. He was the ruthless Saul of Tarsus (see Acts 7:58). If Stephen had not prayed the selfless prayer that he did, the Church of Jesus Christ might not have listed the apostle to the Gentiles among its heroes. Stephen was a "grain of wheat" that fell to the ground and died, only to bring forth "much fruit" (see John 12:24). This martyred seed did indeed bear much fruit: first Paul, as the repeated mention of him in Acts 7:58 to 8:1 seems to imply, and then the vast multitude of both Jews and Gentiles who came to Christ through the ministry of Paul himself.

Questions for Study

1. Is it necessary now to pray for an extended period of time before receiving the baptism in the Holy Spirit? What was the value of the "tarrying meetings" so common in the early part of the twentieth century?

2. The Jews praying at the Wailing Wall (i.e., the western wall of the Temple courtyard area in Jerusalem) have separate areas for the men and for the women. How was that kind of separation changed in the Upper Room before Pentecost and why?

3. What are some of the values of regular times of prayer?

4. What kind of praying caused the place to be shaken in Acts 4:24–31? What does this show us about prayer in times of persecution?

5. How can we help our pastors to give top priority to prayer and ministering the Word?

PRAYER IN THE EXPANDING CHURCH

Severe persecution after the martyrdom of Stephen scattered the believers in all directions. Luke gives us examples of what must have happened in many places when he tells of the ministry of Philip in Samaria and of Peter in Judea. Since the believers faced persecution with earnest prayer (Acts 12:5, for example), we can be sure that by prayer and the leading of the Spirit the Great Commission was carried out just as effectively in places Luke does not tell us about. Acts gives us a few hints of this (see Acts 9:31; 12:24; 15:3; 21:4; 28:14). However, the latter part of the Book of Acts concentrates on the Gentile mission as carried out by the apostle Paul.

Receiving What God Has Already Given

During the scattering of the believers, Philip went to Samaria and preached there (Acts 8:4). And in that city, a glorious spiritual awakening occurred. Evil spirits were exorcised, miracles took place, and many people experienced supernatural healing. There was great joy throughout the city. However, the Holy Spirit had not fallen on any of them.

When the apostles in Jerusalem heard that Samaria had accepted

PART 2

Chapter 10
Prayer in
the
Expanding
Church

the word of God, they sent Peter and John to them. When they arrived, they prayed for the Samaritan believers to receive the Holy Spirit, because He had not come upon any of them; they had simply been baptized into the name of the Lord Jesus (Acts 8:14–16).

That these people were genuinely saved can hardly be doubted. They had believed and had been baptized, both men and women (see Acts 8:12,16). There was no hint of doubt in Peter and John that the Holy Spirit might not be for these new believers. It was Peter himself who on the Day of Pentecost had announced, "The promise is for you and your children and for all who are far off—for all whom the Lord our God will call" (Acts 2:39). The Pentecostal experience still rested freshly and powerfully on Peter and John. To them, it was virtually unthinkable that any born-again believer should continue long without the infilling of the Spirit. But through what means or process might these new believers enter into a similar Pentecostal experience? Scripture provides a succinct answer: When Peter and John arrived, "they prayed for them that they might receive the Holy Spirit" (Acts 8:15). It is of no little significance that Peter and John prayed as they did—that the Samaritan believers "might receive" (receive actively, take).[1] There was no request to God to give them the Holy Spirit since the Spirit had already been given. He had not been given when John earlier wrote, "Up to that time the Spirit had not been given, since Jesus had not yet been glorified" (John 7:39). Of course, by the time he and Peter visited Samaria, Jesus had been glorified and the Holy Spirit had indeed been given (see Acts 2:33). Therefore, the need of the Samaritan believers was simply that they themselves would find faith in their hearts to receive this gracious gift.

Peter and John's prayer was accompanied by the laying on of hands. Some scholars think this practice was limited to the apostles, especially where receiving the Holy Spirit is concerned. Yet the experience of an obscure disciple,

---

[1]For a discussion on this, see Stanley M. Horton, *What the Bible Says About the Holy Spirit* (Springfield, Mo.: Gospel Publishing House, 1976), 137.

PART 2

Chapter 10
Prayer in
the
Expanding
Church

Ananias, disproves this contention. His instructions about going to Saul of Tarsus included the information that Saul had been praying and "in a vision ... seen a man named Ananias come and place his hands on him" (Acts 9:12). The ministry of laying on of hands was not confined to a select few, but was and still is for the many who minister to needs, possibly even for every Spirit-filled believer.

The laying on of hands seems to have been a special means for stimulating the faith of those for whom prayer was made. There was no mystical transmission of power, yet the act symbolized the giving of the Holy Spirit by the Father. The result of the praying and laying on of hands was exactly what should have been expected: "They received the Holy Spirit" (8:17).

Scripture does not record all that took place when the Samaritans received the Spirit, although it is obvious there were certain outward manifestations. "When Simon saw that the Spirit was given at the laying on of the apostles' hands, he offered them money" (Acts 8:18). That he witnessed something of significance can hardly be doubted, considering his unsanctified eye for franchising and marketing (see Acts 8:9–11,18–19). In light of other accounts of receiving the Holy Spirit subsequent to conversion, it becomes quite evident that Simon saw the Samaritans speak with new tongues and overflow with joyous exaltation and magnification of God. (See Acts 2:11; 10:46; 13:52; 19:6.)

When people have accepted Christ as Savior, our immediate concern should be that they be filled with the Holy Spirit. Indeed, our concern should be more with their ability to receive than with God's ability to give. As we pray earnestly that new converts will enter into this experience, it is appropriate, when faith has risen, to lay hands upon them, expecting that God will give the gift He has promised all believers.

Receiving God's Direction

When people truly pray, God listens and sets in motion those forces necessary to the answer. Sometimes the answer is dependent upon the readiness of other individuals to hear God's instructions and to carry them out. Through

■■■■■■
PART 2

Chapter 10
Prayer in
the
Expanding
Church

divine intervention Saul had come face to face with both
Jesus and himself, and he was totally disarmed (see Acts
9:3–4). In utter agony of soul he prayed. Although God
had supernaturally intervened in capturing Saul's attention,
He used one of his lowly servants, Ananias, to complete
the spiritual transformation, telling him, " 'Go to the house
of Judas on Straight Street and ask for a man from Tarsus
named Saul, for he is praying' " (Acts 9:11). Prayer accomplishes many things; but God often uses people to bring
the answer. What we cannot do, God will do by miraculous
intervention in answer to prayer. But what we can do, God
will often use us to do. We wonder what the outcome
would have been for Saul if Ananias had not been attentive
to God's prompting and instructions. And we also wonder
if some desperate souls are not sometimes deprived of
God's intentions for them because of the unwillingness or
unpreparedness of His servants to be agents of His revelation.

It was of fundamental importance for Saul to pray. Furthermore, the divine process in bringing individuals to this
place seems ever necessary, "for it is God who works in
you to will and to act according to his good purpose" (Phil.
2:13). The consequences of Saul's prayer are beyond comprehension. Never has a believer been more completely
surrendered to God's will and used more effectively in
reaching the world for Christ. But Ananias was God's agent
for getting Saul moving in the right direction. What words
of encouragement his message to Saul must have been:
" 'Brother Saul, the Lord—Jesus, who appeared to you on
the road as you were coming here—has sent me so that
you may see again and be filled with the Holy Spirit' " (Acts
9:17). But beyond that, Saul (who became Paul) was one
of a very few people in history who were totally dominated
by God's will (see Acts 22:14).

When we come face to face with Jesus, and as we pray
with utmost sincerity, we can expect God to direct us. And
God's method of direction may very likely be through one
of His servants.

Receiving Knowledge of God's Will

While Peter was in Lydda, Dorcas, a woman "who was
always doing good and helping the poor" (Acts 9:36), died

at nearby Joppa. Her friends washed her body in preparation for her burial. Knowing that Peter—who by now had gained a reputation as one who was used by God to work miracles—was not far away, they sent messengers requesting him to come. Upon his arrival, the mourning widows who had been blessed by Dorcas' benevolence flooded Peter with testimonials about her caring generosity. It is also quite possible that they hopefully entreated him to seek her restoration to life.

PART 2

Chapter 10
Prayer in
the
Expanding
Church

How does the Lord's servant respond to such a request? How does one proceed when faced by such an impossibility? Peter's natural inclination might have been to write off the pleading widows as hysterical and irrational, wanting to escape their sorrow and loss. Or he could have chosen to reason them out of their hope for Dorcas' restoration and simply offer them solace and comfort. Peter did neither. Instead, he "sent them all out of the room; then he got down on his knees and prayed. Turning toward the dead woman, he said, 'Tabitha [Dorcas], get up.' She opened her eyes, and seeing Peter she sat up" (Acts 9:40).

To understand the course of action Peter chose, we must trace his steps from the time he had first met Jesus. At the very outset he had heard Jesus instruct the Twelve, " 'As you go, preach this message: "The kingdom of heaven is near." Heal the sick, raise the dead' " (Matt. 10:7–8). Peter had witnessed innumerable miracles at the Lord's hand, including the raising of the widow's son (Luke 7:11–16), Jairus' daughter (Luke 8:41–42,49–56), and Lazarus (John 11:1–44). Beyond all that, Peter had a personal revelation of Jesus' divinity (Matt. 16:13–17): He had witnessed the glory of God on the Mount of Transfiguration (Matt. 17:1–7), and he had personally seen the Lord after His resurrection (1 Cor. 15:5). Add to all this Peter's fresh post-Pentecost experiences—the healing of the lame man at the temple gate (Acts 3:1–9), the miraculous and untimely death of Ananias and Sapphira as he confronted their deceit (Acts 5:1–10), and his very recent experience with Aeneas, who at his command had risen from an eight-year bout with paralysis (Acts 9:32–34)—and you begin to understand why Peter elected to take a course vastly different from the one that would have ordinarily been taken. He

PART 2

Chapter 10
Prayer in
the
Expanding
Church

had sat at Jesus' feet; he had moved from faith to faith; he had been filled with the Holy Spirit; and in answer to his own prayer and obedience to God he had witnessed the working of God's mighty power. Forearmed then—even in the face of death itself—Peter did not hesitate to consult with God.

Before he dared act in such a serious situation, he had to consult God (v. 40). It had not yet been revealed to Peter that God would choose to work this miracle. Seeking the will of God by fervent prayer, without distraction or interruption, Peter prayed until he knew God's will. For any who dares attempt the impossible, there is no other course. To act apart from a sure conviction of God's will is to court folly, disgrace, and shame; but to act in the light of God's revealed will is pure faith, which brings great glory to God. Once the will of God is known with certainty, it remains only to act in harmony with that will. Peter turned to the lifeless woman, saying, "Tabitha, get up" (v. 40). Then the miracle already determined in heaven became reality on earth: "She opened her eyes, and seeing Peter she sat up" (v. 40). What a glorious restoration, we say, and it was that indeed; yet it was more than that. It turned out to be the key to the hearts of a vast multitude: "This became known all over Joppa, and many people believed in the Lord" (v. 42).

God does care about our earthly sorrows and losses, and sometimes He intervenes in the usual course of nature; but His chief concern is not with the temporal. The eternal destiny of many souls in Joppa was no doubt the reason for a divine response to Peter's prayer. From Peter's experience there is much instruction for the one who would be used of God to meet human need. When confronted with the humanly impossible, consult with God to learn His will. Then, beware of over-rationalizing as faith is put to the test. Do not act presumptuously; make sure you have heard the voice of God before you act. Give faith opportunity to grow until you can believe God for the utterly impossible. When you are certain God has spoken, do not fear to act. When the miracle has taken place, give all the glory to God; allow the supernatural work to be a means of bringing the lost to Christ.

Receiving a Remarkable Answer to Prayer

PART 2

Chapter 10
Prayer in
the
Expanding
Church

When people walk in such light as they have and pray earnestly to God, they are rewarded. Cornelius, a Roman centurion, was such a person. He was probably what the Jews of that time would consider a "sympathetic uncircumcised" alien or, possibly, a partial proselyte.[2] He was a man who was "respected by all the Jewish people" (Acts 10:22), despite the fact that he was a Gentile. It is evident also that he had heard about Jesus and knew about His death, resurrection, and ascension, as well as the baptism in the Holy Spirit (see Acts 10:36–38). This surely inspired his determined pursuit of God. The Jews thought Gentiles could hardly have the same access to God that they did. But God doesn't show favoritism (Acts 10:34), as Peter was shortly to learn.

At Caesarea there was a man named Cornelius, a centurion in what was known as the Italian Regiment. He and all his family were devout and God-fearing; he gave generously to those in need and prayed to God regularly. One day at about three in the afternoon he had a vision. He distinctly saw an angel of God, who came to him and said, "Cornelius!" Cornelius stared at him in fear. "What is it Lord?" he asked. The angel answered, "Your prayers and gifts to the poor have come up as a memorial offering before God. Now send men to Joppa to bring back a man named Simon who is called Peter. He is staying with Simon the tanner, whose house is by the sea" (Acts 10:1–6).

The credentials of this Gentile were impressive: (1) He was devout—pious and godly. (2) He feared God; not only did he have faith in the true God, but he wanted to please Him and receive anything He had. (3) He was mindful of his household and shared his knowledge of God with them.

---

[2]Medieval rabbis sometimes called these interested foreigners "proselytes of the gate," because they stood at the gate of Judaism but did not fully enter in to become a proselyte or full convert. They listened to and believed the Old Testament Scriptures in the synagogue, but had not accepted circumcision and did not follow the dietary laws. See R. A. Stewart, "Proselyte," J. D. Douglas, ed. *The New Bible Dictionary* (Grand Rapids: Wm. B. Eerdmans Pub. Co., 1962), 1047.

PART 2

Chapter 10
Prayer in
the
Expanding
Church

(4) He was generous to the poor. (5) He consistently prayed to God.

We have no indication from the text what Cornelius may have included in his prayer. But we may deduce his prayer from what happened. The words of the angel who visited him may give us a clue: "Bring back a man named Simon" (Acts 10:5). It is not difficult to deduce that from his heart Cornelius must have prayed for someone to help him know what to do. It seems probable that, since all the Spirit-baptized believers were Jews, Cornelius may actually have been praying about becoming a full proselyte of (convert to) Judaism with the hope of receiving the promised salvation and infilling of the Holy Spirit.

Cornelius walked in the light he had received, but in his spirit he seems to have perceived, as honest and earnest people do, that God had prepared something more for him and his household. Within his heart was a hunger for a greater experience of God, and this was his pursuit. It was likely that as a "God-fearer," he had heard the prophet Jeremiah's declaration of the Lord's great promise: " 'You will seek me and find me when you seek me with all your heart' " (Jer. 29:13). In any case, he was soon to know its fulfillment, as well as that of Jesus' corroberative teaching: " 'Blessed are those who hunger and thirst for righteousness, for they will be filled' " (Matt. 5:6).

In this hour of all-but-universal darkness one cheering gleam appears: within the fold of conservative Christianity there are to be found increasing numbers of persons whose religious lives are marked by a growing hunger after God Himself. They are eager for spiritual realities and will not be put off with words. ... They are athirst for God, and they will not be satisfied till they have drunk deep at the Fountain of Living Water.[3]

Cornelius received his answer in a rather remarkable way; it involved both an angel (Acts 10:3) and a man, Peter (Acts 10:5–6). The ministry of angels in bringing answers to prayer will be considered in chapter 14, but let it here

---

[3]A. W. Tozer, *The Pursuit of God* (Harrisburg, Penn.: Christian Publications, Inc., 1948), 7.

be noted that God will employ whatever means necessary to provide an adequate answer to the sincere seeker.

Answers to prayer sometimes come slowly because the divinely chosen means of answering involves a person who has yet to learn some lessons in responding to God's voice. Before God could answer Cornelius' prayer, Peter had to become a prepared messenger (this alone was a project of major proportions). God answers a praying believer, and frequently He uses another praying believer to carry the answer. Consequently, "about noon the following day as they [the men sent to Peter by Cornelius] were on their journey and approaching the city, Peter went up on the roof to pray" (Acts 10:9). No particular reason is given for Peter's praying at this hour (for morning, afternoon, and sunset were the prescribed times among Jews). Very likely he did so from habit and a desire for personal communion with God. When we pray, we give God opportunity to speak, and we are more disposed to hear. Peter's praying precipitated a revelation of immeasurable import for both himself and the entire Church: God is impartial, as willing to bless the Gentile world with the gospel as He is the Jewish world (see Acts 10:34–35).

How much depends on our praying cannot be measured. But if Cornelius had not prayed, the door to the Gentiles might have remained closed longer, though not permanently, for God's promise of blessing has always been to all peoples on earth (see Gen. 12:3; 18:18; 22:18; 26:4; 28:14; Gal. 3:8). And if Peter had not prayed, again perhaps a delay would have prevailed—at least until God found another believer who would obey His directives. But Cornelius prayed, and Peter prayed, with the glorious result that Peter entered the door to the Gentile world, and Cornelius and his household experienced the fullness of the Holy Spirit, even while the gospel was being preached to them the very first time (they did know about the gospel before this; see Acts 10:36–37,44–48).[4]

From this passage on prayer we learn several lessons. God takes note of godly devotion and sets in motion those

PART 2

Chapter 10
Prayer in
the
Expanding
Church

---

[4]For a discussion on this, see Horton, *What the Bible Says,* 157–158.

PART 2

Chapter 10
Prayer in
the
Expanding
Church

forces that bring about answers to the prayers of righteous people. A consistent prayer life and communion with God open the door for His special guidance and direction. When people pursue God, regardless of their position or obscurity, they will find Him. Patience is necessary when we pray, for in answering our petitions God often employs other humans in whom and through whom He must work. Prayer is the greatest force available for influencing lives—and ultimately history.

Receiving Deliverance through United Prayer

The forward movement of the Church is largely dependent upon its leadership, much as conquest by an army depends on its officers. Satan is not oblivious to this reality; so he strikes hardest where it counts most. Even as God chooses to work through people to accomplish His purposes, so Satan employs human emissaries to gain his ends. Herod Agrippa I was his accomplice in seizing and imprisoning Peter. Herod supposed that James and Peter were the two pillars upon which the infant Church rested, and that if they were eliminated the whole structure would collapse. So he had James arrested and executed; and because he saw it pleased the Jews, he arrested Peter, placing him under tight security. "So Peter was kept in prison, but the church was earnestly praying to God for him" (Acts 12:5). Herod, because of his depravity, was not aware that he was in reality contending with the Almighty.

Once again we note the awesome power of prayer. Until prayer is made, Satan has the upper hand. We should remember that fact in this day when church leadership is under vicious attack. The Early Church, beset with great concern over James' death and Peter's imprisonment, became very serious in their praying. They did not half-heartedly pray, as we tend to do, but they kept "earnestly praying." It was fervent prayer. Of considerable significance is the fact that the Church as a whole did the praying. There is a time and place for individual, private prayer; but there is also a time for the whole Church to shoulder the burden. When the mission for which the Church exists is threatened, it is time for the whole Church to pray. So the

PART 2

Chapter 10
Prayer in
the
Expanding
Church

young Church joined in praying for a single thing: that Peter might be spared for the sake of the Church and the world. The prayer was specific. Specific praying, in the will of God, results in specific answers. Such praying refines our petitions, eliminating prayer so general that we hardly have any way of knowing when it's answered. Specific praying puts the supplicant's faith to the test and inclines him toward discovering the will of God before the petition is made, or at least toward being willing to submit to that will if there is any uncertainty about what it is.

The urgency of Peter's situation required a speedy answer. Immediate prayer was called for. Delay was tantamount to accepting Herod's verdict. He would act at the earliest convenient moment. Providentially, the Jewish holy days delayed him in his evil intent, giving a little space for the Church to pray. Had the Church failed, the consequences would have been fearsome. But the Church did pray. And because of that, there was supernatural intervention. Chains fell off. The guards were not alert, or could not see the escaping prisoner. Gates opened of their own accord. Peter was free!

From the account of Peter's deliverance we learn several lessons about prayer. We should not be surprised when church leaders are attacked; earnest prayer for leaders is always in order. When attacks against the Church are of such severity that its divine mission is likely to be hindered, the corporate body should join in earnest, prompt, and constant prayer. Prayer should be for well-defined and specific needs. It should be governed by the will of God, as revealed in His Word, and by a willingness to submit once that will is truly known. We see also that God may answer earnest prayer in impossible situations even when those praying are not really expecting an immediate answer. (Notice how they answered Rhoda when she said Peter was at the door, "You're out of your mind. It must be his angel" [Acts 12:15].)

Receiving Direction to Send Out Laborers

From the inception of the Church, missions has been its priority. Missions is the heartbeat of God himself (see John

PART 2

Chapter 10
Prayer in
the
Expanding
Church

3:16; Luke 19:10). As the Church draws nearer to His heart, missions rests heavier upon its heart. "While they were worshiping the Lord and fasting, the Holy Spirit said, 'Set apart for me Barnabas and Saul for the work to which I have [already] called them.' So after they had fasted and prayed, they placed their hands on them and sent them off" (Acts 13:2–3). The verb "to worship" comes from the Greek *leitourgeō*, the root of our word "liturgy." Its usage in Acts 13 seems to suggest a mingling of praise and prayer. Add to that the fasting, and you confront an intense and united devotion to the Lord. In such a setting, vision is born and people find divine direction for their lives.

Just how the Holy Spirit spoke to the gathered company, we are not told; obtaining the necessary guidance is of more consequence than is the means for obtaining it. There is an ever-present inclination to overemphasize the means of the divine direction at the expense of the all-important directive. This is not to say that we ought not concern ourselves with the means, for not to do so might easily result in a failure to recognize and receive the guidance. It was not until young Samuel was instructed on how to receive divine guidance that he was able to recognize and receive it (see 1 Sam. 3:1–14). Acts 13 says only, "the Holy Spirit said." There are several possibilities of how this word was conveyed: (1) by means of a strong impression on the heart of one or more of the leaders (cf. Acts 8:29; 9:15–16), (2) through a vision (cf. Acts 9:10; 10:3,10–16; 16:9), (3) through a prophetic gift (cf. Acts 15:13,28,32; 21:11). In connection with the third possibility, great caution must be used, for there is only scant evidence pointing to this means in Scripture. Donald Gee, a highly respected British Bible scholar, wrote, "It can be affirmed that there is not one single instance of the gift of prophecy being deliberately resorted to for guidance in the New Testament."[5]

Paul and Barnabas had already been called by the Lord. Now as a direct result of ministering to the Lord and of fasting, the church at Antioch was encouraged to release them from their local duties and send them out. It is at

---

[5]Donald Gee, *Concerning Spiritual Gifts* (Springfield, Mo.: Gospel Publishing House, 1949), 44.

least probable that the gathered group prayed according to the Lord's instructions, "Ask the Lord of the harvest, therefore, to send out workers into his harvest field" (Matt. 9:38). The consecration of the first missionaries was preceded by prayer and fasting. Even as ministering to the Lord and fasting prepared the church to hear the Spirit's command, so fasting and praying were part of the sending process. "After they had fasted and prayed, they placed their hands on them and sent them off" (Acts 13:3). The work to be done was a spiritual work. Methods and practices of ordinary people would not—and will not—suffice. Guidance for a church must be spiritual. Its sending forth must be spiritual. The work must be in the power of the Spirit. When a church engages in spiritual activity, it sets the stage for spiritual ministry and outreach. From Antioch, Paul and Barnabas went out to reach their world with the gospel and to establish a missionary pattern worthy of emulation in all generations.

Several lessons can be learned from this passage. Church leadership does well to give priority time to spiritual exercise, especially prayer, worshiping the Lord, and fasting. Learning to receive and follow the Spirit's direction in selecting and sending forth laborers is essential to effective missionary ministry. The Holy Spirit is the source of divine direction, regardless of the means He may employ, and He works best in an atmosphere of praise and prayer. When the Spirit is vitally involved in directing a church, its outreach mission becomes the primary concern.

Experiencing Confrontation of Satanic Powers

Confronting satanic forces is not the time to begin getting serious about prayer. And though such visible confrontation may be occasional, the battle rages constantly. Every time a believer bows in prayer, there must be a consciousness of the great conflict of which he or she is a part: "Our struggle is not against flesh and blood, but against the rulers, against the authorities, against the powers of this dark world and against the spiritual forces of evil in the heavenly realms" (Eph. 6:12). Paul was a person of prayer who joined other believers in corporate interces-

PART 2

Chapter 10
Prayer in
the
Expanding
Church

PART 2

Chapter 10
Prayer in
the
Expanding
Church

sory prayer. It was only through this preparation that he could be used to confront satanic powers in Philippi.

On the Sabbath we went outside the city gate to the river, where we expected to find a place of prayer. We sat down and began to speak to the women who had gathered there. . . . Once when we were going to the place of prayer, we were met by a slave girl who had a spirit by which she predicted the future. She earned a great deal of money for her owners by fortune-telling. This girl followed Paul and the rest of us, shouting, "These men are servants of the Most High God, who are telling you the way to be saved." She kept this up for many days. Finally Paul became so troubled that he turned around and said to the spirit, "In the name of Jesus Christ I command you to come out of her!" At that moment the spirit left her (Acts 16:13,16–18).

Acts 16:13 and 16 are the only verses in the New Testament in which the Greek *proseuchē* ("prayer") means "a place of prayer." Philippi had no synagogue, because the number of adult male Jews living there was too small, being less than ten;[6] there was only a "praying place" by the Gangites River. So Paul and his company headed for the spot where needy people regularly met with God. So should it be today. The place of prayer, whether the house of God or the closet at home, should be honored and sought. Prayer and worship gain not only the attention of heaven, but in some inexplicable way they also attract and excite the world of unholy spirits. The presence of Jesus often provoked demonic response (Matt. 8:28–32; Mark 1:23–24; 3:11; Luke 4:41). So it should not be thought strange that when earnest prayer is made, the forces of darkness rise up to do battle.[7] It is then, more than at any other time, that they are threatened, engaged, and defeated (see Eph. 6:12–18).

Paul's prayer likewise brought demonic opposition and then glorious deliverance. As the group proceeded to the place of prayer, a young slave girl, possessed by an evil spirit, took up her shout about the mission of the evan-

---

[6]Horton, *The Book of Acts,* 193.

[7]See Appendix 2, "Contemporary Experience of Spiritual Warfare in Prayer."

gelists. Scripture says she earned money for her owners by predicting the future and telling fortunes. It was thought by the pagans that such persons spoke truth by the inspiration of some god. In reality, she spoke by inspiration of the father of lies (John 8:44). Satan frequently conceals his true nature so that he may more effectively deceive.

Paul, equipped and armed by the Holy Spirit and freshly endued through prayer, finally ordered the demon to leave the girl, bringing the wrath of her masters upon himself and his companion Silas. Satan is no less real today than he was then—as those who engage in earnest prayer quickly discover. Yet the praying person has nothing to fear. "The weapons we fight with ... have divine power to demolish strongholds" (2 Cor. 10:4).

We learn some significant lessons about prayer from this passage. A place of prayer, where believers can gather, is of great importance. Prayer may draw the forces of evil to do battle, and at times they may manifest themselves in strange ways. Therefore, the believer needs to be Spirit-filled and ready always to confront evil forces head-on. Yet we need not fear what Satan can do, as long as we ourselves maintain a vital relationship with God. Satan's captives must be set free, and prayer is the powerful means of deliverance.

An Unexpected Response

For delivering the demon-possessed girl and consequently depriving her masters of their livelihood, Paul and Silas were beaten and thrown into prison. Even so, midnight found them "praying and singing hymns to God, and the other prisoners were listening to them" (Acts 16:25). Sometimes the fate of people who pray is not pleasant. Prayer does not guarantee immunity from trouble. At times it even seems to invite trouble. Yet the Scriptures assure us, "A righteous man may have many troubles, but the Lord delivers him from them all" (Ps. 34:19).

The servants of the kingdom can be a mystery to those outside the kingdom. At midnight, their feet held tightly in wooden stocks, their backs bruised and bleeding, and their bodies suffering indescribable discomfort in a damp, inner dungeon, which was probably insect-infested, Paul

PART 2

Chapter 10
Prayer in
the
Expanding
Church

PART 2

Chapter 10
Prayer in
the
Expanding
Church

and Silas began praying and singing praises to God. It is not the place that sanctifies the spirit, but the spirit that sanctifies the place. From the depths of the praying soul come genuine "songs in the night" (Job 35:10), even in the midst of suffering. No clue is given as to the content of the prayer of the two dedicated missionaries. Did they pray for their own deliverance, remembering Peter's miraculous escape under similar circumstances? Did they pray for their jailers' conversion? Whatever their petitions and praise, God responded suddenly and in a totally unexpected way. Though He sent an angel to quietly deliver Peter, he delivered Paul and Silas by means of an earthquake.

A prayer of trusting commitment, accepting whatever God sends as His answer, will prevent misguided praying. God sees the panorama, we see a few of its details. It is of utmost importance in all circumstances to pray "Your will be done." Such a prayer in no way limits God; instead, it opens the door for Him to act in His own matchless wisdom. Had God delivered Paul and Silas in the same way He had delivered Peter, it is unlikely that the jailer and his household would have found salvation.

Several lessons should be learned from this experience of Paul and Silas: In the darkest night, prayer and praise are both possible and productive. The best guarantee of escape from present suffering is to ask the Lord, who reigns over all our circumstances, to gain His purposes and receive all the glory as a result of our deliverance. When God does intervene supernaturally in our suffering, we need to discern His intent, which may very well extend beyond our need to that of others. If we face our difficult circumstances with the right attitude, they can become the means of grace to lost souls.

Praying a Benediction

Parting prayers are often difficult. Paul had just finished his charge to the Ephesian elders who had journeyed some twenty-eight miles to Miletus to meet him for the last time. He had told them that they would never see his face again (Acts 20:25), and they were sorrowing over the prospect

PART 2

Chapter 10
Prayer in
the
Expanding
Church

(v. 38). "When he had said this, he knelt down with all of them and prayed" (v. 36). Prayer is the best guarantee for the future. It unites hearts that miles may separate, and it is the glue that holds us together though we be far apart.

Here is a pattern for farewells, whether the separation be by physical space or by death. In faith we commend each other to God, even as Jesus commended His spirit to the Father as He was dying on the cross (see Luke 23:46). We do well to pray the benediction of Numbers 6:24–26, whether in our own words or those of Scripture: "'The LORD bless you and keep you; the LORD make his face shine upon you and be gracious to you; the LORD turn his face toward you and give you peace.'"

From this Acts account we learn that prayer is in order on every occasion. Praying together is a bond that cements the Christian family. Praying a benediction on the occasion of separation from those we love or hold dear is a privilege. Notice how Paul's final greetings in his letters usually included a benediction.

Receiving a Revelation

Prayer is appropriate on every occasion, but it is never more urgent than in the time of crisis. Sailing to Rome, a prisoner in the custody of the centurion Julius, Paul was in physical jeopardy, along with the crew, the passengers, and the other prisoners (see Acts 27:1–20). It was Paul's fourth experience of shipwreck (those mentioned in 2 Cor. 11:25 are earlier).

After the men had gone a long time without food, Paul stood up before them and said: "Men, you should have taken my advice not to sail from Crete; then you would have spared yourselves this damage and loss. But now I urge you to keep up your courage, because not one of you will be lost; only the ship will be destroyed. Last night an angel of the God whose I am and whom I serve stood beside me and said, 'Do not be afraid, Paul. You must stand trial before Caesar; and God has graciously given you the lives of all who sail with you.' So keep up your courage, men, for I have faith in God that it will happen just as he told me. Nevertheless, we must run aground on some island" (Acts 27:21–26).

PART 2

Chapter 10
Prayer in
the
Expanding
Church

Lesser individuals give way to despair when the storm threatens life itself—but not Paul. One might suspect, from the reference to Paul's abstinence, that he had entered into a deliberate fast in behalf of the life-threatening circumstance. A closer examination, however, hardly supports that understanding. The Greek word *asitia* is a medical term for "loss of appetite," meaning literally, "without food." "After the men had gone a long time without food [because of a loss of appetite], Paul stood up before them and said. ..." (The "Fast" mentioned in 27:9 was probably the Day of Atonement, which all good Jews would have observed.)

Whether Paul ate during the early days of the storm, we can safely conclude that he maintained a constant communion with God throughout the ordeal. Whether he concerned himself greatly over his own welfare, he knew for certain that he was destined to reach Rome (cf. Acts 19:21; 23:11). The believer's praying is affected by his confidence and assurance. Most likely Paul prayed for the safety of his shipmates. It is not easy to pray for those who bring trouble on themselves after rejecting our counsel (see 27:9–11,21). However, those who pray and commune with God gain the ascendancy over personal rejection and rebuff. And their presence, like Paul's, may ultimately bless those who originally dimissed them. Although Satan may cause our seas to rage, the believer's God can calm the storm or deliver from it.

The result of Paul's praying was his bold announcement in the face of apparently impending death: "Now I urge you to keep up your courage, because not one of you will be lost; only the ship will be destroyed" (27:22). This was no presumptuous "positive confession," nor was it merely hopeful aspiration. It was a statement of fact based on divine revelation. Often people who pray come to know by supernatural means.[8] This shouldn't be considered strange in view of the omniscience of the God we serve.

---

[8]While in prayer, a pastor was strongly impressed to tell a certain lady in the community that she had come to her last opportunity to receive Christ. Meeting her and her husband in a local grocery store, he conveyed the word to her as gently as he could. She responded by saying she had tried church, but was not interested. The following day, while driving to work very early, she was struck by another car and killed instantly.

Through Paul's praying came (1) revelation and (2) preservation. By a special angelic revelation he understood the future beyond the present adverse circumstance. By divine intervention he, along with his shipmates, was preserved from terrible destruction.

Paul's experience on the way to Rome teaches several lessons. In the midst of the storm we must maintain communion with God, refusing the despair of unbelief. What God reveals to us in the day, we must not doubt in the night. When we have truly heard from God, we can declare with confidence what He is about to do.

PART 2

Chapter 10
Prayer in
the
Expanding
Church

Receiving Assurance for Healing

There is to be a supernatural presence with God's servants. Mark's Gospel predicts it: " 'They will pick up snakes with their hands; and when they drink deadly poison, it will not hurt them at all; they will place their hands on sick people, and they will get well' " (Mark 16:18).[9] Paul witnessed what Jesus had promised. Earlier on the island of Malta he was bitten by a venomous snake, yet escaped unharmed (Acts 28:5). Now he sees another verification that God heals through His servants.

[Publius'] father was sick in bed, suffering from fever and dysentery. Paul went in to see him and, after prayer, placed his hands on him and healed him. When this happened, the rest of the sick on the island came and were cured (Acts 28:8–9).

What is the secret of supernatural healing through a servant carrying the gospel message at God's command? We see four significant elements in the brief reference to this healing: Paul (1) went in, (2) prayed, (3) placed his hands on him and (4) healed him.

Publius was the chief official of the island of Malta (Melita), where Paul and his companions were stranded after escaping their sinking ship. His father lay sick with a high

---

[9]Some ancient manuscripts of the Gospel of Mark end at 16:8, but many manuscripts do have 16:9–20. It is possible that the end was accidentally torn off the original manuscript that Mark himself wrote and that later he wrote vv. 9–20 as a summary of what had been contained in the original ending.

PART 2

Chapter 10

Prayer in
the
Expanding
Church

fever and dysentery. To Paul, any person's need was God's opportunity. The islanders had shown the castaways unusual kindness. Now it was Paul's turn. He went in to see the sick man (v. 8). The servant of God should also be a good Samaritan. Paul prayed for the man. What greater service can we render the sick and suffering than to pray for them. Yes, we may seek to make them comfortable; we may minister counsel and care (and we should do both), but let it never be forgotten that we minister best by prayer, for then we open the door for divine intervention and provide credibility for the gospel we preach.

How should we pray in such a case? Do we pray for the person who is in such desperate need, or do we pray for ourselves to be channels for God's provision? Perhaps both. Our effective contact with people is governed largely by our vital contact with God. Prayer teams us up with Him who turns the humanly impossible into divine reality.

After praying, Paul laid his hands on the man. Until God lays His hand of anointing on us, we accomplish little by placing hands on others. Paul prayed until he was assured God's hand was on him. Then he acted. And the man was healed. Certainly Paul had no healing powers of his own, any more than we do today. But he was God's agent. It was by the hand of God that he wrought the miracle (see Luke 11:20). We are to be His ambassadors, carrying the credentials of His endorsement and acting in His stead. Consequently, when Paul laid his hands on the man, it was as though God himself had done it. The results were immediate. The fever vanished. The dysentery ended. The man was well. But that was not all. Soon the good news spread and others came to be healed (v. 9). And without a doubt, Malta had a spiritual awakening of no small consequence.

We learn from Paul's part in the healing of Publius' father that we ought to go where there are needs that can be met only by a supernatural God. We must pray until we sense God's hand upon us and His direction for us. Then we can lay hands upon the sick with the confidence that we are acting in Christ's stead.

It is noteworthy that the prayers of the Early Church lack mention of many of the things we often pray for, such as temporal provisions. The kingdom of God, its spread and outreach, was paramount. These commissioned servants had learned well the instructions of their Lord: "Seek first his kingdom and his righteousness, and all these things [food, clothing, material provisions] will be given to you" (Matt. 6:33). Through the medium of prayer we seek first that Kingdom.

PART 2

**Chapter 10
Prayer in
the
Expanding
Church**

Questions for Study

1. What is the purpose and value of the laying on of hands in prayer?

2. Why is it more important to pray for knowledge of God's will than for a miracle that is needed?

3. Why is a consistent prayer life necessary if we want God's guidance and direction?

4. What is most necessary if we are to be victorious in spiritual warfare against demon powers?

5. What does the Bible mean when it says *Paul* healed the father of Publius on the Island of Malta?

6. Under what circumstances will God answer the prayer of a person who is not a Christian?

PAUL ON PRAYER—PART ONE

Lessons on prayer are best learned by praying. Yet much direction, instruction, and correction can be learned from the New Testament's letters to individuals and the various churches. To make references to prayer from these books more manageable, we will in this chapter examine various teachings on the practice of prayer in the Epistles that name Paul as their author. In the next chapter, we will examine Paul's prayers themselves, with the intent of encouraging all believers to pray with the great Apostle and thereby experience what he envisioned as the privilege of all believers. And finally we will examine Hebrews and the General Epistles.

Few individuals have prayed as effectively and powerfully as the apostle Paul. His recorded prayers probe such heights and plumb such depths that anyone who reads them is awed by the contrast. Further, beyond his recorded prayers are his insights and instructions on prayer, to which anyone who desires to have a more effective prayer life should give earnest heed.

An Intercessor for Believers

Almost without exception, those who pray are keenly aware of their own weakness and shortcomings, especially as they seek to pray according to God's will. Only the foolhardy and the presumptuous lack this awareness. Paul has strong words of encouragement for us:

The Spirit helps us in our weakness. We do not know what we ought to pray for, but the Spirit himself intercedes for us with groans that words cannot express. And he who searches our hearts knows the mind of the Spirit, because the Spirit intercedes for the saints in accordance with God's will (Rom. 8:26–27).

The child of God at prayer is not on his own. He has a God-appointed Helper, the Holy Spirit. Never is a person more effective and assured than when he prays as the Spirit prays through him. How does the Spirit help us as we pray? The word "helps" is a translation of the Greek *sunanti-lambanō,* meaning "to take part with," "come to the aid of." The Spirit joins us in intercession to fashion prayer that cannot be grasped by human understanding. This Spirit-prompted prayer is a charismatic manifestation in which the Holy Spirit intercedes with groans uttered by the believer from the deepest recesses of the heart. Just as Christ intercedes in heaven for the child of God (Rom. 8:34), the Holy Spirit intercedes within the believer on earth. The burdens and yearnings that cannot be expressed in familiar words have their source in the Spirit himself.

"Weakness" is a translation of the Greek *astheneia,* which means physical, mental, or moral weakness and may include timidity and lack of spiritual insight. The opposite of all such weakness is the power (Gk. *dunamis*) of the Spirit. The Holy Spirit helps believers at the point of their need, their inability (mental weakness) to comprehend the will of the Almighty: "We do not know what we ought to pray for" (v. 26). Yes, we do have the Scriptures to guide us in a general sense, but we need the assistance of the Paraclete, the Helper, to particularize our praying as may be required at the moment. "The Spirit [himself] intercedes for us with groans which words cannot express." What a comfort to know that the Holy Spirit intercedes for us from within! He inspires these unutterable yearnings known only to the One who searches the heart and answers according to the mind of the Spirit which inspired them.

"Groans" comes from the Greek *stenagmos*, which can mean either an unvoiced sigh or a voiced groan. Between verses 22 and 27, three references are made to groans (or sighs). First, all creation sighs together in pain awaiting its restoration to the state lost with the fall of Adam (v. 22). But believers sigh too (v. 23). Though already a new creation spiritually, their bodies are still subject to corruption. So they sigh, waiting for the transformation of an earthly body into a glorified body. Finally, there is the sighing of the Spirit (v. 26). There are times when we are unable to pray, or do not know what we should pray for (because of our weakness). The Spirit acts in our place, interceding for us. As a Paraclete (Helper), He helps us in our weakness at prayer. The sighs of the Spirit are literally wordless; they are sighs too deep for words. Yet along with these sighs the Spirit also intercedes for the saints in a way that agrees with the will of God (v. 27). This intercession God understands. The result is that "God works for the good of those who love him" (v. 28).

Some expositors deny that the sighs of the Spirit can be tongues, or charismatic utterances. Many Pentecostals do see room for the gift of tongues to be involved in the process along with the sighs. The sighs, or groans, however, are inexpressible and are not in words of any kind. They are expressed in the hearts of God's children. Only the Father ("He who searches our hearts") understands them. The Holy Spirit by this means helps us rise above our human inadequacies through His humanly unutterable sighings, which are in harmony with the divine will.

Stanley M. Horton expressed the flow of this passage:

We remain in the weakness of our present bodies.... But the Holy Spirit is with us. Though our experience with Him in the age to come will be beyond anything we know now, He is still with us in person, ready to help us in a real and personal way. Though Paul does not call the Spirit the Comforter, the Paraclete, he certainly sees the Spirit as our Helper here. He is right here to help us in our weakness. In our weakness we often do not understand ourselves or our needs. We want to do God's will, but we do not even know how to pray as we should. The Spirit comes to our aid and makes intercession for us (instead of us) with groanings too deep for words.

These groanings are not expressed in words. . . . But they do not need to be expressed in words. The same God, the same Heavenly Father who knows what is in our hearts also knows what is in the mind of the Spirit. So there is perfect communication between the Father and the Holy Spirit without the necessity of words. Moreover, the Holy Spirit knows what the will of God is, so we can be sure that His intercession is according to the will of God. In other words, we can be sure His prayers will be answered. No wonder Paul says that nothing can separate us from the love of God which is in Christ Jesus our Lord.[1]

A Testimony of the Heart

It would be helpful if all the biblical passages on the content and manner of prayer were clear and subject to no alternative interpretations. But such is not the case. If Paul had given reasons for his statements about the proper attire and covering when a person prays in public, we could determine better if his statements are timeless and universal truths or merely relative to the time in which he lived and ministered. Probably no passage has been as controversial as the one Paul addressed to the Corinthians, who struggled to be a light in one of the most affluent and morally corrupt cities of the ancient world.

Every man who prays or prophesies with his head covered dishonors his head. And every woman who prays or prophesies with her head uncovered dishonors her head—it is just as though her head were shaved. If a woman does not cover her head, she should have her hair cut off; and if it is a disgrace for a woman to have her hair cut or shaved off, she should cover her head. . . . Judge for yourselves: Is it proper for a woman to pray to God with her head uncovered? Does not the very nature of things teach you that if a man has long hair, it is a disgrace to him, but

---

[1]Stanley M. Horton, *What the Bible Says About the Holy Spirit* (Springfield, Mo.: Gospel Publishing House, 1976), 189–190.

that if a woman has long hair, it is her glory?[2] For long hair is given to her as a covering. If anyone wants to be contentious about this, we have no other practice—nor do the churches of God (1 Cor. 11:4–6,13–16).

It is a clear violation of what the Scripture teaches here to say that God is concerned only with attitudes and inner devotion. To dress properly and modestly, both in the community and in corporate worship, is a valid biblical principle for every time and culture. Though it may not be wise to allow cultural considerations to overly influence our understanding and application of biblical teachings, the principle of modesty and propriety must be applied within the context of the times. We are not told to dress and groom ourselves like first-century Jewish Christians, but we, like them, must practice modesty and acceptable behavior.

Paul's declaration that a man should not pray or prophesy with his head covered (11:4) was later contradicted by the canons of the Jews.[3] They do not let a man pray without some kind of head covering because he must, by being covered, show that he is ashamed before God and unworthy to face Him. Is God then offended if a man prays with a cap on his head? Or is it the possible negative reaction of persons present during the prayer that should be our concern? The principle of respect, as when a man removed his hat in the presence of those he wished to honor, must also be a consideration along with modesty and propriety.

Verse 5 introduces an idea that has strong cultural overtones: "Every woman who prays or prophesies with her head uncovered dishonors her head." The usual head covering for women was a piece of fabric or net bag to cover the hair, similar to what is today called a snood (not a veil

---

[2]"The very nature of things" refers not to "Mother Nature" here, but to the customs inherited from our ancestors. Walter Bauer, *A Greek-English Lexicon of the New Testament and Other Early Christian Literature*, 2d ed. trans. by F. Wilbur Gingrich and Frederick W. Danker (Chicago: University of Chicago Press, 1979), 869.

[3]Orthodox Jewish men now wear a hat or skullcap (yarmulke) when in prayer, but there is no evidence that this goes back to New Testament times.

over the face). It was a custom among the Greeks and Romans, and an express law among the Jews, that no woman should be seen in public without the appropriate covering. Public prostitutes defied such customs as a mark of their profession. Consequently, for a woman to appear in public without proper covering was immodest and dishonoring to her husband's reputation.

Verse 13 is an appeal to propriety: "Judge for yourselves: Is it proper for a woman to pray to God with her head uncovered?" To paraphrase the apostle, "Does it make good sense, in the light of cultural and other considerations, for your women to pray in public without their heads covered?" Certainly to conform to the pagan manner of priestesses praying or delivering their pronouncements bareheaded, or having their hair loose and flowing,[4] would be a disgrace to the godly Christian woman.

Paul wrote that the very nature of things, that is, of human customs, teaches that it is shameful for a man to have long hair; on the other hand, it teaches that long hair is a glory to the woman (vv. 14–15). Was the shame a cultural matter, or does God consider long hair on a man to be shameful? The Nazirite vow of dedication to God called for the hair not to be cut (Num. 6:5). There have certainly been times, also in Christian societies, when mature, dignified men wore long hair and wigs. Did the nature of things still teach what Paul said it taught, or is there some intermingling of the term "nature" with cultural respectability? To be dogmatic or contentious on these points would seem to be unchristian (11:16). The principles of modesty, propriety, and respect, however, are principles not to be compromised.

We need to remember that the primary reference in 1 Corinthians 11:3–16 is to customs common to the churches in public prayer and worship. When we come with other believers into the presence of our holy God, our demeanor, attire, and everything about us should testify to decency, moderation, and order. Although the out-

---

[4]Some scholars believe that "uncovered" includes the idea of loose, long, flowing hair. See Gordon Fee, *The First Epistle to the Corinthians* (Grand Rapids: Wm. B. Eerdmans Pub. Co., 1987), 509.

ward cannot compensate for the absence of the inward, the outward often does bear loud testimony to the inward.

Prayer in the Spirit

Paul's intent in his instructions to the Body is to bring order and purpose to spontaneous expressions as individuals pray in the spirit. If followed carefully, these instructions will keep Pentecostal prayer and worship from becoming disorderly.

For this reason anyone who speaks in a tongue should pray that he may interpret what he says. For if I pray in a tongue, my spirit prays, but my mind is unfruitful. So what shall I do? I will pray with my spirit, but I will also pray with my mind; I will sing with my spirit, but I will also sing with my mind. If you are praising God with your spirit, how can one who finds himself among those who do not understand say "Amen" to your thanksgiving, since he does not know what you are saying? You may be giving thanks well enough, but the other man is not edified (1 Cor. 14:13–17).

Paul's overriding concern is edification of the Body and how it can best be achieved. From the context, it is evident that the gift of tongues, while profusely manifested in the Corinthian assembly, was falling short of its God-intended purpose. Tongues were front and center. Tongues were spoken simply for the drama and display. Edification of the Body was disregarded. What then was the solution? Pray! "Pray that he may interpret." Only as tongues-speaking is interpreted can it edify the Body. The gift of interpretation is available to the believer. Therefore, the person who speaks or prays in tongues before the congregation should pray to be able to interpret.

In verse 14, Paul, still speaking about the importance of interpreting what has been prayed in a tongue, explains, "If I pray in a tongue, my spirit prays, but [apart from the gift of interpretation] my mind is unfruitful."

The question, "What shall I do?" (v. 15) follows naturally. That is, what shall I, as one who prays in a tongue in the gathering of believers, do? The answer follows: "I will pray with my spirit [i.e., in tongues] but I will also pray with my mind." Is Paul saying, "I will pray supernaturally in tongues, as the Holy Spirit gives utterance, and I will pray also from my own mind and thoughts"? In light of his previous instruction about praying "that he may interpret," Paul seems to be saying, "I will pray in tongues, and then I will interpret what I have prayed, that the Body may be edified." The same practice applies to singing with the spirit: "I will sing with my spirit, and I will interpret what I sing, so that others may benefit."

Verse 16 sets the seal to this. We might paraphrase Paul's instruction: "If you fail to follow these guidelines requiring you to interpret in the public meeting what you have prayed or sung in a tongue, how shall those who cannot understand what you are speaking say 'Amen' and thus be edified?" Consequently, we see what praying and singing in tongues include: praising God and giving thanks to God. Therefore, when one praises God and gives thanks in a tongue, and then follows his tongues-speaking with the interpretation, having previously prayed that he might interpret, the whole Body is edified because all can now say " 'Amen' to your thanksgiving" (14:16).

The custom of affirming prayer and praise with an assenting "amen" was heard in Jewish as well as Christian worship.[5] Some observers of the Early Church in worship compared the loud chorus of "amens" to the echo of distant thunder. The concurring "amen" of the congregation was regarded as no less important than the prayer itself. (See Rev. 5:13–14; 22:20.)

Public prayer should be more than something one person does in the presence of the congregation. The "amen" in the Early Church was a response by which the people identified themselves with the one praying, assented to what he said, and appropriated his prayer as their own. Thus, when one person led in prayer it was as much community prayer as when they all joined their voices together

---

[5]"Amen" is a Heb. word meaning "surely." It accepts something as being true and valid.

in prayer, for it indicated to the Lord that they were approaching Him collectively as the Body of Christ.[6]

Spiritual Warfare in Prayer

We are in a spiritual conflict. It is imperative that we understand this, for to seek to wage battle against the enemy in the strength of the flesh is to court certain defeat. We do well to remember the words of our Lord to Peter: "Watch and pray so that you will not fall into temptation. The spirit is willing, but the body is weak" (Mark 14:38). "Body" (Gk. *sarx*) alludes to earthly life. Our battles are not fought on an earthly battleground, or with earthly instruments of war. They are waged with weapons of another sort—weapons made effective through God's might.

Though we live in the world, we do not wage war as the world does. The weapons we fight with are not the weapons of the world. On the contrary, they have divine power to demolish strongholds. We demolish arguments and every pretension that sets itself up against the knowledge of God, and we take captive every thought to make it obedient to Christ (2 Cor. 10:3–5).

Even though the believer's weapons are numerous (see Eph. 6:14–17) and prayer is not named among them, it is at least the means whereby the weapons are employed (see Eph. 6:18). Through the enablement of prayer (not by mere human means such as metaphysics, human philosophy, or mental maneuvers), arguments and pretensions are demolished, as well as every high and mighty opposition to the knowledge of God. Arguments against the gospel involve imagination and purely human reasoning. Through prayer and study of the Word of God, the Spirit gives wisdom to demolish them.

"We take captive every thought" (10:5). The believers' warfare involves bringing our entire thought life into conformity with Christ's will. The mind itself is a battleground. Some of our unholy thoughts originate with us; some are planted by Satan; and others are thrown at us by our en-

---

[6]Alexander B. MacDonald, *Christian Worship in the Primitive Church* (Edinburgh: T. & T. Clark, 1934), 108–109.

vironment. We therefore wrestle against our own sinful nature and against active forces of evil. We must firmly resist evil and unwholesome thoughts, seeking rather that the mind of Christ might dwell in us (Phil. 2:5; 4:8). We overcome our adversary by persistently saying no to his temptations (Titus 2:11–12).

Assurance When Prayer Is Not Answered

Does God always heal and deliver us from our distresses when we pray? This agitating question comes to every believer at one time or another. Though we would like a positive answer, we are confronted with such cases as Paul's unremoved thorn in the flesh (2 Cor. 12:7). It is noteworthy that Jesus' healing ministry was directed, with a few exceptions, toward the sinners and the ungodly. The same was true in the ministry of the Early Church. And when believers were in focus, there were several instances when healing—although it is most assuredly a provision of the Atonement—was not forthcoming (see 1 Cor. 11:30; 1 Tim. 5:23; 2 Tim. 4:20). In some instances, the reason is given. In others, we can only conjecture. Paul does state reasons for his continued infirmity.

To keep me from becoming conceited because of these surpassingly great revelations, there was given me a thorn in my flesh, a messenger of Satan, to torment me. Three times I pleaded with the Lord to take it away from me. But he said to me, "My grace is sufficient for you, and my power is made perfect in weakness." Therefore I will boast all the more gladly about my weaknesses, so that Christ's power may rest on me. That is why, for Christ's sake, I delight in weaknesses, in insults, in hardships, in persecutions, in difficulties. For when I am weak, then I am strong (2 Cor. 12:7–10).

In the Corinthian assembly there was also a stated reason for their prevailing weakness, sickness, and death: not "recognizing the body of the Lord" (1 Cor. 11:29). God permitted weakness, sickness, and death in order to correct a problem. It is not likely that any effort at gaining healing would have been fruitful until the cause was remedied. For God to have healed in such cases would have made Him like a parent who ceases to discipline his child before the necessary character trait is formed.

There is much uncertainty about the nature of Paul's distressing problem. Some think it was a physical malady, possibly an annoying eye problem or recurring malaria. Others suppose it was strictly a spiritual matter, basing their assumption on "... a messenger of Satan, to torment me" (12:7). Still others say it was a Judaizer who followed Paul around and caused him problems (cf. Num. 33:55, where "thorns in your sides" are people). Not much is to be gained by forcing any private interpretation. Whatever the problem was, Paul prayed three times that it would be removed. After his earnest praying, he got his answer, not the healing he so sincerely sought but an understanding of the reason for his affliction (see 12:7). He learned that it was in his best interest that his condition persisted. At the same time, God promised to give him the grace to bear it (12:9).

The lesson for believers today is that when sickness or affliction comes to us, we are well-advised to pursue earnestly God's healing, but to keep in mind that even more important than our physical healing is our spiritual state. If healing seems to evade us, though we seek it repeatedly, we should take note of Paul's experience, opening our hearts for understanding from the Lord himself; then He can minister to us according to His wise counsel.

■■■■■■■
PART 2

Chapter 11
Paul on
Prayer—
Part One

A Spirit-filled Life-style

Countless people have entered into a new experience with the Holy Spirit today. They have spoken with new tongues (like the Ephesian elders [Acts 19:6]). They may also have prophesied and witnessed other manifestations of the Holy Spirit. According to David B. Barrett, a top authority on religious demographics, there were at the beginning of the final decade of the 20th century over 353 million Pentecostals and charismatics in the world.

But as it was in Paul's day, particularly in the church at Ephesus, the once vital and glowing experience can easily be exchanged for an unworthy life-style, one which, instead of furthering the gospel, becomes an impediment to its progress. Paul had a remedy for this problem:

Do not get drunk on wine, which leads to debauchery. Instead, be filled with the Spirit. Speak to one another with psalms, hymns and spiritual songs. Sing and make music in your heart to the Lord, always giving thanks to God the Father for everything, in the name of our Lord Jesus Christ. Submit to one another out of reverence for Christ (Eph. 5:18–21).

To Paul's sanctified thinking, this is standard procedure for spiritual advance. Those things which militate against being Spirit-filled must be addressed and eliminated before the Spirit-filled life-style can be achieved and maintained. For example, the believer who argues for the use of wine or any other alcoholic beverage argues at the same time against being Spirit-filled; there is no compatibility between the two. For the sincere seeker after God there is but a single course to follow: "Be filled [be being filled, keep on being filled] with the Spirit." And to be filled with the Spirit requires prayerful attention to that end. The baptism in the Holy Spirit is a vital and viable experience. Nevertheless, if the experience is to have continuing purpose and meaning, it must necessarily result in an ongoing Spirit-led life-style. That life-style encompasses disciplines that avoid hindrances and embrace enhancements to it. The list of practices that Paul intimates will be evidences of the Spirit-filled life-style (5:19–21: meditation, singing, giving thanks, submitting) are at the same time the God-appointed means to that life-style.

Even though some would translate *laloumtes heautois* as "speaking to each other" or "speaking among yourselves," it is not erroneous to understand the meaning to be "speak within yourself." Paul uses a similar line in 1 Corinthians 14:28, "If there is no interpreter, the speaker should . . . speak to himself and God." Therefore we may say that the Spirit-filled life-style is fostered by an inner worship that expresses itself by means of psalms, hymns, and spiritual songs. At first thought we might relate the word "psalms" to Old Testament psalms. Although they need not be excluded, the lack of the article makes the meaning more general, i.e., songs with musical accompaniment in the character of the psalms. The idea of "hymns" here seems to be songs expressing praises to God the Father and Christ.[7] Though not the only intended sense of "spiritual songs," it is quite likely that Paul was indicating here what he spoke of in 1 Corinthians 14:15, "I will sing with my spirit." This is singing the praises of God in an unknown tongue.

First Corinthians 14:26 indicates that these things are manifest as people come together. The very word "psalm" includes musical accompaniment. "In your heart" could just as well be translated "with your heart" or may mean while you are joining in the congregational singing, your heart is also filled with music. Making melody in Old Testament usage involved musical instruments. The following verse, "Submit to one another," also shows that Paul is talking about what is going on in the church body, not just in the individual heart.

Harold Horton observes, "Speaking to *yourselves* . . . 'in . . . spiritual songs,' that is, songs in other tongues sung to cadences dictated also by the Spirit. Speaking—in songs! Speaking to ourselves thus in the Spirit is edifying ourselves. . . . If we speak with tongues we have a well within us in this barren wilderness of a world. Singing thus will start a fountain in the driest desert."[8] "Singing and making music in [or with] your heart to the Lord" seems to mean that psalms, hymns, and spiritual songs flow out from the private sanctuary of the inner man.

Thanksgiving is the very essence of Spirit-filled living; at the same time it is another important means to the Spirit-filled life-style. "Always giving thanks" is the soul's access into the divine presence. It is to be directed toward God the Father, from whence the Spirit comes. And it is to be done in the name of our Lord Jesus Christ, the only means of approach to Him.

Submission is to praying what blood is to the human

---

[7] Cf. New Testament passages, such as Eph. 1:3–10; Phil. 2:6–11; 2 Tim. 2:11–13; Titus 3:4–7, which have the form of hymns.

[8] Harold Horton, *Gifts of the Spirit* (Nottingham, England: Assemblies of God Publishing House, 1934; reprint, Springfield, Mo.: Gospel Publishing House, 1975), 136 (page reference is to reprint edition).

body. Apart from submission, prayer is only a cold and lifeless form. The Greek word used by Paul, *hupotassō,* means to "subordinate," "subject oneself," "yield voluntarily," "submit oneself." Submission undergirds all effective prayer. It is essential to the initial infilling of the Holy Spirit. Apart from its continued practice there can be no Spirit-filled life-style. Submission is the key to admittance into the Holy of Holies. Submission is always the initiative of the one who submits, for it emanates from the core of a person's being, the central will. If imposed or forced, it is not submission at all. Jesus was the epitome of submission. He could say without equivocation, " 'I always do what pleases him [the Father]' " (John 8:29). He said also, " 'Take my yoke upon you and learn from me, for I am gentle and humble in heart' " (Matt. 11:29). "I am gentle and humble in heart" is equivalent to "I am fully submitted to My Father and His will."

"To one another out of reverence for Christ" presupposes the well-spring of all other necessary submission in the Christian community. The fundamental submission is to our Lord himself. Once this is in place, submission within the family of God, according to God's prescribed order (1 Cor. 11:3; Eph. 5:21; 6:9), is quite natural. All lack of submission within the household of faith is traceable to a fundamental rebellion against God. By its very nature, refusal to submit becomes a hinderance to prayer and the Spirit-filled life-style.

Prayer for Any Occasion

Most believers find it easier to pray in the midst of a crisis. But crisis praying without regular communion is like grasping for a life ring whose connecting line has not been maintained. Paul captures the divine intent for our prayer habits as he encourages the Ephesian believers to pray with regularity, intensity, and perseverance.

Pray in the Spirit on all occasions with all kinds of prayers and requests. With this in mind, be alert and always keep on praying for all the saints. Pray also for me, that whenever I open my mouth, words may be given me so that I will fearlessly make known the mystery of the gospel (Eph. 6:18–19).

Dropping the metaphor of the Christian soldier's armor (6:10–17), Paul continues in verses 18 and 19 the idea of the believer's conflict by focusing on the most vital element of all in successful spiritual warfare: prayer. Though prayer is certainly implied in the foregoing instructions on putting on spiritual armor, Paul now specifically advocates a wide-ranging variety of prayer approaches. Since the powers of this dark world and the spiritual forces of evil are always pitted against us, it is imperative that we always pray. The Greek *en panti kairō* means "on every occasion." This is no casual injunction; it is a matter of such vast proportions and consequences that it must be taken up with all resoluteness. To believe that we can contend successfully in this warfare through the power of our puny intellects or the might of our Adamic nature is to discover to our hurt that we are no match for him who "prowls around like a roaring lion looking for someone to devour" (1 Pet. 5:8).

The Greek *dia pasēs proseuchēs* means literally "through every kind of prayer." Verse 18 begins with this phrase, with no separation from the previous passage on the Christian's armor. In reality, Paul was saying, "Put on the full armor of God [6:11], . . . stand firm then [against Satan] [6:14] . . . Take . . . the sword of the Spirit [6:17] with all kinds of prayers [6:18]." It is useless to debate whether we through prayer put on the full armor or take only the sword of the Spirit (the Word of God). Prayer is the instrument of spiritual warfare that makes effective the defensive armor and the offensive weapons.

"All kinds of prayers" includes public as well as private prayer, informal as well as formal, silent as well as vocal, praise as well as petition, planned as well as spontaneous, and in the Spirit as well as with the mind. "Prayers" derives from the Greek *proseuchē;* "requests" comes from *deēsis.* *Proseuchē* represents general prayer and *deēsis* denotes prayer for a specific need. "Requests" implies strong, persistent prayer that perseveres until evil is checked and righteousness prevails. "In the Spirit" is perhaps better translated "through the Spirit." Paul likely has in mind praying in another tongue (see 1 Cor. 14:14). By this means the believer's praying is elevated beyond intellect and offered according to God's will.

Not only are believers to pray at all times under the direction of the Spirit (who knows what to pray for), but they are to be diligent in prayer and petition for "all the saints" in this spiritual warfare. Paul then demonstrates his seriousness as well as his humility by asking for their vigilant prayer for himself. This request for prayer support of one's own ministry ought to be the prime request of every gospel preacher. Satan seeks by every means to stop the mouths of God's servants, either by fear so they cannot speak boldly, or by doubt so they cannot speak authoritatively, or by confused thoughts so they cannot speak clearly.

Prayer Instead of Worry

The Christians in Rome were admonished, "Do not be overcome by evil, but overcome evil with good" (Rom. 12:21). To the Philippian Christians the advice becomes more specific. In the face of difficult circumstances, they were told how to cope: "Do not be anxious about anything, but in everything, by prayer and petition, with thanksgiving, present your requests to God. And the peace of God, which transcends all understanding, will guard your hearts and your minds in Christ Jesus" (Phil. 4:6–7).

The prevailing tone of the letter to the church at Philippi is joy. There was genuine need for the encouragement. Paul was in prison. The Philippian Christians were suffering at the hands of a hostile world. There were false teachers who sought to entice the Philippians to follow a false gospel. Yet Paul could say, "Do not be anxious about anything." "Anxious" is from the Greek *merimnaō,* meaning to "be anxious about," "be unduly concerned," or "have a distracting care about something." "Not . . . about anything" is the major emphasis of the admonition, for *mēden* is the first word in the sentence: "Nothing be anxious about." Not one thing! We cannot help having cares or concerns—employment, health, loved ones, fellow believers. But we are not to be harassed by those cares, as though we carried their full weight ourselves.

But it is inadequate to exhort a person not to be anxious. To do so may only impose a greater anxiety. An antidote

must be provided, so Paul prescribes the means for overcoming anxious care: "In everything, by prayer and petition, with thanksgiving present your requests to God" (4:6).
Thanksgiving should be an essential element of all praying.
It is the means of expressing appreciation for what God
has already done on our behalf, and of expressing faith for
what we anticipate He will do in answer to our prayers.
The fact that "your Father knows what you need before
you ask him" (Matt. 6:8) is another reason for giving Him
thanks, for He will always answer our prayers in such a
way as to meet our real needs. It is also true that He desires
us to present our requests to Him. We do not make our
requests to give Him new information, but rather to exercise our faith in obtaining from His hand.

Such praying not only obtains answers to the concerns
which generated our anxieties, but results in a state of mind
every child of God should experience: "the peace of God."
It is that deep inward repose of the soul, identified as "the
peace of God" because it is communicated and sustained
by Him. It grows out of a spiritual mind-set, for "the mind
of sinful man is death, but the mind controlled by Spirit is
life and peace" (Rom. 8:6). Peace is the blessed fruit of
having replaced anxiety with supplication and prayer. "You
will keep in perfect peace him whose mind is steadfast,
because he trusts in you" (Isa. 26:3). Prayer is rewarded
with God's peace, a peace "which transcends all understanding" (4:7). The ungodly cannot perceive it, for it is
beyond their comprehension. It is also beyond the believer's comprehension, for even the godly who enjoy the
blessed experience cannot quite grasp how light breaks in
upon their darkness in such a mysterious yet real way,
bringing with it a tranquility defying explanation. "The
peace of God . . . will guard your hearts and minds in Christ
Jesus." The Greek *phroureō* ("keep" or "guard") is a mil-
itary term used by the guarding done by a whole garrison
of soldiers. It describes the sense of security the believer
experiences when he places all his concerns in God's hand.
It is more than mere protection; the Holy Spirit keeps a
watchful guard and benevolent custody over our hearts
and minds so that no disturbing influence may pass through

PART 2

**Chapter 11
Paul on
Prayer—
Part One**

and upset our inner serenity. R. Finlayson preserves the counsel of an earlier writer:

If your mind be overcharged or overwhelmed with trouble and anxiety, go into the presence of God. Spread your case before him. Though he knows the desires of your heart, yet he has declared he will be sought after; he will be inquired of to do it for you. Go, therefore, into the presence of that God who will at once tranquillize your spirit, give you what you wish or make you more happy without it, and who will be your everlasting Consolation, if you trust in him. He will breathe peace into your soul, and command tranquillity in the midst of the greatest storms.[9]

The peace of God, mediated by the Holy Spirit in response to prayer and supplication, "will guard your hearts and your minds in Christ Jesus."

Prayer for Leaders

Good advice can well be repeated. Colossian believers and Ephesian believers needed the same encouragement to pray. What was good for believers in Colosse and Ephesus in the first century is still good for believers around the world today. Note the similarity of Colossians 4:2–4 to Ephesians 6:18–19.

Devote yourselves to prayer, being watchful and thankful. And pray for us, too, that God may open a door for our message, so that we may proclaim the mystery of Christ, for which I am in chains. Pray that I may proclaim it clearly, as I should (Col. 4:2–4).

The Greek *proskartereō,* translated "devote yourselves," means to "persevere in," "spend much time in," or "be continually steadfast with a person or thing." The word is used in Acts 1:14 to describe how the disciples together held on in prayer immediately prior to choosing a replacement for the fallen Judas. Jesus himself prayed similarly when He spent entire nights in prayer before making im-

---

[9]H. D. M. Spence and Joseph S. Exell, eds., *The Pulpit Commentary* (Grand Rapids: Wm. B. Eerdmans Pub. Co., 1950), vol. 20, *Philippians,* by R. Finlayson, 177.

portant decisions or appointments (e.g., Luke 6:12 and Matt. 26:36–44). The same word is used in Romans 12:12, where Paul exhorts believers to be "faithful in prayer."

"Watchful" is a translation of the Greek *grēgoreō*, meaning "to keep awake," "to be spiritually alert," "to be vigilant." Jesus used the same word when he chided the sleeping Peter, James, and John to "watch and pray" (Matt. 26:41). The message is simple and direct: Be always praying; keep your heart focused on the subject of your prayers, lest you be diverted and as a conseqence fail in your purpose. And while you're praying in this manner, do not neglect giving thanks.

Once again the apostle urges his personal appeal upon the church: "praying at the same time for us as well" (4:3, NASB). Paul was at the time a prisoner in Rome, as a result of violent Jewish opposition; and yet he did not lose sight of his holy calling and mission. His passion to preach the gospel was not diminished, although his opportunity to do so was greatly limited. Therefore he solicited the prayer help of fellow believers. Prayer for spiritual leaders must be a priority for all believers. In fact, all leaders need our intercession: kings, presidents, governors, and those in lesser public offices. But of all those for whom we should intercede, none are more worthy (cf. 1 Tim. 5:17–18) or stand in greater need than preachers of the gospel. Their message is more important than that of statesmen or kings. So when Paul asks the Colossians to intercede for him, it is that he may speak the mystery of Christ with greater boldness. The intercession of every saint should be that preachers may be delivered from all limitations and hindrances in the proclamation of the gospel.

"That I may proclaim clearly" is a request with more meaning than may appear at first. Besides "proclaim clearly," the Greek *phaneroō* means to "reveal," "make known," "teach." Paul's desire is that he will not only be given an open door to proclaim the gospel, but that in his proclamation there will be God-given clarity in the manifestation of the mystery hidden to previous generations, but which has already been revealed to Paul (see Col. 1:25–26). And what Paul desired, every preacher of the gospel should covet most earnestly, remembering the words of our Lord:

"The Spirit gives life; the flesh counts for nothing. The words I have spoken to you are spirit and they are life" (John 6:63).

Instructions in Prayer

Paul customarily makes a theological statement and then proceeds to clarify, explain, and apply the truth for the recipients of his letter. But on one occasion, as he wrote to the Thessalonians, he changed his approach. In a staccato of instruction, he lays out concise commands to be followed by all believers: "Be joyful always; pray continually; give thanks in all circumstances.... Do not put out the Spirit's fire; do not treat prophecies with contempt. Test everything. Hold on to the good.... Brothers, pray for us" (1 Thess. 5:16–21,25). Most of these pungent instructions relate to prayer—for twentieth-century as well as first-century believers. No conditions or contingencies qualify the commands. In the midst of tribulation or triumph, they are all to be followed.

Two manuscripts of note[10] add the words "in the Lord" to "be joyful always," thus relating the command to prayer (cf. Phil. 4:4). True joy springs from a vital relationship with the Lord. It is His joy within which enables us to be joyful always. The way to be joyful always is to pray continually. People would rejoice more if they prayed more. "Continually" does not mean to be constantly uttering formal prayers. Rather, it echoes Ephesians 6:18—"Pray in the Spirit on all occasions with all kinds of prayers and requests." We should keep scheduled times of prayer, but we must also be instant in prayer as the need arises or as the heart has opportunity to turn toward its Master. Paul does not say that believers should do nothing else but pray; yet nothing we do should hinder an attitude or spirit of prayer.

What an integral part of prayer is thanksgiving! It should always accompany prayer (Phil. 4:6); it grows out of faithful prayer. Prayer leads into God's presence, and who cannot

---

[10]F^P [also called F$_2$], Codex Augiensis; G^P [also called G$_3$], Codex Boernerianus, both from the ninth century A.D.

give thanks there? "All circumstances" covers the entire sphere of life, the good and the evil, the victories and the defeats, the joys and the sorrows. Nothing is omitted. This parallels the exhortation to give thanks for everything (Eph. 5:20). Our thanksgiving is faith's acknowledgment that God works in all things for our good in the end; so thanksgiving is always the will of God in Christ Jesus. (See the definition of "thanksgiving" in the Introduction; Paul may have been suggesting that a constant attitude and expression of thanksgiving is one way of praying without ceasing.)

It is commonly understood that Paul is alluding to the Spirit's working in the gifts when he says, "Do not put out the Spirit's fire," especially the publicly manifested utterance gifts (cf. 1 Cor. 14:39); it is also appropriate to apply the admonition to our personal prayer lives. We must guard against suppressing those God-inspired times of private praying in unknown tongues and those gentle nudges of the Spirit to intercede for various concerns He may bring to our attention.

Paul also solicits their prayers (cf. Rom. 15:30–32). Believers need the prayers of each other (cf. Gal. 6:2). Our prayers make possible God's intervention in our lives as well as the lives of others. How many tragedies might be averted, how many problems might be solved, how much more effective preaching might be, how much more may be accomplished for the Kingdom, if believers intercede in prayer for God's ministers.

An Avenue for the Spread of the Gospel

The success of the gospel depends on believers' prayers more than most of us realize. It is an evil of major proportions to neglect intercession for the rapid and effective spread of the gospel. " 'Ask the Lord of the harvest, therefore, to send out workers into his harvest field' " (Matt. 9:38). Paul's final instructions on prayer to the Thessalonians was to that end: "Pray for us that the message of the Lord may spread rapidly and be honored, just as it was with you. And pray that we may be delivered from wicked and evil men, for not everyone has faith" (2 Thess. 3:1–2).

"Spread rapidly" is an allusion to the races run in a stadium. Paul pictures the word of the Lord already in the race and desires that it shall run mightily until it gains the appointed crown or is "honored, just as it was with you [the Thessalonian believers]." He perceives that prayer is the enabling propellant, thrusting the word of the Lord toward its intended goal: the conversion of the unregenerate. Apart from prayer the race is lost. The second part of the petition relates to the first. Wicked and evil men obstruct, or at least seek to obstruct, the advance of the gospel. "Wicked" (from the Gk. *atopos*) means "out of place," "injurious," "morally evil." Such faithless and evil people are ever present to oppose the Word of the Lord, either by ridicule or by otherwise hindering the messenger. Paul perceived, and we are wise to believe, that the answer to this problem is ever the same: freedom through the prayer of God's people.

Prayer for Everyone

Prayer should be offered for everyone. Not that every person can be mentioned by name, but all groups and classes of people should be included in our praying. There will, of course, be specific names mentioned within each circle, whether ethnic group, inner city addicts, homosexuals, or secular authorities. It is this last group that Paul singles out as one that should not be overlooked in our praying.

I urge, then, first of all, that requests, prayers, intercession and thanksgiving be made for everyone—for kings and all those in authority, that we may live peaceful and quiet lives in all godliness and holiness. This is good, and pleases God our Savior, who wants all men to be saved and to come to a knowledge of the truth. For there is one God and one mediator between God and men, the man Christ Jesus, who gave himself as a ransom for all men . . . I want men everywhere to lift up holy hands in prayer, without anger or disputing (1 Tim. 2:1–5,8).

It is not easy to determine the precise difference between "requests, prayers, intercession, and thanksgiving." There are, however, distinctions that suggest ways the believer can approach the throne of God. "Requests" (Gk.

deēseis) are petitions or burdened requests that God will meet a lack or need in the life of the person for whom prayer is made. "Prayers" (Gk. *proseuchas*) are general requests for gaining essential needs, both spiritual and temporal. "Intercessions" (Gk. *enteuxeis*) speak of petition to a superior, e.g., a king. For the believer, intercession is petitioning an Almighty God to meet the needs of others. "Thanksgiving" (Gk. *eucharistias*) denotes a prevailing attitude of thankfulness and gratitude as prayer is lifted toward heaven; a prayer of praise always pleases the Lord.

It is probable that the apostle gives directions here for public worship, and that the words may be thus paraphrased: *"Now, I exhort, first of all that,* in the public assemblies, *deprecations* of evils, and *supplications* for such good things as are necessary, and *intercessions* for their conversion, and *thanksgivings* for mercies, *be offered in behalf of all men*—for heathens as well as for Christians, and for enemies as well as for friends."[11]

The essence of our praying should be twofold: (1) for those in authority and (2) for peaceful and quiet lives. Believers do well to pray not only that leaders may rule in justice and equity, but that they will be protected from rash and evil influences, that they will effect peace by their administration, and that they themselves will be saved (v. 4). Furthermore, the prayer for rulers has peace with godliness and holiness as its end. Believers should always pray for a social and political atmosphere in which they can live in faith, godliness, and obedience to God, without having to contend with pagan magistrates. Praying for secular leaders is pleasing to God because His salvation is for all mankind, the noble and powerful as well as the poor and lowly.

We come now to a concept that is foundational to all true faith and also to prayer itself: "There is one God and one mediator between God and men, the man Christ Jesus" (v. 5). The God to whom we come in prayer is the only God. There can be no other, for this One fills eternity and

---

[11]Adam Clarke, *The Holy Bible Containing the Old and New Testament with a Commentary and Critical Notes,* vol. 6 (London: Ward, Lock & Co., n.d.), 560–561.

infinity. He was so concerned about humanity that He provided His Son as the one and only Mediator to reconcile us to himself. He desires the salvation of all, and no one perishes but by one's own neglect. We come to the one and only God through the one and only Mediator, the man Christ Jesus, for our salvation. So it must be for every human being, regardless of social or political stature.

How does Paul apply this basic truth of the Christian faith? What should be our behavior and devotion in light of the eternal reality of divinely provided salvation? Because there is one God, with whom we must be reconciled, and because there is one Mediator through whom we can gain this reconciliation, Paul says, "I want men everywhere to lift up holy hands in prayer, without anger or disputing" (v. 8). "Also" (v. 9) means "in the same way." Therefore, women as well as men must present holy or dedicated hands, with a pure spirit. A synecdoche, "hands" stand for the whole being, one's very life-style. "To lift up holy hands" was a common custom among both Jews and pagans. To lift up or spread out the arms and hands while praying denotes entreaty and request. In this way, Paul shows us how to pray effectively. We are to come to God, humble ourselves for our sins, present as our sacrifice the Lamb of God, offer holy lives in worship and praise to Him, and then expect to enjoy access into His presence. Petitions expressed as we enter His presence with His righteousness will receive a response. For women there is the additional request for modest dress with decency and propriety.

Attitudes are absolutely critical if our prayers are to be answered; therefore, Paul advocates the avoidance of "anger or disputing." There can be no unforgiving or vindictive spirit, no reasoning or dialogues that militate against simple faith. "I want men everywhere," said Paul, "to lift up holy hands in prayer, without anger or disputing." This was certainly characteristic of Paul's prayer and should be of ours.

Questions for Study

1. Under what circumstances is it important for us to look to the Holy Spirit to intercede for us in sighs too deep for words? How do we know the Spirit is doing this?

2. How should we apply 1 Corinthians 11:4–6 to our own day?

3. When is it necessary for praying in tongues to be interpreted?

4. What should we do when God's answer to our repeated prayers is no?

5. Why is it important to pray in the Spirit on all occasions?

6. What is the cure for anxiety?

7. What is included in the peace of God?

8. What part does thanksgiving have in prayer and why?

9. The early Christians expected persecution, but Paul still urged them to pray that they might lead peaceful and quiet lives. Why?

PAUL ON PRAYER—PART TWO

Paul's praying was born out of his own experiences. What he had so well learned through his pursuit of God became the passion of his prayer for the churches. "The one who truly prays will have keener insight, will form sounder judgment, will evolve more intelligent plans, will achieve a greater mastery of situations, will sustain more creative relationships with people, than he ever could without prayer."[1] Paul was an effective witness and preacher because he was effective in prayer.

Why Paul included his prayers in his letters might be questioned. Certainly it was not done to impress his readers with his personal devotion and spirituality; nor was it done merely to fill up space in literary epistles. But because Paul was writing to his readers rather than addressing them in person, his regular habit of praying for them would naturally accompany his admonition and encouragement. We should remember also that he wrote these letters under the inspiration of the Holy Spirit. The Spirit directed him to include these prayers as part of the instruction God wanted all believers to have. Through Paul's example we

---

[1]Albert Edward Ayd, in R. L. Brandt, *Praying with Paul* (Grand Rapids: Baker Book House, 1966), 7.

can learn how to come into God's very presence with confidence. Paul's prayers also help to bring revelation of God's will for His people, and they present a pattern of prayer worthy of emulation. When we study his prayers and enter into their spirit, it is possible to pray them meaningfully along with Paul.

Praying the recorded prayers of Paul helps us express to God the deepest part of our beings. These dynamic and beautiful prayers introduce us to a whole new world. They help us peer into the depths of eternity, and at the same time they transport us from the mundane and mediocre levels of Christian existence to the height of divine revelation. Every believer who desires an effective prayer life is wise to commit all of Paul's prayers to memory and to make them an ongoing part of his daily devotions.[2]

Praying To Know God Better

Paul's prayer for the Ephesian believers (Eph. 1:15–21) expresses God's highest will for every one of His children. Both here and later in the epistle, Paul prays, with great unction, that the Ephesians might grow stronger spiritually through the help of the Holy Spirit (cf. Eph. 3:16). We all need to pray for each other—and for ourselves—that there might be a great work of the Spirit in each one of us.

For this reason, ever since I heard about your faith in the Lord Jesus and your love for all the saints, I have not stopped giving thanks for you, remembering you in my prayers. I keep asking that the God of our Lord Jesus Christ, the glorious Father, may give you the Spirit of wisdom and revelation, so that you may know him better. I pray also that the eyes of your heart may be enlightened in order that you may know the hope to which he has called you, the riches of his glorious inheritance in the saints, and his incomparably great power for us who believe. That power is like the working of his mighty strength, which he exerted in Christ when he raised him from the dead and seated him at his

---

[2]I have personally done this, maintaining the practice with great advantage and delight for over a quarter of a century.—R. L. B.

right hand in the heavenly realms, far above all rule and authority, power and dominion, and every title that can be given, not only in the present age but also in the one to come (Eph. 1:15–21).

With the introduction "for this reason," Paul refers to some previous verses, verses which contain three spiritual blessings that belong to believers through Christ. First, "In him we have redemption through his blood, the forgiveness of sins, in accordance with the riches of God's grace" (v. 7). Second, "In him we were also chosen, having been predestined according to the plan of him who works out everything in conformity with the purpose of his will" (v. 11). Third, "Having believed, you were marked in him with a seal, the promised Holy Spirit, who is a deposit guaranteeing our inheritance, until the redemption of those who are God's possession" (v. 13). Redeemed, chosen to give praise to God (v. 12), and made recipients of the promised Holy Spirit—these are the truths that Paul wanted the Ephesian believers to understand and act upon.

The Ephesian believers for whom Paul was praying had likely been worshipers of the goddess Artemis (see Acts 19:23–34). No doubt as pagans they had prayed to her. But that had all changed, and what a contrast they must have seen in Paul's petitions addressed to "the God of our Lord Jesus Christ, the glorious Father" (v. 17)! We do well to identify the God to whom we pray by addressing Him as He is described by the inspired writers of Scripture.

Immediately we confront somewhat of a mystery: Is not Jesus himself God? Unquestionably the Scriptures declare it (see Matt. 1:23; John 20:28; Heb. 1:8). But though Jesus is indeed the Son of God and therefore God himself, He is at the same time the Son of Man, and therefore both God and Man. That is, He held within himself a full set of divine qualities and a full set of human qualities in such a way that they did not interfere with each other. It was from the human perspective that Jesus prayed to God the Father. His entrance into the human level (see Phil. 2:5–8) necessitated His praying at the human level.[3]

---

[3]Examples of His praying as a man are dealt with in chap. 7.

Having established the identity of Him to whom he addressed his prayer, Paul moved from identity to affirmation of character: "the glorious Father" ("all-glorious Father," Phillips). "Glory" is more than merely brilliance, or brightness; it encompasses all that God is—His nature, His character, His being. Giving glory to God does not impart to Him something He does not already have; instead, it acknowledges the honor that is rightfully His (cf. Isa. 42:8,12). "Glory" is the unfathomable essence of God, which makes Him worthy of all praise. When one discerns God's glory, even to a limited degree, one's praying enters completely new dimensions (cf. Exod. 33:18 through 34:8). To this all-glorious God, and to Him only, Paul addressed his petitions, knowing that God was unquestionably capable of responding to the profound requests he would articulate.

Paul's prayer for the Ephesian believers can be summarized simply, "God, cause them to understand." Paul himself expresses the burden of his heart in this prayer. There is a discernable relationship between one's experience and one's burden. What Paul had experienced, he desired that others would also experience. He had come to know eternal reality through "the Spirit of wisdom and revelation"; the eyes of his heart had been enlightened so that he knew the hope of God's calling, the inheritance God envisioned for His people (including Paul) and the power available to gain these glorious ends. Paul wanted his Ephesian friends to have the same experience, praying that God would give them "the Spirit of wisdom and revelation," so that they would know the glorious Father better.

Whether the word "spirit" is the Holy Spirit or the human spirit "of wisdom and revelation" has been debated. Whichever interpretation is followed, the human spirit, when moved upon by the Holy Spirit, experiences wisdom and spiritual revelation. "Wisdom" means more than judgment or intuition derived from human mental processes, no matter how brilliant it may be. This is a divine wisdom, such as Isaiah foresaw in the coming Messiah: "The spirit of the LORD will rest on him—the Spirit of wisdom and of understanding, the Spirit of counsel and of power, the Spirit of knowledge and of the fear of the LORD" (Isa. 11:2).

Whereas wisdom issues in right judgment, revelation issues in right knowledge. Revelation has two aspects: the divine and the human. In relation to God, it is the unveiling, or uncovering, of knowledge exclusive to God's province. In relation to the human, it is the application of the faculty of insight to such unveiled spiritual truth. Paul's desire to introduce the Ephesians to the God of all wisdom, knowledge, and power inspired his eloquent prayer.

Christ yearns to inspire His Church like He inspired Paul, giving it the same passionate desire for a more complete knowledge of God. We cannot have more confidence that we are praying in God's will than when we petition with Paul for a greater understanding and knowledge of Almighty God for ourselves and our fellow believers. This knowledge is entirely outside the grasp of human nature. "The man without the Spirit does not accept the things that come from the Spirit of God, for they are foolishness to him, and he cannot understand them, because they are spiritually discerned" (1 Cor. 2:14). Yet this divine revelation can be received by everyone willing to acknowledge the existence of a communicating God. "We have not received the spirit of the world but the Spirit who is from God, that we may understand what God has freely given us" (1 Cor. 2:12). Only God can give us the eyes of a seer. "'No eye has seen, no ear has heard, no mind has conceived what God has prepared for those who love him,'—but God has revealed it to us by his Spirit" (1 Cor. 2:9–10).

In other words, obtaining this knowledge of God is not a matter of hard mental toil; as A. W. Tozer observed: "The teaching of the New Testament is that God and spiritual things can be known finally only by a direct work of God within the soul. However theological knowledge may be aided by figures and analogies, the pure understanding of God must be by personal spiritual awareness. The Holy Spirit is indispensable."[4]

The term "revelation" has suffered violence in the house of its friends. Consequently, its use frequently provokes suspicion and distrust. What divisions, what grief, what

---

[4]A. W. Tozer, *That Incredible Christian* (Calcutta: Evangelical Literature Depot, 1964), 91.

anguish, what heartache, what contentions, what ruin, have come to the Church by those who abuse this divine gift! But shall we reject revelation because charlatans employ a counterfeit for their own ends? Certainly not! Instead it should intensify our efforts to experience what is trying to be imitated.

So what are we to understand as Paul's intent when he petitioned God as he did? He meant coming to revealed knowledge other than by ordinary means. He meant coming to revealed knowledge through an act of God, by His Spirit. He meant having our spiritual perception sharpened by the Spirit so we can recognize the genuine from the counterfeit. How great is our need for genuine revelation. Without it we see only an outline in the shadows; with it we see almost face to face. Without it we know about Him; with it we truly know Him. Without it He seems far removed; with it we perceive that He is gloriously near. Revelation spells the difference between cold, dead orthodoxy and warm, living spirituality.

The qualifying phrase "that you may know *him* better" leaves no room for the strange or the spurious. Definite bounds are set within which revelation knowledge is valid: (1) that you may know "the hope to which he has called you," (2) that you may know "the riches of his glorious inheritance in the saints," and (3) that you may know "his incomparably great power for us who believe."

Paul carries his petition yet a step further: "that the eyes of your heart may be enlightened." The heart, in the Hebrew language, included the inner mind and understanding. Our natural understanding cannot discern or comprehend spiritual truth by itself. But enlightened eyes of the heart, awakened by the Holy Spirit, bring genuine divine revelation. This is not some mysterious occultic unveiling of the previously unknown, but an energizing of truth already revealed in the Word but not yet grasped by one's spiritual consciousness. All of us, for one reason or another and to one degree or another, are much like Israel, of whom it was said, "Even to this day when Moses is read, a veil covers their hearts" (2 Cor. 3:15). Or we are like the Emmaus disciples who "were kept from recognizing him [Jesus]" (Luke 24:16).

In none of these lofty petitions is there a hint of concern or desire for anything to gratify the human senses. Yet we get the sense of someone so enraptured with a God-given perception of the believer's ultimate end that he longs to share the revealed promise of blessings to come. Paul had seen the other world as mortals have seldom seen it (see 2 Cor. 12:1–4), and he strongly desired that others might, by the Spirit, glimpse the glorious prospect. How we need to pray with Paul to these ends!

Receiving the Fullness of God

What an inspiration to compare Paul's physical circumstances with the content of his prayer! While writing the Book of Ephesians, he was a prisoner in Rome (see Eph. 3:1,13). Even with the privilege of receiving visitors and moving about with some freedom, he was constantly under guard. We would not fault him for voicing prayer for his complete freedom. Yet he is more concerned about freeing people from sin and helping them grow spiritually. His own physical restraints were nothing compared with the bondage of those without Christ.

For this reason I kneel before the Father, from whom his whole family in heaven and on earth derives its name. I pray that out of his glorious riches he may strengthen you with power through his Spirit in your inner being, so that Christ may dwell in your hearts through faith. And I pray that you, being rooted and established in love, may have power, together with all the saints, to grasp how wide and long and high and deep is the love of Christ, and to know this love that surpasses knowledge—that you may be filled to the measure of all the fullness of God (Eph. 3:14–19).

In this second of Paul's prayers for the Ephesians, we observe an upward progression, leading step by step to the ultimate state of being "filled to the measure of all the fullness of God." Paul's passion for the Church's spiritual progress is never more clearly evident than in this passage. His petitions indicate not only his cherished objectives, but also his unquestioned conviction that only through divine enablement could they be obtained. Until we pray with similar conviction, seeking the same divine enablement, we come short of the glorious heights that God has intended for us.

"I kneel" (v. 14) can be understood in either of two ways: (1) Paul was speaking of his physical posture when praying; (2) he was describing his heart attitude toward God. In some cultures, people show respect for those of higher rank by standing in their presence rather than being seated. In other cultures, bowing or kneeling is the proper body position in the presence of highly esteemed persons. Should God be treated with any less respect than a fellow mortal? It may be, however, that Paul was not as concerned about the posture of his body as he was about the attitude of his heart. Whatever the case, kneeling in the presence of the Lord suggests deliberate and serious prayer, approaching God with reverence and holy fear.

Whereas Paul identified God as "the God of our Lord Jesus Christ, the glorious Father" in his earlier prayer (Eph. 1:17), his identification here simply says, "I kneel before the Father, from whom his whole family in heaven and on earth derives its name" (3:14–15). Paul here emphasizes the whole community of dedicated believers, whether already in heaven or still on earth, as making up one family, deriving its name from God and looking to Him as the supplier of all its needs.

All four of the petitions in this prayer are interrelated and each enhances the one preceding. While we might hope to progress through the four petitions in one mighty ascent, that is no more possible than advancing from infancy to adulthood in a single day. "The child must still grow up by degrees, and there is no 'chair lift' to yonder glorious elevation. . . . Each step is introduced with a 'that' [KJV], and each 'that' points back to the conditions which make possible the next step in the ascent. There is no bypassing and no starting halfway up the stairs. Every step is necessary to the one above it and dependent on the one below it."[5]

---

[5]Brandt, *Praying With Paul,* 55.

Paul's first petition is verse 16: "That out of his glorious riches he may strengthen you with power through his Spirit in your inner being." "Out of" (Gk. *kata*), a term appearing at least fifteen times in Ephesians alone, here suggests a means of measuring. That is, God's ability to provide for the need of the inner person is measured by the vastness of His own resources, His own glorious riches. This heavenly medium of exchange cannot be compared with any earthly medium of exchange, nor can the currency of earth ever afford the resource necessary to the inner person. The riches of the Almighty are not measured in terms of gold, but of glory. Gold may meet the need of the temporal, perishing body, but only glory will satisfy the needs of the eternity-bound soul. All that the inner person needs is available "according to his [unlimited] glorious riches." So Paul makes his claim for everything his inner being may need; his assurance that he will receive more than enough is the existence of the inexhaustible glorious riches of God. We have the privilege of making the same claim.

Prayer, for Paul, was the single means of joining the supply—God's glorious riches—with the overwhelming need of the inner person. He was especially mindful of a particular facet of those glorious riches that would address the need: His power. The believer is strengthened by miraculous power conveyed by God's Spirit.

The second petition is the first part of verse 17: "That Christ may dwell in your hearts through faith." The preceding petition lifts us to this next step in the stairway toward God's ultimate. "Dwell" (Gk. *katoikeō*) means "to make a home," "settle down to stay," or "live permanently." Until Christ makes His permanent home in our hearts, there is little progress toward love in the measure of "all the fullness of God." "Through faith" is not included here by accident. "All the relationships between man and God rest on this bedrock. By his own faith Abraham dwelt in tabernacles; by our faith Christ dwells in our hearts."[6] The reality of Christ dwelling in our hearts is attainable not by human might and determination but only as the Holy Spirit accomplishes it in response to our praying.

---

[6]Ibid., 59.

The third petition is the latter half of verse 17 and continues through verse 19: "That you, being rooted and established in love, may have power, together with all the saints, to grasp how wide and long and high and deep is the love of Christ, and to know this love that surpasses knowledge." While we may not yet perceive it, we are listening here to the praying of a great apostle who, in his own pursuit of God, had left far behind the lowlands of spiritual mediocrity and had climbed the mount of spiritual insight and revelation; from the mountaintop, removed from the world below, he was awed by the almost indescribable sight of his magnificent God. No longer was Paul's view restricted. He had seen God in all His ineffable glory and beauty. Never again could he be satisfied with resting at the foot of the mountain. Nor could he selfishly revel in his present state, for with his whole being he desired the same for all believers. And so he prayed with passion.

This third step flows naturally out of the second, for where Christ is at home within, there also His love abides, opening to us unlimited horizons. Love is at once the fertile soil of the soul and the ground of our spiritual attainment.

"Grasp" (Gk. *katalambanō*) means "to take eagerly," "to seize," "to make one's own," "to possess." Love is the enabling and qualifying force. Apart from it our spiritual limbs are paralyzed; we cannot ascend to the heights where God's fullness is experienced. We may view those heights in the distance with longing eyes, but like the elusive end of the rainbow, they are beyond our grasp. Our limited view of God is our chief handicap. God's greatness may loom before us, like a majestic but distant mountain peak, but we have hardly set foot in its vacinity. Yet, both God and Paul beckon us to make the climb.

What then is this thing of four dimensions (width, length, height, and depth) that attracts us? Most assuredly it is something hidden from the natural eye. It is far beyond the grasp of anyone who does not know God through Christ in a personal way. Some have thought that divine love is the unmeasurable aspect of God that the Spirit wants us to comprehend. That is no doubt part of the consideration, and though the very next statement singles out love by itself ("... and to know this [extraordinary] love [of Christ] that surpasses knowledge"), the context hardly allows this conclusion. Although there can be no question that God desires His children to grow in love, for God is love, we err when we think we understand God if we know about love. "Beyond God's love but encompassing it is His fullness—the breadth, the length, the depth and the height of Him—all that He is."[7] This is what Paul had discovered when he prayed; and this was his prayer concern for the family of God.

The last petition in Paul's prayer is the latter half of verse 19: "That you may be filled to the measure of all the fullness of God." Here is the summit! After our inner being has been strengthened with His might by the Spirit, after Christ has become at home in our hearts, and after we have begun to possess God's glorious fullness, only then is the highest peak in Christian experience our possession. The lowlands, with their subtle downward pull, are far behind; a final step will transport us to the coveted goal: to be filled with the fullness of God. That is something unlimited. That is the brilliant mountain peak—being above the clouds—the loftiest height of all. A person cannot pursue a more precious treasure. How utterly insignificant are earth's treasures by comparison. However, note that just as in the case of the light that God shines in our hearts, "we have this treasure in jars of clay to show that this all-surpassing power is from God and not from us" (2 Cor. 4:7).

What is this fullness upon which we are to fix our sights and to which we are to direct our most earnest prayer? It is conformity to the image of the Son of God. For of Him it is written, "God was pleased to have all his fullness dwell in him [Christ]" (Col. 1:19); and "in Christ all the fullness of the Deity lives in bodily form, and you have been given fullness in Christ, who is the head over every power and authority" (Col. 2:9). Nothing more of God's fullness and nature could have been wrapped in human form, nor could God have been more fully revealed to His creatures, for

■■■■■
PART 2

Chapter 12
Paul on
Prayer—
Part Two

---

[7]Ibid., 60.

██████████

PART 2

Chapter 12
Paul on
Prayer—
Part Two

Jesus was the "the exact representation of [God's] being," the very expression of His substance (Heb. 1:3).

Praying for Deepened Love

As certainly as the ocean tides are influenced by the moon, so are our behavior and practices influenced by our praying. Prayer is immeasurably more than a form of spiritual therapy. Its purpose is far loftier than a mere sense of well-being. In its purest form it is the will of a person rising to a level with the will of God; in that union we can perform the will of God. The will of God for all believers could not be set forth more clearly than it is in this prayer.

This is my prayer: that your love may abound more and more in knowledge and depth of insight, so that you may be able to discern what is best and may be pure and blameless until the day of Christ, filled with the fruit of righteousness that comes through Jesus Christ—to the glory and praise of God (Phil. 1:9–11).

God's will for the Philippian believers, and for us today, is *agapē* love—love in its highest and purest form, though still in its infancy and consequently unperfected. Unlike *philos* love (affection or fondness and sometimes shallow), *agapē* love is poured "into our hearts by the Holy Spirit" (Rom. 5:5) and draws its nourishment from Him alone. Truth is its tutor; wisdom its guide. Satan's temptations cannot destroy it, nor can the enticing words of the false lover make it waver. It has unimagined potential. *Agapē* love prompted Paul's prayer, just as it should motivate our prayer. Paul's impassioned heart desired its superabundant and continual increase, knowing that where love abounds, there is every good work.

The words "in knowledge and depth of insight" should be treated as a unit, since together they represent a compound quality of love. To seek to separate knowledge and insight is like separating Siamese twins, for they are so nearly identical. "Knowledge" (Gk. *epignōsis*) is a strengthened form of *gnōsis* and indicates a full knowledge, a greater participation by the knower in the object known, which influences him the more powerfully. Paul seems to have in mind a spiritual sensitivity, a spiritual sixth sense. The Greek word *aisthēsis,* translated "insight," is found only here in the New Testament. It means "perception," "discernment," "moral experience." It involves moral understanding that intuitively perceives what is right and unconsciously shrinks from what is wrong. Through it a person becomes rich in every moral experience. Spiritual sensitivity and discernment are the supreme needs. Without them, we are too easily found among those "who call evil good and good evil, who put darkness for light and light for darkness, who put bitter for sweet and sweet for bitter. Woe to those who are wise in their own eyes and clever in their own sight!" (Isa. 5:20–21). But with that spiritual sense and discernment we join the ranks of those "who by constant use have trained themselves to distinguish good from evil" (Heb. 5:14).

Apart from Spirit-quickened spiritual sensitivity and discernment, we are unable to "discern what is best." Therefore, Paul's prayer "that your love may abound . . . in knowledge and depth of insight" precedes his prayer "that you may be able to discern what is best." "Discern" (Gk. *dokimazō*) indicates something more than mere understanding. It is to discover the best of something and accept it with approval after it has been tested (like metal) and found superior.

However, it is one thing to judge right from wrong, but quite another to act on that judgment: Approval of the best is most loudly proclaimed by performance, and approval also charts the course for performance; in other words, approval of the best prompts performance of the best. Apart from the ability to discern or discover what is best, there is no ability to perform excellence. *Agapē* love, Paul perceived, was far superior to any excellence approved by the Law (cf. Rom. 2:18). It enabled its possessor to sense and discern what would please the object of its love, and then to perform the action (as the Law could not do). The Law shouted, "This is it; do it or die!" Love whispers, "This is it. I would rather die than not do it."

Spiritual excellence consists of many virtues, the first of them being purity. "Purity" (Gk. *eilikrinēs*), according to some linguists, literally means "tested by the sunlight." In other words, we have a moral and ethical purity that can be examined in the strongest light without displaying a single flaw, or imperfection. It also means "unmixed," "free from impurities." It was also used of a sincerity that was free from wrong, selfish, or underhanded motives. The world has a way of detecting impurity and insincerity. So does God. Nothing has such a discordant voice as insincerity, and nothing provokes more disdain. Purity combined with sincerity, however, is the queen of virtues, the mother of all respect. Its fountainhead is love. Let purity and sincerity reign, and both God and people will esteem and honor the person who shows them.

Purity has a noble twin: blamelessness. "Blameless" (Gk. *aproskopos*) describes an ideal relationship that does not cause offense, a relationship primarily between us and God. *Agapē* love, abounding in spiritual sense and discernment, removes all barriers and keeps one from causing offense; where love is, offense is as hurtful to the offender as it is to the offended. To avoid causing offense by being blameless is to be righteous indeed.

Impurity, insincerity, and offense cannot produce the fruit of righteousness; but combine purity and sincerity with a blameless spirit and you have a heart that can yield no evil fruit. This prayer reaches its glorious climax with a pronouncement of the end toward which the whole prayer is aimed: "filled with the fruit of righteousness that comes through Jesus Christ—to the glory and praise of God" (v. 11). Fruit denotes character rather than service:

There is an almost uniform distinction made in the New Testament between works and fruit; the former pointing to service, and fruit to character. Therefore, ... fruit refers not to what we do but to what we are; not to Christian activity, but to our likeness to Christ; not to our relation to men, but to our condition of soul.[8]

We may be inclined to plead, "Such high goals, how can I reach them? How can I have *agapē* love? How can I discern what is best? How can I be morally and ethically

[8]W. Graham Scroggie, *Paul's Prison Prayers* (Grand Rapids: Kregel Publications, 1981), 33.

pure in a way that does not give offense? How can I be
filled with the fruit of righteousness?" There is but a single
answer. Begin to pray as Paul prayed:

I consider everything a loss compared to the surpassing greatness
of knowing Christ Jesus my Lord, for whose sake I have lost all
things. I consider them rubbish, that I may gain Christ and be
found in him, not having a righteousness of my own that comes
from the law, but that which is through faith in Christ—the
righteousness that comes from God and is by faith. I want to
know Christ and the power of his resurrection and the fellowship
of sharing in his sufferings, becoming like him in his death, and
so, somehow, to attain to the resurrection from the dead (Phil.
3:8–11).

At first glance, this passage may not be perceived as a
prayer; yet it echoes the sweet music of life's highest purpose. To express the desire to know the power of Christ's
resurrection and the fellowship of His sufferings is prayer
indeed. The soul that fully grasps Paul's meaning here may
be shaken by a sense of being subjected to the keenest
scrutiny. Nothing exposes one's imperfections like the perfections of another. No one provokes emulation like the
person who excels.

On review is the exemplary Paul. The spotlight is focused
on the recesses of his being. Whoever dares step into that
light is at once aware of his own spiritual poverty. What
soul ever voiced such searching expression of desire and
at the same time such obvious distrust of past attainment?
Here is a scene almost too sacred for our faint hearts: a
mighty soul on the stretch, but mingling such provocative
confessions that we wince in shame and wonder at our
own complacency. Feel the intensity of his cry: "And so,
somehow, to attain ..." (v. 11); "Not that I have already
attained all this ..." (v. 12); "I do not consider myself yet
to have taken hold of it ..." (v. 13). In an instant we spot
our own deficiency. We may have been so completely
absorbed with past experiences and attainments that we
had not given a second thought to the possibility that we
really had not yet arrived. Now upon second thought, not
only do we recognize that we have been acting as though
we had arrived—we find that we disembarked at the wrong

port. Yet in full view is the chief of the apostles (2 Cor. 11:5; 12:11), the mightiest of the saints, and he is completely aware of overwhelming personal shortcoming (cf. 1 Tim. 1:15). No doubt this is the identifying mark of greatness, for we unveil our spiritual stature by our attitudes toward the past and our hopes for the future.

For Paul there was always something beyond. There was something beyond the revolutionizing experience on the Damascus Road and even something more than the earnest of Straight Street. Not long before was an Arabian desert of revelation, and after that a straight path that rose ever upward toward the unsearchable knowledge of Christ's resurrection power. Nevertheless, when he contemplated his Master, Paul knew there was still more. He had suffered, but not as His Master had. He knew a measure of dying, but he was not yet like Him in His death. Nor would he feel he had attained until he had gone the entire course. One lap of the race was no victory. He would reserve his boasting until the final lap was run.

Unlike Paul, most of us vicitimize ourselves with a dream world. The song of our soul is, "If I am dreaming, let me dream on." And until something drastic happens, we are content to dream. We must be shocked back into reality lest we continue to dream our fantastic and fatal dreams. To feel we have attained is to preclude the possibility of further attainment.

The fact is—and it can be stated without fear of convincing exception—not one of us has yet "attained." Beyond us there is more, more than eye has seen or ear heard, more than any sage has ever told. In Paul's spiritually enlightened mind, knowing Christ "and the power of his resurrection, and the fellowship of sharing in his sufferings" (v. 10) was predicated on the most vital of all spiritual relationships. We make knowing Him altogether too casual a thing, and thereby admit to our own inferior knowledge of Him. We mistake a mere introduction to Him for the full knowledge of Him. We have become the unwitting victims of a deplorable ignorance. But there is a way out. It is to pray with Paul's absolute and unflinching purpose of heart: "That I may gain Christ and be found in Him."

But what does it mean to "gain Christ"? "Gain" (Gk.

kerdainō) is the same word translated "gain" in Matthew 16:26: "What good will it be for a man if he gains the whole world, yet forfeits his soul?" As one gains Christ, he so completely appropriates or receives Christ that the gentle Master becomes the pre-eminent power in and over his whole being and his circumstances. One thing, and only one, was counted as gain by Paul. All else was loss, rubbish (v. 8). True value in life had nothing whatsoever to do with Paul's proud lineage, his noble religious background, his education under the famous Gamaliel, his superior knowledge, his unparalleled zeal and deeds, or his seemingly flawless outward righteousness. All this was mere tinsel, fool's gold, compared to the greater riches he had found: "the surpassing greatness [absolute superiority] of knowing Christ Jesus my Lord" (v. 8). Gaining Christ, in Paul's own inspired words, meant to "be found in him, not having a righteousness of my own that comes from the law, but that which is through faith in Christ—the righteousness that comes from God and is by faith" (v. 9). To use other biblical comparisons for this relationship, gaining Christ means being joined to Him as the Head (Eph. 4:15), wed to Him as the Husband (John 3:29), and built upon Him as the sure Foundation (1 Cor. 3:11). There can be no intimate knowledge of Christ while there is the least bit of dependence on any other thing. Paul knew this, but we do not. This is the perpetual battleground and the glaring reason for our snail-paced spiritual growth. We struggle constantly with a human tendency to take pleasure in our own righteousness; we try to gain Christ by offering the worthless coupons of our self-righteousness, rather than the legal tender of heaven's treasury, the righteousness of Christ.

"Gaining Christ" is not a once-for-all act. It is so easy to revert to the well-worn paths of the past, to begin right and end wrong, to begin in the Spirit but try to finish in the flesh (Gal. 3:3). With Paul, we must also constantly practice accurate "considering." "I consider everything a loss . . . and consider them rubbish" (Phil. 3:8). To consider otherwise is to court disaster and to alienate ourselves from Him. The moment we begin considering our own right living, our church faithfulness, our benevolent acts, our avoidance of certain evils—at that moment a wedge is driven between us and Him, until we repent and our "considering" is corrected.

Gaining Christ is the absolute prerequisite to knowing Him. The second petition in this great prayer is strictly contingent upon the first. "I want to know Christ" can never happen until we make Him Master of our lives. The "knowing," of which Paul spoke and toward which he was striving, went far beyond ordinary mental comprehension. It was more than recounting Christ's highest acts and noblest deeds, more than acquaintance with the facts of His life, more than intellectual conviction of His reality, more than knowledge gained by hearing or reading. It was complete identification with Him. It was identification with the same power that raised Christ from the dead. It was identification with the same sufferings that He suffered. It was identification even to the point of becoming like him in His death.

At first glance there is a rather strange order in Paul's expressed desire to know Christ: "I want to know ... the power of his resurrection and the fellowship of sharing in his sufferings ... and so, somehow, to attain to the resurrection from the dead." However, there is a logic in this sequence. This is the path Christ walked. We discern His footprints at each stage, and having made the journey with Paul, we find ourselves standing with the impassioned Apostle gazing upon the One whose face was set toward Gethsemane, a judgment hall, a whipping post, a cursed tree, a garden tomb, and finally Easter morning! Consequently, we cry with Paul, "I want to know Christ." Resurrection was the capstone of Christ's ministry. But before He arose, He died. And before He died, He suffered. And before He suffered, He had lived and ministered by resurrection power. Did He not say, "The reason my Father loves me is that I lay down my life—only to take it up again. No one takes it from me, but I lay it down of my own accord. I have authority to lay it down and authority to take it up again" (John 10:17–18).

"I want to know him" is really the essence of all of Paul's prayers. All other petitions are but facets of this greater petition. Ignorance is the direct opposite of knowledge. It is the ignorance in all of us that alienates us from the life of God. The person who knows Him not at all is the greatest loser of all. Paul describes such persons as "darkened in their understanding and separated from the life of God because of the ignorance that is in them due to the hardening of their hearts" (Eph. 4:18) Paul wanted no part of this spiritual ignorance; he wanted to know Christ. He understood that to know Christ is to partake of the very life of God; to know the power of His resurrection is to partake of life more abundantly.

It seems that too many believers have stopped far short of God's highest and best. We seem content with the faintest spiritual pulse. Yet how many of us know the power of His resurrection? We hardly know that such a thing exists, to say nothing of knowing it in actual operation. "The power of his resurrection" is the mightiest manifestation of omnipotence, for at its base is the principle of life itself. This power finds its most fertile soil in the valley of death. In fact, it cannot be demonstrated or fully experienced apart from death. But to be dead without it is to be dead eternally. Paul desired to walk the same path his Lord had walked; yet he realized that to do so he had to have the same power. Without it he could not know the fellowship of His suffering, nor conform to His dying, nor attain to His rising. Neither can we! From "the power of his resurrection" we advance to "the fellowship of sharing in his sufferings." What a prayer this is! Humanly, we make every effort to avoid and escape suffering; we think him masochistic who invites suffering. Yet Paul was no masochist. He knew that suffering was necessary to resurrection—but not all suffering, only the suffering exemplified by the Savior.

It is commendable if a man bears up under the pain of unjust suffering because he is conscious of God. But how is it to your credit if you receive a beating for doing wrong and endure it? But if you suffer for doing good and you endure it, this is commendable before God. To this you were called, because Christ suffered for you, leaving you an example, that you should follow in his steps. "He committed no sin, and no deceit was found in his mouth." When they hurled their insults at him, he did not retaliate; when he suffered, he made no threats. Instead, he entrusted himself to him who judges justly (1 Pet. 2:19–23).

The Savior's sufferings are easily identified, for they were always in behalf of others and never because of His own faults or sins. They were always according to the will of God; they were always vicarious; they were always redemptive. The fellowship of sharing in His suffering then necessarily involves suffering according to the same pattern and toward the same end. Can we drink of this cup? Are we ready to be baptized with this baptism? (Cf. Matt. 20:22–23 and Mark 10:38–39.) Dare we align ourselves with Paul in his prayer? Only when by the spirit of wisdom and revelation the eyes of our minds are enlightened to see with Paul, and with Christ himself, the grand finale of it all.

Suffering introduces its victims to death; it even helps prepare one for death. "Although he [Jesus] was a son," the writer of Hebrews says, "he learned obedience from what he suffered" (Heb. 5:8). Paul says, "Christ Jesus ... 'became obedient to death—even death on a cross' ['the death of a common criminal,' Phillips]" (Phil. 2:8). Suffering as Christ suffered makes dying as Christ died possible. Before we can even faintly probe the meaning of Paul's prayer for becoming like the Savior in His death, we must examine that death. Surely the dying that Paul envisioned was something more than merely physical. Physical death is hardly a worthy goal, and death by crucifixion is a lesser one. But "His death" was a different death. Many a person has died, and not a few by crucifixion; yet no one has died as Jesus died. Physical death was the least (although important) part of His dying. It was only a visible demonstration of something profoundly spiritual and invisible. Here was love at its ultimate purpose.

How can we explain it? How can we comprehend it? Listen to Moses pleading for his guilt-laden people and you get some notion of this dying: " 'Oh, what a great sin these people have committed! They have made themselves gods of gold. But now, please forgive their sin—but if not, then blot me out of the book you have written' " (Exod. 32:31–32). Paul's prayer for becoming like Jesus in His death must

■■■■
PART 2
Chapter 12
Paul on
Prayer—
Part Two

have been at least in part his experience already when he wrote concerning Jews who had rejected Christ, "I could wish that I myself were cursed and cut off from Christ for the sake of my brothers, those of my own race" (Rom. 9:3). That is, he would have been willing to give up his own salvation and spend eternity in the lake of fire if that would have guaranteed the salvation of those Christ-rejecting Jews. He knew that was impossible; nothing he could do would save them. But that is how much he loved them.

Paul's desire for death was not morbid. Instead, it reflected his perfect understanding of the pathway to resurrection and to the matchless glory he saw in resurrection. Not unlike his Lord, "who for the joy set before him endured the cross, scorning its shame" (Heb. 12:2), Paul, also enraptured by visions of what lay ahead, was not only willing to walk the same path, but made it his chief pursuit.

The resurrection, viewed with such desire by Paul, can hardly be limited to the final resurrection of the righteous dead. Several translations echo the sense of the Amplified New Testament: "That if possible I may attain to the [spiritual and moral] resurrection [that lifts me] out from among the dead [even while in the body]" (Phil. 3:11).

What mountaintops of spiritual splendor and revelation have we missed by our failure to recognize the present attainable aspects of the resurrection? That there are such aspects, even though we may have only a few slight clues, should provoke the most vigorous pursuit. Our inability to conceive of them should be no deterrent. Our lack of knowledge is simply an indication that God has veiled them in obscurity for the good pleasure of our discovery. But we do not want to be like the prospector in Robert Service's poem, "The Spell of the Yukon," preferring the thrill of the search to the object of the search:

> There's gold and it's haunting and haunting;
> It's luring me on as of old.
> Yet it isn't the gold I am wanting
> So much as just finding the gold.[9]

---

[9]Robert Service, *Collected Poems of Robert Service* (New York: Dodd, Mead & Co., 1940), 5.

"It is the glory of God to conceal a matter," wrote the wisest of men, adding, "to search out a matter is the glory of kings" (Prov. 25:2). And we, as spiritual "kings and priests," search best when by persistent prayer we say with Paul, "I want to know Christ and the power of his resurrection and the fellowship of sharing in his sufferings, becoming like him in his death, and so, somehow, to attain to the resurrection from the dead" (Phil. 3:10–11).

Praying to Understand God's Will

As has been observed, prayer, to be effective, must be in agreement with God's will. Until the divine will is determined, there can be little expectation of receiving positive answers to our prayers. God's children struggle when they misunderstand this point. For them the knowledge of God's will is a riddle, the solution being so difficult they almost give up hope of discovering it. Yet we dare not accuse God of making His will beyond discovery. Why would He who desires that we perform His will subtly conceal it from us? Has it ever broken upon our hearts that while finding the will of God is often a puzzle to us, capturing our will is the chief pursuit of God? Once we begin to perceive this, we are ready for the breakthrough of a lifetime. Paul knew the importance of understanding God's will and what He was doing in the world. Paul commended the Colossian believers for the fruit of the gospel that had been produced in them since the day they had heard it. He also took note of their love in the Spirit, which is a prerequisite to knowing the will of God. "For this reason" (Col. 1:9), since the day he had heard about them, he hadn't stopped praying for them.

We have not stopped praying for you and asking God to fill you with the knowledge of his will through all spiritual wisdom and understanding. And we pray this in order that you may live a life worthy of the Lord and may please him in every way: bearing fruit in every good work, growing in the knowledge of God, being strengthened with all power according to his glorious might so that you may have great endurance and patience, and joyfully giving thanks to the Father, who has qualified you to share in the inheritance of the saints in the kingdom of light (Col. 1:9–12).

Love is an activity of the will. "Whoever has my commands and obeys them, he is the one who loves me" (John 14:21), said the Master. Just as faith without works is dead, being by itself, so love without works is dead, also being by itself. The evidence of love in the Spirit is the complete dedication of the will. Love for God knows no greater demonstration than abandonment to His will. When we commit ourselves to the full performance of God's will, without self-protecting reservations or specific knowledge of that will, we are readied for a revelation of that divine will. To demand that we know before deciding to act is to admit distrust; and distrust obstructs revelation.

In God's design and method, there is a fixed order: willing, knowing, doing. " 'If anyone chooses to do God's will, he will find out whether my teaching comes from God' " (John 7:17). People are prone to tamper with this order. We wish to know before we commit ourselves to do. Like Jacob, we wrestle fiercely through the night, unwilling to yield, while at the same time God wrestles for complete submission. "It is God who works in you to will and to act according to his good purpose" (Phil. 2:13). Let the problem of "willing" be settled, and the problem of knowing will fade into insignificance.

God's most coveted treasure is a person with a committed will. David was such a person. Why did God set aside protocol and instead of choosing the eldest of Jesse's sons to succeed Saul as king of Israel, choose the youngest? We acknowledge the indisputable right of the sovereign God to do this, but we believe that His sovereignty is always compatible with His just and reasonable nature. Though we mortals with our finite limitations may not comprehend His reasons, we must insist that He has them. Anything less would deprecate His character.

Samuel the prophet had gone down to the house of Jesse under divine orders to anoint a new king. When the eldest son Eliab appeared, the prophet's immediate reaction was, " 'Surely the LORD's anointed stands here before the LORD' " (1 Sam. 16:6). But Samuel was looking through human eyes.

■■■■■■■
PART 2

Chapter 12
Paul on
Prayer—
Part Two

He saw height of stature and a kingly countenance. No doubt he saw also a well-groomed, well-trained man of war possessing distinctive leadership abilities. But God thundered in Samuel's ear, " 'I have rejected him.' " Why? " 'The LORD does not look at the things man looks at. Man looks at the outward appearance, but the LORD looks at the heart' " (1 Sam. 16:7). There was a quality missing in Eliab, and it was the major determining factor. The same quality was missing in seven of Jesse's sons, despite the fact that all of them were men of ability and renown. Samuel could anoint none of them, for God had rejected them. Yet when David, the most unlikely prospect because of his youth, was brought in from the shepherd's fields and presented to Samuel, there was no shadow of uncertainty. Instantly the voice of heaven insisted, " 'Rise and anoint him; he is the one' " (1 Sam. 16:12).

What made the difference? It was something God saw in David's heart. Was it that David had a more complete knowledge of God's will? Certainly not. What then about this unpretentious lad attracted heaven's attention? One thing—a will wholly committed to his Maker. Paul erased all doubt forever when under the Spirit's inspiration he said, "After removing Saul, he made David their king. He testified concerning him: 'I have found David son of Jesse a man after my own heart; he will do everything I want him to do' " (Acts 13:22).

There is only one obstacle that keeps God from doing through us all that He desires—our will. Combine a dedicated will with a sincere seeking after a knowledge of God's will, and no force in heaven or earth can hinder God. We do not have to persuade God to make His will known. All we need do is make it possible. "We have not received the spirit of the world," wrote Paul to the Corinthians, "but the Spirit who is from God, that we may understand what God has freely given us" (1 Cor. 2:12). God has freely given. We need only avail ourselves of the proper means for receiving. "The man without the Spirit does not accept the things that come from the Spirit of God, for they are foolishness to him, and he cannot understand them, because they are spiritually discerned" (1 Cor. 2:14). The Colossians by their love in the Spirit had made the revelation of

God's will possible; Paul's prayer to the Colossians was a part of the process by which it was made known. The knowledge of His will is realized when the human will submits in the love of the Spirit. But His will is not actually entered into until it is done "through all spiritual wisdom and understanding" (Phil. 1:9). "Spiritual wisdom and spiritual understanding" here are almost identical with "the Spirit of wisdom and revelation" that makes it possible to know God better (Eph. 1:17). It becomes evident immediately that we can be filled with the knowledge of His will only by a spiritual operation.

Knowledge is the fruit of the learning process. And an aspect of learning is the process of comparison. How often did the Master Teacher say, "The kingdom of heaven is like . . ."? That which we already know is a stepping stone toward that which we do not know. Knowledge, we may say, is the key to greater knowledge. The knowledge of basic arithmetic is necessary to the knowledge of algebra, and the knowledge of algebra is necessary to the knowledge of the higher mathematics of differential and integral calculus. So it is in the things of God. The person who has no starting point can make no progress. The person who is not born again by the Holy Spirit has not learned the ABCs of spiritual knowledge. Therefore, the language of the Spirit is as meaningless to him as sign language is to a blind man. The Holy Spirit is our teacher in the knowledge of God's will; and His teaching process is very similar to the natural learning process. Only the raw material is different: "words taught by the Spirit, expressing spiritual truths in spiritual words" (1 Cor. 2:13). So spiritual experience is an absolute requirement. Until there is a spiritual eye, there is no spiritual seeing. Jesus' word to Nicodemus establishes this beyond all doubt: "No one can see the kingdom of God unless he is born again" (John 3:3). The groundwork had been laid with the Colossian Christians; spiritual life and knowledge were already present. Now it was but a matter of moving from relative emptiness to the place of fullness—Paul "asking God to fill [them] with the knowledge of his will."

For us today, it is no different. The will of God is that we be filled with the knowledge of His will. However, we must pray and desire with Paul that it will be so, for only then do we permit the Spirit to teach us, expressing spiritual truths in spiritual words until we are filled with that supreme knowledge. "That you may live a life worthy of the Lord and may please him in every way: bearing fruit in every good work, growing in the knowledge of God" (Col. 1:10). Life and knowledge have much in common. Christ's life reflected His knowledge. Our knowledge is reflected in our life. On one occasion, Jesus "had to go through Samaria" (John 4:4); He would be meeting a woman there to tell her he was the Messiah. On another occasion the Jews "plotted to take his life" (John 11:53). But Jesus had knowledge of this and "therefore . . . no longer moved about publicly among the Jews" (11:54). On yet another occasion Jesus said, " 'In any case [whatever the opposition], I must keep going today and tomorrow, and the next day—for surely no prophet can die outside Jerusalem' " (Luke 13:33). His knowledge motivated His life.

Paul's prayer that the Colossian believers be filled with the knowledge of God's will was plainly predicated on the premise that this knowledge would result in a worthy life. Notice the relationship between the two petitions: (1) "to fill you with the knowledge of his will" (2) "that you may live a life worthy of the Lord." We are to be filled with the knowledge of God's will in order that we may live worthy of the Lord. "All true action must spring from knowledge: worthy conduct from sound creed: Christian ethics from Christian doctrine: right doing from right thinking: morality from theology."[10] "That you may live a life worthy of the Lord" is the crux of the entire prayer. In it is reflected the consuming passion of the apostle's heart and the burden of all his labors. All that follows is but elucidation and the means of fulfilling that goal.

"That you may please him in every way" would be taken grossly out of context if it were construed to mean the Christian is also to please everyone. Indeed, quite the opposite is true; the Christian's objective is to please only One. The *Twentieth Century New Testament* renders the

---

[10]Scroggie, *Prison Prayers,* 49.

phrase, "and so please God in every way." To walk worthy of Christ is to please God, even as Christ described His daily life on earth: " 'I always do what pleases him' " (John 8:29).

The starting point in a worthy life is "bearing fruit in every good work [or activity]." In fact, a worthy life and good works are almost identical. Good work or activity requires careful examination, for the biblical meaning has been all but lost in a maze of human interpretations. Bearing fruit in every good work is not the product of mere human wisdom and understanding. We think in terms of bread for the hungry, water for the thirsty, shelter for the homeless, clothing for the naked, and healing for the sick. We cannot envision anything more. But when "the knowledge of his will through all spiritual wisdom and understanding" begins to unfold, our vision suddenly begins to take in new horizons. We begin to see that the goodness of a work or effort is measured by the source from which it springs and the end toward which it aims. Acts of human kindness performed for a merely temporal objective may reflect the lingering image of the benevolent, compassionate God; but they are hardly worthy of the designation "good work" as set forth in this prayer. Good, in the absolute sense, is God. Jesus said, " 'There is only One who is good,' " that is, God (Matt. 19:17). Thus good work must be in line with God's nature and God's will.

Consider the work of Him who "went around doing good and healing all who were under the power of the devil, because God was with him" (Acts 10:38). It cannot be denied, nor should it be overlooked, that Jesus ministered to various temporal needs. He healed the sick on every hand. When the throngs that followed Him were hungry, He fed them, for He realized that they might collapse (Matt. 15:32). But when they wanted to make Him their king because He appeared to be the solution to their temporal needs, He turned upon them with a passion and said, " 'I tell you the truth, you are looking for me, not because you saw miraculous signs but because you ate the loaves and had your fill. Do not work for food that spoils, but for food that endures to eternal life' " (John 6:26–27). God's work always has an eternal end in view. It concerns itself more with the Bread of Life though it does not neglect bread for the hungry, more with the Water of Life though it does not neglect water for the thirsty, more with a city whose Builder and Maker is God though it does not neglect shelter for the homeless, more with robes of righteousness though it does not neglect clothing for the naked. Nor should we, in our zeal to bring Christ into human lives, neglect these things (cf. Matt. 25:34–46).

But there is a vast difference between good works of faith and good works without faith. Yet the difference is seldom discerned. The good works of faith are always pleasing to God, for they spring from the God-life within. Good works without faith may spring from human aspiration alone. The good works of faith spring from the knowledge of His will. Eternal good work is always performed unto the Lord, though it may enrich the lives of people. It is labor of the highest kind. It is the devotion of Mary as contrasted with the devotion of Martha. It is the sacrifice of Abel as opposed to the sacrifice of Cain. It is the praying of the Savior as compared with the praying of the Pharisee. It is the wisdom Paul preached over against the wisdom of this world.

There is a blessed compensation for fruitfulness in every good work: "growing in the knowledge of God" (Col. 1:10). Knowledge of God's will leads to good work; good work, in turn, leads to a growing knowledge of God. In the first instance, knowledge is the seed; in the second, knowledge is the fruit. God's knowledge is complete and absolute; our knowledge (of Him especially) is incomplete and gained by degrees. God's knowledge knows no increase, but our knowledge must. Otherwise our spiritual growth will be stunted.

An older Texas couple had spent all their years in poverty on their ranch. One day oil was discovered on their land and they were suddenly transformed from near poverty to wealth. The rancher learned that $500,000 was on deposit for him in the local bank. Returning home, he announced to his wife, "Ma, we're rich! We've got half a million dollars the bank! What would you like to have most of all? You name it and I'll get it." The wife pondered for a moment and then declared her greatest wish. "This old ax is killing me," she said. "What I want most of all is a new ax for choppin' wood for the kitchen stove."

The woman could have drawn on vast riches. She could have had a new stove and a new kitchen and done away with the ax altogether. But her knowledge, limited by her poverty-striken life, kept her from realizing what was available to her. Similarly, the knowledge of God's will determines our spiritual progress and opportunity.

We have seen that the knowledge of God comes by revelation. Now we observe it comes also by participation. This is no conflict of truth, but simply additional light on the first truth. While knowledge of God's will launches us into a worthy walk evidenced by fruitfulness in every good work, the same worthy walk and fruitfulness become a booster rocket to speed our spiritual progress and perfect our knowledge of Him. Furthermore, this knowledge is inward and absolute, rather than outward and questionable. It is the knowledge of the heart, the treasure most coveted by saint and sage. No object of earth is a worthy stumbling block to our utmost pursuit.

With increased knowledge of God comes practical demonstration of that knowledge. We know Him as the God of glorious power only as that power expresses itself in us. Paul says we are "strengthened with all power" (Col. 1:11), or we are, as the phrase has been otherwise translated, "with all power being empowered" (J. B. Rotherham). We do the receiving; God does the empowering. In us the power is displayed, but God is its source. Power has little meaning until it is translated into expression. Jesus announced to the Early Church, "You will receive power . . . and you will be my witnesses" (Acts 1:8). Being witnesses gives expression and meaning to the enduement of power. Wherever the power is, there will also be a demonstration of the power. Make way for the knowledge of God, and His glorious might will express itself.

We are prone to think of God's glorious might only in terms of powerful preaching, mighty miracles, supernatural deliverance, and the like. Yet the Apostle sets forth an altogether different concept. To his enlightened understanding, the inward manifestation of power was as important as the outward, perhaps more so. He understood (and may God enlighten us to understand with him) that it takes more glorious power to be patient than to preach, more might to be longsuffering with joyfulness than to perform immediate miracles, and more divine energy to give thanks than to prophesy. This is not to diminish preaching, miracles, or prophecy, but great preaching without great patience exposes humanity and conceals divinity. Great miracles of deliverance without great longsuffering with joyfulness unveils fleshly weakness and hides His glorious power. Great prophesying without great thanksgiving betrays ignorance and casts a shadow on the knowledge of God.

The knowledge of God's will in all spiritual wisdom and understanding issues in a worthy life and fruitfulness in every good work. From this blessed fountain flows an ever-increasing stream of the knowledge of God that gives practical evidence of itself in great endurance and patience, joyfully giving thanks to the Father. Therefore, with understanding and earnest desire let us pray day by day that we might live a life worthy of the Lord and be pleasing to Him in every way, bearing fruit in every good work, growing in the knowledge of God, being strengthened with all power according to His glorious might so that we will have great endurance and patience, joyfully giving thanks to the Father, who has qualified us to share in the inheritance of the saints in the kingdom of light.

Questions for Study

1. What does Paul's addressing God as "the glorious Father" show about his concept of God?

2. What was the relationship between the heart and the mind in Hebrew thinking? In what sense does the heart have eyes?

3. How did Paul's circumstances as a prisoner in Rome affect the content of his recorded prayers?

4. What did Paul expect "God's glorious riches" to supply?

5. How can we gain the spiritual sensitivity and discernment that are such supreme needs?

6. What does it mean to "gain Christ" and how are we to do so?

7. Why does a person who has been a Christian many years still need to pray "I want to know Christ"? What does knowing Christ involve?

8. How can we become like the Savior in His death?

9. Why is it so important to will to do God's will even before we pray to know what that will is?

10. What does it mean to live a life worthy of the Lord?

PART 2

**Chapter 12
Paul on
Prayer—
Part Two**

PRAYER IN HEBREWS AND THE GENERAL EPISTLES

Confidence to Approach the Throne

In a single verse in the Book of Hebrews we have a strong word of encouragement for every praying child of God: "Let us then approach the throne of grace with confidence, so that we may receive mercy and find grace to help us in our time of need" (Heb. 4:16; read also vv. 14–15). To gain a proper understanding of this fantastic assurance, we must look first at the word "then," which links the promise to the preceding truth: Christ is the believer's great high priest. Jesus the Son of God is in heaven (v. 14) with the Father. Yet there is something very personal and tender about this Mediator, seated at the right hand of the Father (see Acts 2:33; Rom. 8:34). He can "sympathize with our weaknesses" because He was "tempted in every way, just as we are—yet was without sin" (v. 15). Though He was without sin, in His earthly life He felt the reality of testing and temptation. He is sympathetic toward "our weaknesses," weaknesses of health, temperament, commitment, service. He knows the precise force of every evil temptation that may test us. Therefore, He loves and protects us

PART 2

Chapter 13
Prayer in
Hebrews
and the
General
Epistles

as "the apple of his eye" (Zech. 2:8).[1] Because Jesus is God's own Son, because He is at the Father's right hand in heaven, because He is uniquely qualified to empathize with our weaknesses—we are able to approach the throne of grace with confidence.

We ought to come with confidence into the divine presence for two reasons: (1) to receive mercy and (2) to find grace to help us in our time of need. Our first need is for mercy, since every one of us is by nature and deed a sinner. Sin always has a deserved and certain judgment—death. Yet "mercy triumphs over judgment" (James 2:13). We must first "receive mercy" from the only One qualified to dispense it, the One who voluntarily died in our place. Then we can come with confidence, without fear of rejection or reprisal, and receive it freely at His hand. Having received mercy, and with it the privilege of coming with confidence into His presence, we are offered a second privilege: to plead for grace at the very throne of grace and find it as our help "in the time of our need." All of human existence is a "time of need"; yet grace continues to be available and abundant. God's grace was sufficient for Paul (see 2 Cor. 12:9). It is sufficient also for each believer today.

Criteria for Coming to God

Prayer is the soul coming to God. But spoken words, addressed to Deity, do not automatically receive a hearing and a response. There are criteria that God requires of those who come to Him, who truly have His ear and access to His compassionate heart. "Without faith it is impossible to please God, because anyone who comes to him must believe that he exists and that he rewards those who earnestly seek him" (Heb. 11:6).

"Not everyone has faith" (2 Thess. 3:2). Yet only persons of faith can please God. Faith is an absolute prerequisite to all fruitful praying. It is essential, however, that faith be

---

[1]"The apple of the eye" refers to the pupil (conceived of as a sphere). We are very protective when someone tries to touch our eye, wanting to damage it. God is just as concerned over His people.

PART 2

Chapter 13
Prayer in
Hebrews
and the
General
Epistles

clearly understood, lest it be confused with some lesser and inadequate virtue. "Faith," says Hebrews 11:1, "is being sure of what we hope for and certain of what we do not see." Other translations add clarity to the definition. "Faith is the assurance of things hoped for, the conviction of things not seen" (RSV). "Faith means that we have full confidence in the things we hope for, it means being certain of things we cannot see" (Phillips). True faith presupposes an object upon which it stands. The Christian faith is fixed upon the Word of God and upon the God of the Word; it is this faith that pleases God. The praying person must believe that the God of the Bible exists and is truly all the Bible represents Him to be: the great "I AM" (Exod. 3:14). The believer who prays effectively must live constantly in the conviction that this "I AM" is the infinite, eternal, self-existent, ever-present, faithful God by whose energy, bounty, and providence all other beings exist.

Believing that God can do anything, however, is not enough. "Even the demons believe that—and shudder" (James 2:19). Faith that effects change must comprehend not only the existence of a divine Supreme Being, but it must also perceive God's intense interest in His creatures, even to the extent of rewarding "those who earnestly seek him." He desires children who deeply long for His presence. "Earnestly seek" (Gk. *ekzēteō*) means "to seek out or after," "to search for," "to desire to get." The faith that brings pleasure to God and gains His attention is that faith which motivates its possessor to move toward God, to search Him out for the purpose of fulfilling His divine will, to investigate His nature in order to comprehend His fullness, and to desire His superintendence of all of life's affairs.

Prayer for Wisdom in Trials

The truly humble person is painfully conscious of human limitations, especially in the face of trials and tests. As such a believer moves into the spiritual realm, the limitations of human wisdom are even more conspicuous. Knowing that all of life for the believer is spiritual warfare and that human, or natural, weapons will not pull down the strong-

PART 2

Chapter 13
Prayer in
Hebrews
and the
General
Epistles

holds that must be destroyed (2 Cor. 10:4), one is keenly aware of the need for help from a supernatural source:

If any of you lacks wisdom, he should ask God, who gives generously to all without finding fault, and it will be given to him. But when he asks, he must believe and not doubt, because he who doubts is like a wave of the sea, blown and tossed by the wind. That man should not think he will receive anything from the Lord; he is a double-minded man, unstable in all he does (James 1:5–8).

The preceding verses of James 1 identify "testing" as the subject under consideration. The Greek *peirasmos* (v. 2) includes the trials, tests, and temptations, divinely permitted or sent, which come upon God's children. The justification for asking for God's wisdom is that we might understand and use the trials and tests to the advantage of our spiritual development. Wisdom is the right use of knowledge. A person may know a great deal, and yet not be wise. Wisdom chooses the best ends, and the best means of reaching those ends. It is not simply doing the right things, but doing the right things at the right time. The truly wise person regards the glory of God as the purpose of life and makes his actions and words means to that end. Knowing how to use trials and tests so that they produce the greatest degree of Christian perfection requires more than the natural faculty of good judgment. This perfecting process results as supernatural wisdom reveals to the suffering believer the divine intent, the relationship between the process and the fulfillment of God's purpose. Such wisdom is available, but on request: "He should ask God." There is no other source. Neither the counselors of the world, nor the mental acumen of the believer, is capable of it. But for "the only wise God" (1 Tim. 1:17, KJV; cf. Rom. 16:27), it is the reality and expression of His nature. The receiving of such wisdom, however, is conditional: "But when he asks, he must believe and not doubt" (v. 6). "Doubt" (Gk. *diakrinō*) means "to be at odds with one-self," "waver." It suggests not so much a weakness of faith as a lack of faith. The wavering, or doubting, receive nothing from the Lord (v. 7). A double-minded person (v. 8) is "of two souls . . . one for earth, and another for heaven."

PART 2

Chapter 13
Prayer in
Hebrews
and the
General
Epistles

. . . He will not give up earth, and he is loath to let heaven go."[2] Such an individual does not gain access to God's wisdom "because he . . . is like a wave of the sea, blown and tossed by the wind" (James 1:6). But the one of fixed faith finds heaven's response, and by the infusion of God's wisdom is able to gain advantage from even the worst of life's offerings. Joseph is a good example. With the wisdom of God plainly evident, he was able to announce after years of the most severe trials and tests, "You intended to harm me, but God intended it for good" (Gen. 50:20).

Prayer that Warrants Response

Any thoughtful study on prayer must confront the reality of unanswered prayer. What person has not had a prayer "refused," or at least answered differently than was asked? Even so great a prayer warrior as Elijah did not always obtain the answers he desired (see 1 Kings 19:4–8). It is fortunate that God in His great wisdom and love for His people does not always answer according to their requests, for to do so would be to their hurt or destruction. James uncovers an elementary reason for unanswered prayer.

When you ask, you do not receive, because you ask with wrong motives, that you may spend what you get on your pleasures. . . . Submit yourselves, then, to God. Resist the devil, and he will flee from you. Come near to God and he will come near to you. Wash your hands, you sinners, and purify your hearts, you double-minded. Grieve, mourn and wail. Change your laughter to mourning and your joy to gloom. Humble yourselves before the Lord, and he will lift you up (James 4:3,7–10).

"You ask with wrong motives." "Wrong motives" (Gk. *kakōs*) means "badly," "wrongly," "wickedly." We ask wrongly when we pray for anything outside the will of God. Neither will God answer prayers motivated by selfish desires, "that you may spend what you get on your pleasures." He will not listen to the prayer of persons seeking

---

[2]Adam Clarke, *The Holy Bible Containing the Old and New Testament with a Commentary and Critical Notes,* vol. 6 (London: Ward, Lock & Co., n.d.), 761.

PART 2

Chapter 13
Prayer in
Hebrews
and the
General
Epistles

position, pleasure, honor, power, or riches. "Pleasures" (Gk. *hēdonē*) speaks of gratification of natural or sinful desires, of sensual delights. To pray for that which pleases our own sensual desires is contrary to God's will and could lead to spiritual disaster.

The remaining instructions (vv. 7–10) give guidelines for praying rightly (not amiss) and, consequently, warranting God's response.

"Submit yourselves, then, to God." A wholehearted yes to God is a prerequisite to all effective praying. Early in the prayer pattern Jesus taught, His disciples were to say, "Your will be done on earth as it is in heaven" (Matt. 6:10). It is always appropriate to give expression to that prayer, since His will is always a person's highest good. However, it should not be used as a cover for a lack of faith.

"Resist the devil, and he will flee from you." Submission to God always precedes successfully resisting the devil. As powerful as Satan is—and it is a mistake to underestimate his power (see Eph. 6:12)—God will not allow him to overcome the believer who, having submitted to God, continually resists the evil one in the name of Jesus and through the merit of His shed blood.

"Come near to God and he will come near to you." What a blessed and encouraging promise! God promises to come near to all who turn from sin, calling on Him in true repentance. With Him come His presence, His grace, His love, and His blessings. There must be effort on a person's part to invite action on God's part. We are free agents and must choose to initiate the action if we desire God to come near to us. At the same time, God is not passive, for He is the initiator, the One who seeks out His creation (see Gen. 3:8–9): "It is God who works in you to will and to act according to his good purpose" (Phil. 2:13).

"Wash your hands, you sinners, and purify your hearts, you double-minded." Every sincere seeker after God, intending to draw near to Him, is confronted with his own evil ways and must deal with them directly. The psalmist perceived this when he wrote, "Who may ascend the hill of the LORD? Who may stand in his holy place? He who has clean hands and a pure heart" (Ps. 24:3–4). Jesus reminded His disciples of the need for perpetual cleansing from daily defilement (see John 13:2–14). "Purify your hearts, you double-minded" parallels the previous statement. A complete break from sin is absolutely essential if our prayers are to receive a divine response. Those who seek God's approbation and blessing cannot maintain allegiance to two worlds. Double-mindedness invites damnation. It must be repented of until the heart is pure, having a single-minded desire to serve God. Paul further admonishes us to do our part by crucifying the flesh, the old sinful nature (Gal. 6:24). We must flee from sexual immorality (1 Cor. 6:18); hate what is evil; cling to what is good (Rom. 12:9). Yet we cannot do it all ourselves. It takes the blood of Jesus to bring the full cleansing we need (1 John 1:7). The believer who desires to approach God must take seriously John's admonition, "If we confess our sins, he is faithful and just and will forgive us our sins and purify us from all unrighteousness" (1 John 1:9).

"Grieve, mourn and wail." "Grieve" (Gk. *talaipōreō*) means "to be wretched," "to realize one's misery." "Mourn" (Gk. *pentheō*) means "to be sad," "to have sorrow for sin." "Wail" (Gk. *klaiō*) means "to sob," "to wail aloud," "to lament as over the dead." The apostle's burden is to see genuine heart-grief and wholehearted repentance. "The sacrifices of God are a broken spirit; a broken and contrite heart, O God, you will not despise" (Ps. 51:17). How very needful is such contrition in the church of our day.

"Change your laughter to mourning and your joy to gloom." The theme is still repentance and sincere contrition. There is a definite echo of Matthew 5:4 ("Blessed are those who mourn") and Luke 6:25 ("Woe to you who laugh now for you will mourn and weep").

"Humble yourselves before the Lord, and he will lift you up." There is hope. No matter how bad the situation may appear, if one follows the instructions for a pure relationship with God, answered prayer will lift him to victory.

The prescription is appropriate for all people, everywhere, at any time. Each of the seven guidelines is a vital facet of prayer, leading to the desired end: He will lift you up. These instructions fit like a letter in an envelope. The first instruction, "Submit to God," is balanced by the seventh, "Humble yourselves before the Lord." Inserted in

PART 2

**Chapter 13
Prayer in
Hebrews
and the
General
Epistles**

PART 2

Chapter 13
Prayer in
Hebrews
and the
General
Epistles

that envelope are four related instructions and promises. "Resist the devil" and "Come near to God." Then the promises: "The devil will flee" and "God will come near." But resisting the devil and coming to God must always honor the submission-humility envelope. Likewise, washing the hands (putting away outward sins) must be balanced by a purified heart (inner attitudes), still in the submission-humility envelope. Finally, there is a joy in submitting and humbling oneself before God. It is the joy of knowing sins have been forgiven and that one is in right relationship with God. Humility and repentance bring joy as we submit to God in everything.

Powerful, Effective Prayer

The Book of James contains much practical advice on how to pray. The instructions on prayer for healing are especially meaningful to Pentecostals. We believe that God still heals. For those who do not, this passage is merely historic, applying only to the first-century believers. But we take the promises of God for the healing of sickness, illness, and affliction as God's commitment to do today what He has done in the past—if we meet His requirements.

Is any one of you in trouble? He should pray. Is anyone happy? Let him sing songs of praise. Is any one of you sick? He should call the elders of the church to pray over him and anoint him with oil in the name of the Lord. And the prayer offered in faith will make the sick person well; the Lord will raise him up. If he has sinned, he will be forgiven. Therefore confess your sins to each other and pray for each other so that you may be healed. The prayer of a righteous man is powerful and effective. Elijah was a man just like us. He prayed earnestly that it would not rain, and it did not rain on the land for three and a half years. Again he prayed, and the heavens gave rain, and the earth produced its crops (James 5:13–18).

Prayer for healings of various kinds is undeniably taught in Scripture. However, little attention is given to specific teaching on obtaining healing. It is possible that more healings would be witnessed if more attention were paid to the scriptural injunction: "Is any one of you in trouble? He

PART 2
Chapter 13
Prayer in
Hebrews
and the
General
Epistles

should pray." "In trouble" (Gk. *kakopatheō*) means "to suffer misfortune," "to bear hardships patiently." In light of the succeeding verse, "Is any one of you sick . . .," the use of *kakopatheō* seems not to include physical malady or disease, but is instead an allusion to sufferings outside the body. The believer so affected is instructed to pray for his own misfortune; God may remove the hardship or provide grace to bear it. Of course, other believers are encouraged to undergird the suffering one: "Carry each other's burdens" (Gal. 6:2). But the sufferer should himself touch God in behalf of his need. C. Jerdan describes well the meaning and intent of the instruction:

The believer must not allow his trials to exasperate him. Instead of swearing over them, he should pray over them. That is a graceless heart which, when under the rod, challenges God's sovereignty, or impugns his justice, or distrusts his goodness, or arraigns his wisdom. The child of God prays always, because he loves prayer; and especially when under trial, because then he has special need of it. . . . Even to tell God of our trials helps to alleviate them. Prayer brings the soul near to him who bears upon his loving heart the burden of his people's sorrows.[3]

Good health and contentment with circumstances are reasons for a happy disposition. "Is anyone happy? Let him sing songs of praise." Into the life of every believer will come times to pray in affliction and times to sing praise. We should neglect neither. But, since it seems to be human nature to be quicker to express complaint than gratitude, we should give special attention to praise. The Book of Psalms is full of exhortations to sing praise (Pss. 32:11; 33:1–3; 81:1–2; 89:1; 92:1–4; 98:4–6; 100:1; 101:1; 144:9; 149:1,5; 150:6, for example). We need to praise Him for His wonderful works, the heavens that declare the glory of God, the beautiful sunsets, the glories of nature, and above all, the blessings of salvation. Nor should we forget the everyday blessings, such as faithful friends, a good meal,

[3]In H. D. M. Spence and Joseph S. Exell, eds., *The Pulpit Commentary* (Grand Rapids: Wm. B. Eerdmans Pub. Co., 1950), vol. 21, *James,* by E. C. S. Gibson, 80.

PART 2

Chapter 13
Prayer in
Hebrews
and the
General
Epistles

the completing of a task, and so many other things that too often we take for granted.

"Is any one of you sick?" (v. 14). "Sick" (Gk. *astheneō*) means literally "without strength," "weak," "powerless." It may include the thought of being diseased, unhealthy, infirm, disabled, feeble, or, in some contexts, timid, spiritually weak, or morally weak. Whereas the believer in trouble is himself to pray, the sick person is instructed to "call [invite, call on] the elders of the church to pray over him. . . ." The sick person obviously needs the prayer support of others, for in such a time of weakness, often both physical and spiritual, he may be unable to exercise the faith necessary for obtaining the healing. The elders (Gk. *presbyteroi*), which the sick person was to call and who should go to the sick person at home (or in the hospital), were individuals raised up and qualified by the Holy Spirit for ministry and teaching in a local church. The Greek can include going to the elders, though that is not the primary meaning. Sometimes the title represented an appointed office; in other instances, elders were other leaders esteemed for their maturity, spiritual experience, and evident demonstration of the gifts of the Spirit. There was usually more than one in a local church (note the plural), so the term need not be limited to the senior pastor, although one would normally think first of the primary spiritual leader in time of need.

The instructions for these praying elders are brief and uncomplicated: Let them "pray over him and anoint him with oil in the name of the Lord." Interestingly, one manuscript reads, ". . . anoint him with oil in *The Name."* [4] The use of the name shows this anointing with oil was certainly not done with any expectation that the oil would bring the healing, but rather that the oil was a symbol of the Spirit by whom healing would be administered.

"If he has sinned, he will be forgiven" (v. 15). The question arises, By what means or process are the sins forgiven? There is a suggestion that the sickness for which deliverance is requested might be related in some way to a sin

---

[4]Manuscript B, Codex Vaticanus. (Probably a copyist's omission.) The name of the Lord Jesus Christ is undoubtedly meant.

PART 2

Chapter 13
Prayer in
Hebrews
and the
General
Epistles

practiced or committed. James 5:16 is closely connected with v. 15. The conjunction *therefore* (Gk. *oun*), found in many great manuscripts, implies that the sins would be forgiven if the preceding directions were followed. Accepting this, we understand that the sins committed are forgiven through the process of the sick confessing their sins (departures from the way of righteousness, either unintentional or willful) to those who pray for them (not necessarily one who has the office of elder). The well, in turn, are to confess any sins to the sick lest there be any hindrance to their prayers; then they are to pray for one another so that the sick may be healed and restored. Though mental and spiritual illnesses can be included, the word "healed" clearly has its primary meaning of being cured of physical ailments.

The use of present imperatives indicates that confessing to one another and praying for one another is to be the continuous practice of believers, thus keeping an atmosphere where people will more readily healed.

Disposing of the sin does not automatically result from confession, although confession is the required initial step. "He who conceals his sins does not prosper" (Prov. 28:13). If the sin continues even after it is confessed, the sick one may need more than forgiveness. Deliverance may be needed. Therefore, "powerful and effective" prayer (James 5:16) is required. The confession described here is that of Christians to one another, not to a priest. If persons have injured one another, they must confess and ask forgiveness of those against whom they have sinned. Sins of a public nature should be publicly confessed, so that all the injured may be involved in the forgiveness. At times it is advisable to confess our sins to a praying and prudent minister or friend who may help us plead for God's mercy and pardon. James, of course, is not advocating our telling in detail every word or action we are conscious is wrong. His point is that when confession is necessary for our reconciliation with others or for gaining a free and quiet conscience, we must be ready to obey the injunction.

To illustrate the results of powerful and effective prayer, and to encourage the elders called to pray for a sick person, James recalls Elijah, one of the most effective men of prayer

PART 2

**Chapter 13
Prayer in
Hebrews
and the
General
Epistles**

in the Bible (see chapter 5). And because the natural tendency may be to place such people on a pedestal, considering them a superior breed, impossible of imitation, James makes it clear that he was human "just like us." He was not free from the burden of his humanity: He too wrestled with the weakness of the flesh; he too experienced human frailty and its consequences. But he prayed, and God heard him. Therefore, we, like Elijah, ought to pray for the need at hand with utmost confidence that Elijah's God will heed our earnest cry for help.

Hindrances to Prayer

Human relationships play a meaningful role in effective praying. Improper or impaired relationships can short-circuit the divine connection and prevent answers to prayers. Peter specifically addresses relationships in the home: "Husbands, . . . be considerate as you live with your wives, and treat them with respect as the weaker partner and as heirs with you of the gracious gift of life, so that nothing will hinder your prayers" (1 Pet. 3:7).

Peter mentions three areas in which husbands must honor their wives if they want their prayers to be effective. First, they must "be considerate." They should behave toward their wives with full knowledge of what God expects of them. They should understand the purpose for which marriage was instituted: that husband and wife might be one flesh, or fellowship, both physically and spiritually. They should treat their wives with full knowledge of what Scripture defines as a proper relationship between two believers: showing kindness, love, unselfishness; honoring one another above self; displaying the fruit of the Spirit.

Second, husbands must "treat them with respect as the weaker partner." "Weaker" probably has the meaning of "less prominent" (as in 1 Cor. 12:22–23) and does not have the primary reference to the woman's physical strength. Scientists would not agree that she is weaker physically, at least in regard to her stamina and her ability to endure pain. But she was the less prominent member of the team in the Jewish and Greco-Roman culture of the first century. Even today when the wife is not as dependent on the husband and social conditions have changed, this is still often true. What Peter expects here is that the husband will not make arbitrary decisions nor will he fail to give consideration to his wife's opinions and desires. Rather, he should give her special recognition, honor, and respect, recognizing how much he depends on her. Husbands should show understanding also by not taking offense at minor failings and by putting the welfare of their wives before their own. In this way, husbands will love their wives "just as Christ loved the church and gave himself up for her" (Eph. 5:25).

Finally, husbands must "treat them . . . as heirs" with them "of the gracious gift of life." The believing wife is a full-fledged member of the family of God. In Christ there is neither male nor female (Gal. 3:28). Spiritually the husband and wife are equals. They share salvation, spiritual life, and all God's gifts on the same basis—by grace through faith. Neither one merits anything more than the other in the sight of God. Thus the husband should show consideration by encouraging the wife to exercise faith and claim spiritual gifts, ministries, and blessings. In the family, the gender differences are still there, of course, but they should be the ground for loving consideration, mutual respect, and sincere appreciation. If the husband acts with authoritarianism, if he bullies, threatens, or shows an arrogant, domineering spirit toward his wife, he does violence to the oneness of the Body of Christ (1 Cor. 12:27), robs the work of Christ of its true meaning, and becomes a hindrance to answered prayer.

Not practicing these principles in the home will hinder a man's prayers. "Hinder" (Gk. *egkoptō*) is derived from words meaning "to cut down or out," "to cut off." In the New Testament it means to "check," "hinder," or "block." The primary reference here is to the husband's prayers; as a corollary, however, the wife's prayers as well are hindered or blocked by conflict, abuse, or lack of love on her part. As companions in their spiritual pilgrimage, a husband and wife should do all they possibly can to encourage and assist each other. They should together guard against domestic disagreements and confrontations that extend indefinitely (see Eph. 4:26). Both need to be alert so that

PART 2

Chapter 13
Prayer in
Hebrews
and the
General
Epistles

PART 2

Chapter 13
Prayer in
Hebrews
and the
General
Epistles

nothing that might occur will detract from private prayer, family prayer, and especially prayer for each other (cf. 1 Cor. 7:5). When family relationships are right and edifying, prayer by the spiritual leader in the home, as well as by all members, will be effective.

Peter addresses yet another hindrance to prayer: Pride. It is doubtful that any hindrance ranks higher. Pride is the enemy of all prayer. It puts a person ahead of God. It clouds one's vision; it perverts one's values. It promotes division; it attracts divine displeasure—for God opposes the proud. Instead of pride, humility is the clothing of sincere believers.

> Young men, . . . be submissive to those who are older. All of you, clothe yourselves with humility toward one another, because, "God opposes the proud but gives grace to the humble." Humble yourselves, therefore, under God's mighty hand, that he may lift you up in due time. Cast all your anxiety on him because he cares for you (1 Pet. 5:5–7).

Humility is vital to prayer; it dare not be overlooked. True humility is more than saying words. It is a gentleness reflected when the younger submits to the mature and believers generally submit to one another. It is an outward garment that announces an inner virtue. In New Testament times, slaves tied on a white cloth or apron over their clothing so all would know they were slaves.[5] Believers who wear the fabric of humility announce emphatically, "We are servants of Jesus Christ," following Him in the spirit of John 13:4–5.

Humility is so foreign to self-exalting human nature that one must strive constantly to maintain this Christlike character. Pride champions independence and self-sufficiency, unwilling to recognize a need for God's intervention in personal affairs. In the younger and inexperienced, pride encourages insubordination and rebellion; in leaders, it encourages despotism. But humility, springing from self-

---

[5]Charles Bigg, *A Critical and Exegetical Commentary on the Epistles of St. Peter and St. Jude,* The International Critical Commentary (Edinburgh: T. & T. Clark, 1902), 191; J. N. D. Kelly, *A Commentary on the Epistles of Peter and Jude* (New York: Harper & Row, 1969), 206.

PART 2

Chapter 13
Prayer in
Hebrews
and the
General
Epistles

denial (Mark 8:34), acknowledges total dependence on God, no matter what one's station in life.

One good way of humbling oneself is given in verse 7: "Cast all your anxiety on him because he cares for you." The proud, self-sufficient person never asks for help from anyone, not even God. Therefore, the very act of casting one's anxiety upon God expresses dependence, a need of God's help. The ultimate in submission and humility is the total relinquishing of life's perplexities, problems, and burdens to Him who truly cares and can turn them to our advantage and spiritual growth.

"Anxiety" (Gk. *merimna*) speaks of worry or undue concern. Anxiety pulls our thoughts and emotions in several directions at once, resulting in undue worry, uneasiness, apprehension, tension, and distress. It shows a lack of trust in God, and often results from ambitious pursuit of temporal, material things, worldly power, or status. So we humble ourselves by going to God in prayer, throwing upon Him the whole burden of our anxiety, worry, sorrow, and perplexities. And with good reason—because He cares for us. "Cares" as a verb used impersonally (Gk. *melei*) means "to have a genuine concern that is pleased to do something in a loving way." It matters to God about you. Hence we understand that the anxieties that burden us matter to Him, even to the extent that when we bring them to Him He either joins with us in carrying them or bears them on His own (see Matt. 8:17; 11:28–30).

Another hindrance to prayer, obviously, is sin. Without exception, all effective praying by believers is governed by fellowship and relationship, first with God and then with fellow believers. Sin, wickedness, evil, is the arch-enemy of this fellowship and must necessarily be dealt with appropriately.

If we claim to have fellowship with him yet walk in the darkness, we lie and do not live by the truth. But if we walk in the light, as he is in the light, we have fellowship with one another, and the blood of Jesus, his Son, purifies us from all sin. If we claim to be without sin, we deceive ourselves and the truth is not in us. If we confess our sins, he is faithful and just and will forgive

PART 2

Chapter 13
Prayer in
Hebrews
and the
General
Epistles

us our sins and purify us from all unrighteousness (1 John 1:6–9).

"Fellowship" (Gk. *koinōnia*) means "participation," "partnership," "sharing in common." Inherent in the word is the idea of being woven together, as strands of a cord. Having such a relationship with the Lord depends on the believer's walking "in the light."

The contrast here is a walk in darkness versus a walk in the light. The sinner walks in darkness. For him there can be no fellowship with God since there is no compatibility between darkness and light, between sin and the God who is Light. Walking in the light requires total obedience to the will of God as revealed in the Bible. It results in fellowship with God himself. Yet no one is sinlessly perfect (v. 8), for we contend endlessly with a fallen nature and commit sin through ignorance and human weakness, if not deliberately. If we sin while trying to walk in the light, "the blood of Jesus, his Son, purifies us from all sin" (v. 8). There is also a remedy if a believer sins willfully: "If we confess our sins, he is faithful and just and will forgive us our sins and purify us from all unrighteousness" (v. 9).

Confession of sin is mandatory if the believer is to continue in unbroken fellowship "with the Father and with his Son, Jesus Christ" (v. 3). And that fellowship is absolutely essential if a believer is to pray with the assurance of having audience with the Creator.

Assurance that a Prayer Has Been Heard

The believer's confidence in receiving answers to prayer is predicated upon his assurance that he is heard; his assurance that he is heard springs from his knowledge that he is asking in the right way—according to God's will. Therefore, our discovery of the will of God is a first step to effective prayer.

This is the confidence we have in approaching God: that if we ask anything according to his will, he hears us. And if we know that he hears us—whatever we ask—we know that we have what we asked of him. If anyone sees his brother commit a sin that does not lead to death, he should pray and God will give him

PART 2

Chapter 13
Prayer in
Hebrews
and the
General
Epistles

life. I refer to those whose sin does not lead to death. There is a sin that leads to death. I am not saying that he should pray about that (1 John 5:14–16).

Every person who prays can know with the utmost confidence that whenever prayer is offered according to the divine will, audience before the mercy seat is assured. Asking is the believer's prerogative. Sometimes there is no receiving simply because there is no asking (James 4:2; see also Matt. 7:7). On the other hand, the asking is heard only if it is compatible with the good pleasure of the Hearer. There is an asking which is from wrong motives (see James 4:3).

Yet after asking, and asking with right motives, we must be concerned about finding God's will in relation to our praying. How is it discovered? Of primary importance is the question, Does the prayer conform to clear commands of Scripture? It is foolish to pray for anything that is forbidden by God's Word. For example, to pray for God's approval on the marriage of a believer to an unbeliever would be to pray contrary to God's will (see 2 Cor. 6:14). On the other hand, we can be assured we are praying in His will when we ask to be filled with His Holy Spirit (see Luke 11:13). Primarily, the will of God is set forth in His Word (1 Thess. 4:3; 5:18; 1 Pet. 2:15; 4:19). When that will is unclear, for example, concerning a particular circumstance or situation, it is certainly in order to pray, "Your will be done."

A believer's asking should not fail to include any member of the Body who may commit a sin "that does not lead to death." Admittedly, the passage may be variously interpreted, particularly in light of the next statement, "There is a sin that leads to death. I am not saying that he should pray about that." Many interpreters identify the "sin that leads to death" with the sin "against the Holy Spirit" (Matt. 12:32). Others feel the reference is to sin which may be punishable by temporal death (such as murder) or to any sin which God chooses to punish by death.

The position of A. Plummer seems to come nearest to the right interpretation for the "sin that leads to death."

The prayer of one human being can never cancel another's free

PART 2

Chapter 13
Prayer in
Hebrews
and the
General
Epistles

will. If God's will does not override man's will, neither can a fellow-man's prayer. When a human will has been firmly and persistently set in opposition to the Divine will, our intercession will be of no avail. And this seems to be the meaning of "sin unto death;" willful and obstinate rejection of God's grace and persistence in unrepented sin.[6]

Although such may be the case at rare times, it is far more likely that when we earnestly entreat for the sinning brother, God, who is full of mercy and compassion, will "give him life." (See also James 5:20.)

Personal Edification through Prayer

It is most fitting that our study of prayer in the Epistles should leave us with this note: "You, dear friends, build yourselves up in your most holy faith and pray in the Holy Spirit. Keep yourselves in God's love as you wait for the mercy of our Lord Jesus Christ to bring you to eternal life" (Jude 20–21). The instruction is quite simple and basic: Build yourselves up. Instead of listening to ungodly men who had given themselves over to evil desires (v. 19), believers were encouraged to build up themselves, as well as each other, in the most holy faith (that is, in the revelation handed down by Christ and the apostles [v. 20]). Today, such development requires consistent study of God's Word as we seek to know the truth and teachings of Scripture. This is a privilege of, as well as an assignment for, every believer.

The present participles in the Greek of verse 20 act as imperatives and call for continuous action that is parallel. That is, while building ourselves up in (and by means of)

---

[6]H. D. M. Spence and Joseph S. Exell, eds., *The Pulpit Commentary* (Grand Rapids: Wm. B. Eerdmans Pub. Co., 1950), vol. 22, *1 John,* by A. Plummer, 142. I once confronted a brother who had caused a split in a small and struggling congregation. It became necessary to deal rather firmly with him, but afterwards I was distressed for having confronted the man so straightforwardly; so I began to pray earnestly for him. As I prayed day after day, however, a growing conviction settled upon my spirit that my praying was in vain, and that the man had sinned "a sin that leads to death." To my knowledge the man has not served God from that day to this.—R. L. B.

PART 2

Chapter 13
Prayer in
Hebrews
and the
General
Epistles

the holy faith, we should make it our practice to "pray in the Holy Spirit." The Word and the Spirit are both necessary. As we pray by the enabling power of the Holy Spirit, He inspires our hearts, illuminates our minds, and energizes us to be able to stand against the enemy of our souls and the false teachers who would tear down our faith (cf. Rom. 8:26–27; Eph. 6:18). In all likelihood, this is a direct reference to praying in the language given by the Spirit, in another tongue (cf. 1 Cor. 14:15,18). However, it must certainly include all prayer springing from the life and power of the Holy Spirit.

Throughout the examples of prayer in Acts and in the teachings on prayer in the Epistles, the Holy Spirit plays a prominent role. His presence is either implied or mentioned directly as energizing the praying of the Spirit-filled believer. The pattern remains the same today. This divine Paraclete, or Helper, given to assist all believers after Jesus returned to the right hand of the Father, is the key force in a dynamic and effective prayer life. Do not put out the Spirit's fire, but invite Him to revolutionize your life through inspired praying.

Questions for Study

1. What is our confidence as we approach the throne of grace?

2. What does James indicate are the right motives that should be expressed in our requests to God?

3. Who has the responsibility to call the elders of the church to pray for the sick and anoint with oil? Is there anything in the Bible that might indicate any exceptions to this?

4. What does Peter indicate is the greatest hindrance to prayer and why?

5. What does it mean to walk in the light?

6. Why is mercy needed and how can we be sure of obtaining it?

PART
3

Prayer In Contemporary Practice

PART 3: PRAYER IN CONTEMPORARY PRACTICE

— Chapter Fourteen —

ANGELIC INTERVENTION

No study of prayer having an eye to contemporary practice is complete without specific consideration of the ministry of angels in bringing answers to the prayers of believers. The Greek *angelos* can denote either a human or a heavenly "messenger." In the New Testament, however, it is used almost exclusively for heavenly beings (exceptions are Luke 7:24; 9:52; and possibly Rev. 1:20). These supernatural beings serve at God's command. In heaven their mission is to praise and worship God (Rev. 4:11–12). They give themselves without reservation to doing His will (Ps. 103:20); in fulfilling that will in behalf of those God loves, they "always see the face" of the Father (Matt. 18:10).

Angels are neither imaginary nor mythical. Though they participate in the mystical, they are not unreal. Though they appear mysteriously at times in dreams and visions (see Matt. 1:20; 2:13), at other times they become tangible beings in the physical, human world. Because God is the Creator and because He alone can create, He is able to give them physical bodies for the sake of temporary appearances to people. In their encounter with Lot (Gen. 19:1–4), angels ate as ordinary men and even prepared to sleep. Sometimes, as in the instance before us here, the one to whom the angel appeared did not know if he had

349

seen a vision or a physical being, until after the angel was gone.

Angels are sent from heavenly realms; yet their ministry to men and women often transpires unrecognized. We may suspect their intervention in supernatural protection and provision, but then hesitate to claim angelic visitation because we do not fully understand how the invisible realm intermingles with the physical. Nor do we need to understand completely the means that God uses to bring answers to our prayers. Just to know that there are angelic messengers who carry out the bidding of the Father, often in answer to prayer, is sufficient substance on which our faith can stand firm. Though the expression of prayer has a very human and physical aspect, communion between the believer on earth and the divine God of the universe reaches from the lower realm to the higher and links heaven and earth.

It should be noted that nowhere in Scripture are believers exhorted to pray for angelic intervention; nor are we instructed or allowed to pray to angels (Rev. 19:10). Angelic intervention is strictly at God's initiative. We are not to demand activity by angelic beings, but simply to recognize that such may happen as we engage in earnest prayer. Some will experience this form of an answer to prayer;[1] others will not. Yet the prayers of all believers are heard. "If we know that he hears us—whatever we ask—we know that we have what we asked of him" (1 John 5:15). God does not show partiality in how He sends the answer to prayer, but He knows that what may be helpful to some is totally unnecessary for others.

Whenever people seek to understand and explain the mysteries of the supernatural world, caution must be exercised and the study restricted to the biblical record. While it is important to give proper recognition to the possibility of angelic intervention when prayer is offered, it is equally important to avoid extremes that are the fruit of human imagination or the by-product of erroneous biblical interpretation.

---

[1]See Appendix 3, "A Contemporary Angelic Appearance."

The ministry of angels in behalf of God's people is affirmed in the Book of Hebrews: "Are not all angels ministering spirits sent to serve those who will inherit salvation?" (Heb. 1:14). Angels are involved in God's providential ordering of human affairs (Dan. 12:1). They are extremely active in the divine work of preparing the way for sinners to be reconciled to God (Acts 10:3–4). They declare God's word (Luke 1:26–28) and do His work on earth (Matt. 13:41). They participate in bringing God's salvation to mankind: they were present during Christ's birth (Matt. 1:20–24; 2:13,19–20; Luke 1:26–38; 2:9–15), ministry (Matt. 4:11; Mark 1:13; Luke 22:43), resurrection (Matt. 28:2,5; John 20:12), and ascension (Acts 1:10–11). They will play an important role in end-time events (see, for example, Matt. 24:31; Rev. 9:15) and will return with Christ at His second coming (Matt. 25:31).

The dispatching of angels is heaven's prerogative and benediction. They are fully obedient to the God who sends them forth. Some interpreters have erroneously taught that the believer may dispatch angels, but there is no biblical authority to support the claim. Our principal concern in this chapter is to discover how angelic intervention may occur in response to prayer. We understand that angels do function apart from human praying, but our focus here is their function as it relates to prayer.

Angels and Prayer in the Old Testament

There are many instances of angelic intervention in the Old Testament. However, only a limited number of them are directly related to prayer. Rather than speculate on the other episodes featuring the presence of angels, we will confine ourselves to those clearly marked by prayer.

Praying is not uncommonly related to spiritual warfare, but we generally understand spiritual warfare to be with forces of evil. However, Jacob contended with "a man," that is, an angel (Gen. 32:24). Whether the man was an angel dispatched by the Lord or the Lord himself in human form may not be as easy for us to decide as it appears to have been for Jacob, who said of his experience, "I saw God face to face" (Gen. 32:30).

So Jacob was left alone, and a man wrestled with him till daybreak. When the man saw that he could not overpower him, he touched the socket of Jacob's hip so that his hip was wrenched as he wrestled with the man. Then the man said, "Let me go, for it is daybreak." But Jacob replied, "I will not let you go unless you bless me." The man asked him, "What is your name?" "Jacob," he answered. Then the man said, "Your name will no longer be Jacob, but Israel, because you have struggled with God and with men and have overcome." Jacob said, "Please tell me your name." But he replied, "Why do you ask my name?" Then he blessed him there. So Jacob called the place Peniel, saying, "It is because I saw God face to face, and yet my life was spared" (Gen. 32:24–30).

It is not important that we discern between God and His angelic messengers, except when we worship (Rev. 19:10). For Jacob, the confrontation was of great consequence. He recognized that the being with whom he wrestled was capable of blessing him, and in his particular circumstance he understood he could not survive without that blessing.

At the same time Jacob wrestled with the angel, it seems the angel also struggled with him—or possibly Jacob wrestled with himself. His great problem was more within himself than in gaining mastery over the angel, for the angel was God's messenger for his blessing. But Jacob was too "strong" to receive that blessing. Until he could yield, he was not prepared to be blessed. The obstacle to be overcome was Jacob: the deceiver, the supplanter, the devious one.

The angel wrestled long and hard, for he was there to minister to Jacob. All night the battle raged. Not until Jacob's hip, the symbol of his human strength, was wrenched[2] did he finally yield to the angel. The moment Jacob broke—and it took a long and anguish-filled night to get to that point (v. 26)—he gained the desired blessing: "Your name will no longer be Jacob, but Israel, because you have struggled with God and with men and have overcome" (v. 28). "Overcome" whom? the angel? God? No. Jacob had over-

---

[2]Heb. *teqa'*—"was dislocated."

come Jacob; and to that end he had wrestled with the angel. If need be, God may still dispatch His angel to wrestle with us and impart a blessing. The Jacob in us, deceiving and devious, may tend to dominate our lives and make us victims of our old Adamic nature. *Lord, send your angel!*

Jacob responded with his own query, "Please tell me your name" (v. 29). This should not seem strange, for who, after such a revolutionizing encounter, would not want to identify the mysterious being with whom he had struggled? Jacob's question was met with the angel's question, "Why do you ask my name?" As much as a human can comprehend the divine, his name was already evident in what had taken place. Jacob needed nothing more. This was no ordinary angel (v. 30); Jacob had met *the* Angel of the Lord. He showed that he understood, for he named the place Peniel, "the face of God." The struggle of intercessory prayer always tells us more about ourselves than about God. It brings us to the point of recognizing our sinfulness, our spiritual weakness, our lack of any merit of our own. Paul understood this truth and wrote, "When I am weak, then I am strong" (2 Cor. 12:10).

Moses was the leader of the Israelites as they trekked through the wilderness on the way to the Promised Land. But there was another guide. Moses had no question about who that guide was. Having come to Kadesh, Moses asked the king of Edom to let Israel pass through his country. Though the request was denied, it contains a testimonial to God's faithfulness in sending an answer to prayer: " 'When we cried out to the LORD, he heard our cry and sent an angel and brought us out of Egypt. Now we are here at Kadesh, a town on the edge of your territory' " (Num. 20:16).

It is probable that Moses purposely used an expression which might be understood as either angel or messenger, because he could not explain to the king of Edom the true relation of the Lord to his people. At the same time it was in the deepest sense true (cf. Exod. 14:19; 32:34), because it was the uncreated angel of the covenant, which was from God, and yet was God (cf. Gen.

32:30; Josh. 5:15; 6:2; Acts 7:35), who was the real captain of the Lord's host.[3]

The point of the Numbers 20 passage for our interest is the fact that the angelic intervention was in response to Israel's prayer: "We cried out to the LORD." When the people of God find themselves in bondage to governments dominated by evil men, their prayers are most certainly heard; God will in His own wisdom and time intervene, even to the extent of employing angels to effect the necessary deliverance. In later years, when the Israelites were again dominated by another group of people, this time the Philistines, God again heard their cry. The prayer for national deliverance was to begin to have an answer through a God-sent child: Samson.

The record of Samson's birth as an answer to the heart cry of a barren wife contains several miraculous elements, including an angelic announcement of a special child to be born. God was at work in behalf of His people, and the appearance of the Angel of the Lord was confirmation of the fact.

Again the Israelites did evil in the eyes of the LORD, so the LORD delivered them into the hands of the Philistines for forty years. A certain man of Zorah, named Manoah, from the clan of the Danites, had a wife who was sterile and remained childless. The angel of the Lord appeared to her and said, "You are sterile and childless, but you are going to conceive and have a son. Now see to it that you drink no wine or other fermented drink and that you do not eat anything unclean, because you will conceive and give birth to a son. No razor may be used on his head, because the boy is to be a Nazirite, set apart to God from birth, and he will begin the deliverance of Israel from the hands of the Philistines." Then the woman went to her husband and told him, "A man of God came to me. He looked like an angel of God, very awesome. I didn't ask him where he came from, and he didn't tell me his name. But he said to me, 'You will conceive and give birth to a son. Now then, drink no wine or other fermented drink

---

[3]H. D. M. Spence and Joseph S. Exell, eds., *The Pulpit Commentary* (Grand Rapids: Wm. B. Eerdmans Pub. Co., 1950), vol. 2, *Numbers*, by R. Winterbotham, 254.

and do not eat anything unclean, because the boy will be a Nazirite of God from birth until the day of his death' " (Judg. 13:1–7).

While the biblical record does not explicitly indicate that Manoah and his wife prayed for a child, the implication is there; the burden of barrenness in a Jewish home would quite naturally provoke prayer (cf. Gen. 25:21 and 1 Sam. 1:10–11). In this instance God sent His angel not only to assure Manoah's wife that He would heal her barrenness, but to give her specific instructions about her time of pregnancy and the kind of life her son was to lead.

The description of the angel by the mother-to-be is noteworthy. "A man of God came to me. He looked like an angel of God, very awesome" (v. 6). "Awesome" is a translation of the Hebrew *nora'*, a passive participle meaning "to be reverenced," "held in honor," "held in awe." Encountering an angel, especially the Angel of the Lord (cf. Ex. 33:20; Acts 7:38), was indeed an awesome experience, requiring the utmost reverence. Gideon's experience was similar: "When Gideon realized that it was the angel of the Lord, he exclaimed, 'Ah, Sovereign Lord! I have seen the angel of the Lord face to face!' But the Lord said to him, 'Peace! Do not be afraid. You are not going to die' " (Judg. 6:22–23).

The ministry of the angel who visited Manoah's wife was twofold: (1) to convey God's promise to her—"You are going to . . . have a son," and (2) to give specific instructions regarding the son who was to be born—"No razor may be used on his head, because the boy is to be a Nazirite, set apart to God from birth."

While it is implied that the angel visited Manoah's wife in response to prayer, there being no direct statement, there is no doubt about the second angelic appearance coming in response to prayer. Manoah entreated the Lord to send again "the man of God" that he might give further instruction on rearing the child that had been promised. Manoah may not have believed his wife had seen an angel. Angels are not men, for they are identified as "spirits" (Heb. 1:14) and spirits do not have flesh and bones (Luke 24:39). Yet when they appear to people, angels can appear as either ordinary or extraordinary men. That angels can appear as humans is evident in both Testaments (cf. Heb. 13:2).

Manoah prayed to the LORD: "O Lord, I beg you, let the man of God you sent to us come again to teach us how to bring up the boy who is to be born."

God heard Manoah, and the angel of God came again to the woman while she was out in the field; but her husband Manoah was not with her. The woman hurried to tell her husband, "He's here! The man who appeared to me the other day!"

Manoah got up and followed his wife. When he came to the man, he said, "Are you the one who talked to my wife?"

"I am," he said.

So Manoah asked him, "When your words are fulfilled, what is to be the rule for the boy's life and work?"

The angel of the LORD answered, "Your wife must do all that I have told her. She must not eat anything that comes from the grapevine, nor drink any wine or other fermented drink nor eat anything unclean. She must do everything I have commanded her."

Manoah said to the angel of the LORD, "We would like you to stay until we prepare a young goat for you."

The angel of the LORD replied, "Even though you detain me, I will not eat any of your food. But if you prepare a burnt offering, offer it to the LORD." (Manoah did not realize that it was the angel of the LORD.)

Then Manoah inquired of the angel of the LORD, "What is your name, so that we may honor you when your word comes true?"

He replied, "Why do you ask my name? It is beyond understanding.".... And the LORD did an amazing thing.... As the flame blazed up from the altar toward heaven, the angel of the LORD ascended in the flame. Seeing this, Manoah and his wife fell with their faces to the ground. When the angel of the LORD did not show himself again to Manoah and his wife, Manoah realized that it was the angel of the LORD (Judg. 13:8–21).

Even after considerable conversation with the angel who appeared as a man, Manoah did not realize that it was the Angel of the Lord. The encounter had been much like the encounter of one man with another. So Manoah asked him to stay and enjoy the hospitality of a special meal that he would provide. The angel refused to eat their food, however, suggesting rather that they prepare a burnt offering to the Lord. This should have let Manoah know that there was something unusual about this angel, but he still looked at him as a "man of God" (that is, a prophet) and asked his name, "so that we may honor you when your word comes true" (v. 17). Fulfilled prophecy was one of the authentications of a true prophet (Deut. 18:21–22; 1 Sam. 9:6). Manoah clearly did not have as much discernment as his wife did (v. 6).

In one sense Manoah's request was denied. In another it was answered, for "beyond understanding" (v. 18) is from the Hebrew *pel'i,* meaning "wonderful," "marvelous." It is a form of the same word used by Isaiah in his prophecy of Jesus: "He will be called Wonderful [Heb. *pele*']" (Isa. 9:6). Then when Manoah obeyed and made an offering to the Lord, all doubt about the identity of this "angel" who had appeared in answer to Manoah's prayer was cleared away. For we read, "The LORD did an amazing thing while Manoah and his wife watched. As the flame blazed up from the altar toward heaven, the angel of the LORD ascended in the flame." Thus, the Lord and the Angel of the Lord are identified (vv. 19–20). Then Manoah and his wife realized that this was the Angel of the Lord and that they had seen God (vv. 21–22). This is another Old Testament indication that the special manifestations of *the* Angel of the Lord were preincarnate appearances of the divine Son of God. He is the one Mediator between God and mankind (1 Tim. 2:5). Manoah and his wife may not have fully understood this, but his wife did understand the Lord had accepted their sacrifice and was the One who had shown them all these things.

Daniel also had encounters with angels. They usually appeared to him during times of intense prayer and waiting upon God. Their mission each time was of monumental consequence, since they consistently relayed to him a revelation concerning the end times. We will not deal with the content of the visions and the understanding given to Daniel, but we will rather note some significant facts concerning the heavenly messengers who visited him during his times of prayer.

While I, Daniel, was watching the vision and trying to understand it, there before me stood one who looked like a man. And I heard a man's voice ... calling, "Gabriel, tell this man the meaning of the vision." As he came near the place where I was standing, I was terrified and fell prostrate. "Son of man," he said to me, "understand that the vision concerns the time of the end" (Dan. 8:15–17).

Daniel had been praying for understanding of a vision which had come to him. In response to his prayer he testified, "There before me stood one who looked like a man." A voice spoke identifying the man as the angel Gabriel, "hero or strong one of God."[4] As was commonly the case in Old Testament angelic appearances, Daniel felt an awesome fear, and with good reason, for he was confronted by a being only a little lower than God. He knew that no human being could see God and live.

While I was still in prayer, Gabriel, the man I had seen in the earlier vision, came to me in swift flight about the time of the evening sacrifice. He instructed me and said to me, "Daniel, I have now come to give you insight and understanding. As soon as you began to pray, an answer was given, which I have come to tell you, for you are highly esteemed. Therefore, consider the message and understand the vision (Dan. 9:21–23).

Again Gabriel appeared as a "man," or as a "person," as the Hebrew 'ish may mean. As in the first appearance, his mission was to "give ... insight and understanding." Though the angel that came to Daniel brought divine revelation and new truth, angelic appearances today would be for other purposes. Whether it be Moroni of Mormonism, or another angel who claims to add to or take away from the revelation of Holy Scripture, he is to be denounced and rejected. The apostle Paul declared it boldly, "Even if we or an angel from heaven should preach a gospel other than the one we preached to you, let him be eternally condemned" (Gal. 1:8). Satan, who himself "masquerades as

---

[4]Others take the meaning of Gabriel to be "God has shown himself strong." This is the first time an angel is identified by name.

an angel of light" (2 Cor. 11:14), still employs his evil angels to hinder and destroy the work of God.

At that time I, Daniel, mourned for three weeks. . . . I looked up and there before me was a man dressed in linen, with a belt of the finest gold around his waist. His body was like chrysolite, his face like lightning, his eyes like flaming torches, his arms and legs like the gleam of burnished bronze, and his voice like the sound of a multitude.

I, Daniel, was the only one who saw the vision; the men with me did not see it, but such terror overwhelmed them that they fled and hid themselves. So I was left alone, gazing at this great vision; I had no strength left, my face turned deathly pale and I was helpless. Then I heard him speaking, and as I listened to him, I fell into a deep sleep, my face to the ground.

A hand touched me and set me trembling on my hands and knees. He said, "Daniel, you who are highly esteemed, consider carefully the words I am about to speak to you, and stand up, for I have now been sent to you." And when he said this to me, I stood up trembling.

Then he continued, "Do not be afraid, Daniel. Since the first day that you set your mind to gain understanding and to humble yourself before your God, your words were heard, and I have come in response to them. But the prince of the Persian kingdom resisted me twenty-one days. Then Michael, one of the chief princes, came to help me, because I was detained there with the king of Persia. Now I have come to explain to you what will happen to your people in the future, for the vision concerns a time yet to come" (Dan. 10:2; 5–14).

The final angelic appearance to Daniel, as in each of the earlier instances, followed prolonged and earnest fasting and prayer. Daniel's description of the heavenly being has parallels with the "son of man" John saw (Rev. 1:13–15). Whoever Daniel's messenger was—whether the Lord himself or more likely Gabriel, who had already appeared twice—he was a messenger with news from another world (cf. Heb. 1:14).

The experience of Daniel's angelic visitor, as he was coming in response to Daniel's prayer for understanding, holds a weighty meaning. In answer to earnest prayer, God may dispatch an angel immediately. Yet even angels must combat unseen forces which confront and withstand God's messengers of mercy. The existence of extremely powerful evil beings is real. In this case, one was called "the prince of the Persian kingdom" (v. 13). So powerful was he that he delayed the answer to Daniel's prayer for twenty-one days, during which time a second angel, Michael, was dispatched to help get the answer through to Daniel.[5] With Michael taking up the conflict, Gabriel was able to fulfill his God-ordained mission to Daniel. Humans have little or no idea of the conflict in the heavens concerning earthly events and persons. It is probable that Paul was referring to such conflict when he wrote, "For our struggle is not against flesh and blood, but against the rulers, against the authorities, against the powers of this dark world and against the spiritual forces of evil in the heavenly realms" (Eph. 6:12).

Angels and Prayer in the New Testament

Angelic intervention is not confined to Old Testament appearances. In fact, the reports of angelic intervention were remarkably common in the New Testament era. An appearance often occurred as a direct result of prayer, while at other times angels were sent on a special mission apart from any prayer by saints, for example, the angels who appeared at Jesus' empty tomb (Luke 24:4–5).

Angels are never occupied with trivia. When they do appear, it is with high purpose. "When the time had fully come, God sent his Son" (Gal. 4:4). But there was much more to the advent of the Messiah than a mere statement of the event. There was prophecy and preparation. A forerunner for the Savior was part of the great salvation plan, and an angel played a part in announcing that.

In the time of Herod king of Judea there was a priest named Zechariah ... [and] his wife Elizabeth.... Both of them were upright in the sight of God, observing all the Lord's commandments and regulations blamelessly. But they had no children, because Elizabeth was barren; and they were both well along in

---

[5]Michael, "who is like God," is the only other angel identified by name in the Bible. Jude 9 calls him "the archangel" or chief angel.

years. Once when Zechariah's division was on duty and he was serving as priest before God, he was chosen by lot, according to the custom of the priesthood, to go into the temple of the Lord and burn incense. And when the time for the burning of incense came, all the assembled worshipers were praying outside. Then an angel of the Lord appeared to him, standing at the right side of the altar of incense. When Zechariah saw him, he was startled and gripped with fear. But the angel said to him: "Do not be afraid, Zechariah, your prayer has been heard. Your wife Elizabeth will bear you a son, and you are to give him the name John. He will be a joy and delight to you, and many will rejoice because of his birth, for he will be great in the sight of the Lord.... He will go on before the Lord, in the spirit and power of Elijah, to turn the hearts of the fathers to their children and the disobedient to the wisdom of the righteous—to make ready a people prepared for the Lord." Zechariah asked the angel, "How can I be sure of this? I am an old man and my wife is well along in years." The angel answered, "I am Gabriel. I stand in the presence of God, and I have been sent to speak to you and to tell you this good news" (Luke 1:5–15; 17–19).

It cannot be positively said that the praying of Zechariah, or even the praying of the people, precipitated this angelic appearance, though there is no question that prayer set the stage for the supernatural happening. The people were praying outside the Holy Place (v. 10) while inside Zechariah was offering incense (a form of prayer) in fulfillment of his priestly role in the temple. The angel who appeared to Zechariah was Gabriel (v. 19), who identified himself without any request that he do so. He had been sent by God on a special mission to announce "good news" (v. 19). To Zechariah he revealed, " 'Your prayer has been heard. Your wife Elizabeth will bear you a son, and you are to give him the name John' " (v. 13).

The nature of Zechariah's prayer is uncertain. Was he praying for a son (vv. 6–7), or was he praying for Israel's redemption (vv. 16–17)? In any case, the birth of John was an answer to both prayers. According to Scripture, believers are surrounded by angels, sent by God to watch over them (see Ps. 91:11). But in our usual condition we do not perceive their presence. Zechariah and other saints of

Holy Scripture possessed that sensitivity and receptivity, which come only through earnest engagement in prayer.

Jesus received the ministry of angels. In Gethsemane, on the threshold of His sacrificial death for our sins, our Lord prayed the most intense and agonized prayer of His earthly mission. He was facing the unmeasured agony of being made sin (the word "sin" in the Heb. also means a sin offering, cf. Isa. 53:10) for us (see 2 Cor. 5:21), a burden beyond human ability to bear. Believers have the promise, "God . . . will not let you be tempted beyond what you can bear. But when you are tempted, he will also provide a way out so that you can stand up under it" (1 Cor. 10:13). In the face of Christ's almost unbearable burden, He too was tempted, but not beyond His endurance. God made a way to bear it. He sent an angel to strengthen Him: "[Jesus] withdrew about a stone's throw beyond them, knelt down and prayed, 'Father, if you are willing, take this cup from me; yet not my will, but yours be done.' An angel from heaven appeared to him and strengthened him" (Luke ·22:41–43). What encouragement this is for us when we confront life's impossibilities. Surely we can count on God to send His angels "to serve those who will inherit salvation" (Heb. 1:14). At the moment of our greatest need, prayer brings a strength beyond human ability, whether it comes in the form of an angel or through the ministry of the blessed Holy Spirit.

Even after the Holy Spirit had been given as a special help to believers, God did not cease to use angels. Should we consider it strange then when such experiences still happen? Certainly not![6]

Now an angel of the Lord said to Philip, "Go south to the road—the desert road—that goes down from Jerusalem to Gaza." So he started out, and on his way he met an Ethiopian eunuch, an important official in charge of all the treasury of Candace, queen of the Ethiopians. This man had gone to Jerusalem to worship, and on his way home was sitting in his chariot reading the book of Isaiah the prophet. The Spirit told Philip, "Go to that chariot

---

[6]See Appendix 3, "A Contemporary Angelic Appearance."

and stay near it." Then Philip ran up to the chariot (Acts 8:26–30).

While it is not stated that Philip's encounter with the angel was preceded by prayer, it is reasonable to believe that Philip, like all active witnesses in the Early Church, was a man of much prayer who constantly sought God's direction. Visible angelic intervention is certainly the exception rather than the rule. In Philip's case, however, it was probably necessary because of the prevailing circumstance. The Spirit-prompted Samaritan revival no doubt occupied Philip's time and attention. Yet in God's broader perspective, it was of more consequence to the Kingdom that the Ethiopian eunuch receive the gospel (before he returned to his homeland) than that Philip remain in Samaria. Therefore God dispatched an angel with a specific command: "Go south."

Of special interest in this passage is the role of the angel and the Spirit in giving direction to Philip. The angel captured Philip's attention and gave him instruction to head out into the desert between Jerusalem and Gaza. When he was obedient to this direction, the Spirit gave further instructions. When an angel of the Lord directs in a specific way, the result is a meaningful and productive ministry (see Acts 8:30–38).

Another case of guidance from an angel and obedience on the part of people took place at Caesarea. Cornelius was "devout and God-fearing," regular in his prayers. As he prayed, he most certainly expressed his strong and continuing desire for divine direction in his quest for God.

At Caesarea there was a man named Cornelius. . . . He and all his family were devout and God-fearing; he gave generously to those in need and prayed to God regularly. One day at about three in the afternoon he had a vision. He distinctly saw an angel of God, who came to him and said, "Cornelius!" Cornelius stared at him in fear. "What is it, Lord?" he asked. The angel answered, "Your prayers and gifts to the poor have come up as a memorial offering before God. Now send men to Joppa to bring back a man named Simon who is called Peter. He is staying with Simon the tanner, whose house is by the sea (Acts 10:1–6).

God did not dispatch an angel to Cornelius to preach the gospel to him; nor is it the ministry of angels to do so. That is the responsibility laid upon men and women. Angels may have a related ministry, but not evangelism itself. They may set the stage for evangelism, they may guide toward salvation, but they do not do the actual evangelism.

The purpose of the angel's message to Cornelius was twofold: (1) to assure him that he had an audience in heaven and (2) to direct him to send men to Joppa. What assurance must have come to Cornelius as he heard the angel say, "Your prayers and gifts to the poor have come up as a remembrance before God" (v. 4)! Gabriel conveyed a similar message to Zechariah: "Your prayer has been heard" (Luke 1:13). A similar assurance has been confirmed to many devout believers after earnest prayer. When people seek God with all earnestness of heart, God responds, even using His angels if necessary. "You will seek me and find me when you seek me with all your heart" (Jer. 29:13).

Peter was kept in prison, but the church was earnestly praying to God for him. The night before Herod was to bring him to trial, Peter was sleeping between two soldiers, bound with two chains, and sentries stood guard at the entrance. Suddenly an angel of the Lord appeared and a light shone in the cell. He struck Peter on the side and woke him up. "Quick, get up!" he said, and the chains fell off Peter's wrists. Then the angel said to him, "Put on your clothes and sandals." And Peter did so. "Wrap your cloak around you and follow me," the angel told him. Peter followed him out of the prison, but he had no idea that what the angel was doing was really happening; he thought he was seeing a vision. They passed the first and second guards and came to the iron gate leading to the city. It opened for them by itself, and they went through it. When they had walked the length of one street, suddenly the angel left him (Acts 12:5–10).

The praying of the Early Church invited divine intervention. Angels may not always come into one's life as dramatically as this, but the account is sufficient evidence of the reality of Hebrews 1:14: "Are not all angels ministering spirits sent to serve those who will inherit salvation?" Prayer may bring angels into the picture, seen or unseen. The lesson for us is unmistakable: In times of dire emergency and extreme confrontation with evil, the Church must pray until God intervenes in His own way, dispatching an angel if need be.

When the deliverance was accomplished, Peter could testify of a miraculous intervention, not because he had caused it to happen, but because he had obediently followed each instruction and leading of the miracle-working angel. Note the activities of the angel who visited Peter:

1. The angel struck Peter, no doubt to awaken him.
2. The angel called on Peter to act: "Quick, get up!"
3. The angel struck Peter "and the chains fell off from Peter's wrists."
4. The angel told Peter to get dressed: "Put on your clothes and your sandals."
5. The angel gave instructions for the escape: "Wrap your cloak around you, and follow me."
6. The angel caused the iron prison gate to open by itself.
7. The angel led Peter to freedom.

What a testimony of deliverance Peter had to share! Yet he had nothing of which to brag. The heaven-sent angel, in behalf of the One who had sent him, was the prime mover in this supernatural intervention.

An angel appeared to the apostle Paul in a dire situation. Paul was on his way to Rome to stand trial before Caesar. Departing from Crete at a time when safe sailing was highly uncertain, the ship was caught in a wind of hurricane force. The situation became so desperate that all on board gave up hope of being rescued. We must assume that Paul, for whom prayer was a constant habit, was much in prayer during the frightening and horrendous voyage. His epistles are full of encouragements to pray. To the Philippians he declared, "Do not be anxious about anything, but in everything, by pray and petition, with thanksgiving, present your requests to God" (Phil. 4:6). To the Thessalonians he wrote, "Pray continually" (1 Thess. 5:17).

After the men had gone a long time without food, Paul stood up before them and said: "Men, you should have taken my advice not to sail from Crete; then you would have spared yourselves this damage and loss. But now I urge you to keep up your courage, because not one of you will be lost; only the ship will be destroyed. Last night an angel of the God whose I am and whom I serve stood beside me and said, 'Do not be afraid, Paul. You must stand trial before Caesar; and God has graciously given you the lives of all who sail with you' " (Acts 27:21–24).

This mighty prayer warrior no doubt wrestled with God in the dark of night, praying for his own safety and for the safety of his shipmates. But even though he had already been assured that he was going to Rome (Acts 19:21; 23:11), as the storm continued raging for many days, Paul, along with the others, "finally gave up all hope of being saved" (27:20). James reminded us that "Elijah was a man just like us" (James 5:17). So was Paul. In the midst of that awful hurricane "northeaster" (27:14), which threatened to destroy both men and ship, even Paul was afraid. Jewish leaders in more than one place had tried to kill Paul. Would the wind and sea succeed where they had failed? Paul, Luke, and all the rest were in despair.

But God was faithful. He dispatched an angel with a message of hope and assurance, even in the midst of almost certain destruction. The Williams translation gets the exact sense of the Greek when it gives the angel's first words as, "Stop being afraid, Paul."[7] Paul would indeed stand before Caesar. More than that, everyone on board the ship would be saved.

We might ask, Why didn't God simply halt the storm and permit the ship to sail on? Or why didn't God preserve the ship from the fury of the storm. Or why would God permit His servant such an agonizing experience? Suffice it to say that in everything that happened God was glorified. The sailors learned that they should have heeded God's servant in the first place. They learned also that Paul's God was indeed God. The islanders who received the shipwrecked crew and passengers witnessed the mighty power of God and heard the gospel. And Paul, in due time, got to Rome.

Some great lessons in prayer are contained in this ac-

---

[7]A Gk. negative command in the present tense means to stop doing something you are already doing.

count. When trouble overwhelms, pray. When men will not listen to your words, pray. When storms threaten to destroy, pray. When all hope seems gone, pray. No matter how evil the situation, pray. No matter who or what precipitated the problem, pray. Prayer is the proper response to any of life's vicissitudes.

Questions for Study

1. What is the meaning of "angel" and how does this relate to their function with respect to prayer?

2. Who takes the initiative in angelic intervention and what does that mean to us?

3. What do you learn from the Old Testament examples of angels who ministered to those who prayed?

4. Do you agree with the author's statement: "Angels are never occupied with trivia"? Explain your answer.

5. Under what circumstances especially may we count on God to send His angels "to serve those who will inherit salvation"?

PRAYER AND REVIVAL

The relationship between prayer and revival is not routinely recognized by all students of past revivals. Some see prayer only as a burden God places on the hearts of His people when he is about to send revival; His people must be prepared for the coming of the sovereignly sent revival. According to this theological perspective, God sends revival when He chooses, and no amount of prayer can change the divine intention preordained in heaven.

Pentecostals, however, see a direct relationship between prayer, revival, and bringing the lost to Christ. No one, of course, can change God's ultimate will by prayer, by bargaining, or by any other means. Yet God has clearly indicated His desire that His children should pray (Prov. 15:8), asking for those things they need and even desire (Matt. 6:7–13; Mark 11:24). When these desires are in line with His will, we can confidently expect an answer. A loving Heavenly Father would not encourage His children to pray and bring their petitions to Him only to have them ignored and continually denied.

Though God's ultimate will does not change, and cannot be changed by any human being, God has chosen to accomplish that will through the prayers of His children. So one of the primary purposes of prayer is to bring human

369

desires into conformity with divine intention and will. To know God is to know His will. Evangelism, or bringing disobedient and rebellious people back to obedient submission to their Maker, is at the center of God's ultimate will: God is "not wanting anyone to perish, but everyone to come to repentance" (2 Pet. 3:9). When winning the lost moves beyond intellectual affirmation to an all-consuming passion and into prayer, echoing the very heartbeat of God, the Spirit will begin to move in revival power. We need those "times of refreshing" that God has promised to people who repent and turn to Him (Acts 3:19).

Even though the Old and the New Testaments both contain accounts of supernatural intervention that can be called revivals, some oppose such happenings today, claiming that they play upon emotions and lead to spiritual instability and irrational behavior.[1] These same critics also object to the emphasis on crisis experiences, frequently stressed in revivalism. Yet the results of biblical revivals and the dramatic moving of the Spirit in response to intercessory prayer throughout the intervening centuries are evidence of a divine pattern for building and maintaining the vitality of Christ's Church. Church history records increased growth and the rebirth of a new commitment following special periods of religious revival. Moral and social transformation have accompanied the major revivals, in Bible times as well as in subsequent periods.

In its strict definition, "revival" denotes a restoration of spiritual fervor and vitality after a period of decline. It is God's will that His people love Him with all their heart, soul, mind, and strength (see Mark 12:30; Luke 10:27). Any falling away from that wholehearted commitment calls for revival. God's people must ever be encouraged to make that love and commitment fuller and stronger. Then, with the church revived, there will be the winning of the lost

---

[1]A story is told of a boy who urged his father to go to a revival meeting. The father said, "I don't need that excitement. I'm established." Later, one cold morning the family car would not start. The father tinkered with a few things and then said, "I don't know why this car won't start." The boy replied, "I know, Dad—it's established!"

■■■■■■■

PART 3

Chapter 15
Prayer
and
Revival

to Christ.[2] The "dead in . . . transgressions and sins" (Eph. 2:1) need a quickening of new life, a resurrection. When we pray for a revival of believers that leads to the salvation of sinners, we know we are praying in God's will.

Is there a sense of a burden lying upon men's hearts which will not give them rest, but which makes them agonize in prayer? If not, then the night is not far spent, a deeper darkness still awaits us. For what use would a revival be if we are not prepared for it? It would pass over us without doing its work.[3]

There is great advance of the Kingdom through revival. Through revival spiritual life is renewed, revitalized. In the spiritual experience of a congregation or of individuals within it, there is an ebb and flow of commitment and intensity. As prayer times become less frequent and the desire to commune intimately with the Lord wanes, spiritual vitality cools and must be revived. Would to God there were no such thing as lukewarmness in the believer's life! Consequently, each believer and each congregation must be challenged constantly to seek for revival and a greater yieldedness to the Holy Spirit. Providentially, prayer is that key to personal and corporate revival.

Revivals are seldom preceded by an awakening of the entire Church or local congregation to a sense of need. Instead, the burden and the agony of intercession fall upon the hearts of the few devout souls who, feeling the need, begin to entreat God in prayer for revival. As the burden is faithfully presented to God in prayer, the sense of spiritual need and concern for a careless and apathetic church becomes an agonized cry, "How long, O God? How long?" When the prayer becomes persistent and intense, God responds to the cry that He has ordained to bring in the revival He is wanting to send.

All human attempts to create or work up a revival are doomed to failure. There may be activity, but only a heaven-

---

[2]Charles G. Finney, *Lectures on Revivals of Religion* (New York: Fleming H. Revell Co., 1868), 15–16.

[3]James Burns, *Revivals: Their Laws and Leaders* (London: Hodder and Stoughton, 1909; reprint, Grand Rapids: Baker Book House, 1960), 71 (page reference is to reprint edition).

sent revival can accomplish anything of lasting value. If this is true, must we wait helplessly until God in His sovereign will decides to revive His Church? Certainly not! He is ever ready and willing to revive His people. He waits only for their urgency and desperation to reach the point that He can send a revival to hungry hearts that will accomplish the purpose for which He revives His people: to further advance His kingdom.

Prayer opens our hearts and minds to a sense of not only our own need but also the world's. It prepares the soil of the soul for the seed of the Word. Revival then is the spiritual harvest. The burdened and persistent intercession of God's people pleading for a revival is the surest sign that revival is on the way. Revival is not the result of humanly-devised methodology. It is a matter of hunger, intercession, prayer, and confession of need. We should pray, "O Lord, revive your work, and let the revival begin with me," until the answer comes.

Revival in the Old and New Testaments

The revivals of the Old Testament recount Israel's renewed zeal to obey God. There was renewal and recommitment after Solomon's prayer of dedication upon completion of the temple (2 Chron. 7:1–11). There were revivals in the days of Samuel, Asa, Jehoshaphat, Hezekiah, and Josiah. Ezra records the revival that occurred following years of praying for a return from captivity and the rebuilding and dedication of the temple (Ezra 9:1 to 10:14). Yet in all the revival instances of the Old Testament, there is no command to evangelize or reach out to Gentiles. It seems that the wayward Israelites were constantly being called to return to obedience and acknowledgment of God's claim upon them as His chosen people.

New Testament revivals add a dimension that has been a pattern for the Christian Church down to the present. Evangelism is made easier as a result of true revival. It is true that God's people need to be revived; but they are revived that they might be a part of the great work of the Kingdom: rescuing the lost from the dominion of Satan. Believers play a part in sharing the divine plan of salvation.

" 'For God so loved the world that he gave his one and only Son, that whoever believes in him shall not perish but have eternal life' " (John 3:16). And as the Son of God was about to return to glory, having completed His mission of dying for the whole human race, He said to all who were or would be His spiritual brothers and sisters, " 'Go into all the world and preach the good news to all creation' " (Mark 16:15).

Evangelism is more effective when preceded by spiritual awakening. It has been said that before a church can reach out and win the unsaved, there must first be a renewal and preparation of believers, from the pastor to the newest convert. It would be wonderful if churches could always maintain a high spiritual level. But, perhaps due to human nature, perhaps due partly to the pressures of the world around us, every congregation needs renewal from time to time. We need to be brought into that place of one accord that the Book of Acts mentions so frequently.[4] Then, as revival leads to evangelism, the results will not be disappointing. This does not mean, of course, that a believer must wait for revival to sweep the congregation before telling others about the peace and eternal life Christ has provided through His death and resurrection. In fact, when a believer steps out in winning souls, in obedience to the Great Commission, this will bring a sense of the need for power and for personal revival. This will stir the believer's heart to prayer, and personal revival will be sure to come as well as the salvation of souls.

The greatest revival recorded in the New Testament began on the Day of Pentecost. In fact, the entire Book of Acts is a record of personal revival (enduement with power) and effective witnessing. The Early Church prayed for boldness to witness in the face of persecution (Acts 4:29). "After they prayed, the place where they were meeting was shaken. And they were all filled with the Holy Spirit and spoke the word of God boldly" (Acts 4:31). As a result of these re-

---

[4]Someone has compared the Holy Spirit's work to the concentration of the rays of the sun through a magnifying glass. The Holy Spirit does work in a general way, just as the sun warms. But when the Holy Spirit can work through a united local body, the fires of revival begin to burn.

peated refillings and enduements with power, many sinners were converted and added to the Body of Christ (see Acts 2:41,47; 5:14; 11:24).

Revival in Recent History

The relation between prayer and the revivals of the Bible has been well-documented in Bible commentaries. We now look briefly at the importance of prayer in some of the later moves of God, especially since the Protestant Reformation of the sixteenth century. Religious literature of the medieval church contains many accounts of monastics who devoted their lives to personal prayer and intercession. To the extent that these individuals combined their personal spiritual quests with evangelism, we do have historical accounts of revivals which brought the lost to Christ and reformed the moral climate of the times. Francis of Assisi (twelfth century), Savonarola (fifteenth century), and Madame Guyon (seventeenth and eighteenth centuries) are examples of Catholic spiritual leaders who saw notable revivals (as renewal and as evangelism) in response to devout prayer that God would reverse the corruption and moral decay of the time.

Historians traditionally concentrate on the public aspects of events. Private letters and pronouncements may shed light on background influences, but such private statements, unless substantiated by additional unrelated sources, are held to be opinions and private interpretations. Consequently, prayer is frequently omitted as preceding and precipitating revival. Yet the perceptive reader can make some logical deductions from references to increased devotion, ministerial callings, concern over the decay of contemporary society, and reports of supernatural confrontations with deity. Increased devotion to Christ and His Church develops as a prayer habit matures and intensifies. The certainty of a divine call to spiritual leadership comes from personal communion with God. A growing burden for the ungodly state of society leads to intercessory prayer. Repeated supernatural evidences of God's presence in the affairs of devout believers affirms a personal relationship nurtured through prayer.

Martin Luther is recognized as the major figure of the Protestant Reformation (beginning in the sixteenth century). Yet there were significant awakenings of spiritual fervor before his time, leading to the conclusion that prayer and personal devotion played a significant part in reviving nominal Christians and bringing sinners to accept Christ as Savior.

PART 3

Chapter 15
Prayer
and
Revival

The Brethren of the Common Life, founded in the Netherlands in the fourteenth century, are a good example of those who began praying and pressing for reform and revival. According to church historians, they were noted for their piety (i.e., commitment to the devotional life) and holy life-style. Their influence, propelled by prayer and personal communion with the Lord, continued into the seventeenth century when many of the Brethren welcomed the Protestant Reformation and joined hands with Lutheran reformers.

The eighteenth century witnessed outstanding revivals, both in England and in America: the Great Awakening in America and the Methodist Revival under the Wesleys in England. Historians record that during the Great Awakening, fifty thousand persons (one-fifth of the population of New England) were added to the Church as new believers.

The prayer and preaching of Jonathan Edwards contributed much to the Great Awakening in New England. Prior to the beginning of the revival in 1734, religion was in sad decline. The devotion and fervor of the Pilgrim settlers of a century earlier had cooled. Unconverted persons who made no profession of salvation were admitted to church membership. As in Old Testament days of decline, God chose a man to carry the prayer burden and proclaim the call to repentance. Edwards described his conversion experience as a personal relationship with God that continued throughout his revival ministry:

There came into my soul . . . a sense of the glory of the Divine Being; a new sense, quite different from any thing I ever experienced before. . . . I thought with myself, how excellent a Being that was, and how happy I should be, if I might enjoy that God, and be rapt up to him in heaven, and be as it were swallowed up in him for ever! I . . . prayed in a manner quite different from what I used to do, with a new sort of affection. . . . From about that time . . . my mind was greatly engaged to spend my time in reading and meditating on Christ, on the beauty and excellency of His person, and the lovely way of salvation by free grace in Him. . . . The sense I had of divine things would often of a sudden kindle up, as it were, a sweet burning in my heart; an ardour of soul, that I know not how to express.[5]

Edwards' continuing practice of prayer and communion with the Lord is matched by the testimony of David Brainerd in his memoirs. This great man of prayer spent entire days praying and fasting for the native New England Indians. A typical example follows:

Jan. 1, 1744. In the morning, had some small degree of assistance in prayer. Saw myself so vile and unworthy that I could not look my people in the face, when I came to preach. O my meanness, folly, ignorance, and inward pollution!—In the evening, had a little assistance in prayer, so that the duty was delightful, rather than burdensome. Reflected on the goodness of God to me in the past year, etc. Of a truth God has been kind and gracious to me. . . . O that I could begin this year with God, and spend the whole of it to *his glory,* either in life or death![6]

After years of praying and suffering physically without seeing results, Brainerd finally saw revival come to the Indians in 1745. "I stood amazed at the influence which seized the audience almost universally; and could compare it to nothing more aptly than the irresistible force of a mighty torrent. . . . Almost all persons of all ages were bowed down with concern. . . . A principal man among the Indians, who before was most secure and self-righteous, and thought his state good, . . . was now brought under solemn concern for his soul, and wept bitterly."[7] Revival eventually came

---

[5]"Personal Narrative," *The Works of Jonathan Edwards* in Walter Blair, et al., *The Literature of the United States* (Chicago: Scott, Foreman and Co., 1953), 131.

[6]*Memoirs of the Rev. David Brainerd* (New Haven: E. Converse, 1822), 123.

[7]Ibid., entry for August 8, 1745.

in response to persistent praying. Yet Brainerd paid the ultimate price for his devoted ministry to the Indians. He died at age twenty-nine, having spent his life praying for their salvation.

The outbreak of revival in England followed that in America by only a few years. In fact, John and Charles Wesley, along with their fellow evangelist George Whitefield, had witnessed the miraculous turn to God in the American Awakening. But the revival in England began with a small group at Oxford University called the Holy Club. Whitefield described in his journal a meeting of Holy Club members and other seekers on January 1, 1739: "Had a love-feast with our brethren and spent the whole night in close prayer, psalms and thanksgiving."[8] John Wesley described the same prayer meeting with additional details:

The power of God came mightily upon us, insomuch that many cried out for exceeding joy and many fell to the ground. As soon as we were recovered a little from that awe and amazement at the presence of His Majesty, we broke out with one voice, "We praise Thee, O God, we acknowledge Thee to be the Lord."[9]

The established church in England was no more spiritual than the American church at the same time. There was drunkenness among the clergy as well as among the entire population. Popular entertainment was vulgar and obscene. Brutal and savage mobs roamed the streets, engaging in violence and immorality; the mobs openly opposed the message preached by the Wesleys and Whitefield. England, like Western society today, was desperately in need of revival.

John Wesley has been called the "Horseman of the Lord." In a day when there were no hard-surface roads, he traveled by horseback an average of eight thousand miles a year, preaching no less than a thousand times every year. With such a busy schedule, how did he find time to pray? Yet pray he did! Although Wesley's journal is primarily an account of his public ministry, there are sufficient references

---

[8]Colin C. Whittaker, *Great Revivals* (Springfield, Mo.: Gospel Publishing House, 1984), 49.

[9]Ibid., 49.

to prayer to indicate that this great man of God was a man of great prayer. He rose every morning at 4 A.M.—even after a preaching service the night before. He frequently preached an early morning service outdoors, sometimes at 5 A.M. and then the evening service around 6 P.M. This schedule accommodated the long work days of the common people to whom he ministered. The intervening time was spent preaching at jails and institutions and at other activities, "improving the time." Prayer was no doubt a high priority then and during the many hours on horseback. Two representative passages from Wesley's *Journal* are germane:

Saturday, 10 [September 1743].—There were prayers at St. Just in the afternoon, which did not end till four. I then preached at the Cross to, I believe, a thousand people, who all behaved in a quiet and serious manner. At six I preached at Sennan ... and appointed the little congregation (consisting chiefly of old, grey-headed men) to meet me again at five in the morning. But on Sunday, 11, a great part of them were got together between three and four o'clock: so between four and five we began praising God.[10]

Saturday, 30 [December 1780].—Waking between one and two in the morning, I observed a bright light shine upon the chapel. I easily concluded there was a fire near, probably in the adjoining timber-yard. If so, I knew it would soon lay us in ashes. I first called all the family to prayer; then going out, we found the fire about a hundred yards off, and had broken out while the wind was south. But a sailor cried out, "Avast! Avast! the wind is turned in a moment!" So it did, to the west, while we were at prayer, and so drove the flame from us. We then thankfully returned, and I rested well the residue of the night.[11]

Along with the call to evangelism and ministry, God gives the burden to pray. To be successful, the ministry must be bathed in prayer.

The names of leaders and revivals begin to proliferate at the beginning of the nineteenth century. But prayer was

---

[10]John Wesley, *Journal* (Chicago: Moody Press, n.d.)
[11]Ibid.

still the stimulating force behind each significant move of the Spirit. Toward the end of the eighteenth century, morals and religion had undergone a widespread decline. The college campuses were no exception. Schools like Harvard, Yale, and Princeton, first founded as religious training institutions and headed at times by some of the leaders of the Great Awakening, were no longer true to their original mission. The colleges were centers of atheism and unbelief. Spiritually and morally, conditions on campuses and in society generally were deplorable.

The decay of the times became a burden of prayer for over a dozen men in the New England region. They called for a nationwide "Concert of Prayer," asking God to intervene; ministers of many denominations participated. Reports of revival—called by some the Second Great Awakening—began circulating. The events on college campuses were especially noteworthy.

Students on the various campuses began Christian fellowships. They were persecuted at first, but gradually the tide turned. "They committed themselves to mutual watchfulness, ardent prayers, frequent fellowship, mutual counsel and friendly reproof. In most cases, they were tiny societies. For example, three students at Brown University formed a 'college praying society,' which met weekly in a private room."[12] Timothy Dwight, the grandson of Jonathan Edwards, became president of Yale in 1796 and led a return to vital Christian experience; one third of the student body made a profession of faith in 1802. That same year, half the students leaving Yale entered the ministry. Similar stories of revival came from other campuses: Amherst, Dartmouth, Princeton, and Williams. The commitment to prayer, by even a small group on each campus, resulted in dynamic evangelism and many conversions. The revival and awakening continued to touch generation after generation of students on many campuses, as devout administrators and faculty were chosen with care. The collegiate sermon became a regular part of student worship, and campuswide prayer days were scheduled in each term.

---

[12]J. Edwin Orr, *Campus Aflame* (Glendale, Calif.: Regal Books, 1971), 25.

On a summer afternoon in 1806, at Williams College in Massachusetts, five students met off campus for private prayer. On their return to campus, a sudden thunderstorm forced them to take shelter under a haystack. While they waited for the storm to pass, they prayed about a way of reaching the lost of the world with the message of salvation. The eventual result of that Haystack Prayer Meeting was the formation of the first American missions society, a pattern of cooperative missionary endeavor followed by many church groups since that time.

The college awakenings in the United States were but part of a worldwide awakening at the same time. Yet their continuing impact through committed graduates who took their places as leaders in society was monumental. Today's Christian colleges and Bible institutes have a rich heritage as well as a grave responsibility to uphold.

Charles G. Finney was one of America's foremost evangelists. He was born in 1792 into a home having no Christian influence. He became first a school teacher and then an apprentice in a law office in New York State. As he studied for the bar exam, he discovered that the Bible was the foundation for American law. Purchasing his first Bible to help him prepare for a law career, he became convinced that the Bible was the very word of God. At the age of twenty-nine, he surrendered his life to Christ and left his planned career to preach the gospel. He was licensed to preach at the age of thirty-one. Revival immediately accompanied his preaching. People were swept into the kingdom of God in revival after revival. One of his most famous was held in Rochester, New York, in 1830. One hundred thousand persons were reported as being added to area churches as a result. A contemporary, Lyman Beecher, said of the supernatural move: "That was the greatest work of God, and the greatest revival of religion, that the world has ever seen, in so short a time."[13]

Prayer was the primary ingredient in Finney's success. Everything he did was preceded by prayer. On one occasion, when he was teaching a class at Oberlin College, he

---

[13]L. G. Parkhurst, Jr., *Charles G. Finney's Answers to Prayer* (Minneapolis: Bethany House Publishers, 1983), 125.

was asked a question about a biblical passage. Confessing that he did not know the answer, Finney immediately knelt down and prayed before the class. He then rose to give the answer the Lord had given him.

Finney's classic work, *Lectures on Revivals of Religion,* contains whole chapters on the subject of prayer and its importance in revival: "Prevailing Prayer," "The Prayer of Faith," "The Spirit of Prayer," and "Meetings for Prayer." From "The Spirit of Prayer" comes this affecting passage:

Oh, for a praying church! I once knew a minister who had a revival fourteen winters in succession. I did not know how to account for it till I saw one of his members get up in a prayer meeting and make a confession. "Brethren," said he, "I have been long in the habit of praying every Saturday night till after midnight, for the descent of the Holy Ghost among us. And now brethren," and he began to weep, "I confess that I have neglected it for two or three weeks." . . . That minister had a praying church.[14]

For the believer who earnestly desires an effective prayer life for evangelistic outreach, the writings of Charles G. Finney rank second only to the Bible.

In spite of Finney's preaching and the Spirit's work in reclaiming lost souls and putting spiritual vitality into the communities Finney was invited to, the cycle of spiritual decline had set in by the 1850s. In his noteworthy volume, *Revivals: Their Laws and Leaders,* James Burns observes, concerning the decay and ungodliness of the times:

Sick in soul, men turn with a sigh to God. . . . Slowly this aching grows, the heart of man begins to cry out for God, for spiritual certainties, for fresh visions. . . . Within the Church itself, also, through all its days of defection, there have been many who have not bowed the knee to Baal, who have mourned its loss of spiritual power, and who have never ceased to pray earnestly for a revival of its spiritual life. . . . Gradually, however, the numbers are found to increase; prayer becomes more urgent and more confident. . . . Longing for better things becomes an intense pain; men begin to gather in companies to pray; they cease not to importune God day and night, often with tears, beseeching Him

---

[14]Finney, *Lectures on Revivals,* 99–100.

PART 3

Chapter 15
Prayer
and
Revival

to visit with His divine power the souls of men, and to pour into the empty cisterns a mighty flood of divine life.[15]

The great revivals associated with D. L. Moody began with prayer, when a contemporary, Jeremiah Lanphier, experienced just what James Burns described. Feeling a strong burden for the sad spiritual state all around his downtown New York mission, Lanphier invited acquaintances to join him in a noonday prayer meeting every Wednesday. At the first prayer meeting on September 23, 1857, six persons were present. The second week, there were twenty; on the third Wednesday, forty. The noon meetings were changed from weekly to daily. The attendance grew to a hundred. Other prayer meetings were held at other locations. By January 1858 attendance at the original location was so large that simultaneous prayer was scheduled in three different rooms. The majority of those attending were businessmen. Marked by fervent and continual prayer, the revival came to be known as the prayer meeting revival. The revival meetings and multiplied conversions are reported in the many accounts of Moody's ministry. Every level of society was affected. Colleges where Moody preached experienced marvelous visitations. The revival was marked by lay influence. In the two years of 1858 and 1859, one million conversions were reported in a total population of thirty million. Another million church members were revived. The revival was interdenominational, with participation from all the major Protestant groups. These ten features of the revival were noted in *The Methodist Advocate* of January 1858:

(1) [F]ew sermons had to be preached, (2) lay people were eager to witness, (3) seekers flocked to the altar, (4) nearly every seeker had been blessed, (5) experiences enjoyed remained clear, (6) converts were filled with holy boldness, (7) religion became a daytime social topic, (8) family altars were strengthened, (9) testimony given nightly was abundant, and (10) conversation was marked by a pervading seriousness.[16]

---

[15]Burns, *Revivals,* 33.
[16]Whitaker, *Great Revivals,* 84.

■■■■■
PART 3

Chapter 15
Prayer
and
Revival

However, the cycle of revival and decline of religious fervor continued. By the end of the nineteenth century, even though the results of Moody's ministry were still evident, American society was in need of another divine visitation. The mainline churches as a whole had lost their evangelistic zeal, expecting to change the world through political and social action rather than through the return of Christ to set up His millennial kingdom. The few who believed they were living in the end times and that the Second Coming was imminent felt impelled to win their generation to Christ before it was too late. They began intensive study of Scripture, praying that God would show them how they might evangelize their generation and give them the spiritual power to turn a sinful generation back to God.

Although there were significant revivals in the twentieth century apart from the Pentecostal outpouring, there is little dispute that the Pentecostal revival has been the greatest single dynamic in transforming a lethargic Christianity into an evangelistic force reaching around the world. Charles Fox Parham began preaching a holiness and healing message in 1889. His study of the Word and the biblical accounts of revival and evangelism sent him on a search for biblical truth that had been lost. He was especially interested in what others were teaching about the Holy Spirit. In the fall of 1900, he opened a Bible school in Topeka, Kansas. His fascination with the doctrine of the Holy Spirit led him in December of the same year to give students of the school a special assignment: determine from a close study of Scripture the evidence for the baptism in the Holy Spirit. The study was accompanied by extended times of waiting upon the Lord. The study concluded that the baptism in the Spirit provided power for service and that speaking in tongues was the single outward evidence that always accompanied the Baptism experience.

Beginning with a watchnight service on December 31, students began receiving the experience and speaking in tongues. Parham and his Spirit-filled students began sharing their new-found experience wherever people would listen. Miraculous healings took place in some of the meetings, confirming to the hearts of many what they were reading in Scripture.

At the same time Parham was preaching the Pentecostal message in the Midwest, a group began meeting in Los Angeles to pray for a spiritual awakening. They prayed for a full restoration of New Testament Christianity and a last-days outpouring of the Holy Spirit. William J. Seymour, a Baptist holiness preacher who had sat briefly under Parham's teaching, shared his beliefs about the Holy Spirit with the group holding meetings in a decrepit building on Azusa Street. Many disagreed with Seymour's teaching, as they had with Parham's, but the outpouring continued. Events at the meetings were spontaneously ordered by the Spirit, and the number grew as word spread concerning what God was doing.

Many of the early Pentecostals were strongly opposed to church organization or association with any denomination. But with the proliferation of independent preachers with sensational practices and questionable theology, the more level-headed participants became concerned that abuses would dissipate and destroy the great spiritual work that had begun. In April 1914, a group of about three hundred Pentecostals met in Hot Springs, Arkansas, to form the Assemblies of God, a group that would eventually become the largest of several Pentecostal groups born in the early twentieth century. As with the preceding revivals since the Protestant Reformation, the Pentecostal revival was birthed from a prayer burden that rested heavily on a handful of devout and seeking believers.

The evangelistic outreach accompanying the Pentecostal outpouring has been phenomenal. Millions around the world have been called out of pagan as well as nominally Christian religions to become witnesses and evangelists themselves. The fire of the Spirit has burned back into mainline denominations, originally aflame with vital Christianity themselves.

Prayer—revival—evangelism. The sequence has been the same in all the great revival moves of history, a sequence that should not stop short of evangelism: bringing lost souls to know Jesus Christ. As James Burns notes, revival without evangelism falls short of the needed impact:

Often we say that before we can reach out to win the unsaved we must first have a renewal of grace among our church members and officers, including the pastor. Surely no congregation can ever go too far in seeking the betterment of those whose names appear on the rolls of the home church. But experience shows that the majority of our efforts toward revival without evangelism prove disappointing. . . . People, like their minister, have come closest to God when they have been most actively praying and working for the salvation of their relatives, friends, and neighbors.[17]

PART 3

Chapter 15

Prayer and Revival

Questions for Study

1. What is at the center of God's ultimate will, and why?
2. What is a revival and why are revivals needed?
3. What part does prayer have in bringing a genuine revival?
4. What is the relationship between revival and evangelism?
5. What was special about the Great Awakening in America?
6. How was the Wesleyan revival different from those that preceded it?
7. What were some things Finney experienced and taught about revival?
8. How was the Pentecostal revival of the twentieth century different from those that immediately preceded it?
9. What is the secret of continuing Pentecostal revival?

---

[17]Burns, *Revivals,* 334.

THE DISCIPLINES OF PRAYER: A PRACTICUM

Arriving at a basic theology or understanding of prayer should be a major priority for every believer. A study of biblical examples of effective prayer, as treated in earlier chapters, is also of vital importance. But until the Christian actually engages in prayer in a practical and meaningful way, the theology and study are of limited value. Prayer is not answered because a believer knows how it works, but because he knows personally the One to whom it is addressed.

Prayer is a love matter before it is anything else. It is not the finding of right methods, techniques, or processes to persuade God to do what we desire. The highest form of prayer is the love relationship of two hearts (the believer's and God's) beating as one. Walking with God in the sweet communion of prayer is a continuing relationship. It is certain that God hears the panicked cry for help and deliverance from disaster or calamity. But to deliver the believer from tribulation so he can settle back into his apathetic routine is not God's purpose in answering prayer. The crisis may be His way of saying, "Come to Me; I love you and desire to have a mutual and continuing love relationship."

But how does one develop this love that forms the foun-

PART 3

Chapter 16
The
Disciplines
of Prayer:
A
Practicum

dation of an effective prayer life? The question is especially pertinent in today's affluence and busyness. The cares and comforts of life draw human attachment to everything but God. Nor does this love relationship that covets divine communion with God himself come just for the asking. It must be nurtured and cultivated to maturity. It begins with the regular practice of the various disciplines of prayer and grows, with faithful persistence, into a beautiful love relationship with the Heavenly Father. Prayers are answered when they are sent heavenward via the love line. It is quite inconceivable that a believer could be identified as Spirit-filled, Pentecostal or charismatic, without a life-style in which effective prayer plays a significant role.[1]

The preceding chapters are the foundation for the superstructure of effective prayer. To lay a foundation without erecting the finished structure would be foolish; so the pursuit of the theology and biblical examples of answered prayer are in vain until a day-by-day practice of prayer communion is built upon the foundation. This chapter, therefore, is a practicum providing direction, guidelines, and suggestions for all who would move from the mechanics of prayer into the realm of the divine dynamic, from the abstract and theoretical to the concrete and practical.

Personal Prayer

The serious believer should always be conscious of the nearness of a personal God who desires to communicate with His children. And when the mind and heart are freed from the temporal pursuits that occupy much of our waking hours, they should naturally turn toward the One with whom communion is so sweet. But there is more to Paul's admonition to "pray continually" than that. The Jewish background from which Paul was writing placed great value on the practice of giving thanks to God for everything that comes one's way. Even today, devout Jews sprinkle the entire day with short sentence prayers. The "blessings," or "thanksgivings," usually begin, "Blessed are you, O Lord,

[1]See Appendix 4, "Contemporary Testimonies of Answered Prayer."

King of the universe."[2] In this way a devout Jew expresses a brief thanks to God for everything that happens to him: receiving a kindness, smelling a fragrant flower, watching a beautiful sunset, seeing a rainbow, or seeing God's handiwork in the lightning and thunder of a storm. A sincere expression of thanks to Almighty God is a powerful expression of prayer.[3]

PART 3

Chapter 16
The
Disciplines
of Prayer:
A
Practicum

Human life consists of habits, both good and bad. The most productive habits are the fruit of discipline, practice, and application. Until prayer is a well-established habit and has become a part of the believer's life-style, its genuine fruitfulness is not likely to be of appreciable effect.

The great people of prayer of the Bible were people of fixed prayer habits. David wrote, "Evening, morning and noon I cry out in distress, and he hears my voice" (Ps. 55:17). Of Daniel it is written, "He went home to his upstairs room where the windows opened toward Jerusalem. Three times a day he got down on his knees and prayed, giving thanks to his God, just as he had done before" (Dan. 6:10). Daniel had such a fixed prayer habit that none of life's circumstances was permitted to interrupt it.

Regular prayer was a customary habit among the Jews, for they had three established prayer periods each day. By New Testament times they were nine o'clock in the morning, three o'clock in the afternoon, and sundown. Although for some the practice had deteriorated into nothing more than a ritual (cf. Matt. 6:5,16), for the Early Church it appears that the set times of prayer were worth following. We are told that "Peter and John were going up to the temple at the time of prayer—at three in the afternoon" (Acts 3:1).

There is no New Testament command requiring either a daily number of prayers or a set of times; but there are numerous instructions and examples illustrating the importance of and encouraging the habit of prayer (see Luke

---

[2]Heb.: *Baruch 'Attah, Adonai, Melek Ha-'Olam.*

[3]Marvin Wilson, *Our Father* (Grand Rapids: Wm. B. Eerdmans Pub. Co., 1989), 157; see also Jakob Petuchowski and Michael Brocke, eds., *The Lord's Prayer and Jewish Liturgy* (New York: The Seabury Press, 1978), 21–86.

PART 3

Chapter 16
The
Disciplines
of Prayer:
A
Practicum

18:1; Acts 2:42; 6:4; 10:2; 1 Thess. 5:17). Each believer, on his or her own initiative, should determine and devise a personal prayer habit, for without it, an effective prayer life is unlikely to develop.

Retire from the world each day to some private spot, even if it be only the bedroom.... Stay in the secret place till the surrounding noises begin to fade out of your heart and a sense of God's presence envelops you. Deliberately tune out the unpleasant sounds and come out of your closet determined not to hear them. Listen for the inward Voice till you learn to recognize it. Stop trying to compete with others. Give yourself to God and then be what and who you are without regard to what others think. Reduce your interests to a few. Don't try to know what will be of no service to you.[4]

We humans are so constituted that unless we develop a prayer habit, we tend to become dilatory in our prayer practice. Only by stern personal discipline will prayer have its necessary and rightful place; everything about this modern world militates against a regulated prayer life. The regulation should not be rigid and inflexible, but it should be sufficient to give meaning and direction to praying.

My prayer life[5] was revolutionized when I charted a deliberate course for it. For an extended period I set aside my entire noon hour, five days a week. A definite prayer objective was chosen for each of the five days. The first half of Monday's hour was exclusively for giving thanks, and the second half was for meditation on the person and work of Christ. Tuesday was the time for general requests. Wednesday was dedicated to concentration on the Spirit-filled life. Thursday's praying was related to some Epistle read during the period. Friday was occupied with prayer for special needs.

Monday's thanksgiving, which at the outset required stern discipline, suddenly became a thrilling experience—so thrilling in fact that at times it almost insisted on replacing other periods set apart for petition. Thanksgiving welled

---

[4]A. W. Tozer, *Of God and Men* (Harrisburg, Penn.: Christian Publications, Inc., 1960), 106.

[5]Personal experience of R. L. Brandt.

up on behalf of the petitions of other periods until my soul was as thankful as if the petitions were already answered. Meditation on Christ and His work, the chosen direction for the second half hour, was most delightful and rewarding. It led me down a pathway of new and glorious insight. Tuesday's petitions for general needs took an unexpected turn. Instead of the usual praying for physical, material, earthly, and temporal needs, I found myself almost entirely forgetful of these, and instead constrained to pray Paul's prayers. Wednesday's praying about the Spirit-filled life opened new vistas of truth. Understanding was born concerning the means and the consequence of the Spirit-filled life-style. Predicating prayer on the content of an Epistle resulted in praying on Thursday for things not ordinarily on a prayer list. It was this practice that the Holy Spirit used to direct my attention to Paul's prayers, resulting in a personal prayer revolution and the writing of the book *Praying with Paul.*[6] Friday's period for special requests was essentially for God's children and God's work. There are always urgent needs vying for our interest and attention. These can consume all of our prayer time every day; yet this fault can be avoided by a well-ordered discipline.

A note of caution is in order. There will be special times when the Holy Spirit may burden the believer along a certain line for a day or for an extended period. In such times it is important to move with the Spirit and to set aside a previously charted course. We may return to it in due season, or we may find ourselves directed by the Spirit to follow another course.

In more recent years my praying has been for an hour each morning, generally during a three-mile walk. It has incorporated a rather firmly entrenched order:

1. Thanksgiving and worship
2. Prayer for the president and vice-president of the United States, and their advisers
3. Prayer for the Congress and the Supreme Court

---

[6]R. L. Brandt, *Praying with Paul* (Grand Rapids: Baker Book House, 1966).

PART 3

Chapter 16
The
Disciplines
of Prayer:
A
Practicum

4. Prayer for the governor and lieutenant governor of my state, and for all in government
5. Prayer for all the national officers of our Movement, by name, including the head of our vast foreign missions outreach and his four assistants
6. Prayer for my district superintendent and his assistant, as well as for all the district officers by name
7. Prayer for all the pastors and churches within the district, as well as prayer for specific churches and pastors having special needs
8. Prayer for several of our colleges, including their presidents, faculty, staff, and student bodies
9. Prayer for my spouse, for each of our children and their spouses, and for the grandchildren
10. Prayer for neighbors by name
11. Paul's prayers (memorized)
12. Prayer for an outpouring of the Holy Spirit, and for a manifestation of each of the Holy Spirit's gifts through the body of believers
13. Prayer for special needs, and for God's enablement in my own life and ministry.

While each believer must personalize a pattern of discipline, there are some general practices that are of great value in developing an effective prayer life. One of the most significant is the use of Scripture to guide one's prayer time. There is no prayer practice that is more useful in building one's faith. Let all who pray learn early in their praying to bring into focus specific passages dealing with prayer. The following are excellent examples:

When you pray, go into your room, close the door and pray to your Father, who is unseen. Then your Father, who sees what is done in secret, will reward you (Matt. 6:6).

Do not be anxious about anything, but in everything, by prayer and petition, with thanksgiving, present your requests to God. And the peace of God, which transcends all understanding, will guard your hearts and your minds in Christ Jesus (Phil. 4:6–7).

Let us then approach the throne of grace with confidence, so that we may receive mercy and find grace to help us in our time of need (Heb. 4:16).

PART 3
Chapter 16
The
Disciplines
of Prayer:
A
Practicum

A second practice of general significance is praying in the Spirit. Jude 20, "Pray in the Holy Spirit," is evidently a reference to praying in tongues. First Corinthians 14:14–15 is obviously a reference to praying in tongues: "If I pray in a tongue, my spirit prays, but my mind is unfruitful. So what shall I do? I will pray with my spirit, but I will also pray with my mind." Praying in the Spirit is a most effective way of praying and an effective means of avoiding the tendency for prayer to deteriorate into mere ritual.

It is doubtful if any single spiritual practice of the believer holds more promise of reward than waiting upon God. "Those who hope in the LORD will renew their strength. They will soar on wings like eagles; they will run and not grow weary, they will walk and not be faint" (Isa. 40:31). "Hope in" (Heb. *qawah*) means "to wait for," "to look for with intense, eager expectation." Though the promise of reward is great, learning to wait is not easy. It is an art to be learned and a discipline to be developed.

The fact we place our hope in the Lord implies our waiting for Him to move and then moving along with Him. Our hope causes us to wait patiently and steadfastly, confident that God will decisively act on behalf of His people. It is not simply turning to one's own interests while God takes care of His own business. Instead, it is a time when the focus is on God, not self. It requires the expenditure of time in God's presence, usually in solitude. It involves drawing near to God via meditation and contemplation, and developing an ear to hear the gentle voice of the Holy Spirit (cf. 1 Kings 19:12). Sometimes God interrupts us and gets our attention in a powerful way. More often, waiting for the Lord is long on listening, but short on speaking, and implies a readiness to obey.

Meditation involves musing over God and His Word. It recalls truth from memory and considers and reconsiders it until the one praying or meditating is perfectly aligned with that truth (cf. Ps. 1:2). Contemplation is a state of mystical awareness of God's being, an act of thinking about God with concentration and attention. Developing an ear to hear what God is saying becomes the application and the fruit of meditation and contemplation.

Waiting for God to move develops an inward confidence

PART 3

Chapter 16
The
Disciplines
of Prayer:
A
Practicum

and an expectation of His intervention and revelation. It prepares us to receive what He has for us. "Since ancient times no one has heard, no ear has perceived, no eye has seen any God besides you, who acts on behalf of those who wait for him" (Isa. 64:4). In seeking to develop the art of waiting for God, try a gradual approach. Let it begin with a few minutes of quality time daily. Consistence is important. A particular place and time will aid the process. Body posture is not of consequence, whether it be lying upon one's bed, seated in a comfortable position, or kneeling in a quiet place. Once the habit has been established, the time given to it may be determined by the circumstances, the need, and the Spirit's leading.

Family Prayer

Though under unrelenting siege by the forces of darkness, the home is the divinely ordained basic unit of society. In the home, life's values are communicated and established. Spiritual foundations are there laid. The home is designed by God as the primary learning center:

These commandments that I give you today are to be upon your hearts. Impress them on your children. Talk about them when you sit at home and when you walk along the road, when you lie down and when you get up. Tie them as symbols on your hands and bind them on your foreheads. Write them on the doorframes of your houses and on your gates (Deut. 6:6–9).

The Christian home is the plot in which the seeds of godliness are to be planted. This requires a God-centered atmosphere, which should be initiated and fostered by the husband and the wife, giving serious attention to, among other things, the Word of God, family devotions, table prayers, and bedtime prayers. Could it be that Jesus had the husband-wife union in mind when He said, " 'If two of you on earth agree about anything you ask for, it will be done for you by my Father in heaven' " (Matt. 18:19)?

In the Christian family, the father is to be the spiritual leader. This role is not just his privilege and prerogative; it is his sacred responsibility. He is to teach his children by word and by practice. As a regular practice, he should

PART 3
Chapter 16
The
Disciplines
of Prayer:
A
Practicum

daily lead in family devotions. He should teach his children to pray and to depend upon God in all of life's circumstances. Family devotions when the children are young should be child-oriented, rather than adult-oriented (e.g., no adult expositions). Mother should also have an active part in the spiritual development of the children. Some mothers pray with each child before he or she leaves for school.

Table prayers should accompany every mealtime. Jesus is our pattern: "Taking the five loaves and the two fish and looking up to heaven, he gave thanks and broke the loaves. Then he gave them to the disciples, and the disciples gave them to the people" (Matt. 14:19; see also Matt. 26:26; Luke 24:30; and 1 Tim. 4:4–5). It is noteworthy that even though the great crowd needed a miraculous provision of food, Jesus did not ask for a miracle. He thanked the One who provides for our physical needs; the miracle followed. Spiritual leadership in the home should focus on God as the great Provider (instead of on either the father or the mother as the one who knows how to ask and receive from the Provider). The parent's example of faith and trust will indeed be a model for the growing children, but at the same time they will understand that the glory and thanks always go to the Heavenly Father. Memorized prayers are a help for younger children, but as soon as possible each child should be aided in personalizing prayer; unless this is done, table prayer can easily become a mere form. In the eat-and-run pace of today's family, prayer at mealtime can be a boon to family togetherness. Wise parents will insist that all family members be seated and that prayer be made before any eating begins.

Bedtime prayers play a significant role in a child's spiritual development. They teach dependence upon God, thankfulness for His care and provision, and comfort and security in His benevolent protection.[7]

---

[7]Thomas Lofton, "The Role of the Holy Spirit in Family Worship," in *Conference on the Holy Spirit Digest,* vol. 2, Gwen Jones, ed. (Springfield, Mo.: Gospel Publishing House, 1983), 186–191.

PART 3

Chapter 16
The
Disciplines
of Prayer:
A
Practicum

Congregational Prayer

There is considerable precedent, both in the Old and in the New Testaments, for congregational praying.[8]

The power of congregational praying cannot be exaggerated. If the praying of a single believer avails much, how much more does the praying of a congregation (cf. Acts 12:5 and James 5:16)? If a mere two in perfect agreement in the Spirit can obtain "anything ... ask[ed] for" (Matt. 18:19), what might the outcome be when the entire congregation prays in one accord, united in the Spirit? We have some good illustrative answers: When the congregation prayed upon the release of Peter and John, "the place where they were meeting was shaken. And they were all filled with the Holy Spirit and spoke the word of God boldly" (Acts 4:31). Another time, when the Church kept praying earnestly even without real expectation, "the Lord sent his angel and rescued" Peter from Herod (Acts 12:5–16).

Congregational praying may take various forms. It may include preservice prayer, postservice prayer, and concert praying during the service. It may include regular church prayer meetings as well as special times of fasting and prayer.

Preservice prayer not only prepares the heart for receiving the Word of God, but also creates an atmosphere of the Spirit, enabling participants to minister with a special anointing (Eph. 6:18–19). A set time and place for preservice praying should be announced and advertised. This prayer time requires no structuring, but may simply be an opportunity for those who gather early to wait upon God, to worship, and to place their petitions before the Lord.

Postservice prayer has been a valued tradition in most Pentecostal and charismatic churches. It is deemed vital to the spiritual welfare and progress of the congregation. It may involve prayer for the sick, prayer with those seeking salvation or Holy Spirit baptism, prayer for special needs, and general prayer and worship. Many churches have prayer

---

[8]See 1 Chron. 29:20; 2 Chron. 29:28–31; Acts 1:14,24; 4:24–31; 12:5; 20:36.

rooms adjacent to the sanctuary where the congregation can gather in a somewhat secluded atmosphere for seeking God. In other churches, postservice praying occurs around the altar.[9] Some congregations assign persons who are adept at encouraging and assisting others to oversee such prayer times.

Congregational prayer during the actual service should seek to involve everyone present, even though there tends to be structure and time constraints. Many congregations engage in extended periods of corporate worship and prayer, during which manifestations of the utterance gifts of the Spirit are not uncommon. Prayer is usually led by the pastor, an associate, or a member of the congregation; audience participation by amens and other expressions of worship, indicating agreement with the one leading out in prayer, are expected and contribute to a sense of unity as the body approaches the Lord in worship and petition. On occasion, entire congregations unite in concert prayer. Although there are critics of the practice, it is not without biblical support and precedent (cf. Acts 4:24–30). The practice has been common in the Pentecostal movement from its inception.

For the health and growth of a local church, there is no more useful, powerful, and essential activity than a meeting set apart for the major purpose of prayer. Any church that does not concentrate its energy and attention on such gatherings hardly deserves recognition as a church; indeed, without regularly announced times of meeting for prayer, the organization is more aptly described as a social club. The work of the Kingdom is accomplished by saints who know and utilize the power of praying "in one accord."

Most evangelical churches set aside one night a week for Bible study and prayer. It is common, also, for whole weeks to be given to a prayer emphasis at the beginning of the year, before special revival or evangelistic efforts, or during urgent and recognized needs in the congregation.

Home prayer meetings have played a very significant role, particularly in the early days of the Pentecostal move-

PART 3

Chapter 16
The
Disciplines
of Prayer:
A
Practicum

---

[9]Armon Newburn, "The Significance of the Altar Service," in *Conference on the Holy Spirit Digest,* 168–174.

PART 3

Chapter 16

The
Disciplines
of Prayer:
A
Practicum

ment. "It was in the first home prayer meeting I ever attended that I was filled with the Holy Spirit. It was also in such meetings that I personally learned by experience and observation about the movings and workings of the Holy Spirit."[10] The success of such home prayer meetings depends largely on leadership. Sometimes pastors have discouraged or disallowed this kind of meeting for fear of excesses or fanaticism; and the fears have been justified when members of a group have become divisive and victims of spiritual pride and heresy. But though the danger may exist, the dividends of a properly controlled home-style prayer meeting far outweigh the potential debits.

The wise pastor will attend such meetings himself, both in and outside the church building; or he will delegate a qualified person to be present, not to hold too tight a rein but to participate and give direction as may be necessary. The genius of such meetings is not tight control and restraint, but liberty in the Spirit within biblical limits. Within home-style prayer groups, especially Pentecostal or charismatic, there is a subtle tendency toward unsound and unbiblical exercise of spiritual gifts. Resorting to utterance gifts for guidance is an ever-present temptation and a historically documented danger.[11] Averting the danger and avoiding the pitfall is best accomplished not by disallowing the prayer group, but by training, particularly those in leadership, in sound doctrine and practice.

A mature and developed prayer life can reach unparalleled levels of (1) communion with our Lord and (2) effectiveness in meeting spiritual needs, evident everywhere we turn. But fervent and effective praying does not occur simply because we voice a prayer request. It may begin with elementary pleas for help in a crisis or difficult circumstance, but it must mature through the regular practice of traditional forms of prayer. The practical suggestions of this chapter are not ends in themselves. They are identifiable outward forms of prayer that can be used to grow

---

[10]R. L. Brandt.

[11]R. L. Brandt, *Charismatics, Are We Missing Something?* (Published by and available from the author, 1520 Westwood Dr., Billings, Mont., 59102), 85–99.

spiritually until one becomes intimate with God and an intercessor on behalf of a needy and spiritually dying world.

Questions for Study

1. What is most important if we wish to have our prayers answered?

2. How can we "pray continually"?

3. Why are fixed prayer habits necessary and important?

4. Do you find the prayer habit of author R. L. Brandt an example for yourself? Explain.

5. How much of our praying should be in tongues as the Spirit helps us pray?

6. How long should a person "wait on," or "wait for," the Lord, and why?

7. What guidelines should be given for home prayer meetings?

8. What should characterize family prayers?

9. How can congregational prayer be encouraged and made more effective?

10. How has this study helped you in your prayer life? Have you had answers to prayer since you have been studying this book?

PART 3

**Chapter 16
The
Disciplines
of Prayer:
A
Practicum**

Chapter Seventeen

PROBLEMS CONSIDERED

by Stanley M. Horton

We have seen in previous chapters that Jesus prayed, the apostles prayed, and that the Bible everywhere expects God's people to pray. Jesus said, "When you pray...," not "if you pray...." Not only did He expect us to pray, He commanded us to pray (Matt. 5:44; 9:38; Luke 21:36; John 16:24) and taught His disciples "that they should always pray and not give up" (Luke 18:1). The whole Bible shows we also are to "pray continually" (1 Thess. 5:17), that is, keep in an attitude of prayer, ready for spiritual communication. These exhortations are necessary because we have a natural resistance to prayer.

The Problem of Sin

As has been pointed out early in this book, daily communication with God ("in the cool of the day") was the privilege and joy of Adam and Eve in the Garden of Eden (Gen. 3:8). But when Satan suggested that by disobedience and self-assertion they could be like God, they chose to eat of the forbidden fruit, and sin entered the world. Sin raised a barrier between human beings and God. When Adam and Eve heard the voice of God they ran and hid among the trees and bushes of the Garden. They took God

401

off the throne and put self on the throne. Consequently, sin brought a resistance to prayer.

As time went on, self-exaltation refused to recognize the greatness of God and failed to give Him the place He deserves. People wanted to make a name for themselves (Gen. 11:4). They denied their need for God and wanted to control their own future. They wanted glory for themselves that really belonged to God. This left them with "a natural dislike for prayer."[1]

The Problem of Human Reasoning

Resistance to prayer also shows up in objections raised by human reasoning. Some objections come from believers who are troubled by questions that arise from adverse circumstances or even from their reading of the Scriptures. The prophet Habakkuk had questions. He could not reconcile what he saw around him with what he believed was the character of God. But God did not condemn him for having questions. Habakkuk did the right thing when he brought his questions to God. The Bereans undoubtedly had questions when Paul first preached the gospel to them. But they did the right thing when they "examined the Scriptures every day to see if what Paul said was true" (Acts 17:11).

Some objections come from unbelievers who reject the Bible and depend on their own deductions. Human philosophy that ignores the facts of biblical revelation most often rejects the idea of a personal God who is supreme. Oriental philosophers thought of an impersonal pantheism, everything as a part of God. They sometimes spoke of a "great soul" of the universe, the ultimate ground of all being, which they called Brahma (or Brahman) or atman (as the supreme universal self). However, they reasoned that no one could say with certainty that this "great soul" does or does not exist. Their whole outlook is one of pessimism.[2] More recent western philosophers such as Paul

---

[1] William Edward Biederwolf, *How Can God Answer Prayer?* (New York: Fleming H. Revell Company, 1910), 24.

[2] William Ernest Hocking, *Types of Philosophy* (New York: Charles Scribner's Sons, 1939), 12.

Tillich also make God a "ground of being" and "ground of personality."[3] But such a god has no separate being apart from the material universe and is not a person with whom we can communicate. Nor does it feel, speak, or have purpose or plan. To accept such an idea of God is to make prayer as communication impossible and to make worship a mental exercise, giving us nothing more than psychological illusions of peace.

Actually the reasonings of these philosophers have never satisfied the common people. Oriental religions soon added many gods. Temples in India often have hundreds of shrines dedicated to different gods and goddesses. Western philosophies have not fared any better. Many of them have tried to break down people's confidence in the true God. Many promote atheism. But the result has been that millions have turned to the occult, to fortune-telling, to astrology, and even to Satan worship. On the other hand, the response to the gospel in Africa, Eastern Europe, and many other parts of the world shows that these philosophies and false religions do not satisfy. People will turn to the true God when Christ is presented and they recognize the kind of God He has revealed. Then they will pray.

Unfortunately there are those who claim to believe in a personal God but treat Him as if He were impersonal. Some treat Him as if he were a slot machine, needing only the right coin (that is, the right words) to make Him deliver the answer. They have no thought of God's desire for obedience, love, faithfulness, and devoted service. As Peter Baelz put it, "He would be on a par with the impersonal world which is the object of man's mastery and manipulation. Prayer would no longer be communion, but a piece of applied science. ... If their question 'What is the use of prayer,' means only, 'Does it produce the goods?' the questioner has abandoned the sphere of religion for that of the marketplace."[4] The God revealed in the Bible loves us in a personal way. He is more concerned about giving the

---

[3]Millard J. Erickson, *Christian Theology* (Grand Rapids: Baker Book House, 1986), 306–308.

[4]Peter R. Baelz, *Prayer and Providence* (New York: The Seabury Press, 1968), 30.

answer He sees we need than in gratifying our selfish desires and whims.

The Problem of God's Character

The very greatness of God sometimes raises another ob-
jection or question with respect to prayer. It is hard for
the human mind to grasp the vastness of the universe with
its millions of galaxies, each with billions of stars (and we're
not even sure astronomers have seen the extent of it yet).
God is certainly greater than the universe He created. Then
how could such a great God be concerned over people on
a little planet revolving around a minor star in one of the
lesser galaxies?

Our human thinking may not comprehend it, but the
Bible shows that God has not only a concern for each of
us, but for even the small things and the apparently insignificant events—the hairs of one's head, the fall of a sparrow
(Matt. 10:29–30). Actually, between the awesome galaxies
on the one hand and the subatomic particles on the other,
human beings are about in the middle. In God's infinite
greatness and majesty He can deal with the smallest particle
as easily as with the largest galaxy. Is it any wonder that
even when a million people are crying out to Him, He is
so infinite that He can deal with all of us as if each of us
were the only one praying?

A related question is, How can God deal with the confusion of multitudes of prayers that come up to Him asking
for contradictory things? While some are praying for rain
to save the crops, others are praying for dry weather to
enhance a parade. Two things should be kept in mind here:
Jesus said, "He [our Father in heaven] causes his sun to
rise on the evil and the good, and sends rain on the righteous and unrighteous" (Matt. 5:45). That is, God normally
sends rain on the righteous, who may be praying, and on
the unrighteous, who probably are not praying. Just as we
must accept the seasons, which God has placed in the
natural order of things (Gen. 8:22), so we must normally
accept what takes place in connection with the seasons,
for God set them in motion.

On the other hand, James 5:17–18 reminds us, "Elijah

was a man just like us. He prayed earnestly that it would not rain, and it did not rain on the land for three and a half years. Again he prayed, and the heavens gave rain, and the earth produced its crops." However, it must be pointed out that Elijah's prayers were not for his personal gain or pleasure. Queen Jezebel was trying to root out the worship of the Lord and make the Baal of Tyre the national god of Israel; God used Elijah to bring the people to a decision against her. Elijah's prayers were the expression of his commitment to the Lord and His will.

Notice also that Elijah did not tell God how to send the fire from heaven or the rain that came afterward. He just expressed his confidence in God, and let Him do it. C. S. Lewis talks of what he called a "very silly sort of prayer" where someone prays for a sick person and gives God the diagnosis and tells Him just what He should do to make the person well. Others try to tell God just what to do in the world to bring peace.[5] We must recognize that God knows what is needed, but He wants us to come to Him in prayer and confess our need of Him.

When there are conflicts of human interest we can trust our faithful God, who sees all that is involved, to do what is best. But prayer is not an escape mechanism.[6] We have our part to do also. The farmer who prays for rain must also plow, plant, cultivate, and harvest. The student who prays for God's help in his examinations must also study. The football team that prays to win must also pray that God will help them to develop their skills and enable them to play in a manner that will show their Christian character and witness.[7]

Then, because God sees beyond what we can see, He will sometimes not answer our request because what we ask for might actually keep us from receiving a better answer to our needs or desires. St. Augustine as a youth was

---

[5]C. S. Lewis, *Letters to Malcolm: Chiefly on Prayer* (New York: Harcourt Brace Jovanovich, 1964), 20.

[6]Harold Lindsell, *When You Pray* (Wheaton, Ill.: Tyndale House Publishers, 1969), 59.

[7]John Elliot Wishart, *The Fact of Prayer: Its Problems and Possibilities* (New York: Fleming H. Revell Company, 1927), 221.

a follower of Manichaeism, a syncretistic cult that originated in Persia. He also lived a rather immoral life. When he planned to go to Rome, his mother, the godly Monica, was afraid he would fall to worse temptations there and prayed that God would not let him go. He went anyway. Then he went to Milan where Ambrose[8] influenced him and where in a garden he heard a voice saying, "Take and read." He understood the Bible was meant. The result was his conversion to Christ. In this way Monica's real desire was granted even though the specific prayer she had prayed was not.[9]

We are thankful that God does see and know beyond what we can see and know. He also has all power and nothing is impossible with Him (Gen. 18:14; Jer. 32:17; Matt. 19:26; Luke 18:27); He is sovereign. But we must not carry the idea of His sovereignty beyond what the Scripture teaches. On the basis of their view of God's sovereignty, Muslim philosophers decided that every thought, action, or event is the direct act of God. They see no such thing as cause and effect, since they believe each event is separately caused by God. St. Augustine and John Calvin did not go that far, but by their human reasoning they proposed that since God is sovereign, He has everything under control, and since He knows everything, everything must be predestined in advance. This led to the idea that those predestined to be lost cannot be saved, and those predestined to be saved cannot be lost. This made the warnings of Scripture (see John 15:6; Heb. 2:1,3; 6:4–6; 10:26–29) meaningless. Then some carried the idea of God's sovereignty further and questioned the validity of prayer. They reasoned that if God has everything under control and knows the future, what difference can prayer make? What is the use of praying? But that is a fatalism that is not taught in the Bible.

The real problem with such ideas and questions is that they come from a wrong view of the sovereignty of God.

---

[8]Ambrose, bishop of Milan (374–397 A.D.), was an eloquent preacher and hymn writer, with great political influence. He sought to make the church dominant over the collapsing western Roman Empire.

[9]Wishart, *Fact of Prayer,* 222; see also Lindsell, *When You Pray,* 87.

Proverbs 16:32 tells us, "Better a patient man than a warrior, a man who controls his temper than one who takes a city." In other words, it is better for us who are in the image of God to control ourselves and limit our self-expression for the sake of others than it is to show our power. The whole Bible shows God is not only sovereign, He is sovereign over himself. He is able to control and limit himself. If God were not able to do this, then He too would be just a victim of fate. That He has this ability was shown in a most meaningful way when Jesus, God the Son, not only limited himself but humbled himself and took "the very nature of a servant, being made in human likeness. And being found in appearance as a man, he humbled himself and became obedient to death—even death on a cross!" (Phil. 2:7–8).

When God created Adam and Eve He limited himself by giving them the ability of choice. The very presence of the tree of the knowledge of good and evil in the garden of Eden shows that. God could have programmed us so that we would always do the right thing—but we would have been puppets, machines, automatons. He wanted us to be freely responsive to His love and care. Love must be freely given or it is not love. Similarly salvation is a gift (Eph. 2:8) freely given and must be freely received.

God has not given us freedom in all areas, however. We can choose to eat a salad instead of a dessert, but we cannot chose to stop eating altogether and still live. We can choose to accept God's way of salvation through Jesus Christ or we can choose to reject it, but we cannot choose some other supposed savior or way of salvation and make it to heaven. That option is not open to us (cf. Acts 4:12). Nor is a one-time choice to follow Christ enough. We must continue to make daily choices and keep on following Him (see Luke 9:23). For individually we are not predestined to do so.[10] What is predestined is the way of salvation and the fact that the Church is an elect, or chosen, body.[11] We

---

[10]Biederwolf, *How Can God Answer Prayer?* 111.

[11]Robert Shank, *Elect in the Son: A Study of the Doctrine of Election* (Springfield, Mo.: Westcott Publishers, 1970), 157. (The entire book is worth studying with respect to this question.)

do not have to glorify ourselves. If we just follow along with Jesus, God will glorify us when He comes. Thus, there are natural limitations to our prayers: "We don't pray about eclipses"[12]—we cannot pray for the earth to become flat. And there are spiritual limitations—we cannot pray for God to save people by some other means than through faith in Jesus (Acts 4:12).

When we do believe in Jesus we enter into a fellowship with the Father and with His Son, Jesus Christ (1 John 1:3). The very word "fellowship" includes the idea of partnership. God has given us a part. We must come to Him, and we must come in faith (Heb. 11:6). There is much biblical evidence that God often waits to act until we do our part. We can see this in the ministry of Jesus. When He came to Nazareth "He could not do any miracles there, except lay his hands on a few sick people and heal them. And he was amazed at their lack of faith" (Mark 6:5–6). Apparently they did not show faith by asking or seeking what they needed. When Jesus walked on the water and said, "Take courage! It is I. Don't be afraid," only Peter said, "Tell me to come to you on the water." All the disciples could have walked on the water just as easily, but only Peter asked.[13] Many other examples could be given both from Scripture and experience that God works when people ask.

God has also chosen that believers should be His agents, His servants, in the spread of the gospel and the building of Christ's Church, both spiritually and in numbers. God still deserves all the glory. As the apostle Paul said, "What, after all, is Apollos? And what is Paul? Only servants, through whom you came to believe—as the Lord has assigned to each his task. I planted the seed, Apollos watered it, but God made it grow" (1 Cor. 3:5–6). This does not mean that what we do is not important. "The man who plants and the man who waters have one purpose, and each will be rewarded according to his own labor. For we are God's fellow workers" (1 Cor. 3:8–9). We are also "Christ's ambassadors, as though God were making his appeal through

---

[12]Lewis, *Letters*, 38.

[13]Erickson, *Christian Theology*, 405.

us" (2 Cor. 5:20). What a privilege! What a responsibility! In giving us this privilege and responsibility God has chosen to make prayer the means of communication and the means by which we express our faith. Part of His plan is that prayer should have a place and an influence.[14] Jesus said, "Ask the Lord of the harvest ... to send out workers into his harvest field" (Luke 10:2). He wants us all to be "God's fellow workers"; and that means He works with us and we work with Him. Prayer is the God-chosen means to make this possible.

God's holiness also causes some to wonder how One who is supremely holy can enter into a world so full of sin and answer the prayers of imperfect people such as we are. The Gospel of John gives a simple answer. Jesus, the Living Word who was and is God (John 1:1), was the One through whom God the Father made all things. "In him was life, and that life was the light of men. The light shines in the darkness, but the darkness has not understood it" (John 1:4–5). He is the Light of the World (John 8:12). Just as light is able to shine into darkness without having the darkness contaminate the light, so the Holy God comes into a sinful world without it affecting Him at all. In fact, He has always delighted to do so (see Isa. 57:15).

The Problem of Laws of Nature

Many human philosophers take a mechanistic view of the universe. They suppose that all things are controlled by the laws of nature, and that these laws cannot be changed or broken. Some go as far as to believe that nothing exists but matter and energy and their laws. In this way, they attempt to rule out both God and prayer. Others suppose that we can use these laws for our benefit and that science will solve all our problems, provide all the answers, and give us hope for the future. This scientism is a false hope, however. Scientific advance has created as many problems as it has blessings. Worse yet, evil people take advantage of even the good things and use them for evil purposes. Science cannot deal with sin. All sin has "become utterly

---

[14]Biederwolf, *How Can God Answer Prayer?* 108.

sinful" (Rom. 7:13). Only the blood of Jesus can cleanse it.

Actually there are many things that science cannot deal with. For example, science cannot deal with qualities. It has to treat them in terms of quantities: color in terms of light waves, sound in terms of sound waves. But a person born blind can understand all the physics and mathematics of light waves. That does not mean that he has any idea of what the northern lights, a red tide, or a Monarch butterfly's wing looks like. A person born deaf can understand all the physics and mathematics of sound waves, but without any understanding of what a symphony or a congregation praising God in unison sound like. Nor can science deal with anything unique. It has to classify everything by statistical methods, so it can deal only with repeatables. It cannot deal with something like the Virgin Birth, or any miracle for that matter.

(We find God in the Bible again and again answering prayer by miracles. But miracles do not break natural laws. Natural laws are not like city ordinances. They do not say that something must or should happen. They are simply statements of principles that have been observed, tested by experiments, and, consequently, successfully used to predict processes or events. If something occurs that does not fit the "law," then scientists do further testing and experimentation with a view to changing the law.

There is room in the realm of natural law also for the interaction with other forces. For example, if you drop a ball, the law of gravity—which holds well as a description of what we usually encounter in daily life—indicates it will fall toward the earth with a certain acceleration. And if you catch the ball before it hits the earth, you are not breaking the law of gravity. That law is still operating, and you feel it by the weight of the ball in your hand. But by putting out your hand, you brought your strength into the situation to counteract the effect of gravity. In the same way, the Bible talks about God's mighty hand, that is, His mighty power. So when God answers prayer by a miracle, He simply puts His greater power, His almighty power, into effect. The God who created the universe knows how to do this, and we have the assurance again and again in the Bible that He is, and will continue to be, active in the world.

Prayer, then, must take into account what the Bible says about God's nature, will, and plan. God does hear the simple prayer of a child. But as we grow in God we will keep searching the Scriptures to find out more about Him, more about His will, more about prayer. We will seek the help of the Holy Spirit, since Jesus promised that "he will guide you into all truth" (John 16:13). Where we still have questions, doubts, problems, we can have His help to illuminate the Scriptures and give us the insights we need. He will show us that He is not only able but willing to answer our prayer. He hears us no matter what language we use. He hears us whether we are standing, kneeling, sitting, or in whatever circumstances we may be.[15] He hears us when we pray in spite of the fact we do not feel like praying—or when we do not feel anything at all. We can be open with Him. We can tell him what we really think and feel. But because He loves us, because He wants to use us for His glory, because He has prepared wonderful things far beyond our imagination, He also wants to hear the same prayer of dedication that Jesus prayed: "Yet not my will, but yours be done" (Luke 22:42).

Questions for Study

1. How can we overcome our natural resistance to prayer?

2. As we approach God in prayer, why is it important that we recognize He is a personal God?

3. What can we expect God to do when believers divide in prayer, some praying for and some praying against the same thing?

4. How does God's sovereignty affect His dealings with our prayers?

5. Under what circumstances might God overrule the laws of nature to answer prayer?

---

[15]See Wayne R. Spear, *The Theology of Prayer* (Grand Rapids: Baker Book House, 1979), 18.

CONTEMPORARY APPLICATION OF AGREEING IN PRAYER

The following illustration of agreeing in prayer is told by R. L. Brandt:

Upon graduating from Bible college, I returned to my home community and learned that the church I had attended was in great turmoil. A preacher had come to the church representing himself to be an Assemblies of God minister. However, after having won the hearts of numbers of people, he left the church and started several small churches in the surrounding area. Among those who joined forces with him were my parents and numbers of my friends. As a result of all this, the young people were caught in the crossfire of controversy.

I felt God's call to the ministry, but in the midst of the prevailing confusion I found it difficult to get started. I held a series of services in my own country schoolhouse where my father had been converted. I assisted a friend in pioneering a church for a few months and did some evangelizing, but no door seemed to open for permanent ministry. In the meantime I had become a licensed minister of the Assemblies of God.

Finally, after a whole year had passed, the independent preacher came to me offering an opportunity to be his assistant. It appeared to be an open door, and my parents

413

Appendix 1

Contemporary
Application
of
Agreeing
in Prayer

were elated, feeling this was God's leading for me. However, I was beset with uncertainty. I had pledged my loyalty to my credentialing church, but here was a wide-open door to work with an independent when so far no opportunity had come from the group with which I was affiliated. What should I do? I honestly did not know, even though deep in my heart I wanted God's will.

In this confused frame of mind, I attended the Assemblies of God district council. While there I was asked to meet with the district officiary for the purpose of declaring my intent regarding future ministry. Yet how could I declare my intent when I did not know how to interpret my own circumstances? The evening prior to my scheduled meeting with the district board, I decided I must have counsel. So I requested a meeting with a pastor who was from my home church; his parents, like mine, were also supporters of the independent preacher. If anyone could give me guidance, I reasoned, surely this man who knew the circumstances well would be my most likely source of help.

Following the evening session of the district council, we met in his car, overlooking the lake on the campgrounds, and I shared my heart with him. For perhaps two hours we talked, but rather than finding a solution, it seemed the more we talked the further I was from knowing what decision to make. Just when we seemed to have exhausted all of our abilities to resolve the matter, a most remarkable thing happened. Suddenly, apart from any decision to pray, or to agree in prayer, we found ourselves praying in an unusual fashion. We were carried along by the Spirit in supplication and intercession in a most harmonious fashion. Our hearts were knit together over a single issue: the will of God for my life and ministry. This rather strange new way of praying went on into the night, far beyond midnight.

Then as suddenly as we had been launched into the praying, so suddenly a Presence invaded the car, and in my spirit I heard the message, *Your prayer is heard. The matter is cared for.* I cannot articulate the sense of wonder that filled me. Even so, I did not know yet what decision to make, but now I did not need to know, for I knew God's will would be done. It was 1:30 A.M. when I finally got to my room for the night. The next morning I met the friend with whom I had prayed and told him I felt no burden to pray further over my concern. He agreed.

From that day forward a series of events transpired which were beyond my doing and amazed several people who knew my situation. Within a week I was on my way to a city to pioneer an Assemblies of God church. Enroute, I passed by my parents' farm and found them somewhat disappointed at the turn of events. They thought surely I must have missed God's will; but in the final analysis, each believer must find God's will for himself. For weeks following my arrival in the new community I was in heavenly places in my spirit.

Then I heard a strange thing: The independent preacher from my parents' church, who had invited me to join him, had an unhappy clash with some of his people and left the community, never to return. If I had elected to go with him, I fear my hopes for future ministry might have been forever ended. But because two of us had agreed concerning what we asked of God, I was providentially spared; since that crossroad's experience I have now been in the Assemblies of God ministry for over half a century, having served as pastor, district superintendent, national home missions secretary, and executive presbyter. The Lord is faithful to answer those who ask His leading in spirit-agreement with another believer.

Appendix 1

Contemporary Application of Agreeing in Prayer

CONTEMPORARY EXPERIENCE OF SPIRITUAL WARFARE IN PRAYER

Several Bible college students lived in rooms in the up-stairs of a large private home of a Christian family. On some evenings they would gather in one of the rooms for prayer. As they prayed together one evening, Lester, the son of the landlord, sat downstairs playing the piano. His mother encouraged him to go upstairs and pray with the young men.

"Oh, Mother," he responded, "I have this piano lesson to prepare, and other school lessons. I just don't have time." Nevertheless, in a few minutes he left the piano and joined the prayer meeting. Not a word was passed among the praying students, but at the precise moment Lester joined them, a heavy sense of spiritual warfare swept through the room, almost as though the very demons of hell had en-tered. So strong was the sense that one of the young men ran to the stairway landing and called to Lester's mother for help.

"Plead the blood of Jesus, and keep on praying," she instructed.

Following her advice, the men continued in prayer; in a short while the demonic oppression was lifted, and once

Appendix 2

Contemporary Experience of Spiritual Warfare in Prayer

again the atmosphere became calm and peaceful. No one seemed to know what to make of the strange experience until a week later when Lester related to the college chapel his remarkable experience. After he had decided not to join the others in prayer, he felt strongly urged to do so. He told of the awful battle with evil forces which raged as he obeyed the impression; and that in that prayer meeting he was miraculously freed from something which he had battled for two years.

CONTEMPORARY APPEARANCE OF AN ANGEL

John Weaver was the unpretentious pastor of a thriving church in Bozeman, Montana. He had labored and prayed earnestly for the vast Gallatin Valley where his church was located. On a crisp fall day, he was hunting in a mountain range some distance away. He had come across fresh elk tracks in the shallow cover of snow and was following them, thinking that as he topped a nearby crest the elk might burst into sight.

Stopping to catch his breath so he would be ready to shoot when he topped the ridge, he spied a man in his peripheral vision emerging from a patch of trees across a nearby canyon. He watched as the man, dressed in a hat and business suit, moved in his direction. Momentarily, the stranger disappeared in a patch of forest between them, but no sooner had he disappeared than he suddenly reappeared, to John's wonder and amazement, right where John stood. It would have taken an ordinary man twenty to thirty minutes to walk the distance, but only some twenty seconds had elapsed.

The stranger spoke first. "Do you know who I am?"

Knowing that he had seen something quite out of the ordinary, John replied, "I believe you are an angel, a messenger from the Lord."

419

■■■■■■■■
Appendix 3
**Contemporary
Appearance
of an
Angel**

"Yes, I am," he said, "and the Lord has sent me to talk with you."

Nearby were two rocks. The angel suggested that John sit on one of them; then he sat on the other facing John.

"This is a beautiful area," said the angel. "I have never been here before, but the Lord has sent me to talk with you. Everything that happens here on earth is preparing you for heaven. Life in heaven is in some ways like it is here. We are always learning and serving Him. We delight to do His will. My life is wrapped up in Him. My joy is to serve Him. In fact, I can hardly wait to get back into His presence.

"And, John, He knows all about you. In fact, He knew where you would be today and He sent me here. He knows your family and all the people in your church, and He is concerned about every one. He wanted me to ask you what you want to happen in Bozeman."

John reported that in that moment all of his heart-cry for Bozeman and the Gallatin Valley seemed to burst forth.

In response, the angel said, "You know, John, I could give you all these things right now, but that is not the way we work. We usually use people, and that is what we will do."

While all this was happening, John sensed in his spirit that he was conversing with a kindred spirit, that they were spiritually of the same kind.

Finally the angel said, "John, I'm going back to Jesus' presence. We will look forward to seeing you in heaven soon, but if not, I may visit you again."

John reported that they shook hands, and as the angel was returning to where John had first seen him, he waved and disappeared.

Though John continued his hunt, he walked the mountains so enraptured by his experience that elk hunting, at least for the time being, lost its fascination.

A short time later, John was driving back to Bozeman from Laurel, Montana, where he had conducted a board meeting for a home missions church. As he drove along, praising the Lord, he sensed the Lord's presence in an unusual way and in his spirit heard, *John, do you remember the man who visited you on the mountain?*

"Yes, indeed I do," he responded.

Now, I want you to name one of the things you really want me to do, the Presence seemed to indicate.

And John replied, "Lord, it may be kind of big, but I would like to pay off the debt on the church." In a moment the special sense of the Lord's presence was gone, and John continued his journey, rejoicing in the Lord.

John told no one of his experience, but the next morning about eight o'clock his telephone rang. A couple who were attending his church desired him to come to their home to discuss a matter. Arriving there, he found them reviewing the church's financial report. "Pastor," they said, "we have never done anything like this before, but we have felt strangely impressed that the Lord wants us to pay off the church debt." Immediately they wrote a check for half the amount outstanding and indicated they would pay off the balance after the first of the year.

At that point, Pastor Weaver called the district superintendent of the Montana District of the Assemblies of God,[1] requesting that he come for a mortgage burning. When the superintendent arrived, John told him the entire story, asking if he should also share it with the congregation. They agreed it should be done, so on the following day the story was told to the awe-struck congregation, including the couple who had paid the debt in full. They too heard it for the first time.

---

[1]The district superintendent at the time was Rev. R. L. Brandt

Appendix 3

Contemporary Appearance of an Angel

CONTEMPORARY TESTIMONIES OF ANSWERED PRAYER

There exist many written and oral reports of answered prayer. Although the majority of them are accepted at face value by individuals who believe in the miraculous, there have been instances when a miracle was claimed but later proved to be fraudulent or false. The cause of Christ is hindered rather than helped when humans try to authenticate the message or the messenger by fraudulent means.

The following answers to prayer are more than coincidences. So they require authentication. At the time of this writing, the participant in each of the miraculous answers to prayer is living. Four of the six testimonials are by members of the Executive Presbytery of the Assemblies of God and long-time leaders in the Movement. The other three have been verified by R. L. Brandt, coauthor of this book and also a member of the Executive Presbytery. The testimonies are shared not to bring recognition to the individuals whose prayers were answered but to give glory to God as He authenticates His Word with signs following.

The following situation of nature's yielding for the proclamation of the gospel happened in the ministry of Paul E. Lowenberg, executive presbyter. (Note that the initiative for the prayer was not with Lowenberg.) The story is told in his words.

Appendix 4

Contemporary Testimonies of Answered Prayer

We had pitched our evangelistic tent in an area totally unfamiliar to us. It was, as we soon found out, a very wicked and godless community. God and the church were absent from the thoughts of the residents; there was not a church within miles. We felt strongly impressed to move our tent into this rural area, probably because the need to hear about Jesus Christ was so great.

From the very first service we felt a strong sense of God's presence. The crowds were surprisingly large. Response to the gospel message was amazing. Night after night people came to acknowledge Christ as Savior and Lord. We had planned on a week's meeting, but stayed over four months and saw a church built and dedicated debt-free.

About the second week of the meeting, it began to rain. The rain fell continuously for several days, until the entire countryside was water-soaked. We thought at times that the meetings must end, but we persisted and kept them going. On a Thursday night, in spite of the rain, thunder, and lightning, the tent was full of people. I knew it was impossible to carry on the service under these conditions. A strong wind swayed the tent. The rain poured through the many holes. Thunder and lightning added to the consternation. In my mind I wondered what I should do. I felt God was speaking to me, *Ask Me to stop the wind and rain.*

I raised my voice (there was no sound system) and told the people what I was going to do. The audience was incredulous; they could not believe we would do something so outlandish and irrational. Speaking so all could hear me pray, I told God that if I could not preach the Word to these people because of the storm, they would die and go to hell. I remember saying, "If Calvary means more to You than wind or rain, if these people being saved from hell means more to You than this storm, in Jesus' name stop the wind and the rain. I had hardly said amen when the wind stopped blowing and the rain stopped falling.

The effect on the audience was electrifying. They sat stunned. In that moment Matthew 24:27 flashed across my mind: "For as the lightning cometh out of the east, and shineth even unto the west; so shall also the coming of the Son of man be."

The interesting part of the miracle was that I had not thought to ask God to stop the thunder and lightning. So against the backdrop of brilliant electric flashes and the cannonade of thunder, I spoke on the second coming of Christ. When the invitation was given, the audience moved forward to seek God at the altar. Out of this answer to a simple prayer came a revival that swept across the entire community, resulting in a strong church as a testimony to the faithfulness of God.

The following provision of land for the Lord's work is told by Glen D. Cole, executive presbyter and pastor of Capital Christian Center, Sacramento, California:

After being in Sacramento a short time, it became apparent that the location of Capital Christian Center would not accommodate the growth that God was going to grant. We needed more than the thirteen acres currently available [1978]. We began to pray that God would supply a miracle of property.

In 1979, a Christian businessman was in my office discussing the possible relocation of the church. He had a piece of property on a major freeway that might possibly be available. He asked, "Do you think this is the best piece of land we could obtain on which to build your church? Are you satisfied that this site is God's best for your church?"

To my amazement, I heard myself say, "Yes, I think it is. And I think you should make it a gift to the church because we need a miracle!" My remark probably stunned this Christian businessman, for he stood up and prepared to leave before I could ask permission to pray with him. On his way out of my office, he said, "I'll call you."

Sure enough, at 10:30 the next morning my phone rang. This Christian developer was on the line. He simply announced, "It's yours." A sixty-three-acre piece of prime land became a miracle gift to Capital Christian Center. It was indeed an answer to prayer!

In 1981 construction began on that piece of property, which today houses two hundred thousand square feet of buildings, plus a complete outdoor athletic facility for the

Appendix 4

Contemporary
Testimonies
of
Answered
Prayer

Christian school and church sports programs. Capital Christian Center grew from approximately a thousand in 1979 to six thousand in 1990.

The miracle catapulted the church into an era of faith and expectancy. It was the catalyst that inspired the congregation to believe God for other miracles and answers to prayer. And the miracle goes on day after day.

The tithe on all building monies given during the construction of the facilities was given to missions. Many others around the world have had answers to prayer because of the thousands and thousands of dollars that resulted from the original miracle. Christian ministries and missionaries have been blessed, thousands have been saved, and the answer goes on!

The following is an answer to prayer offered spontaneously for and coincident with the need of G. Raymond Carlson, general superintendent and chairman of the Executive Presbytery, when he was a student:

God has graciously answered many scores of my prayers. He has given wonderful healings, wrought miracles, provided material needs, saved relatives, and has been Jehovah-Jireh [the Lord will provide] over and over again.

I wish to relate a simple but very profound answer to prayer that deeply affected my young life and continues to inspire me to this day. During my Bible school days there were several of us young men rooming on the second floor of a large house. My room was directly at the head of the stairs and was the only one without a working latch.

All of us had been out for thirty minutes one evening. Upon returning the fellows came dashing out of their rooms with a common question: "What happened in your room?" A burglar had gotten into the house and stolen various items from every room except mine. Mine was the most accessible, yet nothing had been touched.

About three days were required for mail to reach me from my parents several hundred miles away. Three days after the break-in, a letter came from my mother in which she asked if anything had happened to my things. She went on to relate how on that very night God had burdened her to pray for my possessions. The burden came at 8 P.M. and

lifted at 8:30 P.M., the exact time that we were away from
our rooms. God had intervened on my behalf as my godly
mother responded to the urging of the Holy Spirit to pray.

Thank God, He answers prayer. And may we act when
He impresses us to pray.

The following provision for an overwhelming financial
need is told by Ronald F. McManus, pastor of First Assembly
of God, Winston-Salem, North Carolina:

During our building program around 1985, we were
extremely tight financially. While we were involved in an
extensive fund-raising campaign, some property adjacent
to us became available. Property was at a premium, and
we had to buy when it became available because we might
not have the opportunity again.

I had been negotiating with the owners. The price of
the property was $110,000. Unfortunately, we did not have
any money to apply toward the purchase, nor could we
borrow against the new property because we already had
a substantial loan from the bank and were raising funds
monthly to cover additional building costs.

Going to the congregation on a Sunday morning, I simply
expressed the need. I explained that the property was available and that we had thirty days to close on it. Otherwise,
someone else was going to buy it. It was property we had
to have for future growth. I asked the congregation to take
an offering envelope and indicate what they believed God
would help them do within the next thirty days to deal
with the situation.

On Monday, when the offering and the pledges were
counted, $60,000 had been given or pledged. We were
$50,000 short. I remember praying on that Monday morn-
ing, "Lord, I don't know what else to do or where to turn,
but I am trusting You to provide a miracle." I knew our
people had done all they were able to do.

At approximately five in the evening, the same day, a
secretary indicated that the pastor of the home mission
work we had begun a couple of years earlier was in the
lobby asking to see me for a few minutes. He walked into
my office with a briefcase in his hand and said, "Pastor, I
have come today because a member of your congregation

■■■■■■■■

Appendix 4

**Contemporary
Testimonies
of
Answered
Prayer**

came to my office a couple of hours ago with this briefcase. He indicated that whatever you needed beyond the offering and commitments yesterday would be in the briefcase."

The home mission pastor had not looked in the briefcase, but had been given a key to it. We set the briefcase on my desk, unlocked it, and counted $50,000 in cash—the exact amount needed for the property. We had a camp meeting that afternoon as we saw God's miracle of provision.

The following is an answer to prayer offered spontaneously for and coincident with the need of Paul E. Lowenberg, now an executive presbyter, early in his ministry.

It was May 1951. In January of that year I had gone to Japan to assist a friend from England who had a burden to start a church in Osaka, a city in ruin. World War II had left it shattered. American bombing had leveled the city. Mile after mile of factories were nothing more than grotesque scenes of twisted steel and silent emptiness. For several months, bombed-out areas served as sites for evangelistic open-air services. At one location, three or four services were conducted daily, drawing large crowds. Finally, we purchased two army barracks from the U.S. government, moved them to a well-located bombed-out area, and established a permanent church.

My visa expired in early May, so plans began to be made for my return to Shreveport, Louisiana, where my wife and twenty-month-old daughter lived. My plane ticket had been purchased earlier, and I was eager to get home, be with my family, and assume my responsibilities at our church. However, my excitement about going home was somewhat dampened by an inner feeling that all was not well concerning my flight. The closer the day of my departure, the more disturbed I became. After much prayer, restlessness, and uneasiness, I concluded I could not fly on the airline whose ticket I held.

Consulting with the airport authorities, I was informed I could either fly as planned or be delayed for approximately thirty days; there were absolutely no seats available on any airline flying out of Japan. I was faced with a stubborn dilemma. Should I take a chance and fly as planned, in spite of the disturbed feelings within, or should I wait thirty days for the first available flight? I was so sure I was hearing the voice of God, I decided to wait. Although I was deeply disappointed, I felt a deep inner peace over the decision.

Because of other transportation problems, I was forced to stay at Haneda Airport in Tokyo for several additional hours. All at once I heard a voice calling my name above the din of a busy and bustling airport. "Lowenberg, Sensi, report to Pan American ticket counter immediately." I rushed to the ticket counter, and to my utter astonishment was informed a seat had been located for me on a Pan American flight later that evening. I was excited and thrilled. In a few hours I was winging my way across the blue Pacific.

Changing planes in San Francisco, my excitement was jolted by the startling newspaper headline, "Tokyo to Anchorage Airliner Crashes in Aleutian Islands." That was my original flight! Anchorage was an intermediate refueling stop. The Holy Spirit had guided unerringly. My life and ministry had been preserved by the intervention of the Spirit.

But that was only part of the story. In a home in a small town of Western Canada, about the time I was to return to the United States, my father became very restless and disturbed about my flight home. Rising at 3 A.M., he informed my mother of his deep concern for me, and that he would give himself to prayer and intercession. My father was a comparatively short man; but when he got on his knees, he could reach all the way to heaven. He gave himself to intense prayer "in the Spirit," appealing for heaven's help whatever the problem was. Though lacking in education, and seventy-five years old, he moved the hand of God all the way from heaven to Haneda Airport in Tokyo, moved his son from one plane to another, though there were no seats available for thirty days, and brought him home safely to his family and his work. To God be the glory!

The following is an account of God's care in the midst of trial, as told by Mel Erickson, missionary to native Americans in North Dakota:

In 1989 our foster daughter ran away from home four

times. When she was picked up by the police on the last occasion, she pleaded child abuse. She was kept from our home, and we were treated like criminals. We were prohibited from contacting her in the shelter where she was staying.

During the fall months we endured numerous hearings and meetings when we were examined and cross-examined concerning our foster daughter's unruly behavior. The authorities refused to consult with our other children, the school, or our church, choosing rather to believe her story. So we had to engage a lawyer to assist us with the proceedings. We wondered how we could ever pay for the attorney's services; we were home missions workers laboring among native Americans, and our income was minimal. We were required to pay $2,500 up front, which we had to borrow. The balance had to be paid not long after that, and we had no idea where the funds would be found. We prayed earnestly for the Lord's help.

Finally, it was Saturday—two days until the due date to pay back the $2,500 loan plus another $2,500 to the attorney. We prayed earnestly that the Lord would meet our urgent need. A couple called, inviting us to dinner at a restaurant. As we were finishing our meal, they related to us that five months earlier they had been strongly impressed to give us a certain amount of money, but had put off doing so. They discussed the matter again a couple of months later, but again delayed doing anything. Then they told how the husband, on the day we had prayed so earnestly, had gone out to do chores. Upon returning to the house, his wife had asked if he still felt they should give the specific amount of money they had previously talked about. When he responded, "Yes," she said, "If we are to do it, we must do it today."

They handed us a check for the exact amount of money needed. The checks were written on Saturday, and the money was delivered on Monday, the due date. We praise God for His faithful answer to our prayer.

The following is told by Herman Rattai, layman of the Pentecostal Assemblies of Canada, Manitoba, British Co-

▬▬▬▬▬

Appendix 4

**Contemporary
Testimonies
of
Answered
Prayer**

lumbia, who experienced deliverance from danger in the
wild as a result of prayer:

I was in Churchill, Manitoba, during the summer of 1977,
managing some construction projects. During the long evenings I would seek out the solitude of a lonely beach. On
one occasion, I decided to drive out of town some ten
miles and go for a walk along a particularly isolated section
of the shoreline. Removing all but my trousers, I made my
way slowly, picking up beautiful shells and fossil-ridden
limestone, placing my finds in small piles to be retrieved
on my way back. At about the one-mile point, I encountered a rock protrusion that halted my progress. So I rolled
up my trouser legs and waded out to a large rock; I sat for
a time watching ships passing by with their cargoes of grain
from the nearby port. For fifteen minutes I viewed with
serene pleasure the placid ocean contrasted with the rug-
ged terrain.

I turned to go ashore, intending to climb to a higher
point and watch the ships coming and going. All of a sudden, to my surprise and astonishment, I spotted three polar
bears on a ledge just above me, only about twenty-five feet
away. I knew at once I was in serious trouble because the
bears were moving toward me. One was a large sow, and
at her side were two cubs. While other species of bear will
kill a human only when provoked or threatened, the polar
bear is known as a man hunter, even when unprovoked.
Natives have an incredible fear of polar bears, for they all
know of someone who, while walking through the wild,
has been literally tracked down and devoured.

Automatically I shouted, "Stop!" At the same time my
brain raced, trying to think of all possible options for escape. I might take off and run for dear life, but the bear
would easily outrun me. I thought of plunging into the
ocean to swim away, but the water was very cold and the
bear could easily outswim me. My third thought was to
throw a rock at the bears and try to defend myself, but I
knew that would be pure folly.

My only remaining option was to pray, and that I did—
earnestly. "Lord, I am prepared to die at any time [and I
really meant it], but I'm not wanting to die at the hand of
a wild beast." So I talked to the bears. Every time the bears

began moving toward me, I shouted, "Stop!" And they did, momentarily. I looked the sow in the eye and said, "Don't you dare come down here because someone is going to get hurt!" I didn't want to tell her who I thought that would be.

I had to walk a few steps toward the bears to get to shore. I proceeded to tell the sow of my predicament. "I have to come toward you to get on shore." As I spoke, I moved slowly toward the shore.

Once ashore, I began walking backwards, all the while talking to the bear. Whenever she moved, I shouted, "Stop!" Finally, when I had covered about half the distance to my vehicle, I turned and ran with all my might. One hundred yards from my car, I turned and saw that they were not following. Arriving at the car, exhausted beyond description, my heart feeling like it would explode, I thanked God for an absolute miracle. Back in Churchill, when I related the story to a local transportation agent, he said, "That was a miracle for sure. No one with a polar bear that close ever walks away."

THE SPIRIT HELPS US PRAY: A BIBLICAL THEOLOGY OF PRAYER

Baelz, Peter R. *Prayer and Providence.* New York: The Seabury Press, 1968.

Barth, Karl. *Prayer.* 2d Edition. D. E. Saliers, ed. Translated by S. F. Terrien. Philadelphia: The Westminster Press, 1985.

Bauer, Walter. *A Greek-English Lexicon of the New Testament and Other Early Christian Literature.* 2d Edition. Translated by F. Wilbur Gingrich and Frederick W. Danker. Chicago: University of Chicago Press, 1979.

Biederwolf, William Edward. *How Can God Answer Prayer?* New York: Fleming H. Revell Company, 1910.

Bigg, Charles. *A Critical and Exegetical Commentary on the Epistles of St. Peter and St. Jude.* The International Critical Commentary. Edinburgh: T. & T. Clark, 1902.

Billheimer, Paul E. *Destined for the Throne.* Fort Washington, Pa.: Christian Literature Crusade, 1975.

Bloesch, Donald G. *The Struggle of Prayer.* San Francisco: Harper and Row, 1980.

Boros, Ladislaus. *Christian Prayer.* Translated by David Smith. New York: The Seabury Press, 1976.

Bibliography

Bounds, E. M. *The Essentials of Prayer.* New York: Fleming H. Revell Co., 1925.

————. *The Possibilities of Prayer.* New York: Fleming H. Revell Co., 1923.

————. *Prayer and Praying Men.* New York: George H. Doran Co., 1921.

————. *Preacher and Prayer.* Chicago: The Christian Witness, n.d.

————. *Purpose in Prayer.* New York: Fleming H. Revell Co., 1920.

————. *The Reality of Prayer.* New York: Fleming H. Revell Co., 1924.

————. *The Weapon of Prayer.* Chicago: Moody Press, 1980.

Brandt, Robert L. *Charismatics, Are We Missing Something?* Published and available from the author, 1520 Westwood Dr., Billings, Mont., 59102.

————. *Praying with Paul.* Grand Rapids: Baker Book House, 1966.

Burns, James. *Revivals: Their Laws and Leaders.* London: Hodder and Stoughton, 1909; reprint, Grand Rapids: Baker Book House, 1960.

Buttrick, George Arthur. *Prayer.* New York: Abingdon-Cokesbury Press, 1942.

Carley, W. *The Book of the Prophet Ezekiel.* Cambridge, Mass.: Cambridge University Press, 1974.

Carlson, G. Raymond. *Prayer and the Christian's Devotional Life.* Springfield, Mo.: Gospel Publishing House, 1980.

Carre, E. G., ed. *Praying Hyde: A Challenge to Prayer.* London: Pickering & Inglis, n.d.

Cassuto, Umberto. *A Commentary on the Book of Exodus.* Translated by Israel Abrahams. Jerusalem: The Magnes Press, The Hebrew University, 1967.

Chadwick, Samuel. *The Path of Prayer.* New York: Abingdon Press, 1931.

Clarke, Adam. *The Holy Bible Containing the Old and New Testament with a Commentary and Critical Notes.* London: Ward, Lock & Co., n.d.

Cornwall, Judson. *Praying the Scriptures.* Lake Mary, Fla.: Creation House, 1990.

Craigie, Peter C. *Psalms 1–50,* Vol. 19, Word Biblical Commentary Series. Waco, Tex.: Word Books, 1983.

Dods, Marcus. *The Prayer that Teaches to Pray.* London: Hodder and Stoughton, 1892.

Dubay, Thomas. *Fire Within.* San Francisco: Ignatius Press, 1989.

Duewel, Wesley L. *Touch the World through Prayer.* Grand Rapids: Zondervan Publishing House, 1986.

Eastman, Dick. *The Hour that Changes the World.* Grand Rapids: Baker Book House, 1978.

Ellul, Jacques. *Prayer and the Modern Man.* Translated by C. Edward Hopkin. New York: The Seabury Press, 1973.

Erb, William H. *The Lord's Prayer.* Reading, Penn.: I. M. Beaver, Publisher, 1908.

Erickson, Millard J. *Christian Theology.* Grand Rapids: Baker Book House, 1986.

Fee, Gordon. *The First Epistle to the Corinthians.* Grand Rapids: Wm. B. Eerdmans Pub. Co., 1987.

Feinberg, Charles L. *The Prophecy of Ezekiel.* Chicago: Moody Press, 1969.

Finney, Charles G. *Lectures on Revivals of Religion.* New York: Fleming H. Revell Co., 1868.

Gee, Donald. *Concerning Spiritual Gifts.* Springfield, Mo.: Gospel Publishing House, 1949.

Gibson, John Monro. *The Gospel of St. Matthew.* London: Hodder and Stoughton, 1900.

Gordon, Samuel Dickey. *Quiet Talks on Prayer.* New York: Fleming H. Revell Co., n.d.

Grenz, Stanley J. *Prayer: The Cry for the Kingdom.* Peabody, Mass.: Hendrickson Publishers, 1988.

Hallesby, O. *Prayer.* Minneapolis: Augsburg, 1931.

Hallimond, John G. *The Miracle of Answered Prayer.* New York: The Christian Herald, 1916.

Heiler, Friedrich. *Prayer: A Study in the History and Psychology of Religion.* London: Oxford University Press, 1932.

■■■■■■
Bibliography

Hertz, J. H., ed. *The Pentateuch and Haftorahs.* 2d Edition. London: Soncino Press, 1972.

Horton, Harold. *Gifts of the Spirit.* Nottingham, England: Assemblies of God Publishing House, 1934; reprint, Springfield, Mo.: Gospel Publishing House, 1975.

Horton, Stanley M. "A Defense on Historical Grounds of the Isaian Authorship of the Passages in Isaiah Referring to Babylon." Th.D. diss., Central Baptist Seminary, Kansas City, Kans., 1959.

_____. *The New Testament Study Bible: Matthew.* Vol. 2. The Complete Biblical Library. Springfield, Mo.: The Complete Biblical Library, 1989.

_____. *What the Bible Says About the Holy Spirit.* Springfield, Mo.: Gospel Publishing House, 1976.

Hybels, Bill. *Too Busy Not to Pray.* Downers Grove, Ill.: InterVarsity Press, 1988.

Jamieson, Robert, A. R. Fausset, and David Brown. *A Commentary Critical and Explanatory on the Old and New Testaments.* 6 Vols. New York: George H. Doran Company, 1921.

Jeter, Hugh. *By His Stripes.* Springfield, Mo.: Gospel Publishing House, 1977.

Jones, Gwen, ed. *Conference on the Holy Spirit Digest.* 2 Vols. Springfield, Mo.: Gospel Publishing House, 1983.

Jones, J. D. *The Model Prayer.* London: James Clarke & Co., 1899.

Keller, W. Phillip. *A Layman Looks at the Lord's Prayer.* Minneapolis: World Wide Publications, 1976.

Kelly, J. N. D. *A Commentary on the Epistles of Peter and Jude.* New York: Harper and Row, 1969.

Knight, Cecil B., ed. *Pentecostal Worship.* Cleveland, Tenn.: Pathway Press, 1974.

Leech, Kenneth. *True Prayer: An Invitation to Christian Spirituality.* New York: Harper & Row, 1980.

LeFevre, Perry. *Understandings of Prayer.* Philadelphia: The Westminster Press, 1981.

Lewis, C. S. *Letters to Malcolm: Chiefly on Prayer.* New York: Harcourt Brace Jovanovich, 1964.

Lindsell, Harold. *When You Pray.* Wheaton, Ill.: Tyndale House Publishers, 1969.

Lockyer, Herbert. *All the Prayers of the Bible.* Grand Rapids: Zondervan Publishing House, 1959.

————. *How I Can Make Prayer More Effective.* Grand Rapids: Zondervan Publishing House, 1953.

Macaulay, J. C. *Devotional Studies in St. John's Gospel.* Grand Rapids: Wm. B. Eerdmans Pub. Co., 1945.

MacDonald, Alexander B. *Christian Worship in the Primitive Church.* Edinburgh: T. & T. Clark, 1934.

Maclachlan, Lewis. *Intelligent Prayer.* With a Foreword by L. W. Grensted. Greenwood, N.C.: The Attic Press, 1977.

Matthew Henry's Commentary on the Whole Bible. 6 Vols. New York: Fleming H. Revell Co., n.d.

McGraw, Louise Harrison. *Does God Answer Prayer?* Grand Rapids: Zondervan Publishing House, 1941.

Memoirs of the Rev. David Brainerd. New Haven: S. Converse, 1822.

Miller, Basil. *Prayer Meetings that Made History.* Anderson, Ind.: Warner Press, 1938.

Mitchell, Curtis C. *Praying Jesus' Way.* Old Tappan, N.J.: Fleming H. Revell Co., 1977.

More, Hannah. *The Spirit of Prayer.* Grand Rapids: Zondervan Publishing House, 1986.

Munyon, Tim, "The Scourge of Individualism." *Advance,* 1 January 1990, 9.

Murray, Andrew. *The Ministry of Intercession.* New York: Fleming H. Revell Co., 1898.

————. *The Prayer-Life.* Garden City, N.Y.: Doubleday, Doran and Co., 1929.

————. *With Christ in the School of Prayer.* New York: Fleming H. Revell Co., 1885.

Bibliography

Myers, Warren and Ruth. *Pray: How to be Effective in Prayer.* Colorado Springs: Navpress, 1983.

Nee, Watchman. *The Prayer Ministry of the Church.* New York: Christian Fellowship Publishers, 1973.

Newburn, Armon, "The Significance of the Altar Service." *Conference on the Holy Spirit Digest.* Vol. 2. Gwen Jones, ed. Springfield, Mo.: Gospel Publishing House, 1983.

Ogilvie, Lloyd John. *Praying with Power.* Ventura, Calif.: Regal Books, 1983.

Orr, James., ed. *International Standard Bible Encyclopedia.* Grand Rapids: Wm. B. Eerdmans Pub. Co., 1939.

Orr, J. Edwin. *Campus Aflame.* Glendale, Calif.: Regal Books, 1971.

Parker, William R. and Elaine St. Johns. *Prayer Can Change Your Life.* Englewood Cliffs, N.J.: Prentice-Hall, Inc., 1957.

Parkhurst, L. G., Jr. *Charles G. Finney's Answers to Prayer.* Minneapolis: Bethany House Publishers, 1983.

Petuchowski, Jakob, and Michael Brocke, eds. *The Lord's Prayer and Jewish Liturgy.* New York: The Seabury Press, 1978.

Poloma, Margaret M. and George H. Gallup, Jr. *The Varieties of Prayer.* Philadelphia: Trinity Press International, 1991.

Ravenhill, Leonard. *Revival Praying.* Minneapolis: Bethany Fellowship, 1962.

Ridderbos, J. *Isaiah.* Translated by John Vriend. Grand Rapids: Zondervan Publishing House, 1985.

Rinker, Rosalind. *Prayer: Conversing with God.* Grand Rapids: Zondervan Publishing House, 1959.

Robinson, Charles E. *Praying to Change Things.* Springfield, Mo.: Gospel Publishing House, 1928.

Sanders, J. Oswald. *Prayer Power Unlimited.* Minneapolis: World Wide Publications, 1977.

Scroggie, W. Graham. *Method in Prayer.* London: Pickering & Inglis, 1955.

_____. *Paul's Prison Prayers.* Grand Rapids: Kregel Publications, 1981.

Seiss, Joseph A. *Gospel in Leviticus.* Philadelphia: Lindsay and Blakiston, 1860; reprint, Grand Rapids: Kregel Publications, 1981.

Shank, Robert. *Elect in the Son: A Study of the Doctrine of Election.* Springfield, Mo.: Westcott Publishers, 1970.

Simpson, Robert L. *The Interpretation of Prayer in the Early Church.* Philadelphia: The Westminster Press, 1965.

Spear, Wayne R. *The Theology of Prayer.* Grand Rapids: Baker Book House, 1979.

Spence, H. D. M. and Joseph S. Exell, eds. *The Pulpit Commentary.* 49 Vols. Wm. B. Eerdmans Pub. Co., 1950.

Spencer, William David and Aida Besançon Spencer. *The Prayer Life of Jesus.* Lanham, Md.: University Press of America, 1990.

Sproul, R. C. *Effective Prayer.* Wheaton, Ill.: Tyndale House Publishers, 1984.

Stedman, Ray C. *Jesus Teaches on Prayer.* Waco, Tex.: Word Books, 1975.

Stradling, Leslie E. *Praying the Psalms.* Philadelphia: Fortress Press, 1977.

Stuart, Douglas. *Ezekiel.* Dallas: Word Books, 1989.

Talling, Marshall P. *Extempore Prayer.* Manchester: James Robinson, 1902.

Thomson, James G. S. S. *The Praying Christ.* Grand Rapids: Wm. B. Eerdmans Pub. Co., 1959.

Torrey, Reuben A. *How to Pray.* New York: Fleming H. Revell Co., n.d.

————. *The Power of Prayer.* Grand Rapids: Zondervan Publishing House, 1955.

Tozer, A. W. *Keys to the Deeper Life.* Grand Rapids: Zondervan Publishing House, 1984.

————. *Of God and Men.* Harrisburg, Penn.: Christian Publications, Inc., 1960.

————. *The Pursuit of God.* Harrisburg, Penn.: Christian Publications, Inc., 1948.

Bibliography

———. *That Incredible Christian.* Calcutta: Evangelical Literature Depot, 1964.

Vincent, Marvin R. *Word Studies in the New Testament.* Grand Rapids: Wm. B. Eerdmans Pub. Co., 1946.

Walker, Lucille, "Prayer in Worship." In *Pentecostal Worship,* ed. Cecil B. Knight. Cleveland, Tenn.: Pathway Press, 1974.

Ward, J. Neville. *The Use of Praying.* Plymouth, England: The Epworth Press, 1975.

Whittaker, Colin C. *Great Revivals.* Springfield, Mo.: Gospel Publishing House, 1984.

Whyte, Alexander. *Lord, Teach Us to Pray.* New York: Doubleday, Doran, & Co, n.d.

Williams, J. Rodman. *Renewal Theology.* Grand Rapids: Zondervan Publishing House, 1990.

Williams, Morris O. *Partnership in Mission.* Revised Edition. Springfield, Mo.: Assemblies of God Division of Foreign Missions, 1986.

Wilson, Benjamin. *The Emphatic Diaglott.* Brooklyn: International Bible Students Association, 1942.

Wilson, Marvin. *Our Father.* Grand Rapids: Wm. B. Eerdmans Pub. Co., 1989.

Wishart, John Elliot. *The Fact of Prayer: Its Problems and Possibilities.* New York: Fleming H. Revell Company, 1927.

Wood, Leon. *Distressing Days of the Judges.* Grand Rapids: Zondervan Publishing House, 1975.

THE SPIRIT HELPS US PRAY: A BIBLICAL THEOLOGY OF PRAYER

OLD TESTAMENT

441

NEW TESTAMENT

THE SPIRIT HELPS US PRAY: A BIBLICAL THEOLOGY OF PRAYER